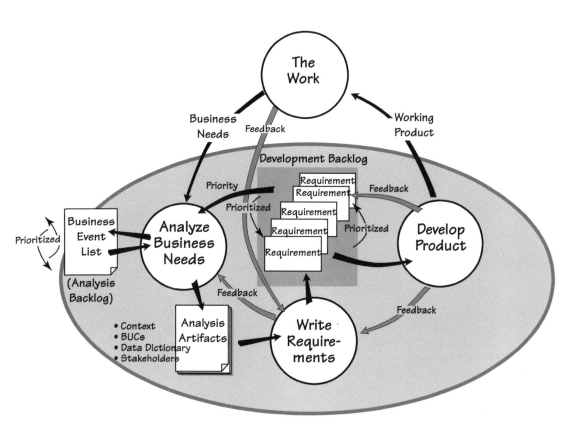

Iterative Requirements Process

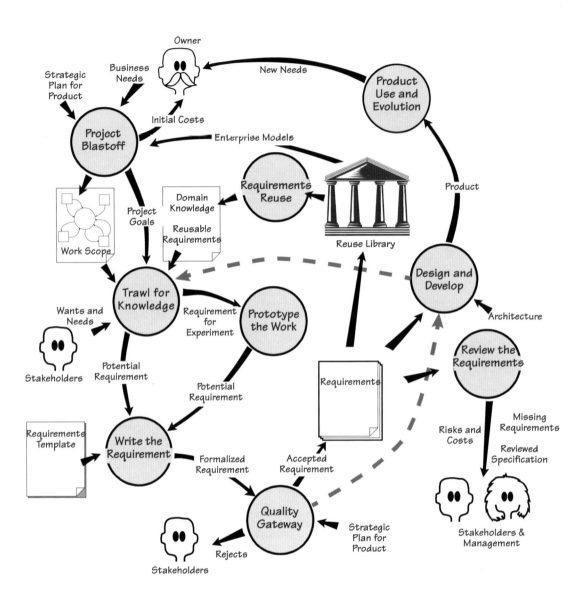

Mastering the Requirements Process

Third Edition

Mastering the Requirements Process

Getting Requirements Right

Third Edition

Suzanne Robertson
James Robertson

✦Addison-Wesley

Upper Saddle River, NJ ● Boston ● Indianapolis ● San Francisco

New York ● Toronto ● Montreal ● London ● Munich ● Paris ● Madrid

Capetown ● Sydney ● Tokyo ● Singapore ● Mexico City

Library of Congress Cataloging-in-Publication Data

Robertson, Suzanne.
  Mastering the requirements process : getting requirements right / Suzanne Robertson, James Robertson.—3rd ed.
      p. cm.
  Includes bibliographical references and index.
  ISBN 978-0-321-81574-3 (hardcover : alk. paper) 1. Project management. 2. Computer software—Development. I. Robertson, James. II. Title.
  TA190.R48 2012
  005.1068′4—dc23

                                                              2012018961

ISBN-13: 978-0-321-81574-3
ISBN-10:   0-321-81574-2
Text printed in the United States on recycled paper at LSC Communications, Willard, OH.

For one generation,

Reginald, Margaret, Nick, and Helen,

and another,

Carlotta, Cameron, and Louise

Contents

in which we discuss a fail-safe way of partitioning the work and so smooth the way for your requirements investigation

in which we come to an understanding of what the business is doing, and start to think about what it might like to do

12   Fit Criteria and Rationale   279

*in which we show how measuring requirements makes them
unambiguous, understandable, communicable, and testable*

Preface to the Third Edition

Why a third edition of *Mastering the Requirements Process*? Because we need it. Much water has passed under the bridge since the last edition of this book was published, and much has happened in the requirements and development world. We have applied the Volere requirements techniques described in this book to many projects; we have received feedback from our projects and those of clients and other practitioners of the Volere techniques; and armed with that knowledge we felt it was time to update our book to reflect the current state of requirements practice. Today's systems, software, products, and services have to be more attractive and more appropriate if they are to be noticed, bought, used and valued. More than ever, we need to be assured that we are solving the real problem. More than ever, we need to be doing a better job with requirements discovery.

New techniques for software development—most noticeably the rise of agile techniques—have changed the role of the requirements discoverer: not the underlying truth of the requirements activity, but the way in which requirements are discovered. Business analysts working with agile teams perform their task differently. Combinations of iterative, incremental, and spiral development techniques require the business analyst to go about the requirements task in a different way.

Outsourcing has increased enormously, which, rather than lessening the requirements burden, means that there is an even greater need to produce accurate, and unambiguous, requirements. If you are planning to send your specification to the far side of the world, you would like to think that your outsourcer will understand it and know exactly what to build.

Despite all these changes in the way in which we develop and deliver our products and services, one underlying fact is still there, and it is this: *If we are to build some software or a product or a service, then it must provide the optimal value for its owner.*

You will see the theme of optimal value developed in this edition, and what it comes down to is that it does not matter how you develop your software, but rather what that software does for its owner that matters. You can finish a project on time and on budget, but if the delivered software brings little benefit to the owning organization, it is a waste of money. Alternatively, you can overspend and be late, but if the delivered product brings several million dollars of value, then it is more beneficial than its cheaper counterpart.

The task of the business analyst is to discover the real business that the software is supposed to improve. This cannot be done at the keyboard simply because software is a *solution*, and to provide a valuable solution you first have to understand the problem—the *real* problem—that it is meant to solve. In this edition we have written about *thinking above the line*. The line in this case comes from the Brown Cow Model (you'll have to read the book to find out what it is) and represents the division between the technological implementations and the abstract, essential world where you discover the real needs. We have written about *innovation* as a way of finding better, more appropriate needs and solutions.

This, then, is the task of the requirements discoverer, and indeed of this edition: to delve more deeply into how we understand our client organizations, and how we find better solutions by discovering and communicating a better understanding of the problem.

London, June 2012

For college instructors who adopt this book for their courses, some of the graphics used herein are available in the **Pearson Instructor Resource Center (www.pearsonhighered.com)** for your use in preparing course materials.

Foreword to the First Edition

It is almost ten years now since Don Gause and I published *Exploring Requirements: Quality Before Design*. Our book is indeed an exploration, a survey of human processes that can be used in gathering complete, correct, and communicable requirements for a software system, or any other kind of product.

The operative word in this description is "can," for over this decade the most frequent question my clients have asked is, "How can I assemble these diverse processes into a comprehensive requirements process for our information systems?"

At long last, James and Suzanne Robertson have provided an answer I can conscientiously give to my clients. *Mastering the Requirements Process* shows, step by step, template by template, example by example, one well-tested way to assemble a complete, comprehensive requirements process.

One watchword of their process is "reasonableness." In other words, every part of the process makes sense, even to people who are not very experienced with requirements work. When introducing this kind of structure to an organization, reasonableness translates into easier acceptance—an essential attribute when so many complicated processes are tried and rejected.

The process they describe is the Volere approach, which they developed as an outcome of many years helping clients to improve their requirements. Aside from the Volere approach itself, James and Suzanne contribute their superb teaching skills to the formidable task facing anyone who wishes to develop requirements and do them well.

The Robertsons' teaching skills are well known to their seminar students as well as to fans of their *Complete Systems Analysis* books. *Mastering the Requirements Process* provides a much-requested front end for their analysis books—or for anyone's analysis books, for that matter.

We can use all the good books on requirements we can get, and this is one of them!

Gerald M. Weinberg
www.geraldmweinberg.com
February 1999

READING
Gause, Donald C., and Gerald M. Weinberg. *Exploring Requirements: Quality Before Design.* Dorset House, 1989.

READING
Robertson, James, and Suzanne Robertson. *Complete Systems Analysis: The Workbook, the Textbook, the Answers.* Dorset House, 1998.

Acknowledgments

Writing a book is hard. Without the help and encouragement of others, it would be nearly impossible, at least for these authors. We would like to take a few lines to tell you who helped and encouraged and made it possible.

Andy McDonald of Vaisala was generous with his time, and gave us considerable technical input. We hasten to add that the IceBreaker product in this book is only a distant relation to Vaisala's IceCast systems. The Vaisala User Group, of which E. M. Kennedy holds the chair, also provided valuable technical input.

Thanks are due to the technical reviewers who gave up their time to wade through some fairly incomprehensible stuff. Mike Russell, Susannah Finzi, Neil Maiden, Tim Lister, and Bashar Nuseibeh all deserve honorable mentions.

We would like to acknowledge our fellow principals at the Atlantic Systems Guild—Tom DeMarco, Peter Hruschka, Tim Lister, Steve McMenamin, and John Palmer—for their help, guidance, and incredulous looks over the years.

The staff at Pearson Education contributed. Sally Mortimore, Alison Birtwell, and Dylan Reisenberger were generous and skillful, and used such persuasive language whenever we spoke about extending the deadline.

For the second edition, Peter Gordon provided guidance and persuasion at exactly the right times. Kim Boedigheimer, John Fuller, and Lara Wysong were invaluable at steering us through the publishing process. Jill Hobbs tamed our faulty grammar and punctuation, and made this text readable. The technical input of Ian Alexander, Earl Beede, Capers Jones, and Tony Wasserman goes far beyond valuable. Thank you, gentlemen, for your insights. And we hasten to add that any remaining technical errors are ours and ours alone.

One would imagine that by the time one got to the third edition, one would not need help. Not so. We gratefully acknowledge the alphabetic trinity of Gary Austin, Earl Beede, and John Capron. Our Volere colleague Stephen Mellor sorted out some of the trickier issues we encountered. Our other Volere colleagues James Archer and Andrew Kendall have helped over the years with their ideas, experience, and meaningful conversations over a glass of wine.

The Pearson crew of Peter Gordon, Kim Boedigheimer, and Julie Nahil were invaluable. We want to point out the special work done by Alan Clements to design the cover. Once again, Jill Hobbs stepped up to tame our grammatical misdemeanors and semantic transgressions.

And finally we thank the students at our seminars and our consulting clients. Their comments, their insistence on having things clearly explained, their insights, and their feedback have all made some difference, no matter how indirect, to this book.

Thank you, everybody.

James and Suzanne Robertson
London, June 2012

Some Fundamental Truths

1

in which we consider the essential contribution of requirements

Truth 1

Requirements are not really about requirements.

Requirements are what the software product, or hardware product, or service, or whatever you intend to build, is meant to do and to be. Requirements exist whether you discover them or not, and whether you write them down or not. Obviously, your product will never be right unless it conforms to the requirements, so in this way you can think of the requirements as some kind of natural law, and it is up to you to discover them.

That said, the requirements activity is not principally about writing a requirements document. Instead, it focuses on understanding a business problem and providing a solution for it. Software is there to solve some kind of problem, as are hardware and services. The real art of requirements discovery is discovering the real problem. Once you do that, you have the basis for identifying and choosing between alternative solutions. In essence, then, requirements are not about the written requirements as such, but rather an uncovering of the problem to be solved.

Incidentally, when we say "business," "business problem," or "work" we mean whatever activity you are concerned with—be it commercial, scientific, embedded, government, military, or, indeed, any other kind of activity or service or consumer product.

Also incidentally, when we say "he" in this book—usually referring to the business analyst—we mean "he or she." We find it too clumsy to keep saying "he or she" or "he/she." Believe us, requirements work belongs equally to both genders.

Throughout this book we have used "he" to refer to both genders. The authors (one male and one female) find the use of "he or she" disruptive and awkward.

Truth 2

If we must build software, then it must be optimally valuable for its owner.

Note that we are concerned with the owner of the end result, and only indirectly the user. This focus seems to run contrary to the usual priorities, so we had best explain it.

The owner is the person or organization that pays for the software (or hardware or any other product you might be building). Either the owner pays for the development of the software or he buys the software from someone else. The owner also pays for the disruption to his business that happens when the software is deployed. On the other side of the ledger, the owner gets a benefit from the software. To describe that relationship very simply, the owner is buying a benefit.

We could say that another way—the owner will not pay unless the product provides a benefit. This benefit usually comes in the shape of providing some capability that was not previously available, or changing some business process to be faster or cheaper or more convenient. Naturally this benefit must provide a value to the owner that exceeds the cost of developing the product (see Figure 1.1).

To be *optimally valuable,* the product must provide a benefit that is in proportion to the cost of the product. In some cases, the product can have a very high cost if the value to the owner is great enough. For instance, airlines are willing to pay significant sums for simulators that ensure their pilots are suitably qualified and skilled; lives will be lost if they aren't. An airline might also pay a lot for an automated check-in system when it will make significant inroads into the cost of getting passengers onto planes. The same airline would pay far less for a canteen staff roster system because, let's face

Figure 1.1

As the software becomes more capable and the cost of construction increases, so does the benefit that the software brings. At some point, however, the cost of construction starts to outstrip the benefit and the project is no longer beneficial.

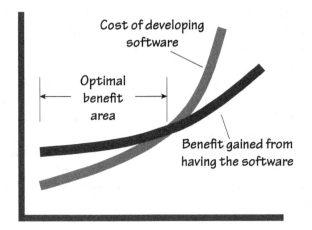

it—that kind of task can be done manually and having a few wrong people in the canteen is annoying but hardly life-threatening.

The role of the requirements discoverer—call him a "business analyst," "requirements engineer," "product owner," "systems analyst," or any other title—is to determine what the owner values. In some cases, providing a small system that solves a small problem provides sufficient benefit for the owner to consider it valuable. In other cases (perhaps many others), extending the system's capabilities will provide a much greater value, and this can be achieved for a small additional cost. It all depends on what the owner values.

This, then, is optimal value—understanding the owner's problem well enough to deliver a solution that provides the best payback at the best price.

Truth 3

If your software does not have to satisfy a need, then you can build anything. However, if it is meant to satisfy a need, then you have to know what that need is to build the right software.

It is worthwhile considering that the most useful products are those for which the developers correctly understood what the product was intended to accomplish for its users, and in what manner it was to accomplish that purpose. To understand these things, you must understand the work of the owner's business and determine how that work should be carried out in the future.

Once these points are understood and agreed to, then the business analysts negotiate with the owner about which product will best improve the work. The business analysts produce requirements that describe the functionality of the product—what it will do; and the quality attributes of the product—how well it will do it.

Without knowing these requirements, there is little chance that any product emerging from the development project will be of much value. Apart from a few fortuitous accidents, no product has ever succeeded without prior understanding of its requirements.

It does not matter which kind of work the owner wishes to do, be it scientific, commercial, e-commerce, or social networking. Nor does it matter which programming language or development tools are used to construct the product. The development life cycle—whether agile, prototyping, spiral, the Rational Unified Process, or any other method—is irrelevant to the need for understanding the requirements.

This truth always emerges: You must come to the correct understanding of the requirements, and have your client agree with them, or your product or your project will be seriously deficient.

Sadly, the requirements are not always correctly understood. Authors Steve McConnell and Jerry Weinberg provide statistics showing that as many as 60 percent of errors originate from within the requirements activity. Software developers have the opportunity to (almost) eliminate these errors. Yet many choose—or their managers choose—to (almost) eliminate the requirements discovery and rush headlong into constructing the (inevitably) wrong product. As a result, they pay many times the price for their product than they would have if the requirements discovery had been done correctly in the first place. Poor quality is passed on in the development life cycle; it is as simple as that.

Truth 4

There is an important difference between building a piece of software and solving a business problem. The former does not necessarily accomplish the latter.

Many software development projects concentrate solely on the software. This might seem reasonable—after all, most software projects manage to produce some software. However, concentrating almost exclusively on the software is a little like trying to build the Parthenon by concentrating on stones. The software, if it is to be valuable to the owner, must solve the owner's business problem.

We build an awful lot of software. Tens (if not hundreds) of millions of lines of code are produced each year. Much of this output contains errors, and most of those are errors of requirements. As a consequence, an awful lot of the world's software simply does not solve the correct problem.

Some development processes are based on the idea of delivering some functionality to its intended users, and inviting them to say whether it solves their problem. If it does not, the software is reworked, and then once again presented for approval. The problem here is that we never know whether the users approve the last delivery because they are satisfied with it or because they are exhausted by the process.

More importantly, it is very difficult for an individual user to understand the broader ramifications of deploying a piece of software. Typically software users do not know enough about the wider business to decide whether this incarnation of software will cause problems in some other part of the business.

And at the risk of repeating ourselves, we cannot stress enough that software is there to solve a business problem. Clearly, then, any development effort must start with the problem, and not with a perceived solution.

Truth 5

The requirements do not have to be written, but they have to become known to the builders.

It often seems that the aim of a requirements project is to produce as large a specification as possible. It doesn't seem to matter that very few readers can understand much of it, and that even fewer have the patience to read it. It appears that the requirements writers believe that their work will be appreciated in direct proportion to the thickness of the specification.

Once produced, this considerable document is then thrown over the wall—or, should we say, forklifted over the wall—to the developers, who are expected to rejoice at the sheer volume of the specification. After all, the more pages it contains, the more chance it has not missed anything—or so the theory goes. Naturally enough, the developers are almost always underwhelmed by this document and either ignore it or willfully comply with it. Either way, the end result is usually unsatisfactory.

Despite this bizarre behavior, there remains a need for requirements, and for those requirements to be communicated to the development team (see Figure 1.2).

Whether the requirements are written or not is beside the point. In some cases it is more effective to verbally communicate requirements; in other cases there is an inescapable need for a permanent record of the requirements.

Despite the efficacy of verbal requirements, we feel that it is not feasible to communicate *all* requirements this way. In many cases the act of writing a requirement helps both the business analyst and the stakeholder to

Figure 1.2

Naturally, there is a need to communicate the requirements to the builders of the product.

completely understand it. As well as improving the understanding, a correctly written requirement provides trace documentation. The rationale of a requirement, or the justification on a story card, documents the team's decisions. It also provides the testers and the developers with a clear indication of the importance of the requirement, which in turn suggests how much effort to expend on it. Additionally, the cost of future maintenance is reduced when the maintainers know why a requirement exists.

Requirements are not meant to place an extra burden on your project, so nothing should be written unless there is a clear need for it. Nevertheless, when the need exists, then the effort involved in writing a requirement is paid back several times over by the precision of the requirement and the reduction in the maintenance effort that is yet to come.

Truth 6

Your customer won't always give you the right answer. Sometimes it is impossible for the customer to know what is right, and sometimes he just doesn't know what he needs.

The requirements activity is traditionally seen as somewhat akin to the task of a stenographer. That is, the business analyst listens carefully to the stakeholders, records precisely whatever it is they say, and translates their requests into requirements for the product.

The flaw in this approach is that it does not take into account the difficulty stakeholders have when they are trying to describe what they need. It is no simple task to envisage a product that will solve a problem, particularly when the problem is not always completely understood. Given the complexity and scale of today's businesses, it is very difficult, indeed, for individuals to understand all appropriate parts of the business.

We also have the problem of *incremental improvements*. It is far too common that when asked about a new system, stakeholders describe their existing system, and add on a few improvements. This incremental approach

Figure 1.3

Sometimes, like
Pinocchio, your
customer does not tell
you the whole truth.

generally precludes any serious innovation, and it often results in mediocre products that fail to live up to expectations.

The business analyst has to perform a juggling act. In some cases he must record the customer's request; in some cases he must persuade the customer that what is being asked for is not what is needed; in other cases he has to derive the requirements from the customer's solution; and in some cases he must come up with an innovation that is not what anyone asked for, but results in a better solution. In all cases, he should think that any stakeholder could be Pinocchio (Figure 1.3) and not believe everything he is told.

Truth 7

Requirements do not come about by chance. There needs to be some kind of orderly process for developing them.

Any important endeavor needs an orderly process. Random applications of steel and concrete do not produce buildings; there is a defined process for designing and erecting such structures. Similarly, there is a defined and systematic process for making movies. Your motorcar was designed and built using orderly processes, and your last airline flight was the result of a set of orderly processes that were followed more or less verbatim. Even artistic endeavors, such as novels and paintings, have an orderly process that the artist follows.

These processes are not lockstep procedures where one mindlessly follows every instruction without question, in the prescribed sequence, and without variation. Instead, orderly processes comprise a set of tasks that achieve the intended result, but leave the order, emphasis, and degree of application to the person or team using the process.

Most importantly, the people who are active in the process must be able to see why different tasks within the process are important, and which tasks carry the most significance for their project.

Truth 8

You can be as iterative as you want, but you still need to understand what the business needs.

Since the previous edition of this book was published, iterative development methods have become much more popular. This is certainly a worthwhile advance, but like many advances these techniques are sometimes overhyped. For example, we have heard people say (and some commit to print) that iterative delivery makes requirements redundant.

Cooler heads have realized that any development technique has a need to discover the requirements as a prerequisite to serious development. In turn, the cooler heads have absorbed requirements processes into their development life cycles. Instead of attempting to do away with requirements, intelligent methods simply approach the requirements need from a different direction.

The real concern—and this applies to any kind of development technique—is to discover what is needed without producing unnecessary, premature, and wasteful reams of documentation.

No matter how you develop your software, the need to understand the customer's business problem, and what the product has to do to solve this problem (in other words, its requirements), remains.

Truth 9

> *There is no silver bullet. All our methods and tools will not compensate for poor thought and poor workmanship.*

While we have a need for an orderly process, it should not be seen as a substitute for thinking. Processes help, but they help the smart people much more than they help people who are not prepared to think. This is particularly true of requirements processes where the business analyst is required to juggle several versions of the requirements, and at the same time imagine what will make the best future software product.

The requirements activity is not exactly easy; it takes thought and perception on the part of the business analyst if it is to succeed. Several automated tools are available to help with this endeavor, but they must be seen as aids and not as substitutes for good requirements practices. No amount of blindly following a prescribed practice will produce the same result as a skilled business analyst using his most important tools—the brain, the eyes, and the ears.

[E]ven perfect program verification can only establish that a program meets its specification. The hardest part of the software task is arriving at a complete and consistent specification, and much of the essence of building a program is in fact the debugging of the specification.

—Fred Brooks, *No Silver Bullet: Essence and Accidents of Software Engineering*

Truth 10

> *Requirements, if they are to be implemented successfully, must be measurable and testable.*

At its heart, a functional requirement is something that your product must do to support its owner's business. A non-functional requirement is the quantification of how well it must carry out its functionality for it to be successful within the owner's environment.

To build a product that exactly meets these criteria, you must be precise when writing requirements. At the same time, you must take into account the fact that requirements come from humans, and humans are not always, and sometimes never, precise. To achieve the necessary level of precision, you have to somehow measure a requirement. If you can measure the requirement using numbers instead of words, you can make the requirement testable.

For example, if you have a requirement that your product "shall be attractive to new users," then you can set a measurement that a first-time user can successfully set up an account within 2 minutes, with less than 5 seconds' hesitation for any item of data for which the user is expected to know—such as his name, e-mail address, and similar items. (Hesitation time is a measure of how intuitive the product is, which is part of its attractiveness to the user.) Naturally, when you measure the requirement this way, your testers can determine whether the product (or in some cases a prototype of the product) meets its need.

It is also safe to say that if you cannot find a measurement for a requirement, then it is not a requirement, but merely an idle thought.

Truth 11

You, the business analyst, will change the way the user thinks about his problem, either now or later.

When you come to understand the requirements, especially when they come from different stakeholders, you start to build abstractions and establish vocabulary. When you present models of the business processes, when you work with the stakeholders to find the essence of the work, when you have clear and measurable requirements, and when you reflect all this truth back to the stakeholders, it will change (for the better) their thinking about their business problem.

Once people have a better understanding of the real meaning of their requirements, they are likely to see ways of improving them. Part of your job is to help people, as early as possible, to understand and question their requirements so that they can help you to discover what they really need.

What Are These Requirements Anyway?

After all that truth, what are these requirements that we keep talking about? Simply put, a requirement is something the product must do to support its owner's business, or a quality it must have to make it acceptable and attractive to the owner. A requirement exists either because the type of product demands certain functions and qualities, or because the client justifiably asks for that requirement to be part of the delivered product.

Functional Requirements

Functional requirements are things the product must do.

A functional requirement describes an action that the product must take if it is to be useful to its operator—they arise from the work that your stakeholders need to do. Almost any action (calculate, inspect, publish, or most other active verbs) can be a functional requirement.

> *The product shall produce a schedule of all roads upon which ice is predicted to form within the given time parameter.*

This requirement is one of the things that the product must do if it is to be useful within the context of its owner's business. You can deduce that owner in this case is an organization that is responsible for maintaining roads safely, and that does so by dispatching trucks to spread de-icing material on roads where ice is about to form.

Non-functional Requirements

Non-functional requirements are qualities the product must have.

Non-functional requirements are properties, or qualities, that the product must have if it is to be acceptable to its owner and operator. In some cases, non-functional requirements—these specify such properties as performance, look and feel, usability, security, and legal attributes—are critical to the product's success, as in the following case:

> *The product shall be able to determine "friend or foe" in less than 0.25 second.*

Sometimes they are requirements because they enhance the product or make people want to buy it:

> *The product shall provide a pleasing user experience.*

Sometimes they make the product usable:

> *The product shall be able to be used by travelers in the arrivals hall who do not speak the home language.*

Non-functional requirements might at first seem vague or incomplete. Later in this book we will look at how to give them a fit criterion to make them measurable and thus testable.

Constraints

Constraints are global requirements. They can be limitations on the project itself or restrictions on the eventual design of the product. For example, this is a project constraint:

> *The product must be available at the beginning of the new tax year.*

Constraints are global issues that shape the requirements.

The client for the product is saying that the product is of no use if it is not available to be used by the client's customers in the new tax year. The effect is that the requirements analysts must constrain the requirements to those that can deliver the optimal benefit within the deadline.

Constraints may also be placed on the eventual design and construction of the product, as in the following example:

> *The product shall operate as an iPad, iPhone, Android, and Blackberry app.*

Constraints are simply another type of requirement.

Providing that this is a real business constraint—and not just a matter of opinion—any solution that does not meet this constraint is clearly unacceptable.

Whatever they are constraining, constraints can be seen as another type of requirement. See Figure 1.4.

The Volere Requirements Process

This book describes a process for successfully discovering, verifying, and documenting requirements. Each chapter covers an activity of the process, or some aspect of requirements gathering that is needed to complete the activity.

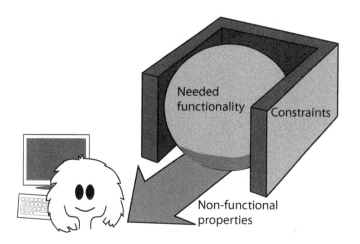

Figure 1.4

The functionality of the end product is restricted by the constraints. The functionality is to the benefit of its user, but it is the non-functional requirements that "deliver" the functionality by making the product usable and acceptable to the users.

"Volere" is the Italian word for "to wish" or "to want."

As you learn more about the Volere Requirements Process, keep in mind that it is meant to be a guide for producing deliverables. What you do with the process is driven by the relevant deliverables, not by the procedures. We would like you to think of the process as a set of tasks that have to be done (to varying degrees of detail) for successful requirements projects, rather than as a lockstep procedure that must be followed at all costs. As you read about each part, think about how you would perform that part of the procedure given your own structural and organizational setup.

What you do with the process is driven by the relevant deliverables, not by the procedures.

To understand the process, it is not necessary to read the book in the presented order, but keep in mind that you may encounter some terminology that assumes knowledge from previous chapters. Your requirements needs will naturally differ from those of other readers, so you may be interested in exploring some aspects of the process before others. Once you are familiar with the basic outline of the process—provided in Chapter 2—feel free to plunge in wherever you feel it will be most valuable.

The Requirements Process

in which we present a process for discovering requirements and discuss how you might use it

This book is a distillation of our experience. In it, we describe a requirements process that we have derived from our years of working in the requirements arena—working with clever people who do clever things, and working on projects in wonderfully diverse domains. We have also learned much from the experience of the many people around the world who use various parts of our techniques.

We developed the Volere Requirements Process and its associated specification template from the activities and deliverables that had proved themselves to be most effective in project and consulting assignments with our clients. The result of this experience is a requirements discovery and specification process whose principles can be applied—and indeed have been applied—to almost all kinds of application types in almost all kinds of development environments.

We want to stress from the very beginning that while we are presenting a process, we are using it as a vehicle for discovering requirements; we do *not* expect you to wave this process around and tell your co-workers that it is "the only way to do things." However, we have high expectations that you will find many useful things from this process that will, in turn, help you to discover and communicate your requirements more productively and accurately. We have personally seen hundreds of companies adapt the process to their own cultures and organizations, and we know of thousands more that have done so.

Our clients who use the Volere Requirements Process are those who develop their products using RUP, incremental, iterative, spiral, Scrum, or other variations of iterative development; more formalized waterfall processes; and a variety of homebrewed development processes. Over the years,

Whether you are building custom systems, building systems by assembling components, using commercial off-the-shelf software, accessing open-source software, outsourcing your development, or making changes to existing software, you still need to explore, discover, understand, and communicate the requirements.

If the right product is to be built, then the right requirements have to be discovered.

Figure 2.1

This map of the Volere Requirements Process shows the activities and their deliverables. We have used a stylized data flow notation. Each activity (the bubbles) and its deliverables (named arrows or documents) are explained in the text. The dotted lines represent how this process is used with iterative projects.

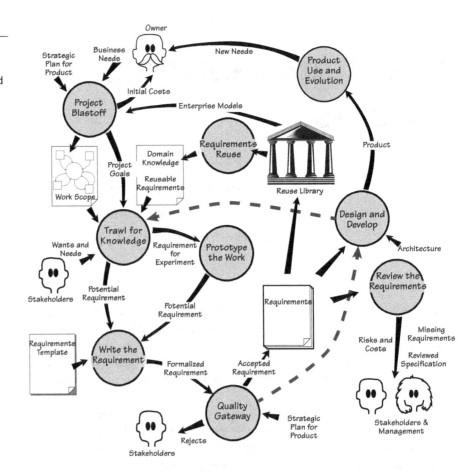

all of these clients agreed with us: If the right product is to be built, the right requirements have to be discovered. But requirements don't come about by fortuitous accident. To find the correct and complete requirements, you need some kind of orderly process.

The Volere Requirements Process is shown in Figure 2.1. Each of the activities included in the figure, along with the connections between them, is described in detail in subsequent chapters of this book.

The Requirements Process in Context

We need to point out—indeed, we need to stress—that this process is not intended to be a waterfall approach. At various stages throughout this book, we will point out how you might modify the process if you are using some kind of iterative development.

Requirements discovery should be seen as a necessary forerunner of any construction activity, but it should also be viewed as something that can be conducted quite quickly, sometimes quite informally, sometimes overlapping with subsequent design and construction activities, but never ignored.

Let's look briefly at each of the activities shown in Figure 2.1, which are covered in more detail in subsequent chapters. The intention of this chapter is to give you a gentle introduction to the process, its components, its deliverables, and the ways that they fit together. If you want more detail on any of the activities, feel free to jump ahead to the relevant chapter before completing this overview.

As we go through the process, we describe it as if you were working with a brand-new product—that is, developing something from scratch. We take this approach to avoid, for the moment, becoming entangled in the constraints that are part of all maintenance projects. Later, we will discuss requirements for those situations when the product already exists and changes to it are required.

A Case Study

We will explain the Volere Requirements Process by taking you through a project that uses it.

The IceBreaker project is to develop a product that predicts when and where ice will form on roads, and to schedule trucks to treat the roads with de-icing material. The new product will enable road authorities to more accurately predict ice formation, schedule road treatments more precisely, and thereby make the roads safer. The product will also reduce the amount of de-icing material needed, which will help both the road authority's finances and the environment.

Project Blastoff

Imagine launching a rocket. 10 – 9 – 8 – 7 – 6 – 5 – 4 – 3 – 2 – 1 – blastoff! If all it needed were the ability to count backward from 10, then even Andorra[1] would have its own space program. The truth of the matter is that before we get to the final 10 seconds of a rocket launch, a lot of preparation has taken place. The rocket has been fueled, and the course plotted—in fact, everything that needs to be done if the rocket is to survive and complete a successful mission.

The key purpose of the project blastoff is to build the foundation for the requirements discovery that is to follow, and to ensure that all the needed components for a successful project are in place. The principal stakeholders—the sponsor, the key users, the lead requirements analyst, technical and business experts, and other people who are crucial to the success of the project—gather together to arrive at a consensus on the crucial project issues.

> " The likelihood of frost or ice forming is determined by the energy receipt and loss at the road surface. This energy flow is controlled by a number of environmental and meteorological factors (such as exposure, altitude, road construction, traffic, cloud cover, and wind speed). These factors cause significant variation in road surface temperature from time to time and from one location to another. Winter night-time road surface temperatures can vary by over 10°C across a road network in a county. "
>
> —Vaisala News

Blastoff is also known as "project initiation," "kickoff," "charter," "project launch," and many other things. We use the term "blastoff" to describe what we are trying to achieve—getting the requirements project launched and flying.

FOOTNOTE 1
Andorra is a tiny principality in the Pyrenees mountains between France and Spain. Only since 1993 has it been

a parliamentary democracy, but it retains its ancient chiefs of state as a coprincipality. The responsibilities of the French prince are now vested with the president of France. On the Spanish side, the "prince" is the bishop of Seo de Urgel.

Andorra became famous in the 1960s for having a defense budget of $4.50, a tale that has become the stuff of legend. Today Andorra's defense budget is zero.

Refer to Chapter 3, Scoping the Business Problem, for a detailed discussion of project blastoff.

The blastoff defines the scope of the business problem and seeks concurrence from the stakeholders that yes, this is the area of the owner's organization that needs to be improved. The blastoff meeting confirms the functionality to be included in the requirements discovery, and the functionality that is to be specifically excluded.

Defining the scope of the business problem is usually the most convenient way to start. In the IceBreaker project, the lead requirements analyst coordinates the group members' discussion as they come to a consensus on the scope of the work—that is, the business area to be improved—and how this work relates to the world around it. The meeting participants draw a *context diagram* on a whiteboard to show which functionality is included in the work, and by extension, which elements they consider to be outside the scope of the ice forecasting business. The diagram defines—precisely defines—the included functionality by showing the connections between the work and the outside world. (More on this in the next chapter.) This use of a context diagram is illustrated in Figure 2.2. Later, as the requirements activity proceeds, the context diagram is used to reveal the optimal product to help with this work.

When they have reached a reasonable agreement on the scope of the business area to be studied, the group identifies the *stakeholders*. The stakeholders are those people who have an interest in the product, or who have knowledge pertaining to the product—in fact, anyone who has requirements for it. For the IceBreaker project, the people who have an interest are the road engineers, the truck depot supervisor, the weather forecasting people, road safety experts, ice treatment consultants, and so on. These people must be identified, so that the requirements analysts can work with them to find all the requirements. The context diagram, by establishing the extent of the work, helps to identify many of the stakeholders.

Figure 2.2

The context diagram is used to build a consensus among the stakeholders as to the scope of the work that needs to be improved. The eventual product will be used to do part of this work.

The blastoff also confirms the *goals* of the project. The blastoff group comes to an agreement on the business reason for doing the project, and agrees that there is a clear and measurable benefit to be gained by doing the project. The group also agrees that the product is worthwhile for the business to make the investment, and that the organization is capable of building and operating it.

It is sensible project management practice at this stage to produce a preliminary estimate of the costs involved for the requirements part of the project—this can be done by using the information already contained in the context diagram. It is also sensible project management to make an early assessment of the risks that the project is likely to face. Although these risks might seem like depressing news, it is always better to get an idea of the downside of the project (its risk and cost) before being swept away by the euphoria of the benefits that the new product is intended to bring.

It is always better to get an idea of the downside of the project (its risk and cost) before being swept away by the euphoria of the benefits that the new product is intended to bring.

The blastoff group members arrive at a consensus on whether the project is worthwhile and viable—that is, they make the "go/no go" decision. It might seem brutal to kill off an embryonic project, but we know from bitter experience that it is better to cancel a project at an early stage than to have it stagger on for months—or years—consuming valuable resources when it has little or no chance of success. The blastoff group carefully considers whether the product is viable, and whether its benefits outweigh its costs and risks.

Alternatively, if too many unknowns remain at this point, the blastoff group might decide to start the requirements investigation with the intention of reviewing the requirements after a short while and reassessing the value of the project.

READING

DeMarco, Tom, and Tim Lister. *Waltzing with Bears: Managing Risk on Software Projects.* Dorset House, 2003.

McConnell, Steve. *Software Estimation: Demystifying the Black Art.* Microsoft Press, 2006.

Trawling for Requirements

Once the blastoff is completed, the business analysts start *trawling* the work to learn and understand its functionality—"What's going on with this piece of the business, and what do they want it to do?" For convenience and consistency, they partition the work context diagram into business use cases.

Each business use case is an amount of functionality needed by the work to make the correct response to a business event. (These terms will be fully explained soon.) A requirements analyst is assigned to each of the business use cases—the analysts can work almost independently of one another—for further detailed study. The analysts use trawling techniques such as apprenticing, scenarios, use case workshops, and many others to discover the true nature of the work. These trawling techniques are described in Chapter 5, Investigating the Work.

Refer to Chapter 4 for a discussion of business events and business use cases, and an exploration of how you might use them.

Trawling means discovering the requirements. The business analysts sit with the IceBreaker technicians as they describe the work they currently do, and their aspirations for work they hope to do. The business analysts

Refer to Chapter 5, Investigating the Work, for details of the trawling activity.

also consult with other interested stakeholders and subject-matter experts—experts on usability, security, operations, management, and so on—to discover other needs for the eventual product. The IceBreaker business analysts spent a lot of time with the meteorologists and the highway engineers.

Perhaps the most difficult part of requirements investigation is uncovering the *essence* of the system. Many stakeholders inevitably talk about their perceived *solution* to the problem or express their needs in terms of the current implementation. The essence, by contrast, is the underlying business reason for having the product. Alternatively, you can think of it as the *policy* of the work, or what the work or the business rule would be if it could exist without any technology (and that includes people). We will have more to say about the essence of the system in Chapter 7, Understanding the Real Problem.

Once they understand the essence of the work, the analysts get together with the key stakeholders to decide the best product to improve this work. That is, they determine how much of the work to automate or change, and what effect those decisions will have on the work. Once they know the extent of the product, the requirements analysts write its requirements. We illustrate this process in Figure 2.3.

The IceBreaker product must not be a simplistic automation of the work as it is currently done; the best of our automated products are not mere imitations of an existing situation. To deliver a truly useful product, the analytical team must work with the stakeholders to innovate—that is, to develop a better way to do the work, and a product that supports this better way of working. They make use of innovation workshops where the team uses creative thinking techniques and innovative triggers to generate new and better ideas for the work and the eventual product.

We look at developing innovative products in Chapter 8, Starting the Solution.

READING

Maiden, Neil, Suzanne Robertson, Sharon Manning, and John Greenwood. *Integrating Creativity Workshops into Structured Requirements Processes.* Proceedings of DIS 2004, Cambridge, Mass. ACM Press.

Michalko, Michael. *Thinkertoys: A Handbook of Creative-Thinking Techniques,* second edition. Ten Speed Press, 2006.

Robertson, Suzanne, and James Robertson. *Requirements-Led Project Management.* Addison-Wesley, 2005.

Figure 2.3

The blastoff determines the scope of the work to be improved. The business use cases are derived from the scope. Each of the business use cases is studied by the requirements analysts and the relevant stakeholders to discover the desired way of working. When this is understood, the appropriate product can be determined (the PUC scenario) and requirements or user stories written from it.

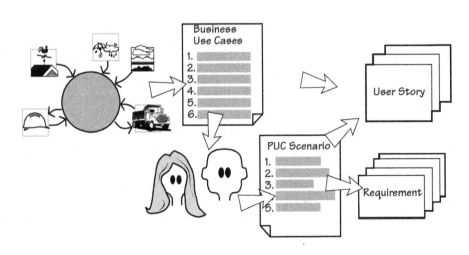

Quick and Dirty Modeling

Models can be used at any time in the Volere life cycle; in Figure 2.1, we show this activity as "Prototype the Work." There are, of course, formal models such as you would find in UML or BPMN, but a lot of the time business analysts can make productive use of quick sketches and diagrams to model the work being investigated. One quick and dirty modeling technique we should mention here is using Post-it notes to model functionality; each note can be used to represent an activity, and the notes can be rapidly rearranged to show different ways the work is done or could be done. We find that stakeholders relate to this way of modeling their business processes, and are always willing to participate with hands-on manipulation of the Post-its to show what they think the work should be. We discuss this kind of modeling more fully in Chapter 5, Investigating the Work.

In Chapter 8, Starting the Solution, we examine how you move into an implementation of the requirements discovered so far. At this point, your models change from being something to explain the current work, to something to explain how the future product will help with that work.

We can now start to refer to this type of model as a prototype—a quick and dirty *representation* of a potential product using pencil and paper, whiteboards, or some other familiar means, as shown in Figure 2.4. Prototypes used at this stage are intended to present the user with a simulation of the requirements as they might be implemented. The IceBreaker business analysts sketch some proposed interfaces and ways that the needed functionality might be implemented—this visual way of working allows the engineers and other stakeholders to coalesce their ideas for the future product.

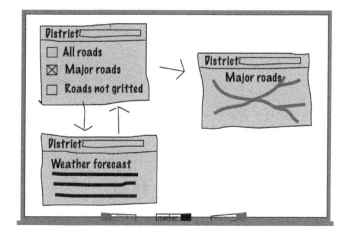

Figure 2.4

A quick and dirty prototype built on a whiteboard to provide a rapid visual explanation of how some of the requirements might be implemented, and to clarify misunderstood or missing requirements.

Scenarios

Scenarios are so useful that we have devoted the whole of Chapter 6 to them. Scenarios show the functionality of a business process by breaking it into a series of easily recognizable steps, written in English (or whatever language you use at work) so that they are accessible to all stakeholders. The IceBreaker analysts used scenarios to describe the business processes and present their understanding of the needed functionality. These scenarios were then revised as needed—different stakeholders took an interest in different parts of the scenario, and after a short time, the business analysts were able to have everyone understand and come to a consensus on what the work was to be.

Refer to Chapter 6 for a discussion about using scenarios.

Once they are agreed, the scenarios become the foundation for the requirements.

Writing the Requirements

A major problem in system development is misunderstood requirements. To avoid any misunderstanding, the analysts must write their requirements in an unambiguous and testable manner, and at the same time ensure that the originating stakeholder understands and agrees with the written requirement before it is passed on to the developers. In other words, the analysts write the requirements so as to ensure that parties at either end of the development spectrum are able to have an identical understanding of what is needed.

Although the task of writing down the requirements might seem an onerous burden, we have found it to be the most effective way to ensure that the essence of the requirement has been captured and communicated, and that the delivered product can be tested. (See Figure 2.5.)

Figure 2.5

The requirements are captured in written form to facilitate communication between the stakeholders, the analysts, and the developers (and anyone else who has an interest). By writing the requirements carefully, the team ensures that the correct product is built.

I want it easy enough so my mother could use it.

The developer doesn't know your mother. How about "A truck driver shall be able to select the correct route within 90 seconds of first encountering the product"?

The IceBreaker analysts start by writing their requirements using business language so that the nontechnical stakeholders can understand them and verify their correctness. They add a *rationale* to the requirements—it shows the background reason for the requirement, which removes much of the ambiguity. Further, to ensure complete precision and to confirm that the product designers and developers can build exactly what the stakeholder needs, they write a *fit criterion* for each requirement. A fit criterion quantifies, or measures, the requirement, which makes it testable, which in turn allows the testers to determine whether an implementation meets—in other words, fits—the requirement.

The rationale and the fit criterion make the requirement more understandable for the business stakeholder, who has on several occasions said, "I am not going to have any requirements that I do not understand, nor will I have any that are not useful or that don't contribute to my work. I want to understand the contributions that they make. That's why I want each one to be both justified and measurable."

Chapter 12 describes fit criteria in detail.

The business analyst has a different, but complementary, reason for measuring requirements: "I need to ensure that each requirement is unambiguous; that is, it must have the same meaning to both the stakeholder who originated it and the developer who will build it. I also need to measure the requirement against the stakeholder's expectations. If I can't put a measurement to it, then I can never tell if we are building the product the stakeholder really needs."

The analysts use two devices to make it easier to write their specification. The first device, the *requirements specification template,* is an outline and guide to writing a requirements specification. The business analysts use it as a checklist of the requirements they should be asking for, and as a consistent way of organizing their requirements documents. The second device is a *shell,* also known as a *snow card.* Each atomic (that's the lowest level) requirement is made up of a number of attributes, and the snow card is a convenient layout for ensuring that each requirement has the correct constituents.

Of course, the writing process is not really a separate activity. In reality, it is integrated with the activities that surround it—trawling, prototyping, and the quality gateway. However, for the purposes of understanding what is involved in putting the correct requirements into a communicable form, we will look at it separately.

Refer to Chapters 10, 11, 12, and 16 for detailed discussions of writing the requirements.

Iterative development methods employ *user stories* as a way of conveying the requirements. The stories are, in fact, placeholders for lower-level requirements; they are augmented during conversations between the developers and the stakeholders to flush out the detailed requirements. In Chapter 14, Requirements and Iterative Development, we look closely at how the business analyst can produce better user stories. Working iteratively does not obviate the need for requirements, but rather seeks to discover and communicate the requirements in a different manner.

The primary reason for wanting written requirements is not to *have* written requirements (although that is often necessary), but rather to *write* them. Writing the requirement, together with its associated rationale and fit criterion, clarifies it in the writer's mind, and sets it down in an unambiguous and verifiable manner. To put that another way, if the business analyst cannot correctly write the requirement, he has not yet understood it.

Quality Gateway

Requirements are the foundation for all that is to follow in the product development cycle. Thus it stands to reason that if the right product is to be built, the requirements must be correct before they are handed over to the builders. To ensure correctness, the quality gateway tests the requirements (Figure 2.6). The IceBreaker team has set up a single point that every requirement must pass through before it can become a part of the specification. This gateway is manned by two people—the lead requirements analyst and a tester—and they are the only people authorized to pass requirements through the gateway. Working together, they check each requirement for completeness, relevance, testability, coherency, traceability, and several other qualities before they allow it to be passed to the developers.

By ensuring that the only way for requirements to be made available for the developers is for those requirements to pass through the quality gateway, the project team is in control of the requirements, and not the other way around.

Chapter 13 describes how the quality gateway tests the requirements.

Figure 2.6

The quality gateway ensures that requirements are rigorous by testing each one for completeness, correctness, measurability, absence of ambiguity, and several other attributes, before allowing the requirement to be passed to the developers.

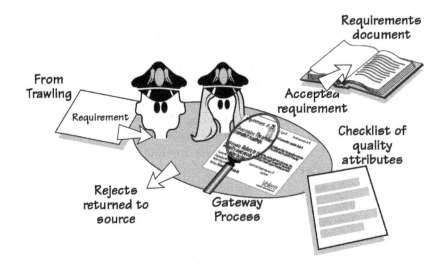

Reusing Requirements

The requirements for any product you build are never completely unique. We suggest that before starting on any new requirements project, you go through the specifications written for previous projects and look for potentially reusable material. Sometimes you may find dozens of requirements that you can reuse without alteration. More often you will find requirements that, although they are not exactly what you want, are suitable as the basis for some of the requirements you will write in the new project.

For example, in the IceBreaker project, the rules for road engineering have not changed much over the years. Thus, the requirements analysts working on various projects do not have to rediscover them, but can simply reuse them. They also know that the business of vehicle scheduling does not change radically over time, so their trawling process can take advantage of some requirements from previous projects.

Similarly, for different projects within your organization, the non-functional requirements are fairly standard, so you can start with a specification from one of the previous projects and use it as a checklist.

The point about reusing requirements is that once a requirement has been successfully specified for a product, and the product itself is successful, the requirement does not have to be reinvented or rediscovered. In Chapter 15, Reusing Requirements, we discuss how you can take advantage of the knowledge that already exists within your organization, and how you can save yourself time by recycling requirements from previous projects.

See Chapter 15 for more on reusing requirements.

Reviewing the Requirements

The quality gateway exists to keep bad requirements out of the specification—it does this one requirement at a time. Nevertheless, at the point when you think your requirements specification is complete (or as complete as you need it for the next activity), you should review it. This final review checks that there are no missing requirements, that all the requirements are consistent with one another, and that any conflicts between the requirements have been resolved. In short, the review confirms that the specification is really complete and suitable so that you can move on to the next stage of development.

This review also offers you an opportunity to reassess the costs and risks of the project. Now that you have a complete set of requirements, you know a lot more about the product than you did at the project blastoff. In particular, you have a much more precise knowledge of the scope and functionality of the product, so this is a good time to remeasure its size. From that size, and from your knowledge of the project's constraints and solution architecture, you can estimate the cost to construct the product.

See Chapter 17, Requirements Completeness, for more on reviewing the specification.

You also know at this stage which types of requirements are associated with the greatest risks. For example, the users might have asked for an interface that your organization has not built before. Or perhaps they want to use untried technology to build the product. Perhaps the developer might not have the people with the skills needed to build the product as specified? By reassessing the risks at this point, you give yourself a more realistic chance of building the desired product successfully.

Iterative and Incremental Processes

One common misconception in the requirements world is that you have to gather *all* the requirements before moving on to the next step of design and construction. In other words, doing requirements means that you employ a traditional waterfall process. In some circumstances this is necessary, but not always. On the one hand, if you are outsourcing or if the requirements document forms the basis of a contract, then clearly you need to have a complete requirements specification. On the other hand, if the overall architecture is known, then construction and delivery can often begin before all the requirements are discovered. We show these two approaches in Figure 2.7, and suggest you consider which one works best for you when working on your own requirements projects. We also have a lot more to say on various approaches in Chapter 9, Strategies for Today's Business Analyst.

On the IceBreaker project, the developers are ready to start building the product, so after the blastoff the key stakeholders select three (it could be any low number) of the highest-priority and greatest-value business use cases. The requirements analysts trawl and gather the requirements for only those

Figure 2.7

Two (of many) variations on development life cycles. At the top of the figure is the traditional waterfall approach, in which the complete requirements document is put together before product development begins. At the bottom of the figure is an iterative process, in which, after a preliminary analysis, the product is developed in small increments. Both approaches achieve the same purpose.

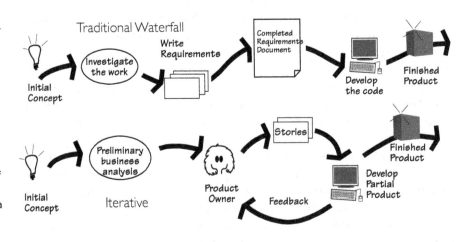

business use cases, putting aside the rest of the work for now. Then, when the first tranche of requirements have successfully passed the quality gateway, the developers start their work. The intention is to implement a small number of use cases as early as possible to get the reaction of the stakeholders—if there are going to be any nasty surprises, the IceBreaker team wants to get them as early as possible. While the developers are building and delivering the first lot of business use cases, the analysts are working on the requirements for the next-highest-priority ones. Soon they have established a rhythm for delivery, with new use cases being implemented and delivered every few weeks.

Requirements Retrospective

You are reading this book about a requirements process, presumably with the intention of improving your own process. Retrospectives, sometimes known as *lessons learned,* are one of the most effective tools for discovering the good and bad of a process, and suggesting remedial action. Retrospectives for requirements projects consist of a series of interviews with stakeholders and group sessions with the developers. The intention is to canvas all the people involved in the project and ask these questions:

- What did we do right?
- What did we do wrong?
- If we had to do it again, what would we do differently?

By looking for honest answers to these questions, you give yourself the best chance of improving your process. The idea is very simple: Do more of what works and less of what doesn't.

Keep a record of the lessons learned from your retrospectives. While humans have memory and can learn from their experience to their advantage in future projects, organizations don't learn—unless you write down the experience. By keeping the lessons learned available in some readily accessible manner, subsequent projects can learn from your accomplishments and mishaps.

"If we did the project again tomorrow, what would we do differently?"

Your retrospective can be very informal: a coffee-time meeting with the project group, or the project leader collecting e-mail messages from the participants. Alternatively, if the stakes are higher, this process can be formalized to the point where it is run by an outside facilitator who canvases the participants, both individually and as a group, and publishes a retrospective report.

The most notable feature of retrospectives is this: Companies that regularly conduct retrospectives consistently report significant improvements in their processes. In short, retrospectives are probably the cheapest investment you can make in improving your own process.

Evolution of Requirements

You start a project with little more than a vision—and sometimes a fairly blurred vision—of the desired future state of your owner's work. (As we have done elsewhere in this book, we use the term "work" to refer to the area of the owner's organization where improvements are to be made, usually by automating or re-automating part of it.)

During the early stages of requirements discovery, analysts deploy models of varying degrees of formality to help them and the stakeholders to learn what the work is, and what it is to be. From this investigation of the work, everyone arrives at the same level of understanding such that the stakeholders find improvements that will be truly beneficial.

It helps enormously when coming to an understanding of the work if the analysts and stakeholders can see the *essence* of the work. The essence is an abstraction of the work that sees the underlying policy of the work without the technology that clouds our vision of what the work actually is. This "thinking above the line," as we call it in Chapter 7, Understanding the Real Problem, is important if the requirements are not to merely replicate whatever it is that exists at the moment, and if "technological fossils" and inappropriate process are not to be inadvertently reimplemented.

The understanding of the work evolves and matures, and at some point it is possible for the stakeholders, guided by the business analysts and the systems architects, to determine the optimal product to improve that work. When this stage is reached, the business analysts determine the detailed functionality for the product (keep in mind that not all of the work's functionality would be included in the product) and to write its requirements. The non-functional requirements are derived at roughly the same time and written along with those constraints that are not already recorded. At this point, the requirements are written in a technologically neutral manner—they specify what the product has to do for the work, but not how the technology will do it.

You can think of these requirements as "business requirements," meaning that they specify the product needed to support the business. Once they are adequately understood, they are released to the designer, who adds the product's technological requirements before producing the final specification for the builders. This process is illustrated in Figure 2.8.

We have said that the requirements evolve, but this process should not be thought of as an inexorable progression toward some known destination. As Earl Beede points out, every time you think of a solution, it causes some new problems that require you to backtrack and revisit some of your earlier work. When we are talking about a requirements process, keep in mind that the process, if it is to be useful, must allow you to move backward as well as forward. Naturally, you would like to spend most of your time moving

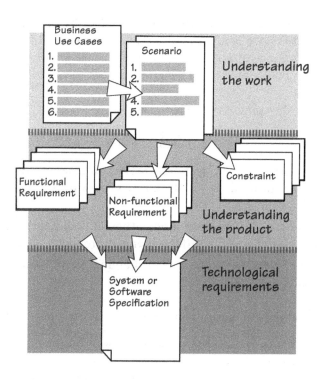

Figure 2.8

The requirements evolve as development of the product progresses. They start out as fairly vague ideas as the analysts and stakeholders explore the work area. As the ideas for the product emerge over time, the requirements become precise and testable. They remain technologically neutral until the designer becomes involved and adds those requirements needed to make the product work in its technological environment.

forward, but don't be too disappointed if you have to return to some things you thought you had put behind you.

The Template

It is easier to write requirements, and far more convenient, if you have a guide to writing them. Appendix A of this book provides The Volere Requirements Specification Template, which is a complete blueprint for describing your product's functionality and capabilities. This template, which is a distillation of literally hundreds of requirements specifications, is in use by thousands of organizations all over the world.

It is convenient to categorize requirements into several types—each of the template's sections describes a type of requirement and its variations. Thus, as you discover the requirements with your stakeholders, you add them to your specification, using the template as a guide to necessary content.

The template is designed to serve as a sophisticated checklist, providing you with a list of what to write about, and suggestions on how to write about them. The table of contents for the template is reproduced here, and we will discuss each section in detail later in the book.

The complete Volere Requirements Specification Template is found in Appendix A.

Our associate, Stephen Mellor, suggests using the template by going directly to the most pressing sections—the ones that seem to you to be most useful—and then revisiting the template as needed. You will probably use most of it, but it is not—really not—a template that you fill by starting on page one and working through to the bitter end. Like any good tool, when used wisely the template provides a significant advantage to your requirements discovery.

Here, then, is the content of the template.

Project Drivers—reasons and motivators for the project

1 **The Purpose of the Project**—the reason for making the investment in building the product and the business advantage that you want to achieve by doing so

2 **The Client, the Customer, and Other Stakeholders**—the people with an interest in or an influence on the product

3 **Users of the Product**—the intended end users, and how they affect the product's usability

Project Constraints—the restrictions on the project and the product

4 **Requirements Constraints**—the limitations on the project, and the restrictions on the design of the product

5 **Naming Conventions and Definitions**—the vocabulary of the project

6 **Relevant Facts and Assumptions**—outside influences that make some difference to this product, or assumptions that the developers are making

Functional Requirements—the functionality of the product

7 **The Scope of the Work**—the business area or domain under study

8 **The Scope of the Product**—a definition of the intended product boundaries and the product's connections to adjacent systems

9 **Functional and Data Requirements**—the things the product must do and the data manipulated by the functions

Non-functional Requirements—the product's qualities

10 **Look and Feel Requirements**—the intended appearance

11 **Usability and Humanity Requirements**—what the product has to be if it is to be successfully used by its intended audience

12 **Performance Requirements**—how fast, big, accurate, safe, reliable, robust, scalable, and long-lasting, and what capacity

13 **Operational and Environmental Requirements**—the product's intended operating environment

14 **Maintainability and Support Requirements**—how changeable the product must be and what support is needed

15 **Security Requirements**—the security, confidentiality, and integrity of the product

16 **Cultural Requirements**—human and sociological factors

17 **Legal Requirements**—conformance to applicable laws

Project Issues—issues relevant to the project that builds the product

18 **Open Issues**—as yet unresolved issues with a possible bearing on the success of the product

19 **Off-the-Shelf Solutions**—ready-made components that might be used instead of building something from scratch

20 **New Problems**—problems caused by the introduction of the new product

21 **Tasks**—things to be done to bring the product into production

22 **Migration to the New Product**—tasks to convert from existing systems

23 **Risks**—the risks that the project is most likely to incur

24 **Costs**—early estimates of the cost or effort needed to build the product

25 **User Documentation**—the plan for building the user instructions and documentation

26 **Waiting Room**—requirements that might be included in future releases of the product

27 **Ideas for Solutions**—design ideas that we do not want to lose

Browse through the template in Appendix A before you go too much further in this book. You will find a lot of information about writing requirements, plus much food for thought about the kinds of requirements you are looking for.

Throughout this book, we will refer to requirements by their type—that is, one of the types as shown in the template's table of contents.

The Snow Card

Whereas the template is a guide to *what* to write about, the snow card is a guide to *how* to write it. Individual requirements have a structure—a set of attributes, where each attribute contributes something to your understanding of the requirement, and to the precision of the requirement, and thereby to the accuracy of the product's development.

Before we go any further, we must point out that although we call this device a card, and we use cards in our courses, and this book is sprinkled with diagrams featuring this card, we are not advocating writing all your requirements on cards. Some good things can be realized by using cards when interviewing stakeholders and quickly scribbling requirements as they come to light. Later, these requirements are recorded in some electronic form; at that time, their component information is filled in. Thus any reference to "card" should be taken to mean (probably) a computerized version.

At first glance, the card might seem rather bureaucratic. (See Figure 2.9.) We are not seeking to add to your requirements burden, but rather to provide a way of accurately and conveniently gathering the needed information—each of the attributes of the snow card makes a contribution. We shall explain these as we work our way through this book.

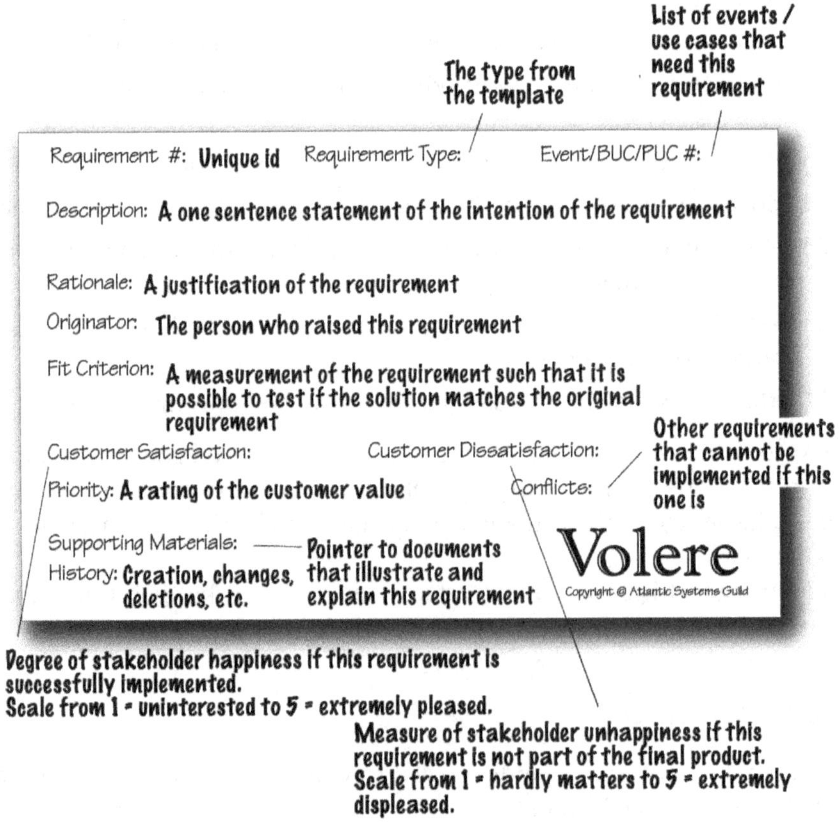

Any number of automated tools are available for recording, analyzing, and tracing requirements.

Figure 2.9

The requirements shell or snow card, consisting of a 5-inch by 8-inch card, printed with the requirement's attributes, that is used for our initial requirements gathering. Each of the attributes contributes to the understanding and testability of the requirement. Although a copyright notice appears on the card, we have no objections to any reader making use of it for his or her requirements work, provided the source is acknowledged.

The type from the template

List of events / use cases that need this requirement

Requirement #: **Unique Id**   Requirement Type: Event/BUC/PUC #:

Description: **A one sentence statement of the intention of the requirement**

Rationale: **A justification of the requirement**

Originator: **The person who raised this requirement**

Fit Criterion: **A measurement of the requirement such that it is possible to test if the solution matches the original requirement**

Customer Satisfaction: Customer Dissatisfaction:

Priority: **A rating of the customer value**   Conflicts:

Other requirements that cannot be implemented if this one is

Supporting Materials: —— **Pointer to documents that illustrate and explain this requirement**

History: **Creation, changes, deletions, etc.**

Volere
Copyright @ Atlantic Systems Guild

Degree of stakeholder happiness if this requirement is successfully implemented.
Scale from 1 = uninterested to 5 = extremely pleased.

Measure of stakeholder unhappiness if this requirement is not part of the final product.
Scale from 1 = hardly matters to 5 = extremely displeased.

Your Own Requirements Process

The itinerant peddler of quack potions, Doctor Dulcamara, sings the praises of his elixir—it is guaranteed to cure toothache, make you potent, eliminate wrinkles and give you smooth beautiful skin, destroy mice and bugs, and make the object of your affections fall in love with you. This rather fanciful libretto from Donizetti's opera *L'elisir d'amore* points out something that, although very obvious, is often disregarded: There is no such thing as the universal cure.

We really would like to be able to present you with a requirements process that has all the attributes of Doctor Dulcamara's elixir—a process that suits all projects for all applications in all organizations. We can't. We know from experience that every project has different needs. However, we also know that some fundamental principles hold good for any project. So instead of attempting to provide you with a one-size-fits-all magic potion, we have distilled our experiences from a wide variety of projects to provide you with a set of foundation activities and deliverables that apply to any project.

We have distilled experience from a wide variety of projects to provide you with a set of foundation activities and deliverables that apply to any project.

The process described in this book is made up of the things you have to do to successfully discover the requirements. Likewise, the deliverables presented here are the foundation for any kind of requirements activity. Our intention is not to say that there is only one true path to requirements Nirvana, but rather to give you the components you need for successful requirements projects.

As you read this book, think about how you can use these components within the constraints of your own culture, your own environment, your own organizational structure, and your own chosen way of product development.

To adapt this process, you should understand the deliverables it produces—the rest of this book will discuss these items in detail. Once you understand the content and purpose of each deliverable, ask how each one (provided it is relevant) would best be produced within your project environment using your resources:

READING
Brooks, Fred. *No Silver Bullet: Essence and Accidents of Software Engineering,* and "No Silver Bullet Refired." *The Mythical Man-Month: Essays on Software Engineering,* twentieth anniversary edition. Addison-Wesley, 1995. This is possibly the most influential book on software development; it certainly is timeless.

- What is the deliverable called within your environment? Use the definitions of the terms used in the generic process model and identify the equivalent deliverable in your organization.

- Is this deliverable relevant for this project?

- How much do you already know about this deliverable? Do you know enough to be able to avoid devoting additional time to it?

- Who produces the deliverable? Understand which parts of the deliverable are produced by whom. Also, when several people are involved, you need to define the interfaces between them.

- When is the deliverable produced? Map your project phases to the generic process.

- Where is the deliverable produced? A generic deliverable is often the result of fragments that are produced in a number of geographical locations. Define the interfaces between the different locations and specify how they will work.

- Who needs to review the deliverable? Look for existing cultural checkpoints within your organization. Do you have recognized stages or phases in your projects at which peers, users, or managers must review your specification?

The generic model describes deliverables and procedures for producing them; our intention is that you decide how you use them.

We also point you to Chapter 9 of this book, entitled Strategies for Today's Business Analyst. This chapter considers how you might approach your requirements projects. We suggest that before you become too involved in the mechanics of requirements discovery, you think about the strategy that is most suitable for you.

Formality Guide

There is every reason to make your requirements discovery and communication as informal as possible. We say "as possible" because it is not so much what you would like as what your situation demands—often the degree of formality will be dictated by factors beyond your control. For example, you may be developing software using contracted outsourced development. In this case, there is a clear need for a complete written requirements specification. In other cases, the way you communicate your requirements can be informal to the point that a portion of the requirements are not written, or partially written, and communicated verbally.

We have included a formality guide to suggest where you might take a more relaxed approach to recording requirements, as well as those times when you should rightly be more systematic with your requirements discovery and communication. These are the conventions you will encounter as you move through this book.

Rabbit—small, fast, and short-lived. Rabbit projects are typically smaller projects with shorter lifetimes, where close stakeholder participation is possible. Rabbit projects usually include a lesser number of stakeholders.

Rabbit projects are usually iterative. They discover requirements in small units (probably one business use case at a time) and then implement a small increment to the working functionality, using whatever has been implemented to solicit feedback from the stakeholders.

Rabbit projects do not spend a great deal of time writing the requirements, but use conversations with the stakeholders as a way to elaborate the requirements written on story cards. Rabbit projects almost always co-locate the business knowledge stakeholders with the business analysts and the developers.

Horse—fast, strong, and dependable. Horse projects are probably the most common corporate projects—they are the "halfway house" of formality. Horse projects need some formality—it is likely that there is a need for written requirements so that they can be handed from one department to another. Horse projects have medium longevity and involve more than a dozen stakeholders, often in several locations, factors that necessitate consistently written documentation.

If you cannot categorize your own project, think of it as a horse.

Elephant—solid, strong, long life, and a long memory. An elephant project has a need for a complete requirements specification. If you are outsourcing the work, or if your organizational structure requires complete, written specifications, you're an elephant. In certain industries, such as pharmaceuticals, aircraft manufacture, or the military, regulators demand not only that full specifications be produced, but also that the process used to produce them be documented and auditable. Elephant projects typically have a long duration, and they involve many stakeholders in distributed locations. There are also a large number of developers, necessitating more formal ways of communicating.

The Rest of This Book

We have described—briefly—a process for discovering, communicating, and verifying requirements. The remainder of this book describes the various activities in this process, along with their deliverables, in some detail. Feel free to jump to any chapter that is of immediate concern—we wrote the chapters in more or less the order in which you would do each of the activities, but you don't have to read them that way.

And please, while you are reading this book, be constantly asking yourself how you will do the things we describe. After all, it is you who has to do them.

We hope find useful ideas, processes and artifacts, in the rest of this book. We also hope you enjoy reading and using it.

Scoping the Business Problem

3

in which we establish a definition of the business area to be changed, thereby ensuring that the project team has a clear vision of what their project is meant to achieve

Let's revisit our fundamental premise: If a piece of software (or any device or service) is to be built, it must be optimally valuable to its owner.

From this statement, you can safely infer that if you are to know what is optimally valuable, you must firstly determine what the owner is actually doing, who he is doing it with or for, and why he wants to do it. To put that another way: What are the scope, stakeholders, and goals? Hold that thought—we will come back to it in a moment.

In the Volere process model, as shown in Figure 3.1, the first activity is the Project Blastoff. It is during this activity—typically a meeting of the key stakeholders—that you decide the key factors that, taken together, determine the viability of the requirements project.

If a piece of software is to be built, it must be optimally valuable to its owner.

Project Blastoff

The blastoff identifies the boundary of the work area the product is to become a part of, and determines the purpose the product is to fulfill. It also identifies the stakeholders—those people who have an interest in the success of the product. Other deliverables from the blastoff qualify the project, and are used as inputs to subsequent requirements discovery activities.

You might know this activity as "project kick-off," "project initiation," "project launch," or any one of the many other names given to it. Whatever you call it, its purpose is to lay the groundwork so your requirements discovery is efficient and effective.

The blastoff produces a number of deliverables. You might be given some of these by your project manager; others, you might have to dig out for yourself. In any event, you need these deliverables if you are to have a successful

Figure 3.1

The Project Blastoff activity lays the groundwork for the requirements discovery activities to come.

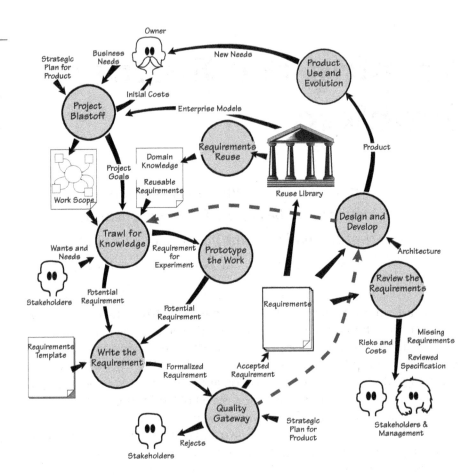

requirements activity. Look through the following list and consider the effect that each of these typical blastoff deliverables would have on your project:

- *Purpose of the project:* a short, quantified statement of what the product is intended to do, and what benefit it brings to the business. This statement of purpose is an explanation of why the business is investing in the project, along with the business benefit it wants to achieve. This justifies the project and serves as a focus for the requirements discovery process.

- *The scope of the work:* The business area affected by the installation of the product. You need to understand this work to specify the most appropriate product.

- *The stakeholders:* The people with an interest in the product. This group includes anyone who has some influence on the outcome or has knowledge needed to uncover the requirements for the product.

- *Constraints:* Restrictions on the scope or style of the product. These items include predetermined design solutions that must be used, constraints on changing the way that business processes are currently implemented, and the time and money that are available for the project.

- *Names:* Any special terminology to be used in this project.

- *Relevant facts and assumptions:* Are there any special facts people need to know? Or are there assumptions being made that may affect the outcome of the project?

- *The estimated cost:* Some of the deliverables from the blastoff provide input to the estimating process and allow fairly good estimates to be made early in the project. This is not really a requirements issue, but as the requirements deliverables are prime input, your project management will thank you for it.

- *The risks:* Possibly a short risk analysis to reveal the main risks faced by the project. Someone skilled at risk assessment should perform this analysis.

Taken together (see Figure 3.2), these deliverables give you enough information to make the final deliverable from the blastoff:

- *Go/no go decision:* Is the project viable, and does the cost of producing the product make it worthwhile? Do you have enough information to proceed with the requirements activity, or should you ask for extra time to gather more information and build a better foundation?

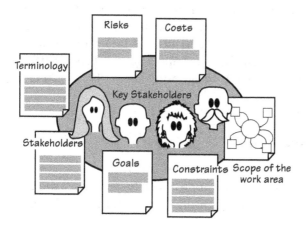

Figure 3.2

The blastoff activity assembles enough information to ensure that the project can proceed smoothly. It also verifies that the project is viable and worthwhile. Most of the outputs serve as the foundation for the trawling activity about to come; the risks and costs are used by project management.

Formality Guide

The blastoff deliverables—especially scope, stakeholders, and goals—are needed by any project, regardless of its size or aspirations for informality. Even a small change to an existing system needs to ask these questions. Any project must have a clear understanding of its goals if it is to avoid wandering aimlessly. Additionally, a project must understand the work to be improved; otherwise, it runs the risk of producing a solution in search of a problem.

In the previous chapter we spoke about rabbit, horse, and elephant projects. These types relate to formality and their differences are as follows.

Rabbit projects should have a sketch of the work scope diagram pinned to the wall close to their user stories; close by should be a list of stakeholders. Finally, written with a broad marker pen on the wall, are the project goals. Rabbits will probably have only a brief blastoff meeting at best, with most of the consensus on the blastoff coming from wikis, phone calls, and other informal interactive means. Despite the relative informality, we cannot stress how important it is to document the work scope, and to ensure that you are thinking about the *work,* and not just the intended product.

Horse projects should be more formal and hold a blastoff meeting; they should also record their deliverables and communicate them to the appropriate stakeholders. Horse projects might benefit from producing a first-cut sketch of the guessed-at product to ensure all stakeholders (we are thinking of the nontechnical ones) understand where the project is headed. This sketch must be destroyed as soon as the stakeholders have confirmed it.

Elephants have a lot to lose by not having the blastoff deliverables firmly in place before proceeding further in the product development process. In most cases, the deliverables are discovered during meetings with the key stakeholders, and the results are recorded and distributed. Elephants should take the additional step of having the quality assurance (QA) people test their blastoff deliverables: Elephant projects are critical, and costly if they make errors, so the foundation of the requirements must be proved to be rock solid. Risk analysis and cost estimation are important to elephant projects; having a clearly defined and properly understood work scope is crucial.

The degree of formality you apply to the blastoff deliverables varies, but that does not stretch to ignoring them. This chapter explains these deliverables.

Setting the Scope

Let's go back to optimal value and the owner.

If the owner is an organization, you have to understand the business processes and aims of that organization, or, as is the case for most projects, the part of the organization your project will affect. If the owner is an individual using some personal computer software or a mobile device app, you still have to understand what that owner is doing, and what he wants to do, if you are to deliver optimal value. In any event, if you want to build something valuable, then you have to understand what the owner values and what he is trying to achieve when he uses your product.

It is unlikely that you will ever have to study the entirety of the owner's business. Almost certainly, you need to examine only part of the business—the part that you will change when you install the product you intend to build. Let's call this part of the business "the work"; the first task in the product development life cycle is to define the precise scope of that work. You need to know which parts of the business are included in the work, and which parts can be safely excluded.

Figure 3.3 illustrates the relationship between different scopes: the scope of the work, the scope of the entire organization within the outside world, and the potential scopes of the product your project is to build.

For the moment, you are intentionally ignoring any proffered solution; until you understand what the solution is to be used for, there is little point in spending time on it. Instead, you should step back and look at the work that the owner values and, most importantly, define its scope.

Step back and look at the work that the owner values, and define its scope.

The scope you are interested in at the beginning of the requirements project is the scope of the owner's work—specifically, the piece of work that the owner would like to change and improve. This work might be a commercial business activity, some scientific or technical work, or a game—anything at

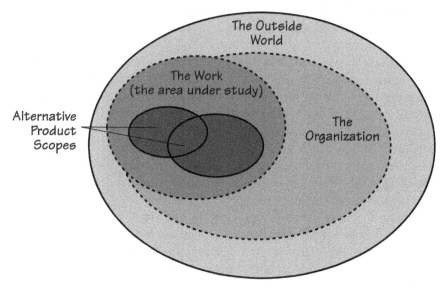

Figure 3.3

The work is the part of the organization that you need to study to discover the requirements. The work is usually connected to other parts of the organization and to the outside world. You must study the work well enough to understand how it functions. This understanding will enable you to come up with alternative scopes for the product and eventually choose the one to build.

all that involves some kind of meaningful activity. The work might be currently automated, it might be manual, or it might take advantage of a combination of these approaches that makes use of several different devices. At this stage it makes no difference whether your product is to be sold to an outside customer or used within your own organization. As long as it involves some processing and some data, we shall refer to it as "work," and you must know the scope of it.

Separate the Work from its Environment

Any piece of work must be connected to at least one other piece of work; there can be no such thing as a piece of work without any external connections. If there were no connections, then the work would be useless; it would not have any outputs. It is also true that any activity within that work is connected to at least one other activity. With that point in mind, you can separate the activities that you are interested in—the ones inside your work—from other activities that hold no interest for you. The latter activities are considered to be outside the scope of your work.

To make this separation, you rely on the simple fact that all activities are driven by data. We spoke a moment ago about activities being connected to other activities, with this connection being a flow of data. That is to say, an activity produces some data and then hands this data on to another activity. When the next activity in turn receives its incoming flow of data, it is triggered to do whatever processing it is meant to do, and produces a different data output, which is in turn sent to another activity. Thus these flows of data are the connections between activities.

By identifying these data connections, you determine the boundary of your interest. To do so, you say that you include in your work area the activity that produces a certain packet of data, but you are not interested in the activity that receives this data packet. By drawing a line to represent your work boundary between similarly coupled activities, you create a partition that eventually includes all the activities that are to be part of your work.

You cannot effectively describe the work area by simply looking at the processors that do the work. The problem is that almost all processors—computers, humans, and mechanical devices—are capable of carrying out more than one type of activity. Nor can you effectively describe the work area using words alone: It is difficult, if not impossible, to accurately describe what to study and what to ignore.

To achieve the optimal value for the owner, study enough of the owner's work to identify what is valuable.

To achieve the optimal value for the owner, study enough of the owner's work to identify what is valuable. Then decide how much effort can be expended to build a product to improve the valuable part of the work. Clearly, if you study too much, then the project will produce less value because you are wasting resources studying unnecessary activities. Conversely, if you study too little of the owner's work, you may fail to achieve the optimal value because you do not know enough about the business to make the correct value decisions.

Let's look at an example of how you can isolate the activities to be studied from those you will ignore. We said earlier that activities have data flowing between them. This simple fact enables you to construct a diagram that shows the data that flows from a non-interesting activity to the collection of activities that you find interesting. A sample of this diagram—called a *context diagram* or a *work scope diagram*—appears in Figure 3.5. Before examining it, however, you need a little background on this diagram.

IceBreaker

IceBreaker is a case study we have put together to illustrate the requirements process. IceBreaker uses data from the environment to predict when ice will form on roads. It then schedules trucks to treat the roads with de-icing material (a salt compound) before the roads can become dangerous. The IceBreaker case study uses subject-matter knowledge from the many ice forecasting and road de-icing systems, and other products produced by Vaisala (U.K.) Limited and Vaisala Worldwide. We acknowledge Vaisala's permission to use its material and the company's kind cooperation. Figure 3.4 depicts a weather station used by IceBreaker.

Imagine IceBreaker is your project. You work for Saltworks Systems, and you are responsible for producing the requirements specification. The first customer for the IceBreaker product is the Northumberland County

Figure 3.4

This weather station transmits data about the weather and road surface conditions to IceBreaker, which uses the information to predict ice formation. These predictions are used to dispatch trucks to treat the roads with de-icing material. Photo of Vaisala Weather Station ROSA courtesy of Vaisala. www.vaisala.com.

Highways Department. Northumberland is a county in the northeast of England, tucked up under the border with Scotland, with serious snow and icy conditions in winter. The Highways Department is responsible for keeping the roads free of ice that is likely to cause accidents; it has agreed to provide expertise and information for you to build the optimally valuable product for the department.

First-Cut Work Context

A lot of activities are carried out as part of the process in which the IceBreaker work predicts whether there is a need to treat a road: A weather forecast is generated, the temperature at the surface of the road is taken, predictions about which roads will freeze are made, trucks are dispatched, and so on. To deliver optimal value, you must determine which of these activities should be studied because they have the possibility for improvement, and which can be safely excluded from the study.

To illustrate your decisions, collect all the activities to be studied and hide them (for the moment) in the central circle. Put the connected activities that are not part of your study outside the circle, and show the data that connects them. Using this approach, our first draft of the context diagram for the IceBreaker work is shown in Figure 3.5.

Figure 3.5

The work context diagram identifies the scope of the work to be studied. It shows the work as a single activity, surrounded by the adjacent systems. The named arrows represent the data that flows between the work and the adjacent systems. The adjacent systems are the activities that you have decided not to study.

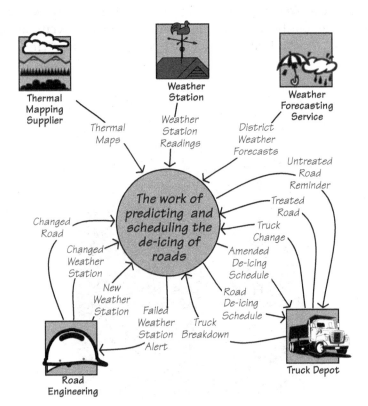

The context diagram shows the work to be studied, as well as those activities you decide not to study. The latter activities are called *adjacent systems*. The purpose of the context diagram is to show the processing responsibilities of the work and the responsibilities of the adjacent systems. But be aware that the responsibilities are in reality defined by the flows of data on the context diagram. As an example, the flow called *Truck Change* advises the work about changes to the de-icing trucks—for example, new trucks that have been added to the fleet, trucks that have been taken out of service, and modifications to trucks that would affect the way that they are scheduled. Why is this flow there? The work needs this information when it allocates a truck to each road that needs treatment as part of the production of the de-icing schedule. But what if you changed this responsibility? What if the depot became responsible for allocating trucks to the icy roads? In that scenario, the flow would be different. In fact, the *Truck Change* flow would not appear on the work context diagram at all, as the activities that are triggered by this data flow have become the responsibility of the adjacent system.

> *The work context shows where the responsibilities of the work and the responsibilities of the adjacent systems start and end.*

This leads to us saying that the data flows around the boundary of the work are the clearest indication of its processing capabilities. By defining these flows, you define the precise point at which the processing of the work ends and that of the adjacent system starts, and vice versa.

One problem commonly arises in setting the context: Often we see product-centric contexts that contain only the intended software product. Remember that you are investigating some work, and the eventual product will become *part* of that work. To specify the most valuable product, you must understand the work into which that product is to be deployed. In most cases, projects that restrict their study to only what they think the product will contain build less useful products; in fact, they often omit functionality that would have been valuable to the owner. As a rule of thumb for commercial projects, if you do not have any humans inside your work context, then chances are that your work context is too narrow.

Also consider the possibility that by enlarging the scope of the work, you find other potential areas for automation or other types of improvements that could be valuable. All too often, before we understand the work, we think of an automation boundary, and we never rethink it. Of course, then the "hard stuff"—the work that we did not intend to automate—is not considered. By casting your net wider, you usually find aspects of the work that would benefit from automation or some other improvement, and in the end turn out to be cheaper than first thought. The moral of the story: First understand the work, and then decide which product is most valuable to that work.

> *The moral of the story: First understand the work, then decide which product provides the best value to that work.*

Scope, Stakeholders, and Goals

Scope is not all there is to getting the requirements project off the ground. To build the right product, you have to understand the extent of the work;

Figure 3.6

The scope, stakeholders, and goals are not decided in isolation from one another. Rather, the scope of the work indicates the stakeholders who have an interest in the work; the stakeholders, in turn, decide what they want the goals of the project to be.

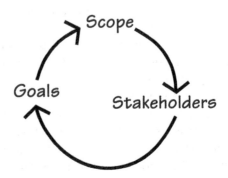

the people who do it, influence it, or know about it; and the outcome that those people are trying to achieve. This is the trinity of *scope, stakeholders, and goals,* as shown in Figure 3.6.

The *scope* is the extent of the business area affected by the product. Because it is defining a part of a real-life organization, the scope points to the *stakeholders*—the people who have an interest in, or an effect on, the success of the work. The stakeholders, in turn, decide the *goals,* which is the improvement the business wants to experience when the product is installed.

There is no particular order to deciding what these factors should be. Most projects start with scope, but it is not obligatory—you use whatever information is to hand first. You have to iterate between the three factors until you have stabilized them, but this is almost always a short process when your organization knows why it wants to invest in the project.

Stakeholders

*Stakeholders
are the source of
requirements.*

The next part of the trinity is the stakeholders. Stakeholders include any-one with an interest in, or an effect on, the outcome of the product. The owner is the most obvious stakeholder, but there are others. For example, the intended users of the product are stakeholders—they have an interest in having a product that does their work correctly. A subject-matter expert is an obvious stakeholder; a security expert is a less obvious stakeholder but one who must be considered for any product that could hold confidential or financial information. Potentially dozens of stakeholders exist for any project. Remember that you are trying to establish the optimal value for the owner, and that probably means talking to many people, all of them are potentially sources of requirements.

The stakeholder map (Ian Alexander calls it an *onion diagram*) in Figure 3.7 identifies common classes of stakeholders that might be represented by one or more roles in your project. Let's look a little more closely at this map.

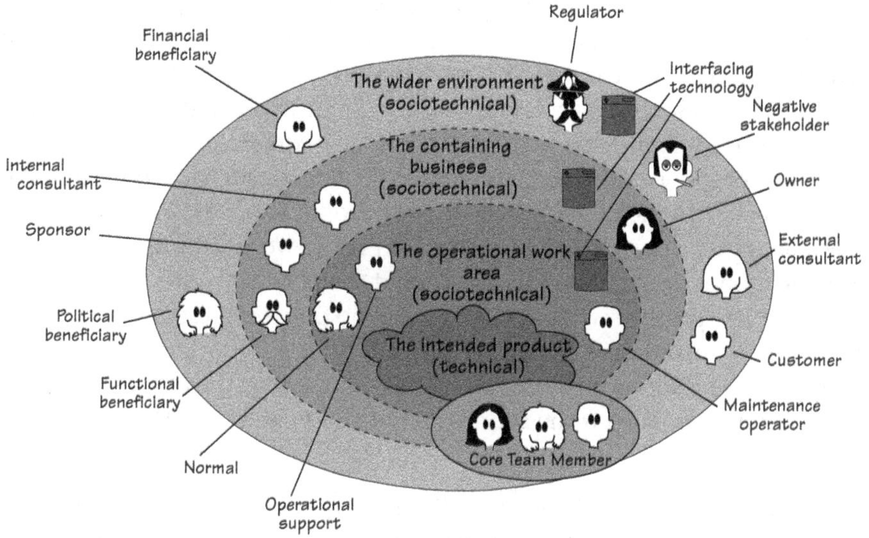

Figure 3.7

This stakeholder map shows the organizational rings surrounding the eventual product, and the classes of stakeholders who inhabit these rings. Use this map to help determine which classes of stakeholders are relevant to your project and which roles you need to represent them.

At the center of the stakeholder map is the *intended product*. Notice that it has a vague, cloud-like shape—this is intentional. At the start of the requirements activities you cannot be certain of the precise boundaries of the product, so for the moment we will leave it loosely defined. Surrounding the intended product is a ring representing the *operational work area*—stakeholders who will have some direct contact with the product inhabit this space. In the next ring, the *containing business,* you find stakeholders who benefit from the product in some way, even though they are not in the operational area. Finally, the outer ring, the *wider environment,* contains other stakeholders who have an influence on or an interest in the product. Note that the detailed and multiple involvement of the *core team members*—analysts, designers, project manager, and so on—is emphasized by the fact they span all the rings.

Because so many classes of stakeholders exist, it is helpful to discuss some of the more important ones. After we have discussed these stakeholders, we will point you at a way of formalizing them with a stakeholder analysis template.

The Sponsor

We have said—often, and it shall be repeated—that the product has to provide the optimal value to its owner. However, for many products you do not, and usually cannot, have direct access to the owner. Many projects are carried out by commercial organizations, which are strictly speaking owned by their shareholders. Naturally enough, you can't go and talk to all the shareholders, nor are you likely to get access to the board of directors. In this case,

READING
For more on stakeholder analysis, refer to Alexander, Ian, Neil Maiden, et al. *Scenarios, Stories, Use Cases Through the Systems Development Life-Cycle.* John Wiley & Sons, 2004.

the usual course of action is to appoint a sponsor for the project to represent the owner's interest; in many cases, the resources for the development of the new product that come from a sponsor's budget. You will find that the sponsor is concerned with project issues, and will be instrumental in setting some of the constraint requirements. We will deal with constraints in a little while.

The sponsor pays for the development of the product.

On the simple basis that "money talks," the sponsor, by paying for the development, has the final say in what that product does, how it does it, and how elaborate or how sparse it must be. In other words, the sponsor is the ultimate arbiter of which product will yield the optimal value.

You cannot proceed without a sponsor. If no one is representing the interest of the organization at large, then there is little point in proceeding with the project. The sponsor is most likely to be present at the blastoff meeting (you should be worried if the sponsor is not there) and is most likely one of these people:

- *User Management:* If you are building a product for in-house consumption, the most realistic sponsor is the manager of the users who will ultimately operate the product. Their department, or its work, is the beneficiary of the product, so it is reasonable that the cost of construction is borne by the departmental manager.

- *Marketing Department:* If you build products for sale to people outside your organization, the marketing department may assume the role of sponsor and represent the eventual owners of the product.

- *Product Development:* If you build software for sale, the budget for its development might be with your product manager or strategic program manager, in which case one of those would be the sponsor.

Consider your own organization, its structure and job responsibilities: Which people best represent the owner? Who pays for product development? Who, or what, reaps the benefit of the business advantage that the product brings? Whose values do you have to consider when you are determining what the end product is to do?

Do whatever you need to do to find your sponsor; your project will not succeed without one.

Let's assume the sponsor (in this case an owner representative) for the Ice-Breaker project is Mack Andrews, the CEO of Saltworks Systems. Mr. Andrews has made the commitment to invest in building the product. You record this agreement in Section 2 of your requirements specification:

> The sponsor of the project is Mack Andrews, the CEO of Saltworks Systems. He has said that it is his goal to develop this product to appeal to a broader range of markets in other countries, including airports and their runways.

There are several things to note here. First, you name the sponsor. It is now clear to everyone on the project that Mack Andrews takes responsibility for investing in the product, and so will be the final arbiter on scope changes. Second, other information is provided about the sponsor that will be used as the project proceeds and may have a bearing on some of the requirements—particularly, the usability, adaptability, and "productization" requirements.

For more details on usability, adaptability, productization, and other types of requirements, refer to the template in Appendix A.

The Customer

The customer buys the product once it is developed, becoming the product's new owner. To persuade the customer to purchase the product, you have to build something that your customer will find valuable and useful and pleasurable.

The customer buys the product. You have to know this person well enough to understand what he finds valuable and, therefore, what he will buy.

Perhaps you already know the names of your customers, or perhaps they are hundreds or thousands of unknown people who might be persuaded to pay for your product. In either case, you have to understand them well enough to understand what they find valuable and what they will buy.

There is a difference between customers who buy for their own use and those who buy for use by others. When the product is a retail product and the customer and the owner are the same person, then that person's own values are of supreme importance to you. Is the customer looking for convenience? Most people are, and if so, you have to discover what the customer is doing that you can make more convenient. How much convenience will he find valuable?

When customers buy for use by others, the owner is presumably an organizational customer. Your interest lies in what the organization is doing, and what it considers valuable. That is, what can your product do that will make the users within the organization more productive, efficient, quicker, or whatever other quality it is seeking?

Even if you are developing open-source software, you still have a customer; the difference is simply that no money changes hands.

You must understand what appeals to your customers, and what they value. What will they find useful? What will they pay for? Understanding your customer correctly makes a huge difference to the success of your product.

For the IceBreaker product, the Northumberland County Highways Department has agreed to be the first customer.[1]

FOOTNOTE 1
The original Vaisala de-icing prediction system was built for the Cheshire County Council. The designers of the product were Thermal Mapping International and The Computer Department. The product is now installed by all counties in the United Kingdom and has thousands of customers overseas in most cold-weather countries. www.vaisala.com.

> *The customer for the product is the Northumberland County Highways Department, represented by director Jane Shaftoe.*

As there is a single customer (at this stage), it would, of course, be advisable to invite her to participate as a stakeholder in the project. This kind of outreach results in the customer being actively involved in selecting which requirements are useful, choosing between conflicting requirements, and making the requirements analysts aware of her values, problems, and aspirations.

Saltworks Systems has further ambitions for the IceBreaker product. In the earlier statement about the sponsor, he said that he wanted an ice forecasting system that could be sold to road authorities and airports in other counties and other countries. If you plan to build the product with this aim, then your requirements specification should include an additional customer statement:

> *Potential customers for the product include all counties in the United Kingdom, northern parts of North America, and northern Europe and Scandinavia. A summary of the requirements specification will be presented to the Highways Department managers of selected counties, states, and countries for the purpose of discovering additional requirements.*

It is clear that the customer must always be represented on the project. Where many potential customers exist, you must find a way of representing them in your project. This representation can come from the marketing department, senior users from one or more of your key customers, or a combination of domain and usability experts from within your organization. We will also later discuss personas as a way of representing the customers. The nature of your product, the structure of your organization, your customer base, and probably several other factors decide which roles within your organization are able to represent the customers.

Users: Understand Them

We are using the term *users* to mean the people who will ultimately be the hands-on operators of your product. The stakeholder map (Figure 3.7) refers to them as *normal operators, operational support,* and *maintenance operators.* For in-house products, the users are typically the people who work for the project sponsor. For personal computer or mobile device products, the user and the owner are often the same person.

The purpose of identifying the users is to understand what they are doing and which improvements they consider to be valuable.

Identifying your users is the first step in understanding the work they do—after all, your product is intended to improve this work. Additionally, you have to learn what kind of people they are so you provide the right user experience (we look at this issue later when we discuss usability requirements). You have to bring about a product that your users are both able to use and want to use. Obviously, the better your understanding of your users, the better the chance you have of specifying a suitable product for them.

Different users make different demands on your product. For example, an airline pilot has very different usability requirements from, say, a commuter buying a ticket on a rail system. If your user were a commuter, then a "person without cash" and a "person with only one arm free" would raise their own usability requirements.

When developing consumer products, mass-market software, or websites, you should consider using a *persona* as the user. A persona is a virtual person who is archetypical of most of your users. By determining the characteristics of this persona to a sufficient degree, the requirements team can know the correct requirements to satisfy each of the personas. You should decide at this stage if you will use personas, but they can be more fully developed later. More information is provided on personas in Chapter 5, Investigating the Work.

The consideration of potential users is vital for agile development. Too many teams operate with only one user asked to supply the requirements for a product, and little or no consideration given to what will happen when the product is released to a wider audience. We strongly urge you to always consider the broadest spectrum of users and, at the very least, to choose user stakeholders from both ends of that spectrum.

Having identified your users, you have to record them. For example, in the Icebreaker project we had users in the following categories:

- Qualified Road Engineers
- Clerks in the truck department
- Managers

For each category of user, write a section in your specification to describe, as fully as time allows, the attributes of your users. Consider these possibilities:

- Subject-matter experience: How much help do they need?
- Technological experience: Can they operate the product? Which technical terms should be used?
- Intellectual abilities: Should tasks be made simpler? Or broken down to a lower level?
- Attitude toward the job: What are the users' aspirations?
- Education: What can you expect your user to know?
- Linguistic skills: Not all your users will speak or read the home language.
- And most importantly, what is it about their work that they most wish to improve?

Also, for each category of user, identify the particular attributes that your product must cater to:

READING

Don Gause and Jerry Weinberg give a wonderful example of brainstorming lists of users in their book: Gause, Don, and Gerald Weinberg. *Exploring Requirements: Quality Before Design.* Dorset House, 1989. Although this text is getting a little long in the tooth, its advice is still relevant. Most of Jerry Weinberg's books are available as Kindle books or at Smashwords.

A persona is a virtual person that is archetypical of most of your users.

- People with disabilities: Consider all disabilities. This, in some cases, is a legal requirement.
- Nonreaders: Consider people who cannot read and people who do not speak the home language.
- People who need reading glasses: This is particularly near and dear to one of the authors.
- People who cannot resist changing things like fonts, styles, and so on.
- People who will probably be carrying luggage, large parcels, or a baby.
- People who do not normally use a computer.
- People who might be angry, frustrated, under pressure, or in a hurry.

We realize that writing down all this stuff seems like a chore. However, we have found that taking the time to record it so other people can read it is one of the few ways for you to demonstrate that you understand it. The users are so important to your cause that you must understand what kind of people they are and which capabilities they have. To wave your hands and say, "They are graphic designers" or "They want to buy books on the Web," falls short of the minimum level of understanding.

Another category of stakeholder in the operational work area is the maintenance operator. Your product is likely to have maintainability requirements, and you can learn about them from this person.

Operational support is another source of requirements relating to the operational work area. Roles that are sources of these requirements include help desk staff, trainers, installers, and coaches.

At this stage, any users you identify are *potential* users. That is, you do not yet precisely know the scope of the product—you determine this later in the requirements process—so you are identifying the people who might possibly use, maintain, and support the product. Remember that people other than the intended users (e.g., firefighters, security personnel) might end up having hands-on contact with your product. It is better to identify superfluous users than to fail to find them all because each different category of user will have some different requirements.

People other than the intended users might end up having contact with your product. It is better to identify superfluous users than to fail to find them all.

Other Stakeholders

There are more people you have to talk to so that you can find all the requirements. Your contact with these people might be fleeting, but it is nevertheless necessary. Any of them may potentially have requirements for your product.

The problem that you often face in requirements projects is that you fail to discover all the stakeholders, and thus fail to discover their needs. This shortcoming may result in a string of change requests when the product is

❝ ❝ Every context is composed of individuals who do or do not decide to connect the fate of a project with the fate of the small or large ambitions they represent. ❞ ❞

—Bruno Latour, *ARAMIS or the Love of Technology*

released to an audience that is wider than at first thought. Naturally, the people who were overlooked will not be happy. Additionally, you must consider that when any new system is installed, someone gains and someone loses power: Some people find that the product brings them new capabilities, and some people are not able to do their jobs the way they used to do them. The moral of the story is clear: Find all parties who will be affected by the product, and find their requirements.

Let's consider some other stakeholders by looking at some candidate categories. You can also see most of these groups illustrated as classes on the stakeholder map shown in Figure 3.7.

We list our stakeholders in Section 2 of the Volere Requirements Specification Template. You can find this template in Appendix A. The list acts as a checklist for finding the appropriate stakeholders.

Consultants

Consultants—both internal to your organization and external—are people who have expertise you need. Consultants might never touch or see your product, but their knowledge becomes part of it. For example, if you are building a financial product, a security expert is one of your stakeholders. He might never see your product, but his expertise—and this is his stake in the requirements—ensures the product is secure.

Management

Consider any category of management. These groups show up on the stakeholder map (Figure 3.7) as classes like *functional beneficiary, political beneficiary,* and *financial beneficiary.* Is it a strategic product? Do any managers other than those directly involved have a stake?

Product managers and program managers are obvious sources of requirements. Project managers or leaders who are responsible for the day-to-day management of the project effort likewise have contributions to make.

Subject-Matter Experts

This constituency may include domain analysts, business consultants, business analysts, or anyone else who has some specialized knowledge of the business subject. As a consequence, these experts are a prime source of information about the work.

Core Team

The core team is made up of the people who are part of the building effort for the product. They may include product designers, developers, testers, business analysts, systems analysts, systems architects, technical writers, database designers, and anyone else who is involved in the construction.

You can also consider the open-source community as stakeholders—they have knowledge about technology and trends in most areas of software.

You can contact these people via open-source forums. They are usually very enthusiastic and ready to share knowledge with you.

When you know the people involved, record their names. Otherwise, use this section of the template to list the skills and duties that you think are most likely needed to build the product.

Inspectors

Consider auditors, government inspectors, any kind of safety inspectors, technical inspectors, or even possibly the police. It may well be necessary to build inspection capabilities into your product. If your product is subject to the Sarbanes-Oxley Act, or any of the other regulatory acts, then inspection is crucial, as are the requirements from the inspectors.

Market Forces

People from the marketing department are probably the stakeholders representing the marketplace. When you are building a product for commercial sale, trends in the market are a potent source of requirements, as is a deep knowledge of the likely consumers. Note the speed at which the smart phone and tablet markets are moving (at the time of writing). Staying ahead of the curve is vital for any consumer product.

Legal Experts

Each year the world is filled with more and more laws—complying with all of them is daunting but necessary. Your lawyers are the stakeholders for most of your legal requirements.

Negative Stakeholders

Negative stakeholders are people who do not want the project to succeed (remember what we said previously about losing power). Although they may not be the most cooperative individuals, you would be wise to consider them. You may find that, if their requirements are different from the commonly perceived version, and you can accommodate their requirements, your opposition could well become your supporters.

You might also consider the people who threaten your product—the hackers, defrauders, and other malevolent people. You will get no cooperation from them, but you should consider how they might mistreat your product.

Industry Standard Setters

Your industry may have professional bodies that expect certain codes of conduct to be followed or certain standards to be maintained by any product built within the industry or for use by the industry.

Public Opinion

Do any user groups for your product exist? They will certainly be a major source of requirements. For any product intended for the public domain, consider polling members of the public about their opinion. They may make demands on your product that could spell the difference between acceptance and rejection.

Government

Some products must interact with government agencies for reporting purposes, or receive information from a government agency; other products have requirements that necessitate consulting with the government. Although the government may not assign a person full-time to your project, you should nevertheless nominate the pertinent agency as a stakeholder.

Special-Interest Groups

Consider handicapped-interest groups, environmental bodies, foreign people, old people, gender-related interests, or almost any other group that may come in contact with your product.

Technical Experts

Technical experts do not necessarily build the product, but they will almost certainly be consulted about some part of it. For the stakeholders from this constituency, consider usability experts, security consultants, hardware people, experts in the technologies that you might use, specialists in software products, or experts from any technical field that the product could use.

Cultural Interests

This constituency is applicable to products intended for the public domain, and especially when your product is to be sold or seen in other countries. In addition, it is always possible in these politically correct times that your product could offend someone. If there is any possibility that religious, ethnic, cultural, political, gender, or other human interests could be affected by or come into contact with your product, then you should consider representatives from these groups as stakeholders for the project.

Adjacent Systems

The adjacent systems on your work context diagram are the systems, people, or work areas that directly interact with the work you are studying. Look at each adjacent system: Who represents its interests, or who has knowledge of it? When the adjacent system is an automated one, who is its project leader or maintainer? If these stakeholders are not available, you might have to read the adjacent system's documentation, or its code, to discover whether it has any special demands for interacting with your product. For each adjacent system you need to find at least one stakeholder.

Finding the Stakeholders

At scoping time, you normally inspect your context model and hold a brainstorming session to identify all possible stakeholders. You do not have to start from scratch; we have constructed a spreadsheet with many categories of stakeholders, along with the kind of knowledge you need to obtain from each person. This spreadsheet (see Appendix B) cross-references the stakeholder map (Figure 3.7) and provides a detailed specification of your project's sociology. Once you have identified the stakeholder, add that person's name to the list. The complete spreadsheet is available as a free download at www.volere.co.uk.

The greatest problem concerning stakeholders is the requirements you miss when you don't find all of the stakeholders.

You will be talking to the stakeholders, so at this stage it pays to explain to them why they are stakeholders and why you need to consult them about requirements for the product. Explain specifically why their input will make a difference to the eventual product. It is polite to inform stakeholders of the amount of their time you require and the type of participation that you have in mind; a little warning always helps them to think about their requirements for the product. The greatest problem concerning stakeholders is the requirements that you miss if you do not find all of the stakeholders, or if you exclude stakeholders from the requirements-gathering process.

See the Stakeholder Management Template in Appendix B, also available as a downloadable Excel spreadsheet at www.volere.co.uk.

Goals: What Do You Want to Achieve?

When you are busy working with your stakeholders on detailed requirements, it is very easy to go *off piste* and either spend time on irrelevancies or miss important requirements.

Your sponsor is making an investment in a project to build a product; to understand the reason behind this investment, you need to determine the precise benefits the project is to deliver. You also need a guide to help you steer your efforts toward those requirements that will make the greatest contributions to the expected business advantage.

In other words, you need to know the goal of the project. You can think of the project goal as the highest-level requirement; all the detailed requirements you collect along the way must make a positive contribution toward that goal.

The project goal is the highest-level requirement.

Spending a little time during the blastoff to ensure that a consensus on the goal of the project has been reached will pay handsome dividends over the course of the project. The goal should be written clearly, unambiguously, and in a measurable way so it quantifies the benefits of the project; this quantification makes the goal testable.

How do you make a clear statement of the goal? Start with a statement of the user problem or background to the project. (We make this problem statement the first part of all our specifications; see the template in Appendix A for a suggested format.) Those stakeholders who represent the user or business side of the organization should confirm that you do, indeed, understand the problem, and that your problem statement is a fair and accurate one.

For the IceBreaker project, the business has given you this background:

"Roads freeze in winter, and icy conditions cause road accidents that may potentially kill people. Predictions at the moment rely largely on guesswork, experience, and phoned-in reports from motorists and the police. Trucks do not always get to the icy roads on time to prevent accidents, or they may arrive far too early, which results in the de-icing material being dispersed by the time the road freezes. Road treatment is sometimes indiscriminate, and this wastes de-icing material and causes environmental damage."

You and your blastoff group must learn and articulate the business problem. Only when that is done can you discover the requirements that make the greatest contribution toward solving the problem.

Once you have a clear understanding of the problem, it is time to move on and look at how the project's goal will solve that problem. We use a three-pronged approach to writing the goal statement, with the three prongs being purpose, advantage, and measurement (PAM).

Purpose

The problem is that ice on the roads causes accidents. The only viable[2] solution to this problem is to treat the roads to prevent the ice from forming (and presumably to melt the ice if it has already formed). Thus you can write the purpose for this project as follows:

> Purpose: To accurately forecast road freezing and schedule de-icing treatment.

The purpose of the project should be not only to solve the problem, but also to provide a business advantage. Naturally, if there is an advantage, you must be able to measure it.

FOOTNOTE 2
There are other solutions, but none of them are viable. Roads could be heated (expensive), roads could be closed (unpopular), motorists could be asked to fit snow chains (unlikely they would comply), or drivers could be asked to learn ice-driving skills (unbelievable).

The purpose of the project is not only to solve the problem, but also to provide a business advantage to the owner of the product created through the project.

Advantage

The business advantage is the reduction—ideally the elimination—of accidents due to ice. The road authorities (your owners) have a charter to maintain their roads in a condition that will make for safe motoring. Thus the owner gets the following advantage from the product:

> Advantage: To reduce road accidents by eliminating icy road conditions.

Measurement

Is this advantage measurable? It can be. The success of your product can be measured by the reduction in the number of accidents where ice is a contributing factor:

> Measurement: Accidents attributed to ice shall be no more than one accident per 10,000 vehicle-miles traveled on all roads in the districts covered by the product.

You have stated a measurable goal, and monitoring the accidents for a winter or two is reasonable. Accident statistics, police reports, and road usage data are already being collected, so you should have no trouble finding data to measure the performance of your product and establish whether it is successful.

But is this a reasonable goal? Is the elimination of most of the accidents due to ice worth the cost and effort of building the product? And where did "one accident per 10,000 vehicle-miles" come from? The Northumberland County Highways Department representative (your initial customer) at the blastoff tells you that this is a target figure set by central government. If it can be achieved the county government will be satisfied, and county officials are prepared to spend money to achieve this target.

Is it viable? One of the reasons for having a blastoff meeting with the key stakeholders present is to answer questions like this. One of the stakeholders is from the National Road Users Association; she assures you that this group's research shows ice treatment is effective and the expected outcome is realistic.

Is it achievable? The stakeholders representing the product designers and builders, the technical experts from the hardware side, and the meteorologist all assure the blastoff participants that the technology is available, or can be built, and that similar software solutions are known by the team.

Note the major aspects of the project goal:

Purpose: What should the product do?

Advantage: Which business advantage does it provide?

Measurement: How do you measure the advantage?

Viable: Given what you understand about the constraints, is it possible for the product to achieve the business advantage?

Feasible: Given what you have learned from the blastoff, is it possible to build a product to achieve the measure?

Achievable: Does the organization have (or can it acquire) the skills to build the product and operate it once built?

Sometimes projects have more than one purpose statement. Look at the customer's statement:

"Road treatment is sometimes indiscriminate, and this wastes de-icing material and causes environmental damage."

This reveals another purpose for the project:

> *Purpose: To save money on winter road de-icing costs.*

The advantage stemming from this purpose is that accurate forecasting reduces the cost of treatment—only roads in imminent danger of freezing are treated. Additionally, by preventing ice from forming on road surfaces, damage to roads is reduced.[3]

The advantage is straightforward:

> *Advantage: Reduced de-icing and road maintenance costs.*

The measurement of reduced costs is always the amount of money that can be saved:

> *Measurement: The cost of de-icing shall be reduced by 25 percent of the current cost of road treatment, and damage to roads from ice shall be reduced by 50 percent.*

Naturally, you need to know the current costs and damage expenditures so that you will know when they have been reduced by 25 percent and 50 percent, respectively. If there is supporting material available, then cite it in your specification:

FOOTNOTE 3
When the water lying in cracks in the road surface freezes, it expands and forces the crack to expand. Eventually, this process results in significant fractures and holes in the road surface.

> *Supporting Materials: Thornes, J. E. "Cost-Effective Snow and Ice Control for the Nineties." Third International Symposium on Snow and Ice Control Technology, Minneapolis, Minnesota, Vol. 1, Paper 24, 1992.*

The engineers also know that applying too much salt compounds to roads damages the environment. By having a more accurate treatment, less material finds its way to the environs of the roads, and less damage results. This means that accurate forecasting gives you another advantage:

> *Advantage: To reduce damage to the environment by unnecessary application of de-icing compounds.*

This advantage can be measured by comparing the amount of de-icing material used by the product with that used at present:

> *Measurement: The amount of de-icing chemicals needed to de-ice the authority's roads shall be reduced to 70 percent of current usage.*
>
> *Supporting Materials: Thornes, J. E. "Salt of the Earth." Surveyor Magazine, December 8, 1994, pp. 16–18.*

Note that the purpose statement results in an advantage and a measurement. If you cannot express an advantage for the purpose, or if the advantage is not measurable, then it should not be part of your specification. For example, suppose the purpose of a project is something vague:

> *Purpose: To improve the way we do business.*

The advantage here is unclear. Does your owner want the business to make more money, or does he want the business processes to function more smoothly? Or something else? The discipline necessary to give the purpose an advantage and a measurement means that fuzzy or ill-defined purposes are far less likely to find their way into your specifications.

You cannot build the right product unless you know precisely what the product is intended to do and how the product's success is to be measured.

You cannot build the right product unless you know precisely what the product is intended to do and how the product's success is to be measured. Whether the organization using the product achieves the target defined by the product purpose may depend on how it uses the product. Obviously, if the product is not used as intended, then it may fail to provide the advantages for which it was built. Thus the statement of project purpose must assume that the resulting product will be used as intended.

When you write the goal, you should make the point that all decisions about the project are driven by it. Make sure everyone understands that if the goal changes during the project, then so do the scope, stakeholders, and any requirements that have already been defined.

Constraints

Constraints (which appear in the early part of the requirements specification template) are global requirements. These restrictions help determine which subset of requirements can be included in the eventual product. Constraints affect decisions about the scope of the product by limiting the amount of time or money that may be spent on the project. Sometimes the constraint is a pre-ordained design decision that limits the way the problem is solved.

You can think of constraints as a special type of requirement that provides some guidance on where to focus your requirements-gathering efforts. These limitations are written as if they were regular requirements. Your management, your marketing colleagues, or your sponsor probably already knows the constraints—the task at blastoff time is to elicit and record them.

See Chapter 13, The Quality Gateway, for more on using the project purpose as a test for relevancy. The Quality Gateway runs each requirement through a series of tests, including relevancy. If a requirement is not in some way relevant to the purpose, it is rejected.

Section 3, Mandated Constraints, of the Volere Requirements Specification Template provides a description of how you record constraints. You can find the template in Appendix A.

Solution Constraints

Your specification should describe any mandated designs or solutions. For example, your management may tell you that the only acceptable solution is one that will run on a tablet device—no other design is allowable. While we caution you against designing the solution before knowing the requirements, perhaps for some overriding reason—marketing, cultural, managerial, political, customer expectations, or financial—only one acceptable design solution exists. If this is the case, then that item should be included in your requirements as a constraint.

Any partner or collaborative applications should also be brought to light and recorded at this time. These are other applications or systems with which your product must cooperate. For example, your product may have to interact with existing databases, reporting systems, or Web-based systems; thus the interfaces to those systems become constraints on your product. Mandated operating systems should also be included in this section of the template.

Off-the-shelf and open-source applications, if they are to be used, or interacted with, are recorded under the "Constraints" heading as well. There may be good reasons for mandating this cooperation—but then again, there may not. Along with your stakeholders, consider whether the decision to incorporate ready-built software is appropriate for your situation.

Project Constraints

Project constraints describe the time and financial budgets for the project. These parameters should be known at scoping time, because they affect the requirements you gather later. If you have a $500,000 budget, there is no point in collecting the requirements for a $1 million product.

Time constraints can be imposed to enable the product to meet a window of opportunity, to coincide with coordinated releases of associated products, to meet the scheduled start-up of a new business venture, or to satisfy many other scheduling demands. If this type of constraint exists, then you should make your team aware of it. Keep in mind that a time constraint is not the same thing as an estimate of the time necessary to complete the project.

Financial constraints indicate how extensive the product may be. They also give you a good indication as to whether the product is really desired by the putative customers. If the budget is impossibly small, it probably indicates that the priority for the project is so low that no one really wants the product. Impossibly small budgets and impossibly short deadlines almost always cripple projects—and there is no reason to think your project would be different.

Financial constraints indicate how elaborate the product may be, and they give you a good idea if the product is really wanted.

Naming Conventions and Definitions

Names are important. Good names convey meaning; poor names do the opposite. Additionally, we have found that every project has names that are particular to it, and this terminology should be recorded to make communication easier, and future understanding more reliable. During the scoping time you begin to collect and record the names, along with their agreed-upon meanings.

Every project has names that are peculiar to it.

Record the names in Section 4, Naming Conventions and Terminology, of the specification template. This glossary serves as a reference point for the entire project. We are always amazed at how many misunderstandings occur simply because no central glossary is available, and how effective good names can be at communicating meaning. It is worth expending effort in this area to ensure smooth communication later on in the project.

For example, the IceBreaker project team added the following definition to their glossary during the blastoff:

FOOTNOTE 4
Weather stations are also used as ice detection systems on airport runways.

Weather station Hardware capable of collecting and transmitting road temperature, air temperature, humidity, and precipitation readings. Weather stations are installed in eight locations in Northumberland.[4]

Starting to define terminology at scoping time has a distinct advantage: You make the words visible. The stakeholders can then discuss them and change them to reflect their consensus of the meaning. Subsequent development activities build on understanding the terminology more precisely and use it as the basis for building a complete data dictionary—see Section 7 of the template.

How Much Is This Going to Cost?

At this point, you have a fair amount of information on which to base your estimates of cost and effort. The needed effort is usually proportional to the amount of functionality contained within the work area, and this relationship makes sense—the more functions done by the work area, the more effort needed to study it and devise a solution.

At this stage you do not know the size of the product—how much functionality it will contain. Also, given the huge variations in the cost of implementing various technological solutions, you are well advised not to attempt (yet) to estimate the complete development cost. However, you know the size (in terms of its functionality) of the work area—or you do if you measure it.

The easiest way to measure the size or functionality of the work area is to count the number of adjacent systems on the context model as well as the number of inputs and outputs. While more accurate ways to measure size have been devised, counting the inputs and outputs is a quick technique that gives you a far better idea of size than merely guessing. If your context has more than 30 inputs and outputs, then it falls into the "average cost per input/output" range of estimating. Your organization has an average cost for gathering the requirements for one input or output. You can determine this cost by going back to previous projects, counting the number of inputs and outputs on the context diagram, and dividing this number into the total cost of that requirements investigation.

A more accurate estimate can be developed by determining the number of business events that affect the work. The number of business events can be identified by inspecting the context diagram. Each business event has an amount of functionality that responds to it, so the number of business events is the determining factor in the cost of the requirements effort. It is, of course, necessary to know the cost to your organization of analyzing the average business event: You can learn this cost by looking at previous projects or, if necessary, running a benchmark. Multiply the cost per event by the number of events to give a reasonably accurate cost for requirements gathering.

More accurate still is function point counting. At this stage you need to have an idea of the data stored by the work. This can usually be identified in a short time if your team includes some experienced data modelers. Function point counting measures the amount and the complexity of the data processed by the work—the inputs and the outputs from the context

Starting to define terminology at scoping time has a distinct advantage: You make the words visible. The stakeholders are able to discuss and change them to reflect the consensus of the meaning.

A brief overview of function point counting appears in Appendix C, Function Point Counting: A Simplified Introduction.

READING

Bundschuh, Manfred, and Carol Dekkers. *The IT Measurement Compendium: Estimating and Benchmarking Success with Functional Size Measurement.* Springer, 2010.

The key consideration is not so much that you use a particular estimating system, but rather that you use a system based on measurement, not hysterical optimism.

model—along with data stored within the work. Enough is known about function points to enable you to find figures for the average cost per function point of requirements investigation for your particular industry.

It really doesn't matter which estimating system you use, but it does matter that you use a system based on measurement, not one based on hysterical optimism. Too much risk is courted by not measuring; there is too much evidence to support the downside of not measuring, and too much known about measuring, to have any excuse for not doing it.

We strongly advocate that all projects take into account the amount of functionality in the work area that they are about to improve. Although some development techniques shun this upfront measurement in favor of time boxing, there is a strong argument to be made for measuring the amount of functionality to be delivered by each iteration. It is always helpful to project management, and the requirements activity, to know (rather than guess) how much effort lies ahead.

Risks

We face risks every day. Just leaving your home to go to work involves some risk—your car won't start, the train will be late, you will be assigned to share an office with a boring person with body odor problems. But still you go to work each day, because you know the risks and consider the outcome (a pay packet or job satisfaction) to be worth the risk. Of course, once you are at work, you might well plunge into projects where you have no idea of the risks involved, and thus no idea whether the outcome is worth braving the risks.

Have you ever worked on a project where nothing went wrong?

Have you ever worked on a project where nothing went wrong? No? Nor has anyone else; something always goes wrong. But did you ever try and figure out ahead of time what could go wrong, and do something to prevent it from going wrong, or at least allow for the mishaps by budgeting for them? This, in its simplest sense, is risk management.

Your blastoff process should include a short risk assessment. Such an assessment is probably outside the remit of the business analyst, and should be done by a competent risk-assessment person. The job is to assess both those risks that are most likely to happen and those risks that will have the greatest impact if they do, in fact, become problems. The deliverables from your blastoff provide input for the risk assessor to identify risks. For each identified risk, the assessor determines the probability of it becoming a problem, along with its cost or schedule impact. At the same time, the assessor determines the early-warning signs—the happenings or conditions that signal a risk is coming to fruition. In some cases where the risks are considered serious, a risk manager is assigned to monitor for the telltale signs that some risks are about to become full-blown problems.

Risk management is common-sense project management or, in the words of our partner Tim Lister, "project management for adults." If your organization is not doing it, then you should prepare for the budget or time overruns that are coming your way. The most noticeable effect of doing risk analysis is that it makes the risks visible to all stakeholders. Once aware of the risks, they can contribute to risk mitigation. Similarly, the risk assessor makes management aware of the risks and their impact if they become problems.

READING

DeMarco, Tom, and Tim Lister. *Waltzing with Bears: Managing Risk on Software Projects.* Dorset House, 2003.

To Go or Not to Go

The deliverables from the project blastoff indicate the viability of your project. When you take a hard look at what these deliverables are telling you, you can decide whether it makes good business sense to press the button and launch the requirements project.

Consider your deliverables:

READING

Tockey, Steve. *Return on Software: Maximizing the Return on Your Software Investment.* Addison-Wesley, 2004.

- Is the product goal clear and unambiguous? Or does it contain fudge words?

- Is the goal measurable? That is, will it give a clear indication when you have successfully completed the project?

- Does the goal indicate an actual benefit to the owner?

- Is it viable? Is it possible to achieve the objectives of the project within the allotted time and budget?

- Have you reached agreement on the scope of the work?

- Are there some risks that have a high probability of becoming problems?

- Is the impact of these risks such that it makes the project unfeasible?

- Is the cost of investigation reasonable given the product's benefit?

- Are the stakeholders willing to be involved?

- Do you have sufficient justification to invest in the project?

- Do you have enough reasons not to invest in the project?

- Is there any further investigation that you should do before launching the requirements project?

The point is to make an objective decision based on facts, not on boundless enthusiasm or giddy optimism. In the book co-authored with our Guild partners, *Adrenaline Junkies and Template Zombies,* one of the essays is called "Dead Fish." A Dead Fish project is one of those where it is known from the moment of inception that it is doomed to failure, and yet no one on the project stands up to say that it is doomed, that it will hang around, smelling badly, long after it should have been thrown out with the other trash. Sadly, Dead Fish projects are all too common—and we urge you to do whatever it takes to not be part of one. A little consideration at this stage can prevent Dead Fish projects from being started; it can also give good projects a flying start.

Other project management techniques can also be brought into play at this time. Sadly, they all have cheesy acronyms, which makes it a little hard for your authors to take them too seriously:

SWOT

The Strengths, Weaknesses, Opportunities, and Threats are listed. These factors are used to evaluate the overall value and risk of the project.

ALUo

The Advantages, Limitations, Unique Qualities, and overcome limitations of proposed options. This technique comes from The Creative Problem Solving Group.

SMART

The project must be Specific, Measurable, Attainable, Relevant, and Time-bound. Management considers if the project is all of these things.

PESTLE

This model looks at the Political, Economic, Sociological, Technological, Legal, and Environmental factors of the project. It is often used in conjunction with SWOT.

CATWOE

This technique comes from Peter Checkland's soft systems methodology and means that you consider the Customers, Actors, Transformation Processes, World view, Owners, and Environment for the project.

Each of these techniques has its adherents, and when used correctly all of them may provide some value. Our intention here is not to discuss these approaches, but rather to provide a pointer to techniques that can be used in conjunction with the deliverables from the blastoff meeting.

Blastoff Meetings

We suggest that the key stakeholders get together for a day or so and derive the deliverables discussed in this chapter. We understand that in many organizations this type of meeting, despite its merit, is simply not possible. Nevertheless, there are other ways to achieve the same results.

While coming together is important, it is the deliverables that really matter. Some organizations come up with these items in other forms—a lot of companies write a business plan or some similarly named document that covers many of the topics we advocate. This is fine as long as you have an objective, quantifiable plan and it is circulated and agreed to by the stakeholders.

Some organizations use feasibility studies as a way of getting their projects started. Of course, the feasibility study must take an honest look at the costs and risks as well as the benefits from the product. Provided the study delivers realistic numbers, it will serve. We make the proviso that all the key stakeholders must have seen and commented on the accuracy of the feasibility study. You don't have to hold a meeting, but you do need to know all the facts that the meeting would deliver.

You don't have to hold a meeting, but you do need to know all the facts that the meeting would deliver.

Summary

The Project Blastoff is about knowing: Knowing what you want the product to do for you, and what it will cost to build it. Knowing the scope of the work that is to be studied so as to gather the requirements for the product. Knowing which people will be involved in the project, and having them know what is expected of them. Knowing the users, which in turn will lead you to knowing the usability requirements for the product. Knowing the constraints on the project—how much money have you got to spend, and how much or how little time do you have to deliver the product? Knowing the words to be used on the project. Knowing whether you can succeed.

The Project Blastoff is about knowing.

The blastoff delivers knowledge at a time that it is most useful. It is at the beginning of the project that crucial decisions—decisions that affect all subsequent stages of the project—must be made. If they are made badly, the project will suffer; if they are made well—and there is no real reason why all decisions cannot be good ones—the project will prosper.

The blastoff deliverables will reappear from time to time in this book. Some of them are used as input to the mainstream requirements activities; none of them is wasted.

Business Use Cases

4

in which we discuss a fail-safe way of
partitioning the work and so smooth the way
for your requirements investigation

The blastoff process, which we described in the previous chapter, establishes the scope of the work—the business area to be studied. This scope—ideally shown graphically as a context diagram—defines a business area, part of which is to be automated by your intended product. In reality, this work scope is probably too large to be studied as a single unit. Just as you cut your food into small bites before attempting to eat it, so it is necessary to partition the work into manageable pieces before studying it to find the product's requirements.

In this chapter we provide heuristics for finding the most appropriate use cases. In later chapters you will see how this process allows you to arrive at the most relevant and useful product to build.

> *Never eat anything bigger than your head.*
> —B. Kliban

Understanding the Work

The product you intend to build must improve its owner's work; it will be installed in the owner's area of business and will do part of (sometimes all of) the work. It does not matter which kind of work it is—commercial, scientific, embedded real-time, manual, or automated—you always have to understand it before you can decide which kind of product will best help with it.

When we say "work," we mean the system for doing business. This system includes the human tasks, the software systems, the machines, and the low-tech devices such as telephones, photocopiers, manual files, and notebooks—in fact, anything that is used to produce the owner's goods, services, or information. Until you understand this work and its desired outcomes, you cannot know which product will be optimally valuable to the owner.

Figure 4.1 presents an overview of how we intend to proceed. You might wish to refer back to this figure while reading the text—it will help smooth the way.

Figure 4.1

The scope of the business problem—the work—is agreed to by the blastoff participants. The scope defines both the work area to be studied and the adjacent systems that surround it. The adjacent systems supply data to the work and/or receive data from it. Business events happen in the adjacent systems—usually the event produces a demand for a service provided by the work. In addition, time-triggered business events occur when it is time for the work to provide some information to the adjacent system. The response the work makes to the business event is called a business use case; it includes all of the processes and data necessary to make the correct response. The requirements analysts study the functionality and data of the business use case with the help of the appropriate stakeholders. From this study, they determine the optimal product to build, and construct a product use case scenario to show how the actor and the product will interact. Once agreement is reached on this product use case scenario, the requirements analysts write the requirements or the user stories for the product.

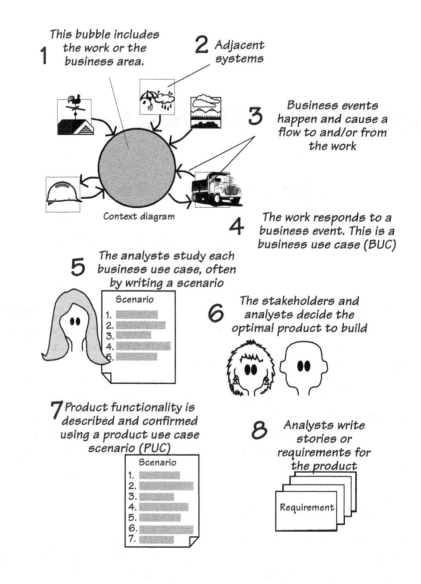

If we have some systematic and observable way of partitioning the work, then we are far more likely to be consistent with the results we get. We turn to *business events* as our preferred way of partitioning. The responses to the business events—we call these *business use cases* (BUCs)—meet the following criteria:

- They are "natural" partitions—each one makes an obvious and logical contribution to the work.
- They have minimal connectivity to other parts of the work.
- They have a clearly defined scope.
- They have rules for defining their scope.

- They have boundaries that can be observed and defined.
- They can be named using names that are recognizable to stakeholders.
- Their existence can be readily determined.
- They have one or more stakeholders who are experts for that part of the work.

Before we examine business use cases, let's look at how different projects need them.

Formality Guide

Rabbit projects should pay particular attention to this chapter. When running an iterative project, it is important to have a rock-solid grasp of the business problem to be solved. We strongly suggest that rabbits make use of business use cases to explore their problem domain before starting to formulate a solution. This approach does not add to the documentation load, and it lessens the time spent delivering inappropriate solutions.

Horse projects should consider partitioning the work area using business use cases as we describe them in this chapter. We have found that the BUC scenarios are a useful working tool for discussing the current and future work with your stakeholders. There is also the possibility of using BUC (and later product use case [PUC]) scenarios as the documentation to pass along to the developers, which allows you to avoid writing many of the detailed requirements. We shall discuss this aspect in later chapters.

Elephant projects should definitely use business events. Given that elephant projects have a large number of stakeholders, clear communication is both important and difficult. We have found that BUC scenarios are an ideal mechanism for discussing the work in geographically distributed teams. Later, the BUC scenarios and their PUC derivatives are maintained as part of the formal documentation. The BUC scenario is also useful for discussing high-level issues with outsourcers.

Use Cases and Their Scope

The term *use case* was coined by Ivar Jacobson back in 1987 as a way to describe an interaction between a system and a user of that system. Jacobson needed to break the system into smaller units, as he felt that object models were not scalable. Thus, to conquer the complexity and largeness of modern systems, he said it was first necessary to partition them into convenient chunks, and that these chunks should be based on the user's view of the system.

READING

Jacobson, Ivar, et al. *Object-Oriented Software Engineering: A Use Case Driven Approach*. Addison-Wesley, 1992.

However, Jacobson left us with some loose ends. For example, his definition of a use case does not indicate precisely where or how a use case starts and ends. In fact, Jacobson's definition of a use case must have left some ambiguity; other authors have written about use cases and very few of them have the same idea of what it is. There are about 40 published definitions of "use case" with almost none of them agreeing. This chaos is unfortunate.

Jacobson also uses the term *actor* to mean a user role, or perhaps another system, that lies outside the scope of the system. The *system* in this usage is presumed to be the automated system under construction (we refer to this item as the *product*). This now leads to a question: How can anyone know what the automated system is to be before having an understanding of the work for which this system is to be used?

If the responsibilities of the actor and the system are established at the beginning of the analysis process, and the requirements gathering focuses on the automated system, how will you ever understand the work the actor is doing or the work the automated product could be doing for the actor?

Think about this: If the responsibilities of the actor and the system are established at the *beginning* of the analysis process, and the requirements gathering focuses on the automated system, how could you ever understand the work the actor is doing, or the work the automated product might be doing for the actor? Failure to understand the actor's true task—which surely happens if you exclude the actor from the analysis study—means that you run the risk of missing opportunities for automation, or automating where a non-automation would be a better solution. You also could be guilty of building products that are not as useful as they might be as well as run the risk of constructing interfaces that ultimately do not satisfy what the actor is really trying to do.

We can rush headlong into a solution, or we can find out what the problem is. The problem is simply the work that you are meant to improve, and the first step is to establish the scope or the extent of this work. If it is to be effective, this work scope must *include* the intended actors and all the work they are doing. Once you have established a satisfactory scope for the work, you partition it into smaller pieces; these pieces are the business use cases.

This chapter discusses the process of partitioning the work. Keep in mind as you are reading it that it probably takes longer to describe each of the steps than it does to actually complete most of them.

The Scope of the Work

Your context diagram shows how your work relates to its business environment.

The work is the business activity of the owner of the eventual product; alternatively, you can think of it as the part of the business that your customer or client wants to improve. To understand this work, it is best to think about how it relates to the world outside it. This perspective makes sense because the work exists to provide services to the outside world. To do so, the work must receive information and signals from the outside world, use these inputs as raw materials, and send information and signals back to the outside world—the customer for such things. This outside world is represented by *adjacent systems,* which comprise the automated systems, people, departments, organizations, and other parties that place some kind of demand on, or make some kind of contribution to, the work.

To locate your work within the outside world, you demonstrate its context by showing how the work connects to the adjacent systems. In other words, your context diagram shows your work in its business environment.

Figure 4.2 shows the context diagram for the work of predicting when roads are due to freeze and scheduling trucks to treat them with de-icing material (this diagram also appeared in Chapter 3). The work is surrounded by adjacent systems that either supply the data necessary for this work, or receive services and information from the work.

The work to be studied must include anything that can be affected by your product. If you are building a product intended to automate part of some existing work, then the scope of the study should include those parts of the existing work—human activities, together with any existing computer systems—that could potentially be changed by the eventual product. For embedded systems, there may be no human activity in your work, but the work scope must include any devices that can be changed or someway

> *The work to be studied must include anything that can be affected by your product.*

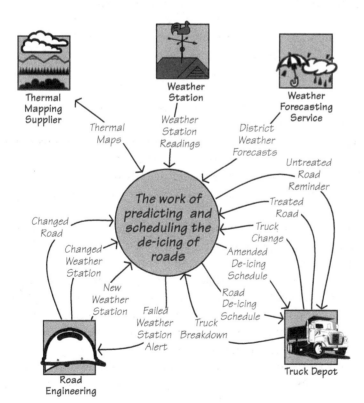

Figure 4.2

The context diagram showing the scope of the work. The central area of the diagram represents the work you are about to study, and the product you eventually build becomes part of this work. The outside world is represented by the adjacent systems— *Weather Station, Truck Depot,* and so on. The named arrows represent flows of information between the adjacent systems and the work.

affected by the current development. Even if you are building an electro-mechanical device, such as an automated teller machine (ATM), and most of the human participation occurs outside the product boundary, your work context must still include the work that the human will be doing with the device.

While we are talking about the work context diagram, note the limited, but nevertheless crucial, aim of the model. This model shows only the flows of information. It does not attempt to show the constraints upon the work, although these limitations may be inferred from the model. Likewise, it does not explicitly show who or what is doing the work, although this information might also be inferred. As is true of most models, the context model is an abstraction that shows a single view. In this case, by highlighting the flows of information, we are able to make better use of the model for determining the business events affecting the work. But first, let's look at one part of the context model in more detail: the outside world.

The work scope includes anything that you are permitted to change, plus anything that you need to understand to decide what can or should be changed.

The Outside World

As we saw earlier, the adjacent systems are those parts of the world that connect to the work by delivering data to it or receiving data from it.

Adjacent systems behave like any other systems: They contain processes and consume and/or produce data. You are interested in them because they are often customers for the information or services provided by your work, or because they supply information needed by your work. You can see these relationships by looking at the data flows on the context diagram. It is through these informational connections that the adjacent systems influence the work.

Within reason, the farther away from the anticipated automated system you look, the more useful and innovative your product is likely to be.

To find the adjacent systems, you sometimes have to venture outside your own organization. Go to the customers for your organization's products or services. Go to the outside automated systems and organizations that supply information or services to your work. Go to the other departments that have connections to the work. Use the guideline that the farther away from the anticipated automated system you look, the more useful and innovative your product is likely to be.

You will usually find that your work is also closely connected to one or more computer systems, often within your own organization, or that you are making an enhancement to an existing computer system. In this case, the computer systems, or the parts that you are not changing, are adjacent systems. The interfaces between your work and the existing computer systems are critical. Although they may prove difficult to describe, you can never know the extent of your work, and eventually the extent of your product, if you do not define these interfaces clearly.

Do not be limited by what you think might be the limits of a computer system. Instead, try to find the farthest practical extent of any influence on the work.

Think of it this way: The adjacent systems are the reason why the work exists; they are customers for the services produced by the work. The work produces these services either on demand or at prearranged times, and when it does so, the work is responding to a business event.

Business Events

Any piece of work responds to things that happen outside it—it's that simple. For the sake of clarity, because we are discussing your owner's work or business, we shall call these happenings *business events*.

Let's look at an example of a business event. You are reading this book, so your authors sincerely hope you paid for it. Let us for the moment suppose that you bought it online. You had already found the book, looked at the sample pages, and decided that you wanted it. At that moment, one of two things could have happened: (1) You could have decided that you had something other to do and abandoned the transaction or (2) you could have decided to buy the book. That moment—that instant when you decided to buy the book—is the business event. Of course, just deciding that you want the book is not quite enough; you have to tell the work that you want it.

You signaled the work by indicating that you wanted to check out (or whatever mechanism your online bookseller has for such things) and provided a credit card and shipping address and so on. This incoming flow of data triggered a response in the bookseller's work, which was to transfer ownership of the book to you, debit your credit card, and send a message to the fulfillment department to ship the book to you. If you bought the book as an e-book, that last step would be replaced by one that started the download.

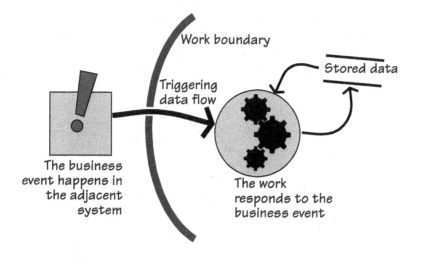

Work boundary

Stored data

Triggering data flow

The business event happens in the adjacent system

The work responds to the business event

Figure 4.3

Business events and their responses: A business event happens at the moment the adjacent system decides to do something, or as part of its work some processing condition occurs. The adjacent system tells the work that the event has happened by sending a triggering data flow. When this stream of data arrives, the work responds by processing the incoming data, and by retrieving and recording stored data.

Another example: You pay your credit card bill at the end of the month—that is a business event as seen from the point of view of the credit card company. The credit card company responds to this event by checking that your address has not changed and then recording the date and amount of your payment.

In these examples, the moment you decide to buy the book and the moment you decide to pay your monthly bill are the business events. There is always some data resulting from the business event (the triggering data flow), which invokes a preplanned response to the event. This response is the business use case.

You as a customer do not own or control either the bookshop or the credit card company. Nevertheless, in both examples you did something to make them respond—they did some processing and manipulated some data. Think of it this way: Those pieces of work have a preplanned business use case that is activated whenever an outside body (the adjacent system) initiates a business event. Figure 4.4 illustrates this idea.

When a business event happens, the work responds by initiating a business use case.

Note that business use cases are triggered by the arrival of a data flow from the adjacent system. In the preceding examples, these data flows were your request to buy the book and your payment slip and check arriving at the credit card company. As a consequence, the responsibility for triggering the business use case lies outside the control of the work. We will return to this point shortly. First, however, let's look at another kind of business event.

Time-Triggered Business Events

Time-triggered business events are initiated by the arrival of a predetermined time (or date). For example, your insurance company sends you a renewal notice a month before the anniversary of your policy; your bank sends you a statement on an agreed day of every month. "The arrival of a predetermined time" may also mean that a certain amount of time has elapsed since another event happened. For example, a computer operating

Figure 4.4

A business event takes place outside the scope of the work, and the work learns that it has happened through the arrival of an incoming flow of information. The work contains a business use case that responds to this business event.

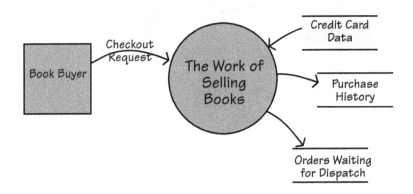

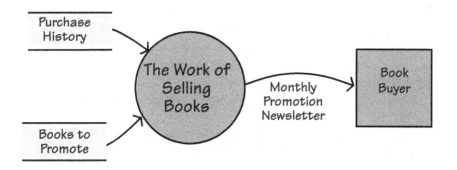

Figure 4.5

A time-triggered business event happens when a prearranged time is reached. This is based on either a periodic occurrence (for example, the end of the month, or a certain time each day), a fixed time interval (for example, three hours since the last occurrence), or a certain amount of time elapsing since another business event (for example, 30 days after sending out an invoice). The normal response is to retrieve stored data, process it, and send some information to an adjacent system.

system may check the available memory 2.4 microseconds after the last time it checked, or you may be sent a reminder that you borrowed a library book six weeks ago.

The usual response to a time-triggered business event is to retrieve previously stored data, process it, and send the resultant information to an adjacent system. Consider the example depicted in Figure 4.5.

Once the predetermined time for the event arrives, the work's response is to do whatever is necessary to produce the output. This almost always involves the retrieval and manipulation of stored data. Once again, we use the response to the time-triggered business event—the business use case—as our unit of study.

Why Business Events and Business Use Cases Are a Good Idea

We may seem to be going to a lot of trouble to describe something that may, at first glance, seem fairly obvious. But this care with the subject is warranted: Our experience has amply demonstrated the value of having an objective way of partitioning the work, and the value of understanding the work itself, before plunging into the solution. The result is that you discover the real requirements, and you discover them more quickly.

Your partitioning of the work will be more objective if you identify the responses to outside stimuli; after all, that is the way your customers see your business. The business's internal partitions—department and processors, whatever they may be—hold no interest for outsiders. Similarly, it is likely that the current partitioning of any system is based on technological and political decisions made at the time the system was built. Those decisions may no longer be valid—at the very least, you should question them and avoid perpetuating them just because they are there at the moment. By looking not at the inside, but from the outside, you get a clearer idea of the most functional way of partitioning the work.

By looking not at the inside, but from the outside, you get a much clearer idea of the most functional way of partitioning the work.

The work's response to a business event brings together all the things that belong together.

The work's response to a business event brings together all the things that belong together. As a result, you get cohesive partitions with minimal interfaces between the pieces. This partitioning gives you more logical chunks of work for your detailed requirements investigation—the fewer dependencies that exist between the pieces, the more the analysts can investigate the details about one piece without needing to know everything about all the other pieces.

There is one more reason for using business use cases, and that is to prompt an investigation of what is happening at the time of the business event.

The "System" Cannot Be Assumed

In many of the texts available today, the existence of a "system" is assumed. That is, the author guesses what he thinks the boundary of the automated system should be, and begins the use case investigation by looking at the actor and the interaction with the automated system, and completely ignores the work surrounding this interaction. *To do so is dangerous and wrong.*

This product-centric way of looking at the problem means that you are ignoring the most important aspect of the automated system: the work that it is meant to improve. By starting with the automated system, projects take a massive gamble that they have, in fact, hit on the right solution, and that they have been able to do so without any study of the problem. Although we seem able to resist the blandishments of the salesman who claims that his particular insurance package will serve all our needs, we have an unhappy tendency to leap at the first automated solution that comes to mind. Looking inward at the solution discourages analysts from asking, "But why is this like it is?" This failure, in turn, leads to "technological fossils" being carried from one generation of a product to the next.

Consider this example: "An insurance clerk receives a claim from a car insurance policy holder and then enters the claim into the automated system." This view encourages the requirements analyst to study the work of the clerk entering the details of the claim into the system. However, if you spend a few moments looking at the real business being done here, you will see that the claim is simply the insurance company's implementation—it is the *accident* that initiates this piece of business. Why is this point important? If you start your business investigation at the real origin of the problem—in other words, you look at what is happening at the time of the business event—you will build a better product. Perhaps it would be feasible to create a product that processes the claim in real time at the scene of the accident. A possible solution for that problem would be a smart phone app that knew where you were, and could take photos of the result of the accident along with the relevant license plates and driver details, and transmit them to the insurance company before the tow-trucks arrive.

Think of the *real* originator of the business event—in this case, it is the driver or owner of the vehicle (not the insurance clerk). What are the driver's aspirations here? He wants to have the vehicle repaired as quickly and effortlessly as possible; his goal is *not* to fill in claim forms and wait for them to be approved.

Another example: "A caller contacts the help desk. The help desk person initiates the use case by asking the caller for details of the problem and logging the call." The use case is the logging, and the actor is the help desk person. Again, this product-centric view misses the real business event—the event that started it all. In this case, it is the initiation of the call to the help desk.

The requirements analyst must look past the obvious, and the current way of doing business, and instead understand the true nature of the work.

Why is it important to find the real origin for the event? If you think of initiating the call as the business event, the correct response is to log the call, use caller ID to identify the caller's equipment, retrieve information on the equipment, and provide it for the help desk person.

Stepping back a little further and seeing the end-to-end business (see Figure 4.6), you would probably decide that the real business event is the malfunctioning of the caller's equipment. When you adopt this perspective, you also think of the equipment making the call for help itself. Perhaps a better understanding of the reasons underlying the malfunction might result in your new product giving the help desk operator historical information that will facilitate him in responding correctly to the call.

Stakeholders often don't ask for these requirements because they are thinking only of an assumed product. It is the task of the accomplished business analyst to look beyond that endpoint, which means understanding the intentions of the adjacent system at the moment it initiates the business event.

Step Back

A security system this time: "The actor receives the shipment and logs it in." Nope. The real business event is the *dispatch* of the shipment; the business use case should log the shipment as it leaves the shipper and monitor its

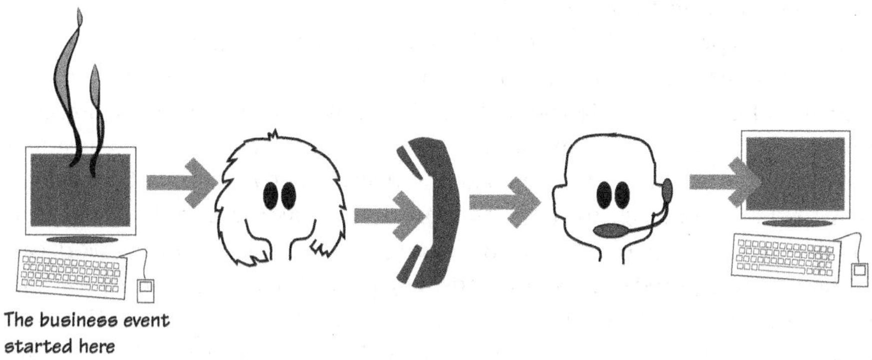

The business event
started here

Figure 4.6

Consider the real end-to-end process. The aim of the diligent requirements discoverer is to look at all the activities and include them in the study. This way, the real business is revealed.

Figure 4.7

Step back and see the end-to-end process, and at the same time, see the real business.

transit and arrival. We need to step back and see the whole business as in Figure 4.7.

By stepping back and seeing the whole of the business process, the business analyst has the best chance of identifying the real work. Conversely, by looking only at the automated system, the analyst is often led down the path of incremental improvements that stakeholders ask for. If you can see the whole spectrum of the business use case from its real inception to its conclusion, you are in a much better position to derive a more appropriate and useful automated product.

Finding the Business Events

Business events are things that happen and, in turn, make the work respond in some way. An event may happen outside the scope of the work (an external event), or it may happen because it is time for the work to do something (a time-triggered event). In the case of an external event, a communication to the work from the outside—represented by the adjacent systems—lets the work know that the event has happened. In the other case, the time-triggered event, the outcome is always a flow to the outside world. In either situation, whenever a business event occurs, there must be at least one data flow to show it on the context diagram.

Figure 4.8 provides the context diagram for the de-icing project. The same diagram appeared earlier in this chapter—for convenience, we repeat it here. Take a look at it and note the information flows that connect the adjacent systems to the work. For example, the flow called *Changed Road* is the result of the event that occurs when the Road Engineering department either builds a new road or makes significant alterations to an existing one. The engineering personnel advise the work of the change so that the scheduling work can update its own stored data about roads. The flow called *Road De-icing Schedule* is the outcome of a time-triggered business event: Every two hours, the work produces a schedule of the roads to be treated and sends it to the *Truck Depot*.

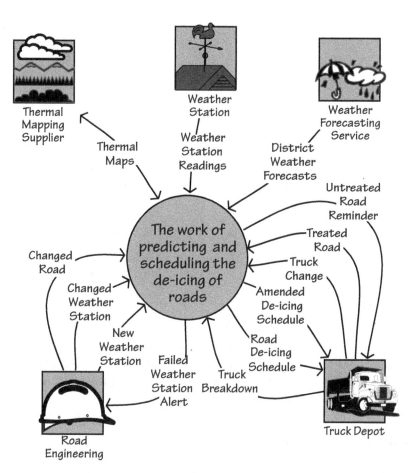

Figure 4.8

The context model for the IceBreaker work. Note the flows of data entering and leaving the work. The analyst uses these data flows to determine the business events.

Each of the flows that enters or leaves the work is the result of a business event; there can be no other reason for an external communication to exist. Looking at each flow, you can determine the business event that caused it. In some cases, several flows may be attached to the same business event. For example, when the *Truck Depot* advises that a scheduled truck has broken down or will be withdrawn from service for some other reason (the input flow is *Truck Breakdown*), the work responds. Because one of the trucks is now out of service, the other trucks have to be rescheduled to compensate for the shortfall, and the resultant outgoing flow is the *Amended De-icing Schedule*.

Each of the flows that enters or leaves the work is the result of a business event.

Table 4.1 shows a list of business events and their input and output flows for the de-icing work. Compare it with the work context diagram in Figure 4.8, and reconcile the business events with the data that flows to and/or from the work.

Admittedly, you need some knowledge of the work to figure out the business events. To this end we advise you to start the process of determining business events during blastoff, when the key stakeholders are present. In

Table 4.1

List of Business Events and Their Associated Input and Output Flows for the Road De-icing Work

Event Name	Input and Output
1. Weather Station transmits a reading	Weather Station Readings (in)
2. Weather Bureau forecasts weather	District Weather Forecasts (in)
3. Road engineers advise there are changed roads	Changed Road (in)
4. Road Engineering installs a new weather station	New Weather Station (in)
5. Road Engineering changes the weather station	Changed Weather Station (in)
6. Time to test Weather Stations	Failed Weather Station Alert (out)
7. Truck Depot changes a truck	Truck Change (in)
8. Time to detect icy roads	Road De-icing Schedule (out)
9. Truck treats a road	Treated Road (in)
10. Truck Depot reports a problem with a truck	Truck Breakdown (in)
	Amended De-icing Schedule (out)
11. Time to monitor road de-icing	Untreated Road Reminder (out)

most situations, you will find the stakeholders know the business events (they may not know them by that name, but they will know what they are). If you do not identify all of the business events during the blastoff, you will see them when you begin to study the work.

Business Use Cases

Business events are useful to partition the work, but it is the work's *response* to the event that now captures the interest of the requirements analyst.

The business use case is the most convenient unit of work to study.

For every business event, there is a preplanned response to it, known as a *business use case* (BUC). The business use case is always a collection of identifiable processes, data that is retrieved and/or stored, output generated, messages sent, or some combination of these. Alternatively, we could simply say that the business use case is a unit of functionality. This unit is the basis for writing the functional and non-functional requirements (we will talk about these requirements in more detail in Chapters 10 and 11).

You can identify one or more stakeholders who are expert in each event.

You can readily isolate the work of a business use case, because it has no processing connections to other BUCs; the only overlap between BUCs is their stored data. As a consequence, different analysts can investigate different parts of the work without the need for constant communication between them. This relative isolation of each business use case makes it easier to identify the stakeholders who are expert in that part of the work, and they can (with your help) describe it precisely and in detail. You can also *observe* the business use case: Business events are known to the stakeholders, and they can show you how the organization responds to any of them. For example, it would not be hard to find someone in your favorite bookshop who can take you through the process of selling a book, or someone in your insurance company who can show you how the company processes a claim. We discuss trawling techniques for this kind of investigation in Chapters 5, 6, and 7.

The processing for a business use case is continuous—it happens in a discrete time frame. Once it is triggered, it processes everything until there is nothing left to do that can logically be done at that time. All the functionality has been carried out, all the data to be stored by the business use case has been written to the data stores, and all the adjacent systems have been notified. You can see an example of this processing in Figures 4.9 and 4.10.

The product you intend to build contributes to the work being done by the business use case. Sometimes the product will do all the work of the BUC, but usually it will do some part of it. Your product does not change the real nature of the work; it just changes the way it is done. Nevertheless, before you can design the product that makes the optimal contribution to the work, you must understand the work. Most importantly, you must understand your client's desired outcome from the work. So for the moment, forget the details and technology of the business use case, and instead look

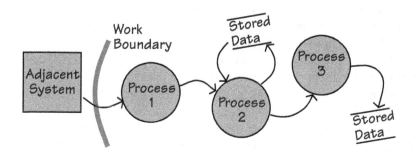

Figure 4.9

The work's response to the business event is to continue processing until all active tasks (the processes) have been completed and all data retrieved or stored. You can think of the response as a chain of processes and their associated stored data. Note that the processes are surrounded by a combination of data stores and adjacent systems.

Figure 4.10

This model uses BPML notation to show the same processing as in Figure 4.9, which uses data flow notation. You are urged to use whichever notation you prefer.

outside the organization to see what kind of response is needed, or wanted, by the organization's customers and suppliers.

Business Use Cases and Product Use Cases

We have stressed the importance of understanding the work, not just the product. By looking at the larger scope of the work, you ask more questions about the business requirements and ultimately build a better product. The following example comes from a recent consulting assignment: The product is to rip a CD into MP3 or some other digital format. When the engineers looked at the technical part of the product (they are engineers, so naturally they are interested in technicalities), they saw a use case that was triggered by the insertion of the CD and then went on to rip the CD. Getting the best musical quality (the engineers were mainly concerned with achieving the desired bit rate for the transfer) seemed to be the most important thing.

We could have considered that to be the final product use case and written requirements for it. But look what happens when you step back and look at the wider context of the real business being done here (the business use case): You see something more.

What is the end user trying to accomplish? What are his aspirations and desired outcomes?

What is the end user trying to accomplish? What are his aspirations and desired outcomes? We define them as "getting the music from the CD into an MP3 player." Thus the real question is not about the technicalities of the assumed product, which is ripping CDs and converting them to MP3 format, but rather about the remainder of the true business.

Part of that business indicates that the end user wants the track names to appear on his MP3 player. Thus adding track names must be part of the BUC, as must adding images of the album cover and artist. The business use case should also allow for the order of tracks to be changed, unwanted tracks to be deleted, and any other organizational changes to the music to be carried out.

By stepping back and looking at the work being done, we were able to find a much better product to build.

So what do you have? At the outset, you have the scope of the work being studied, and the scope is bounded by the communications with the adjacent systems surrounding the work. Business events happen in the adjacent systems when they decide they want some information or service from the work, or they want to send some information to the work. Once the business event has happened and the resulting data flow has reached the work, the work responds. This response constitutes the business use case.

Study the business use case, considering what the work does and what the adjacent system desires or needs. In other words, consider whether the organization is making the correct response to the adjacent system. Once you understand the correct work of the business use case, determine the scope of the product that best contributes to that business use case. As part of this effort, consider whether the adjacent system is capable (or desirous) of making a different contribution to the work than it currently does.

Don't assume the responsibilities of the product and the adjacent systems at the beginning of the project. Instead, derive them from an understanding of the work and from what the external customer considers to be a useful product.

When that is understood, decide how much of the BUC is to be done by the product use case. Specifically, the part of the BUC handled by the automated system is the *product use case* (PUC). Sometimes the functionality of the PUC ends up being the same as that of the BUC (you have decided to automate everything), but often some part of the functionality does not become part of the PUC; you decide that this task is best done by humans.

So here's the thing: the PUC is *derived*. It is not assumed at the beginning of the requirements investigation, but rather carefully arrived at by examining the work. By deriving the PUC from the BUC, you find a more useful product, one that gives better value to its owner. And that surely is the point of your project.

The relationship between PUCs and BUCs is shown in Figure 4.11.

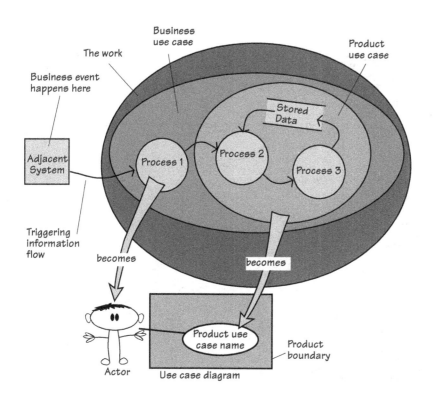

Figure 4.11

The business event is some happening in the adjacent system. The resulting information flow notifies the *work* of the event and triggers a response (the *business use case*). After study, the requirements analysts and the interested stakeholders decide how much of the business use case is to be handled by the proposed product (the *product use case*). Whatever is immediately outside the scope of the product becomes the *actor*, who manipulates the functionality of the product use case within the product. A UML use case diagram is shown for comparison.

Sometimes, for technical reasons, you might choose to implement a business use case with a number of PUCs. Perhaps you wish to subdivide the work inside the computer into smaller pieces, or perhaps you have the opportunity to reuse product use cases that have previously been developed for other parts of the product or for other products, or maybe different types of stakeholders are concerned with only part of the business use case.

The selection of product use cases is somewhat driven by technical considerations. However, if the product is to be recognizable and usable by its intended users, then its PUCs must be based on the original business events and must be traceable back to the business use case.

Actors

When you determine the product use cases, you are also selecting the *actors* who interact with the product.

Actors are the people or systems that interact with the automated product. In some cases, they are adjacent systems that are outside the work—for example, the organization's customers. In other cases, you appoint actors from inside the organization. Figure 4.12 shows the product use cases that were selected for the IceBreaker product as well as the actors that operate each of the product use cases.

Figure 4.12

The product use case diagram for the IceBreaker product, showing the product use cases, the actors involved in each product use case, and the product's boundary. The different notation used for the actors indicates the way they interact with the product. (These distinctions are explained in Chapter 8, where we look at starting the product.)

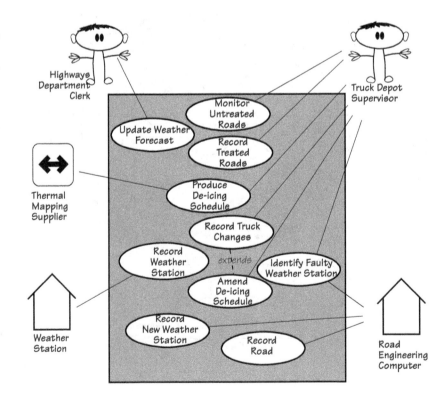

Summary

Business events and business use cases allow you to carve out a cohesive piece of the work for further modeling and study. By understanding the work being done by each of the BUCs, you come to understand the optimal product you can build to support that work.

If you are outsourcing, you might not determine the product use cases, but work instead on the business use cases. These business use cases can then serve as your negotiating document when you ask your outsourcer which parts of them he can deliver as product use cases.

By using business events to partition the work, you take an external view of the work. You are not relying on how it happens to be partitioned internally at the moment, or on someone's idea of how it might be partitioned in the future. Instead, you partition the work according to the most important view of the work: how the outside world (often your customers) sees it. Figure 4.13 is an overview of this kind of partitioning.

The idea of deriving the product use cases from the business use case means your requirements are grouped according to how the work responds to the business event. The result is a natural partitioning of the work, which results eventually in a product that is more responsive to the real demands of the outside world, and thereby optimally valuable to its owner.

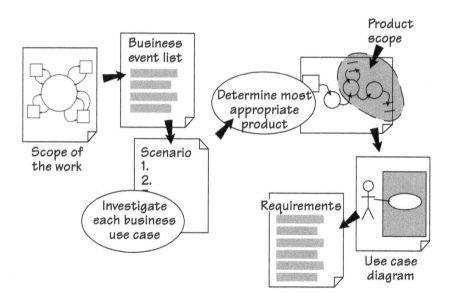

Figure 4.13

The flow of requirements discovery: The response to each business event—the business use case—is examined and an appropriate product determined. The analysts write the requirements for each product use case.

Investigating the Work

5

in which we come to an understanding of
what the business is doing, and start to think
about what it might like to do

The owner's work, for better or for worse, is the starting point of the requirements for any new product you build. Your product is intended to improve the existing work or enable some new capabilities for it. The work might be a small, simple task done by an individual, or it might involve many people and software systems and hardware systems, and make up a significant and critical part of the organization.

Whatever the work, it seems sensible to have a fair understanding of it before attempting any changes. If you charge in and make "improvements" with little or no understanding of what you are changing, then you should hardly be surprised if things do not turn out as they should. In contrast, a little time invested in learning the work will significantly enhance your chances of successfully making a beneficial impact on it. And while you are coming to an understanding of the existing work, you are certain to generate ideas on how to make it better.

In this chapter we discuss how to investigate a piece of work prior to changing it. Normally your change would mean building a software product or some other device to do some or all of the work. This seems a reasonable approach given that when you build a piece of software, you are, in essence, automating a task that if you had enough time, you could do using human labor.

Trawling the Business

We use the term *trawling* to describe the activity of investigating the business. This term evokes the nature of what we are doing here: fishing. Not idly dangling a line while hoping a fish might come by, but rather methodically

Figure 5.1

The business analyst trawls for knowledge by investigating the client's work. The analogy of running a net through the organization is appropriate: You need to sift through much of the business before you can find the best way to improve it.

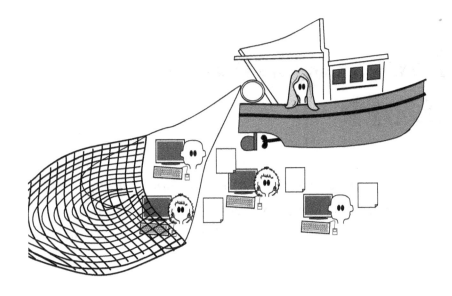

running a net through the business to catch every possible requirement (see Figure 5.1). With a little experience and good techniques, the skipper of a trawler knows where to fish so that he gets the fish he wants, and avoids the ones that he doesn't. The objective in this chapter is to show you some trawling techniques, and give you guidelines on how to get the best from them.

While it is important to uncover the current business, including both its data and its processes, it is also important that you do not spend too much time doing so. Keep in mind that this is the beginning of the analysis process, and you would like to get through this step as rapidly as possible. Also keep in mind that the business you are studying is about to be changed. Given these caveats, we suggest that you study the current business as quickly as possible—you can always come back later to get additional information should it be necessary.

This chapter explores the techniques for discovering the business processes, and the people involved in those processes. Inevitably, you will need a variety of techniques to achieve this feat, and you will find that not all techniques are equally acceptable to your stakeholders. For this reason, it will be necessary to vary your approach to best suit the stakeholders who are providing the requirements.

When you are reading about the trawling techniques, you will see our suggestions on when and how they are used. Use these suggestions to determine for yourself what is most appropriate for your stakeholders, your preferred way of working, and your project. We have included an owl to provide guidance on whether the technique is applicable to your situation.

While it is important to uncover the current business, including both its data and its processes, it is also important that you do not spend too much time doing so.

Formality Guide

The study of the current business is not intended to be a lengthy process. You are encouraged to do it as quickly as possible, and to stop doing it once you have enough information about the current state of the business to enable you and your stakeholders to move on to the next stage. Also keep in mind that requirements are not solutions; you have to learn the requirement before you can find the solution. It just doesn't work the other way round.

Rabbit projects need to understand the work as it currently is, as well as what the work is to be. Because rabbit projects are usually iterative, you are likely to visit the current work in small slices and then proceed to find its essence and ultimately its solution. This cycle is repeated until the product is complete. This iterative way of working should minimize any documentation of the current work. However, that does not obviate the need to *understand* the work.

Some of you will be working on an agile team with a product owner or customer representative. We have found (unfortunately) that a single person is unlikely to have a good enough understanding of the wider business to be able to provide all of the needed information. We suggest you adopt some of the trawling techniques to enhance your iterative team's understanding of the work, and as a result enhance the product you are building.

Horse projects, due to their larger number of stakeholders, probably make more extensive use of apprenticing, interviewing, and use case workshops. These techniques generate some documentation, and while documenting the current work is by no means the objective of the project, it is extremely useful as input to subsequent decisions.

Horse projects are more likely to be dealing with critical infrastructure systems, so knowledge of the work and its goals is important to the project.

Elephant projects, due to their larger number of stakeholders, need to document their findings as they go about trawling for their requirements. Because of the more extensive set of possibilities for elephant projects, we suggest that you read this entire chapter, paying special attention to the "owl recommendations."

Projects using outsourcing are always elephants—they need a formal specification. Additionally, the artifacts produced by investigating the work should be retained for future maintenance.

Trawl for Knowledge

We build products to help us do work. For our purposes, it doesn't matter whether the work is processing insurance claims, analyzing blood samples, designing automotive parts, predicting when ice will form on roads, keeping track of a "things to do" list, controlling a telephone network, downloading music or movies, monitoring a household, manipulating photographs, or one of many other human activities. In all instances, the product that you are being asked to build must improve this work.

Figure 5.2 shows the Volere process and highlights the part where you investigate the work with a view toward discovering the best product to enable or improve that work.

When you are trawling for knowledge, the first task is to investigate and understand the work as it is currently being done. It is not always necessarily to document this information, but you must certainly understand it. Once you have a fair understanding of the current work, then you can derive its essence. That is, you can strip away the current technology to get a clean picture of the real business.

The essential view is then developed in conjunction with the stakeholders to arrive at the requirements for the new product. This is not a laborious process—just a thorough one. We will look at it over the next few chapters.

The trawling activity uses outputs from the project blastoff—the scope of the work, the goals of the project, and the constraints that apply to any solution. The blastoff also identified the stakeholders involved in the project and the potential users. These stakeholders are the people with whom you consult to get an understanding of the work.

Figure 5.2

The trawling activity is central to the requirements process. It uses the outputs of the project blastoff activity as its starting point for investigating the work and accumulating knowledge about it. Over the next few chapters, we will develop this knowledge into requirements for the product to be built. The dotted lines on the diagram indicate how trawling works when you are using iterative development.

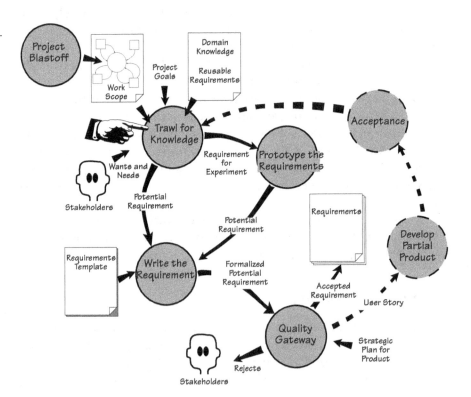

The Business Analyst

The business analyst is also known as a systems analyst, a requirements engineer, and probably several other titles. We use "business analyst" because it is the most commonly used name. Whatever name you use, this person is an investigator and a translator: He has to inspect the work, interview the business stakeholders, understand what they are saying, and then translate that knowledge into a form that can be communicated to and understood by the developers. Initially, the business analyst's task is to record, clarify, and question the current state of the business. Later, as the analysis progresses, the emphasis changes from recording an existing system to thinking about a new one. For the moment, the task of the business analyst is this:

- *Observe and learn the work, and understand it from the point of view of the owner.* As you work with your users, you study their work and question them about what they are doing, and why they are doing it.

- *Interpret the work.* A user's description of some work is not always factual despite the user being the expert on that part of the work. The analyst must filter the description to strip away the current technology, thereby revealing the underlying essence of the work, not its incarnation.

- *Record the results in the form of stakeholder-understandable analysis models.* The analyst must ensure that he and the stakeholders have the same, and agreed, understanding of the work. We suggest using models as a common language for communicating your knowledge to the stakeholders.

There is a lot to know about trawling—and we know that not all trawling techniques are applicable to all projects. The owl gives you guidance on whether the technique is applicable to your situation. By all means, read this entire chapter—but realize that you don't need to use all of the trawling techniques on every project.

Many techniques are available to help with the task of studying the business. We provide you with several choices here because we know that no single technique works in every situation. Instead, you have to select the technique that works best for you at the time. In our discussions of the techniques, we indicate when and why one would be useful. But don't just take our word for it—try to connect each technique to your own situation, and consider where and when each would be most advantageous.

Consider your stakeholders. They are *conscious* of some of their processes and requirements and bring them up early. At the same time, they are *unconscious* of others—things that are so ingrained into the stakeholders' work that they have forgotten they exist, or forgotten how they are done. The techniques that capture the conscious processes may not necessarily work for the unconscious ones. Then there are the *undreamed-of* processes—those functions and features that the stakeholders are not aware they could have.

Undreamed-of needs exist because the stakeholders do not realize they are possible, perhaps because the stakeholders lack sufficient technological sophistication, or perhaps because they have never seen their work in the way that you will show it to them.

Whatever the situation, your responsibility is to bring the conscious, unconscious, and undreamed-of work to the surface.

Trawling and Business Use Cases

Business use case are so fundamental to the requirements activity that we urge you, whatever your situation or project type, to consider doing your requirements trawling one business use case at a time. If you have not already read Chapter 4, Business Use Cases, we encourage you to do so now.

From the work context diagram, you determine the business events and the resulting business use cases. In Chapter 4, we discussed business events, exploring how happenings outside the work cause a response inside the work. This response is a *business use case,* and we suggest that you do your work by studying one business use case at a time.

The business use case is the functionality that the work does in response to a business event. When the triggering data flow enters the work, the work starts to process it. If the triggering data flow arrives via a telephone call, then a person might be there to answer it. Alternatively, an automated telephone system might prompt the caller to identify the nature of the call. In the end, it doesn't matter *how* it is done; the important thing is *what* is done. This functionality is what you study when trawling, as is illustrated in Figure 5.3.

Figure 5.3

Business events are determined using the triggering data flows from the adjacent systems on the context diagram. The business use cases are the work's responses to the business events, and these are studied until the analyst understands the way the work functions.

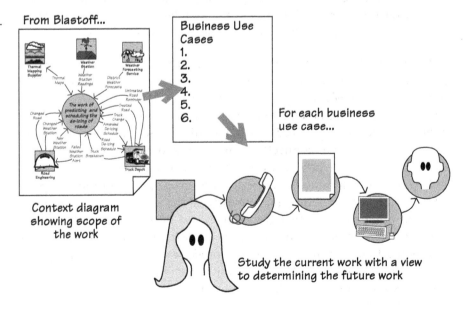

The Brown Cow Model

When you are investigating the work area, there are a number of ways in which you can look at it—*viewpoints*—and there are four really useful ones. We shall demonstrate them using a brown cow.

The Brown Cow Model,[1] shown in Figure 5.4, takes four views of the work; the two axes separate *What* from *How*, and the *Now* from the *Future*.

Let's start in the lower-left quadrant of the model: How-Now. This is sometimes—but not always—the place to start. How-Now shows the implementation of the work as it currently exists, including the physical artifacts, people, and processors used to do the work. You use this view when you need to get enough of a grounding to begin to ask other questions.

When you set out to build some new product, you are not trying to simply duplicate whatever you have at the moment; no gain is realized in doing that. Instead, by eliminating the technological fossils and obsolete organizational procedures from the current situation, you begin to see the pure, unadulterated business problem.

This brings us above the line to What-Now. This abstract view shows the real business policy, or as we prefer to call it, the *essence* of the work. This view is completely technologically neutral, and it shows the business as if no machines, people, or organizational departments existed. We use this view to cleanse our ideas on what the current business is actually doing without inhibiting it by referring to processors and physical artifacts that might not be part of a future implementation.

Moving to the upper-right quadrant, we get to the Future-What view. This view shows the business as your owner wants to have it, but still without the

FOOTNOTE 1

If you are wondering, the name of this model comes from a piece of English elocution. Students being taught to speak correctly with rounded vowels have to clearly enunciate, "How now brown cow?" The first segment of this model is the How-Now segment—hence the Brown Cow name for the model.

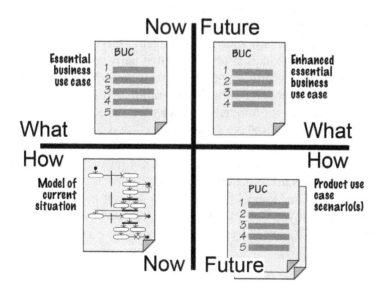

Figure 5.4

The Brown Cow Model. This shows four views of the work, each of which provides the business analyst and the stakeholders with information that is useful at different stages of the requirements discovery process.

technology that might be used to implement that business. It is the purest version of the proposed future state of the business area. The value of this viewpoint is that it shows—so you can discuss with your stakeholders—precisely what the owner would like to do, without worrying about how the technology might do it.

The last quadrant, the lower right, is Future-How. Here you take your idealized view of the future business policy, and augment it with the technology and people needed to bring it into the real world.

It is generally not sufficient to simply have two views of the business—the "as is" and the "to be." These views never get away from the implementation, never see the pure business problem in its true light, and as such are unsuitable for any kind of serious innovation or system development.

The Current Way of Doing Things (How-Now)

Building models as a way of investigating the work is best done when you need to understand a medium-to-large work area for which no documentation exists. This technique is also used when the current users struggle to give you an idea of how the work fits together. It is also useful when you know that there will be a significant legacy from the existing work.

We have mentioned several times—and probably will do so again several times more—the need to understand the work. This is best done by being actively involved in investigating the work rather than by being a passive onlooker.

Despite any bad reputation the current work may have, it is still useful: It contains functionality that is making a positive contribution to the business. Naturally, much of this functionality must be included in any future system. You may implement it differently with new technology, but its underlying business policy will remain almost unchanged. Thus one reason to build a model of the current work is to identify which parts you need to keep.

You can use models to help you understand the work but, paradoxically, you cannot build a model without understanding the work. This paradox follows from the way the modeling activity leads you to ask all the right questions. Any useful model is a *working* model—it is functionally correct in that you can demonstrate the model's outputs are derivable from its inputs. As a consequence, if your model isn't working, it means you simply haven't asked enough questions to get enough right answers (see Figure 5.5). Alternatively, we could say that as the model develops, it becomes increasingly more obvious what you don't know, how much you don't know, and what the business people don't know.

Uh, I have a
few questions.

Figure 5.5

Knowing where to ask questions, and which questions to ask, is almost as useful as knowing the answers. If your model has flows going nowhere, processes without inputs, read-only or write-only data stores, or other breaches of the modeling conventions, then you need to ask your stakeholders more questions about those aspects of the work.

Your models record the work and demonstrate your understanding of it. Because the model is a common language between you and your stakeholders, you can come to have the identical understanding of the situation.

When you model the current work, keep in mind that you are not attempting to specify a new product, but rather merely establishing the work that the users currently do. Most likely the users will describe their work in a way that includes the mechanisms and technology they use to get the work done. These mechanisms are not requirements for the new system—you must look beyond them to see the underlying policy of the users' system. That understanding emerges when you move "above the line" and work with the two segments of the Brown Cow Model above the horizontal axis that deal with *what*, rather than *how*. We shall get to this step in a little while.

Modeling the current system should be done as quickly as possible. Figure 5.6 shows a model of an existing system, built by the authors in conjunction with staff at City University, London. This model was built in about 15 minutes—but we were drinking coffee at the time.

Restrict the amount of detail you include in your models of the current system—there is little point in modeling every tiny facet of something you are about to replace. The ideal model contains enough detail to give you an understanding of the work, and no more. The detail shown in Figures 5.6 and 5.7 is about right. That is, these models show the major parts of the current situation. Such a model would allow the stakeholders to verify that it is a good-enough representation of the work as it stands, and it gives the requirements analyst places to make further inquiries.

READING
Robertson, James, and Suzanne Robertson. *Complete Systems Analysis: The Workbook, the Textbook, the Answers.* Dorset House, 1998. This book demonstrates how to build models of current, future, and imaginary work.

The current work contains many functions that contribute to the continuation of the business. Naturally, these functions must be included in any future work.

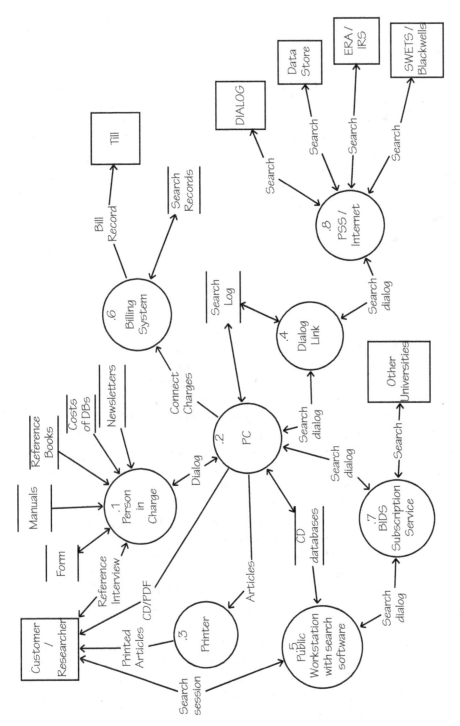

Figure 5.6

City University researchers' process for interrogating commercial databases. This model shows the technology used for the task and was built by the authors working with the user of the process. As the user described the work, the authors modeled and demonstrated their understanding. This model uses conventional data flow notation. Most process models would do the job equally well, so use whichever model you are most familiar with.

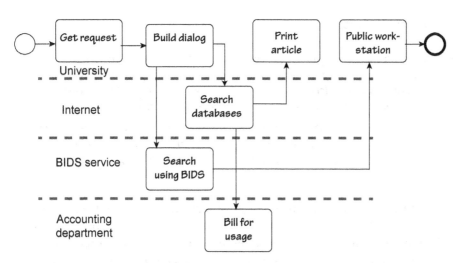

Figure 5.7

A UML activity diagram showing the same piece of work as illustrated in Figure 5.6. Business analysts should use whatever models they feel most comfortable with.

One aspect of the model that should not, within reason, be restricted is the area of the work covered by the model. Here it is almost—and we stress "almost"—a case of "the more, the merrier." Your models should cover all the work that could possibly be relevant to your product, those parts of the business that could contribute to the new product, and those parts where operational problems have popped up in the past. The other areas worth covering are those where the business is not well understood.

The point of having a large scope for models of the current work is that requirements analysis is really *work reengineering.* You specify products to improve work; thus, the more of the work that you study, the more opportunities to improve it that will emerge. The greater the scope of your study, the better your understanding and the better chance you and your stakeholders have of finding areas that will benefit from improvement.

The current model is also used to confirm the work scope. During the blastoff exercise (Chapter 3), you and the stakeholders built a context model to show the scope of the work you intended to study. Any models you build while looking at the current situation should confirm that all of the appropriate parts of the work are included in the context. If at this stage you discover areas that would benefit from your attention, parts of the work that need to be understood, or anything at all that should be included, then now is the time to adjust the context. Such a revision does entail getting the agreement of the stakeholders, but it is better to enlarge the scope now than to end up with a product that lacks important functionality.

Apprenticing

Apprenticing is particularly useful for in-house work. The underlying assumption for apprenticing is that users are currently doing work, and you, as the requirements analyst, have to understand their work. This work could be clerical, commercial, graphic arts, engineering, or almost anything short of brain surgery.

If significant parts of the current work and systems are likely to be reimplemented, then apprenticing is appropriate. Please keep in mind, however, that you will not reimplement the work exactly as is. We recommend that all apprentices refer to the section on essence.

READING

Holtzblatt, Karen, Jessamyn Burns Wendell, and Shelley Wood. *Rapid Contextual Design: A How-to Guide to Key Techniques for User-Centered Design.* Morgan Kaufmann, 2004.

❝ *Nobody can talk better about what they do and why they do it than they can while in the middle of doing it.* ❞

—Hugh Beyer and Karen Holtzblatt. *Contextual Design*

Apprenticing—based on the old idea of masters and apprentices—is a wonderful way to observe and learn the work as it really happens. In this case, the requirements analyst is the apprentice, and the user assumes the role of master craftsman. The analyst sits with the user at the user's place of work, learning the job by making observations, asking questions, and perhaps doing some of the work under supervision. This technique is also sometimes known as "job shadowing."

It is unlikely that many users can explain what they do in enough detail for the business analyst to completely understand the work and thereby capture all the requirements—if you are away from your work, you tend to generalize. Generalizations can be useful, but they do not provide enough detail for them to work every time.

Nor can you expect users to have the presentation and teaching skills needed to present their work effectively to others. Conversely, almost everyone is good at explaining what they are doing while they are doing it.

If the user is doing his job in his normal workplace, he can provide a running commentary and provide details that might otherwise be lost. So if you want to get an accurate explanation of the work, go to the work; sit beside the user in the normal workplace and get a running commentary on the work as it happens. While he is working, the user can describe his task precisely and tell you why he is doing things. If the explanation is not clear, the apprentice asks questions: "Why did you do that?" "What does this mean?" "How often does this happen?" "What happens if this piece of information is not here?" You also get to see the things that can go wrong, and the special cases, and the work-arounds he uses when things are not normal. Through the process of apprenticing, you come to see all the cases and the actions the user takes for each.

Apprenticeship can be combined with modeling. As you observe the work and the user explains it, you sketch a model of the tasks and their connections with the other tasks (see Figure 5.8). As you build your models, feed them back to the user and confirm that they are correct. Naturally you use this feedback to raise questions about any areas of uncertainty.

Figure 5.8

The requirements analyst learns the work while sitting at the user's desk, sometimes building models of the work while learning it.

When you are apprenticing, you are an interpreter as well as an observer. When you are looking at the current work, you must abstract away from what you see to overcome the user's close connection to the physical incarnation of the work. In other words, the artifacts, the technology, and other inputs that are currently used must be seen as a product of a previous designer. Someone, some time ago, decided that was the best way to do the work. But times have changed. Today it may be possible to do things that were impossible yesterday. Better ways may now be available—ways that take advantage of up-to-date technology, that use streamlined processes, that simplify the work or automate some or all of it.

But first you have to abstract. While you are learning the work by seeing it done in real-world conditions, you are abstracting from the current technology to find the underlying essence of the work. We will come back and have a good look at essence a little later.

Business Use Case Workshops

BUC workshops are useful to most projects, and are the most commonly used requirements technique. These workshops look at one slice of the business with the objective of finding the ideal work. You must overcome geographical limitations and ensure that you can assemble the right combination of specialized stakeholders who have an interest in the business use case. These workshops are particularly useful when you are making fundamental changes to the work.

In Chapter 4, Business Use Cases, we discussed business events and how they trigger a response by the work. We called this response a business use case (BUC). We hope that by devoting an entire chapter to business events and business use cases, we have unequivocally signaled the importance of partitioning the work according to how it responds to the world outside it.

Refer to Chapter 4, Business Use Cases, for a complete explanation of business events and BUCs.

READING

Gottesdiener, Ellen. *Requirements by Collaboration: Workshops for Defining Needs.* Addison-Wesley, 2002. Gottesdiener's book covers in detail how to plan and conduct requirements workshops.

Hass, Kathleen, and Alice Zavala. *The Art and Power of Facilitation: Running Powerful Meetings (Business Analysis Essential Library).* Management Concepts, 2007.

See Chapter 3, Scoping the Business Problem, for more on how to discover the relevant interested stakeholders.

Now that you have partitioned the work, the business use case workshop is an effective way of understanding each partition and making improvements. The workshop is where interested stakeholders describe or reenact the work they currently do, and discuss the work they desire to do, for one specific business use case. Your task is to record this work in a way that the stakeholders can understand it and agree that is it an accurate portrayal. As a general rule, we suggest that you use scenarios to show the functionality of the business use case (see Figure 5.9). Later, you will use this recording of the improved work to derive the requirements for the product to support this work.

In Chapter 6, we talk about scenarios as a way of telling the story of the business use case in a fairly structured way. We propose that you use scenarios as part of the business use case workshop—they are easy to understand, and provide a convenient focal point for the workshop. Feel free to peek into Chapter 6, but for the moment it will suffice if you think of a scenario as a tool for breaking the business use case's functionality into a series of steps.

The analysts and the stakeholders work together on a business use case and record the following information:

- The desired outcome for the BUC
- A normal case scenario that describes the work done by the BUC
- Exception scenarios describing what can go wrong and what the work does to correct them (these can be postponed until later if desired)
- The business rules applicable to the business use case
- Sketched prototypes used to help stakeholders visualize the business use case—these throwaway sketches are optional and are not intended to be kept beyond the requirements phase

Figure 5.9

The business use case workshop records the proposed functionality using scenarios and sketched prototypes. The workshop serves as a forum for interested stakeholders to communicate effectively, express their understanding, ask questions, and give their aspirations for the work.

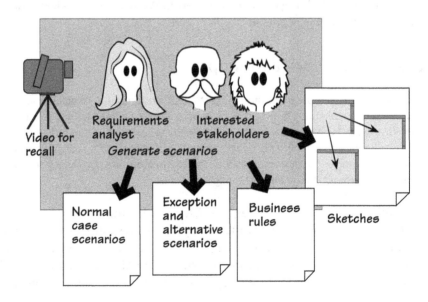

Outcome

The outcome is what the organization hopes to achieve from this business use case, cast in terms of results, not outputs. For example, suppose the business use case is "rent a car to a customer." The desired *outcome* is that the customer drives away in the car of his choice, the rate selected is equitable, the details are recorded, and the transaction is completed with the minimum inconvenience to the customer at minimal cost. The *outputs* of the same business event are the rental document and some recorded data. Achieving the output does not necessarily guarantee the outcome.

Think of outcomes, not outputs.

Note that the outcome is a business objective, not a way of achieving something. Outcomes are expressed from the point of view of the owning organization—what it wants to achieve. The outcome gives your business use case its reason for existing.

The outcome should be able to be written as one sentence along the lines of "When this business event happens, this is what we want to achieve."

Scenarios

Scenarios describe the work being done by the business use case as a series (usually between three and ten) of steps. The scenario is a stakeholder-friendly document that serves as the focal point of the workshop. The steps do not have to be detailed; the intention is not to capture every small part of the business use case, but rather to obtain a business-level picture of the work that stakeholders can use to arrive at a consensus.

The normal-case scenario shows the actions of the business use case if everything works as desired and no mistakes are made, no wrong actions are taken, or no other untoward happening occurs. The intention is for you and your stakeholders to reach consensus on what *should* happen. Other scenarios focus on the exception cases—when unwanted things go wrong—and the alternative scenarios—when the users of the business use case may take some allowable variations on the normal case.

Chapter 6 provides a full treatise on scenarios.

The collection of scenarios represents the interested stakeholders' consensus on what the work should do in response to the business event. We stress again the importance of understanding the work, and not just the product.

Business Rules

The business rules are management prescriptions that transcend and guide the day-to-day business decisions. For example, we discovered these two business rules in the road de-icing project:

The maximum length of a truck driver's shift is 5 hours.

The engineers maintain the weather stations once a week.

These rules come to the surface as the stakeholders discuss the work for each business event. Later they are used to guide the functional requirements and to help to discover the meaning of stored data. Naturally, any product you build must conform to the business rules, and often it is the product that has to enforce them.

There is no set form for the business rules. In most cases you will be able to find, with the help of the interested stakeholders, existing documents that spell out these rules. The rules must, of course, become incorporated into the business use case scenarios and the subsequent requirements.

The business use case workshop gives the interested stakeholders the opportunity to bring out all the relevant business rules.

Interviewing the Stakeholders

Interviewing is used by almost all projects, as it is really a part of all elicitation techniques. Despite its omnipresence, we suggest that you do not use interviewing as your only technique for gathering requirements. Rather, you should conduct interviews in conjunction with the use of other techniques discussed in this chapter.

Interviewing the stakeholders is a technique that is commonly employed, but is not without its problems. The interviewer relies on the interviewee to know—and be able to verbalize—all the necessary knowledge about the work. This method may work very well when people are familiar with the work, but that knowledge is often restricted to their own immediate area. There are likely to be few people in the organization who understand enough of the business to be the sole person to describe it for you. Interviewing also requires some abstraction and communication ability on the part of the interviewee. For this reason, it is wise to avoid relying on interviews as your sole method of gathering requirements; instead, use them in conjunction with other techniques.

That cautionary note notwithstanding, interviewing skills are highly useful in other contexts. For example, a requirements analyst can "interview" a model or a document. The skill here is to know which questions to ask of the model, or more realistically, the appropriate stakeholder for the model.

Some requirements analysts draw up a questionnaire and send it to the stakeholder in advance of the interview. While this preparatory step gives some structure to the subsequent interview, we have found few stakeholders who are motivated enough, or who have time enough, to fill in a questionnaire prior to meeting the analyst. We suggest that you send a brief agenda listing the topics that you wish to cover in your interview along with the planned duration of the interview. This notification at least gives the interviewee a chance to think in background mode, to have needed material close by, or to ask subject-matter experts to be present.

Stakeholders should not remain completely passive during the interview. Instead, do your best to involve them by building models—business event responses, use cases, scenarios, and so on—during the interview. This approach creates a feedback loop between you and your stakeholders, and it means you can iteratively test the accuracy of what you are being told. Follow these guidelines to make your interviews more effective:

- Set the interview in context. This step is necessary to avoid having your stakeholders talk about something irrelevant to your purpose. It also gives them a chance to withdraw gracefully if they have not prepared for the interview.

- Limit the duration of the interview to the time stated in the agenda. We find that interviews running for more than an hour (90 minutes tops) tend to lose focus.

- Have business use cases serve as an anchor for the interview. Users recognize business use cases (although they may not necessarily call them by that name), and it makes for more directed conversations if you talk about their work one business use case at a time.

- Ask a question (more on this in a moment), listen to the answer, and then feed back your understanding.

Feed back your understanding. Build models while you are interviewing the stakeholder.

- Draw models and encourage the user to change them. Plenty of models (e.g., data flow diagrams, activity diagrams, sequence diagrams) are available to help you communicate your understanding of a process. You can also construct data models for information, and mind maps to link different subjects.

- Use the stakeholders' terminology and artifacts, both conceptual and real. If the stakeholders do not use their own language, then you force them to make technological translations into terms they think you will understand. This, sadly, usually leads to misunderstandings. By contrast, if you are forced to ask questions about their terminology, you inevitably make new discoveries.

- Keep samples or copies of artifacts and log them for future reference. Artifacts are the things the stakeholders use in their daily work. They can be real things: documents, computers, meters, spreadsheets, machines, pieces of software. They can also be conceptual things: status, contracts, schedules, orders. Artifacts will inevitably cause you to raise questions when you examine them later.

- Thank the stakeholders for their time and tell them what you learned and why it was valuable. After all, they have lots of other things to do. Talking to you is not the reason they are employed, and they often view the interview as an interruption.

Thank the stakeholders for their time.

> ● Write down what you were told. We guarantee you'll have more questions.

Note taking is almost a skill set of its own. We encourage the use of mind maps as a note-taking device—we talk about these later in the chapter. You might also consider some of the smartpens on the market. These devices record an electronic version of your notes (easy to share with the rest of the team) and some record the voice part of the interview. Livescribe pens are popular at the time of writing, and some others offer similar technology.

Asking the Right Questions

We suggested earlier that the business use case was the ideal unit of work to interview someone about. We also urge you to use the Brown Cow viewpoints (shown in Figure 5.4) as triggers for asking the right questions. Let's look at this process by using an example from the IceBreaker road de-icing project.

Suppose that you have an interview with the Chief Engineer. The business event that you want to explore is *Road Engineering Installs New Weather Station*. Your questions should focus on what the work does to respond to this business event.

Business Analyst: "What happens when your engineers install a new weather station?"

Chief Engineer: "The engineers let us know where the new weather station is located, and we keep a record of it."

BA: "How do you keep a record of the new weather station?"

CE: "I'll show you the spreadsheet that we use; here it is."

BA: "Thank you. I'd like a copy of this weather station spreadsheet. I see that you keep track of the weather station number, geographical coordinates, and installation date. What else do you keep track of?"

CE: "We have another computer system where we have the maintenance history for each weather station. There are some double entries, but that's the way it is."

BA: "Are there any other facts about the weather station that would be useful to you?"

CE: "Well, we would like to know the manufacturer and performance of each weather station."

BA: "What do you mean by performance?'

CE: "Which weather stations need the most maintenance. This would help in planning which new technology we spend our budget on. However we've never been able to do that in the past."

Note that the analyst begins with a "W" word—what, why, where, who— to open up the question and elicit information.

BA: "Would it be acceptable to you if you had a new system that integrates all the information about the weather stations, their maintenance, and their performance?"

CE: "What, you mean all on one screen?"

BA: "Yes, something that makes it possible for you to track a weather station and its lifetime performance."

CE: "That sounds marvelous, but we'd have to check it with some of the engineers."

BA: "Well, once I've made sure that I have all the facts about the weather stations properly defined, then I could do a quick mockup to show the engineers our ideas. How would that be?"

CE: "I like the idea."

BA: "Thanks for your time. I'll go back and review my notes and the samples you have given me, and I'll send you a brief summary of this interview. I might need to phone you with a couple of questions. Then I'll make an appointment to explore the mockup with the engineers. Is this approach all right with you?

CE: "Yes it is. Thank you."

In this interview, the business analyst uses the Brown Cow viewpoints to help explore the business use case. He starts by asking how the work is done now (How-Now) and discovers the spreadsheet and the other computer system for maintenance of the weather stations. He asks, "What else do you keep track of?" to discover the attributes that are recorded (What-Now) when a new weather station is installed. The question about "What other facts" is designed to uncover other facts that are not currently recorded or made use of (Future-What). And raising the idea of an integrated system and a mockup (Future-How) is signaling the chief engineer that there will probably be a better way of doing things once the business analyst has properly understood the business of installing weather stations.

The Brown Cow viewpoints help you explore the business use case as it is now, its essence, and what it might be in the future.

Notice that the business analyst used a lot of *open questions*. These begin with "What," "How," "When," "Where," "Why," or "Who," and they encourage the interviewee to give a detailed answer rather than a "Yes" or "No" answer.

Listening to the Answers

Being a good listener means being able to understand someone else's meaning behind the words that they are using. This is difficult to do because we all have our own view of the meaning of words that is based on our own assumptions, experience, and preoccupations. Also, especially when interviewing someone, we are often afraid of silence and might think, "If I'm not saying anything, then maybe the interviewee will think that I don't know

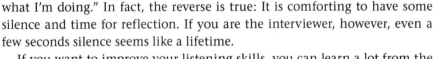

READING
The following are books that provide insights into how to ask better questions and listen to the answers.

O'Connor, Joseph, and John Seymour. *Introducing Neuro-Linguistic Programming.* Conari Press, 2011.

Sullivan, Wendy, and Judy Rees. *Clean Language: Revealing Metaphors and Opening Minds.* Crown House Publishing, 2008.

Weinberg, Jerry. *Quality Software Management. Volume 1: Systems Thinking. Volume 2: First-Order Measurement. Volume 3: Congruent Action. Volume 4: Anticipating Change.* Dorset House, 1992–1997.

what I'm doing." In fact, the reverse is true: It is comforting to have some silence and time for reflection. If you are the interviewer, however, even a few seconds silence seems like a lifetime.

If you want to improve your listening skills, you can learn a lot from the fields of psychology, sociology, and family therapy. These disciplines have realized that to help people with problems, you first have to understand what those people mean by their words and behavior.

In their book *Clean Language,* Wendy Sullivan and Judy Rees talk about the power of "attending exquisitely" to another person's words. One of their hints on improving listening skills is "Put your attention on what the other person is actually saying rather than on the person themselves or what you think they might mean by their words." Another helpful piece of advice: "Repeat back some of their words or phrases exactly as you heard them." By doing so, you demonstrate that you are, in fact, listening to what that person is saying, and this feedback encourages that person to expand further on what he means by his words.

Most of all, if you want to become a better listener, don't talk; develop an appreciation of silence.

Looking for Reusable Requirements

Many of the our projects deliver similar products. That is, if you work for a finance house, then almost all of your projects will deliver some kind of financial system. Given that your organization has been doing this for a number of years, it is likely that someone, at some time, has studied a piece of work that is similar to yours and has written requirements for a product that is similar to yours. You don't have to do it all again when you can borrow from those who have gone before.

Investigating the work is a time when you observe and interpret. The interpretation we are looking for here is one where you see a business process and recognize its similarities with other processes. By making abstractions—that is, by ignoring the subject matter and concentrating on the processes (look at the verbs, not the nouns)—you are often able to interpret one piece of work as having the same functionality as another. This does not mean they have the same subject matter, but rather that they have similarities in the way that both pieces of work are done.

Look for similarities, not differences.

As an example of this, one of our clients, the international section of a bank, had 20 different products. The products ranged from letters of credit, to guaranteed foreign bank loans, to guaranteed funds, and so on. At first glance, the users appeared to handle each of these products differently. However, a common pattern emerged as we studied the work—we were looking for similarities, not differences. We observed that each product was, in fact, a different way of guaranteeing that exporters got paid for their goods in foreign countries. The end result was that we were able to borrow heavily from one project to feed the next. We had to change names and make some alterations to processes, but by and large, by using abstracted requirements from other projects, we were able to save significant project time.

We suggest building abstract models of the work structure—that is, models that do not give specific technological names to things, or use distinctive terminology associated with one part of the organization. Such models also do not apply to any particular user, or use terminology identified with a particular user. They are abstracted from their source—they use categorizations rather than specifics, generics rather than actual instances. Instead of modeling the work the way any single user sees it, they model the *class* of work as all users could see it.

This kind of abstraction enables you to discover whether the same work pattern exists in another part of the organization. It has been our experience that although the names and the artifacts may vary, the same work pattern occurs several times in an organization. We have used the recurrence of patterns first to understand the requirements more quickly, and then to deploy the implementation of one part of the work to suit another part.

Chapter 15 deals with reusing requirements. We suggest that you visit this chapter if you suspect you have the opportunity to reuse requirements and other artifacts from previous projects.

See Chapter 15, Reusing Requirements, for more on patterns.

Quick and Dirty Process Modeling

Quick and dirty process modeling is a technique for building quick models of business processes to gain understanding and consensus about the current work. We find that business stakeholders relate very well to the dynamic nature of these kinds of models.

The technique is useful when much of the legacy system is to be replaced. It can also be used when the stakeholders are geographically dispersed.

Quick and dirty process models simulate the current reality, and of course can be used to model any future processes. They are not formal models in the sense of UML activity diagrams and the like, but rather are put together using whatever physical artifacts are to hand. We find that Post-it notes are the most convenient way to build these models, but they are not confined to that medium (see Figure 5.10).

The technique is more or less to build a process model using large Post-it notes, or index cards, for each of the activities in the process. You can stick the notes onto a whiteboard and draw lines to link them, or if you are using a regular wall, use masking tape to join one note to the next. In the best of all possible worlds, the walls of your office are painted with whiteboard paint

Figure 5.10

With quick and dirty process modeling, the business analyst uses Post-it notes to build an informal model of the work. Large notes are stuck on the wall and linked by masking tape. Naturally, interested stakeholders are partners in this modeling activity.

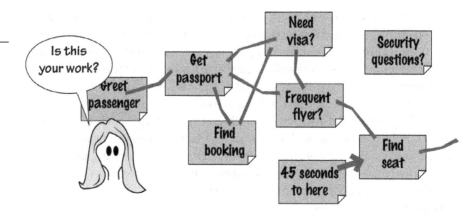

such as IdeaPaint and you can draw and stick and post notes wherever and of whatever you want.

The advantage of using Post-it notes to model the business process is that stakeholders are usually willing to become involved in moving the brightly colored notes around to model their process. If an activity is badly named, it can quickly be replaced by another note with a better name. If something is out of place, it can be moved around with little effort.

But perhaps the most important benefit of using this technique is that when the stakeholders start moving the Post-it notes around, they often discover ways of simplifying their business process. It is not uncommon to find business stakeholders saying things like "If we just move this activity over here, change that one, we could eliminate those two down there." These ideas must be kept and brought into play when we look at the essence of the system and derive a new way of working.

The Post-its models range from simple models where the activities proceed more or less in a straight line, to the rather elaborate Post-it model shown in Figure 5.11.

Please keep in mind that while we are advocating the use of physical models, we are not advocating designing screens and delving into low-level detail—those actions are not appropriate at this stage. The intention of using quick and dirty models here is merely to build a more pliable model of the current and future business processes. Little is to be gained—and, in fact, much is to be lost—if business users turn their hand to designing screens at this time.

However, if you can avoid designing, you can make good use of sketches of screens and other interfaces.

Figure 5.11

A five-meter-long Post-it model built by the air traffic controllers during a workshop. This model is perhaps more elaborate than that needed by many businesses, but it helped the controllers to understand their process much better. *Photo: Neil Maiden.*

Prototypes and Sketches

Prototyping and sketching—they are really the same thing—can be effective techniques for eliciting requirements. The basic idea is to sketch some proposed product, and then reverse engineer the requirements from the sketch. This is a particularly useful approach in the following situations:

- The product has not existed before, and it is difficult to visualize.
- The stakeholders for the product have no experience with either the kind of product or the proposed technology.
- The stakeholders have been doing their work for some time and are stuck in the way that they do it.
- The stakeholders are having trouble articulating their requirements.
- The requirements analysts are having trouble understanding what is required.
- The feasibility of a requirement is in doubt.

When gathering requirements, you ask your stakeholders to imagine what they need their future product to do. The results you uncover are limited by the stakeholders' imaginations and experiences, and by their ability to describe something that for the moment does not exist.

The prototype makes the product real enough to prompt stakeholders to bring up requirements that might otherwise be missed.

66 *Prototypes are requirements bait.* 99

—Steve McMenamin

In contrast, a prototype gives the stakeholder something real, or at least something that has the appearance of reality. The prototype makes the product real enough for stakeholders to bring up requirements that might otherwise be missed. Our colleague Steve McMenamin refers to prototypes as "requirements bait": When stakeholders see the functionality displayed by a prototype, it inspires them to bring up other requirements. In this way, by demonstrating possibilities through prototypes and giving stakeholders a seemingly real experience, you capture the additional requirements—sometimes there are quite a lot of them—that might otherwise have waited until the product was in use to come to the surface. (See Figure 5.12.)

Prototypes are also used to play out the consequences of requirements. You will inevitably come across a strange requirement that has a single advocate who swears he would be lost without it. Who knows whether his requirement is a great idea that will make the product better or merely a complex way of doing something that doesn't need to be done? The prototype does. Building a prototype of hard-to-fathom requirements makes them visible; it gives everyone the opportunity to understand them, discuss them, possibly simplify them, and then decide whether their merits warrant their inclusion in the final product.

We have to emphasize that the prototypes and sketches discussed here are throwaway prototypes; they are not intended to evolve into the finished product. Of course, they might—but that possibility is incidental to your task of requirements gathering.

Figure 5.12

Requirements prototypes are used to display the functionality of a potential product. The prototype is intended to prompt stakeholders to tell you whether you have understood the needed functionality and, as a result of "using" the prototype, to give you additional requirements suggested by it.

In this discussion, we are using the terms "prototype" and "sketch" to mean some kind of simulation of a product that the stakeholders could use to do their work—the work that you envisage they might do in the future. Put simply, you show your prototype and possibly several alternative prototypes—to your stakeholders and ask if they could do their job using a product something like your simulation. If the answer is yes, then you capture the requirements demonstrated by that version of the prototype. If the answer is no, then you change the prototype and ask again.

The stakeholders who must decide whether your prototype is a reasonable demonstration of the proposed work face a somewhat difficult situation. Inevitably, they bring to the prototyping exercise some work-related baggage. They have been doing their job for some time (you probably wouldn't be asking them to test your prototypes if they hadn't), and their perception of their work may differ dramatically from yours. This difference in perspectives requires tact on your part to discover which aspects of reality are uppermost in the minds of the people you are dealing with. Which metaphors do they use for their work, and how do they envision themselves while they are doing their work? In addition, you are asking them how they feel about doing different work—the work that you are proposing for the future. Adopting the new product could mean jettisoning artifacts and ways of working that they feel quite comfortable with. It is no easy task for the stakeholders to turn away from their experience and their comfort, and to accept a new, as-yet-untried way of doing their work.

Which aspects of reality are uppermost in the minds of the people you are dealing with? Which metaphors do they use for their work, and how do they envision themselves while they are doing their work?

This means that you should always try to use prototyping techniques that conform, in some way, to the artifacts and experiences that are most familiar to the stakeholders. This means adjusting your prototyping approach for each work situation.

Build a prototype that relates to the physical anchors in the user's world.

Let's look at some of the possibilities available for requirements prototypes. We can then talk about how they might be gainfully employed. We'll start with the simplest option: the low-fidelity prototype.

Low-Fidelity Prototypes

By using familiar media, low-fidelity prototypes (we also call these "sketches") help stakeholders concentrate on the subject matter. Such things as pencil and paper, whiteboards, flip charts, Post-it notes, index cards, and cardboard boxes can be employed to build effective low-fidelity prototypes (Figure 5.13). In fact, these prototypes may take advantage of anything that is part of the stakeholders' everyday life and do not require an additional investment.

The low-fidelity prototype is a sketch, which is not meant to look all that much like the finished product—this is why such prototypes are called "low-fidelity." This lack of faithfulness to the finished product is both good and bad. The good part is that no one will confuse your prototype with an actual

" To look at structure, the first prototypes are always paper. "

—Hugh Beyer and Karen Holtzblatt, Contextual Design

Figure 5.13

Effective prototyping tools do not have to be complex or expensive.

product—it is obviously built with a minimal investment in time, and most importantly it gives no indication that it is anything other than an easy-to-change mockup. The low-fidelity sketch encourages iteration, and it more or less indicates that you are not expecting to get the right answer on your first attempt. The bad part is that such a prototype sometimes requires more effort on the part of the stakeholder who is testing it to imagine that the whiteboard sketch might potentially be his new product. Nevertheless, the ability to make changes easily and the speed with which you can sketch out a prototype usually help you to bring things to life, thereby assisting stakeholders in taking more advantage of their imaginations.

Prototyping is more convenient, and ultimately more accurate, if done one PUC at a time.

We find that prototyping is more convenient, and ultimately more accurate, if the prototype involves a single business use case (BUC) or a single product use case (PUC); given that the prototype involves some simulated product, we will assume you are prototyping a PUC. We introduced business and product use cases in Chapter 4. Recall that a business use case is an amount of work, triggered by an external business event occurring or by a predetermined time being reached, that takes place in a single, continuous time frame. It also has a known, measurable, testable outcome. The part of the BUC that is to be done by the product is the PUC. Because of its single, continuous time frame, it provides you with an appropriate amount of work as the subject of your prototype.

Let's look at prototyping by examining an example use case. The "Monitor Untreated Roads" product use case, as shown in Figure 5.14, is suitable for our purposes. This use case is triggered periodically when it is time to monitor the road treatment: The engineer checks whether all the roads that have been scheduled to be treated with de-icing material have, in fact, been covered by one of the trucks. Your task is to find all the requirements for this part of the product.

Your aim in building a low-fidelity prototype of this BUC is to unearth the existing requirements that must be carried forward into the new product, along with the new, as yet undreamed-of requirements. Let's assume the engineers are currently working with a system that supplies them with a list of roads, and use that as a starting point.

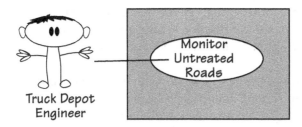

Figure 5.14

The truck depot engineers are responsible for ensuring that all roads in danger of freezing are treated with de-icing material. Use case number 11, "Monitor Untreated Roads," represents this part of the work.

You can quickly sketch a low-fidelity prototype of the current situation, and then begin to explore improvements to it. The prototype focuses on what the product might do; for the moment, it ignores any implementation details.

When you are sketching a low-fidelity prototype, be quick. Demonstrate each requirements suggestion with another sketch, or several alternative sketches. You might intentionally serve up several prototypes of the same PUC, asking for the stakeholders' preferences and possibly more suggestions for alternatives. Once your stakeholders see you are simulating potential ways of solving their problem and realize their input is not only welcome but also necessary, they will almost certainly help you by suggesting their own enhancements and requirements. Our experience is that once you get people involved by making the problem visible, they tend to become more creative and imaginative—so much so that sometimes your problem becomes one of keeping pace with their suggestions.

> *Paper is eminently practical and meets the primary need: It makes it possible to express the structure of the system and makes it hard to overfocus on user interface detail.*
>
> —Hugh Beyer and Karen Holtzblatt, *Contextual Design*

Get started by sketching what the stakeholders[2] might be doing when using the product. Ask the stakeholders what the product could do to contribute to their work, and note their ideas. In the "Monitor Untreated Roads" PUC, stakeholders would probably want the product to provide something like the following information:

FOOTNOTE 2
We say "stakeholders" rather than "users," because there are probably people other than users who are interested stakeholders for any use case.

- Roads that have been scheduled for treatment
- Scheduled roads that have been treated
- Relative positions of roads

Now ask the stakeholders what they would do with this information. At this point you are not trying to design a solution to this immediate problem, but rather want to explore ideas for what a potential product *might* do and what the work *might* be with that product:

- "What is the best way of presenting the needed information?"
- "Is the requested information the right information for the work being done?"
- "Could the product do more or less of the work?"

When you are prototyping, assume that there are no technological limitations. Also, keep in mind that you are designing the work, not the product—you are capturing the things the product might do to help the stakeholders with their work.

Sketch pictures to elicit ideas from the stakeholders. If they are having trouble getting started, then inject some ideas of your own. Ask them to imagine that they are doing the job of monitoring untreated roads. Which other pieces of information would they need to do the job? Can your prototype provide it, or would they have to look elsewhere for information? Is all of the information in the current version of the prototype needed to do the job of monitoring untreated roads?

As the prototyping proceeds and the engineers see your sketches, you may hear the following kind of remark:

> "That's great. Now wouldn't it be great if we could see the major roads that have not been treated for three hours? But only the major roads—the secondary ones don't matter so much. Our current system can't distinguish between major and secondary roads."

How long would it take you to add that requirement to your sketch? About 10 seconds. How long would it have taken to modify the installed product if the engineers had asked for this requirement after delivery? Enough said.

By working with the engineers, you may generate a prototype that is quite different from the product they have at the moment. But that's the point—to change the work, and to discover new and better ways of doing the work. By encouraging the engineers to tell you more and more about the job, you uncover requirements that otherwise would not come to light. (See Figure 5.15.)

Figure 5.15

By drawing this low-fidelity prototype on a flip chart or whiteboard, you help identify requirements for the truck depot engineers. They want the product to highlight the major roads within a district that have not been treated and are in a dangerous condition.

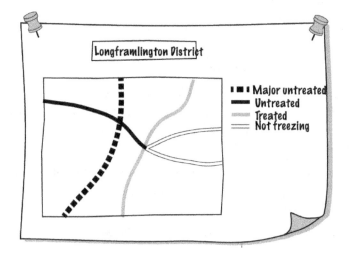

When you sketch a low-fidelity prototype, you demonstrate your ideas to the stakeholders and encourage them to iterate its development by changing and improving your ideas. Recall that a part of the requirements process is inventing a better way to do the work. The prototype is an invention vehicle with which you and your stakeholders to experiment to see how the proposed product could contribute to the new work.

The low-fidelity prototype is not a work of art, but rather an idea-generating device.

A low-fidelity prototype is informal and fast. No one will mistake it for the finished product. Because it is easy to change, stakeholders are willing to iterate, experiment, and investigate alternative ideas.

High-Fidelity Prototypes

High-fidelity prototypes are built using software tools and have the appearance of working software products. They appear to do whatever the use case does, and they display most of the characteristics of working software products. Development of such a prototype gives stakeholders the opportunity to "use" a realistic-looking product and decide whether the product displays the correct requirements.

Because the prototype behaves as the stakeholders would expect the final product to behave, it gives them the chance to explore the *potential* of the product, ideally leading them to suggest improvements and new requirements. But herein lies a problem: Because the prototype looks so much like a working product, the stakeholders may be tempted to concentrate on its appearance and possibly forego making functional improvements. To do so, however, would defeat the purpose of requirements prototyping.

Putting aside the slight risk of stakeholders misunderstanding their role in the prototyping activity, the high-fidelity prototype has a lot to offer. It is interactive, which encourages users to explore its capabilities. The icons and data displayed on the screen are representative of the data and icons used to do the actual work. The stakeholders should feel at home with the prototype: They should be able to open windows, update data, and be told whether they have made an error. In other words, the prototype can be a realistic simulation of the real work.

A high-fidelity prototype allows you to create lifelike work situations, and ask the stakeholders to operate the prototype as if they were doing real work. By observing the stakeholders' reactions and noting their comments, you find even more of their requirements.

An extensive set of high-fidelity prototyping tools is available. Interface builder types of tools incorporate functionality that allows you to easily build screens and simulate functionality. Many of these tools are backed by a database, thereby enabling you to construct small to medium-size working applications.

Content management systems such as Drupal, Alfresco, Joomla, and many more (a lot of them are available as open-source products) allow prototyping of Web-based products. You should also check the CMS capabilities of Share-Point, as this is already available in many organizations. These tools are more than just prototyping tools—the final result may be the full-strength version of the product. Care must be taken to ensure the requirements for the other aspects of the product—security, maintainability, and so on—keep pace with the front end as it is being prototyped.

We will not attempt to list all products that could be used for high-fidelity prototypes. Any such list would be out of date before you picked up this book. We suggest searching the Web and, in particular, the open-source community (sourceforge.net) as the best way to find software suitable for requirements prototyping.

The high-fidelity prototype is effective for discovering usability requirements. As the user attempts to work with it, you observe which parts of the prototype are pleasing and easy to use, and which usability features need improvement. From these observations, the you can write most of the usability requirements.

But let's not get ahead of ourselves. In Chapter 8, Starting the Solution, we look at the interface of the potential product; this is where you concentrate on the usability aspects and other user-experience attributes of the product. High-fidelity prototypes are more commonly used at that point in the development process, so we will defer any more discussion of them until that chapter.

Mind Maps

We use mind maps all the time. We use them for taking notes during interviews, planning projects or actions, summarizing workshops—in fact, anytime we need to have a concise and intelligible record. Mind mapping is a skill that will benefit all business analysts.

A mind map is a combination of drawing and text that attempts to represent information in the same way as your brain does. The mind map imitates your brain storage mechanism by using links between the words and pictures that represent the information.

Figure 5.16 shows a mind map—a friend drew this when she was planning her business. The business provides advice and recipes for people who dine alone. This market segment is unusual—lone diners usually do not have well-stocked larders and fridges, and sometimes they find it hard to buy food in quantities suitable for one person. Additionally, they might not be good cooks. Our friend's business, Good Food for One, provides recipes and advice on cooking when one is on one's own—you can see the business in the mind map.

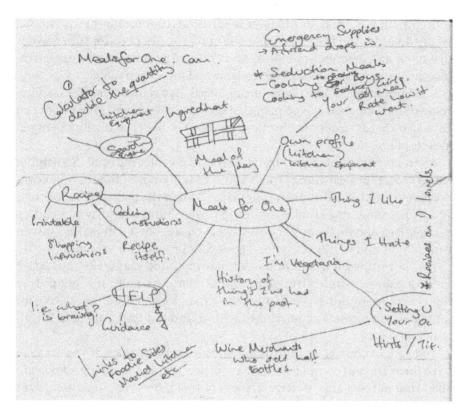

Figure 5.16

A mind map drawn while planning the business Good Food for One. This Web-based business provides recipes, shopping advice, and cooking tips for people who cook and eat alone. *Mind map by Joanna Kenneally. Used by permission.*

Note the quick sketches and the hastily scribbled words in Figure 5.16. Joanna Kenneally, the mind map's author, was in a hurry. She wanted to start her business right away and needed a quick overview of what it would do; she wanted to record all her ideas, and see if they came together to form a viable business.

Mind maps are useful devices for organizing your thoughts. You can see the result of your thinking in one diagram—you get an overview and details at the same time—with each of your subtopics teased out to show divergence and connections. The mind map provides enough information—shown as keywords and links between those keywords—for you to get the overall picture. You can also decide to follow one of the branches, or make decisions based on having all the information laid out in a convenient format. Drawing small pictures on your mind map helps; they obviate the need to have as many words and have the advantage of being more easily remembered than words.

If you do not draw mind maps already, give them a try; nothing bad can happen to you. Start with the page in landscape format, and place your central subject in the center of it. The central idea should be some words, or a strong image, that tells you, or anyone who reads your mind map, what it is about. The first breakdown, or set of radiating lines, shows the major

If you do not draw mind maps already, give them a try; nothing bad can happen.

concepts, themes, ideas, or whatever subdivisions of your subject you choose. Write these ideas on the lines, using one or two words. Look for strong words that name and describe your ideas. And print rather than using cursive writing; the result will be both more readable and more memorable.

Use lines to make links between the ideas. We remember colors, so use colored lines for areas of the map that contain one theme. These lines can have arrowheads to denote direction, but most of the time the link between ideas is bidirectional.

Mind maps cannot always be built from the center outward. Sometimes you get ideas, or hear things when you are taking notes, that have no connection to anything already in your map. Add it to the map anyway, because you will at some stage find a connection. Your mind map may not end up as organized and pretty as some examples you see, but it still makes sense to your mind—and that is the point. Figure 5.17 provides an example.

One last thing on the technique of drawing mind maps: Use the biggest sheet of paper or whiteboard you can find. Borrow a large drawing pad, or flip chart, or anything you can get your hands on. Spread out. Give your mind room to move. Amuse yourself with your mind map. And be as imaginative as you can.

You can, of course, buy software for drawing mind maps if you want to have them on your computer. There are plenty of mind mapping apps available. Your authors almost never use any of them, however, because it takes

READING

Buzan, Tony, and Chris Griffiths. *Mind Maps for Business: Revolutionise Your Business Thinking and Practise.* BBC Active, 2009.

Figure 5.17

A mind map your authors drew when planning an article on innovation and creativity.

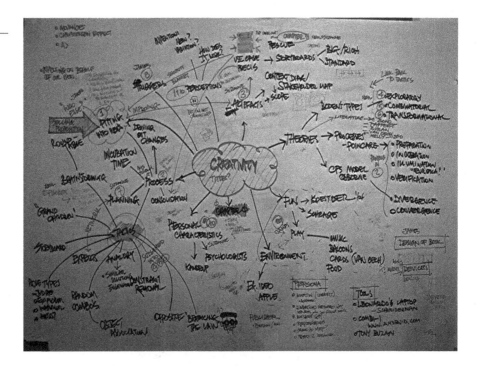

away the sheer spontaneity of using paper and colored pencils. We photograph ours for posterity (as in the case of Figure 5.17).

An alternative technological approach is to use Wacom's Inkling as a way of recording your mind maps, along with your other sketches and handwritten notes. This technology uses plain paper on which you then draw or write, and faithfully records an electronic version of your drawing. It's an impressive tool for those of us who like to sketch and doodle.

We use mind maps for note taking when interviewing stakeholders about their requirements. The benefit of using mind maps in these situations is realized when your stakeholder tells you about features and functions of their work and the new product. Some of these are linked, and many are dependent on others. By drawing your interviews in mind map format, you become more likely to see the connections as well as to spot connections that the client has not made, but should be explained. Think of the mind map as a more versatile note-taking tool—versatile, because you can replace all of the text it takes to establish connections by simply drawing a line.

The best way of learning to draw mind maps is to start drawing mind maps. Use the tips described in this book, or gather examples from the Web to help. But mainly, just start drawing. You will soon see your mind map come to life.

The Murder Book

Your authors spend too much time on airplanes. Reading light literature, particularly crime novels, is a favorite way to pass some of the long hours. Several authors, and in particular Michael Connelly and his Los Angeles detective Harry Bosch, make frequent reference to the *murder book*—a case file for a murder investigation. The murder book includes a trail of every document, interview, photograph, and other items of evidence collected during the investigation.

We often use this same approach with our business analysis assignments: We collect every document and other piece of "evidence" into a binder, sometimes several binders (see Figure 5.18). Like the detectives, our intention is to create a trail of items that can be referred to later from a central repository. Just as detectives often solve murders by going back through the

Figure 5.18

The murder book is a collection of documents and models generated by the requirements discovery project.

murder book, so the business analyst can often find wonderfully useful material from the project murder book.

The technique is simple: Add every document, interview note, model, mind map, user story, and paper prototype—in fact, everything—to the murder book. This assumes, of course, that you have paper artifacts. If everything is electronic, then you have an electronic murder book. Add your artifacts in chronological order, and that's about all there is to the technique—except the part where you need to know something, and the murder book is where you look.

The murder book provides a trail of the story of the development. In the future when problems arise (and they will arise), the solutions to the new problems usually depend on knowing what took place and why things were decided previously in the project. The murder book is intended to be documentation of your development project.

We like this kind of documentation, particularly because it is free. There is no need to write extra material; just collect everything that has been written.

Sometimes you need to go a little further with this kind of record keeping and provide some kind of document register to make it easier for others to find your documents (or whatever form your gathered information is in).

With the availability of excellent search engines, we can see future potential for the majority of documentation being in this form. Instead of you having to spend a huge amount of time filing and cataloguing documents, the search engine finds what you want when you want it.

Video and Photographs

A video or photograph is a way of capturing some moments in time so that you can study them later. It is a particularly useful technique if you want to show the current work to people who cannot visit the stakeholders' workplace. We also take photos of whiteboards—to show the progression of ideas—and find that we often refer back to these images and include some of them in documents.

Video and photographs are especially useful tools for distributed teams.

Video records help fill in the spaces between the paragraphs of more formal written documentation by retaining off-hand remarks, body language, facial expressions (like

Video can be used for studying the business. When users and business analysts participate in workshops and brainstorming sessions, for example, the proceedings may be videoed. Interviews and on-site observations may also be videoed. With this technique, video is used initially to record, and then confirm, the proceedings. In addition, you can show the video to developers who do not get the opportunity to meet face to face with the users.

Video can serve as an adjunct to interviewing and observing the users in their own workplace. Users have their own ways of accomplishing tasks. They have their own ways to categorize the information that they use, and their own ways to solve problems that they have found worked well for them in their particular situation. Thus, by using video to capture the users at work, you also capture their ways of doing their jobs, their concerns, their preferences, and their idiosyncrasies.

Of course, video can be used in a more structured way as well. For example, you might select a business use case and ask the users to work through typical situations they encounter while you make a video recording of them. As they work, the users describe the special circumstances, the additional information they use, the exceptions, and so on. The shrugs, grimaces, and gestures that are normally lost when taking notes are faithfully recorded for later playback and dissection.

Obviously, you must ask permission before you begin to video someone. Keep in mind that whoever you are videoing will initially be very self-conscious in front of the camera, but subjects usually relax after a few minutes and accept the presence of the camera. Do not ask any important questions in the first five minutes, as the answers may be given for the benefit of the camera, and not for the benefit of accuracy.

We suggest that you try video in the following circumstances:

- Video users and developers participating in use case workshops and brainstorms.
- Video interviews and on-site observations.
- Video users at work.
- Video a business event. Ask the users to work through their typical response to an event, and to describe how they do their jobs.
- Send video to other members of a distributed team. We find the impact of video to be more involving for those who cannot see events firsthand.

If video does not seem practical in your environment, then use photographs. We always carry a small camera (the one in your phone is the most convenient) as part of our business analysis kit. During interviews, meetings, and workshops, we photograph stakeholders, whiteboards, flip charts, offices, manufacturing plants, and anything else that we think will be useful in helping us to discover the requirements. We often include photographs in minutes and progress reports. Photos are an effective way of giving people a detailed review without having to write a huge report.

You might also consider other recording devices such as the voice recorder on your smartphone, or a Livescribe smartpen, which acts as a pen and a sound recorder simultaneously.

raised eyebrows), indications of stress in using the program, the ease of using the keyboard, and so on. Since it retains more information than language, which is simply an abstraction of the information on the tape, it retains the information more faithfully. 99

—DeGrace and Stahl

READING
DeGrace, Peter, and Leslie Hulet Stahl. *Wicked Problems, Righteous Solutions: A Catalogue of Modern Software Engineering Paradigms.* Yourdon Press, 1990. This book has been around for a long time, but it has some relevant ideas on video to pass along.

Wikis, Blogs, Discussion Forums

This technique can apply to many types of projects. However, because it requires participation from a number of stakeholders, it is most effective for larger projects.

People love to contribute. The success of Facebook, Twitter, Wikipedia, and blogs demonstrate that, given a chance and a forum, people are happy to spend a little time (sometimes a lot of time) recording their opinions and knowledge. These contributions take many forms—you have probably used several—but for the sake of brevity we shall refer to them all as being posted to *wikis*.

The basic idea of a wiki in requirements discovery is that anyone—and the point is largely that *anyone* can do it—can make a post or edit or add to whatever has already been posted. Some forums keep discussions threaded so you can see it unfold; some allow contributors to overwrite or reorganize whatever they find. Additionally, anyone can add hypertext links to other useful sources of information or make any other kind of change.

Wikis rely on technology, but it is technology readily available to all. You can buy or download free hosting solutions to host your requirements wiki. If your organization will not give you the server space, then many publicly available sites are available. If you take the latter route, check carefully before you post what could be sensitive commercial information in the public domain.

To start a wiki, you seed it with an outline of the proposed product and invite stakeholders to add their piece. Once someone posts an opinion on what the product should do, you will no doubt find others chipping in to support or refute the original posting. Others invariably have their say, which usually results in a substantial collection of information and opinions. Anyone can contribute to a wiki; if a contributor is not one of the stakeholders whom you identified in the blastoff, it doesn't matter. If a person has something to say, you want to hear it, and you want each of your contributors to see what the others are saying.

And it is free, or can be.

The Web is a bountiful source for requirements. Search for your domain of interest. You will likely uncover a lot of information on what other people have done in your domain and, if you are lucky, you will find information that you can readily convert to requirements for your product. At the very least, you will find papers and articles that provide valuable information about your domain. And, like wikis, searching the Web is free.

The Web is a bountiful source for requirements. Search for your domain of interest. You will likely uncover a lot of information on what other people have done in your domain and, if you are lucky, you will find information that you can readily convert to requirements for your product.

Document Archeology

Document archeology is a technique of searching through existing reports and files for underlying requirements. It is best used when you have some existing or legacy system, and plan on modifying or renewing it.

Document archeology involves determining the underlying requirements by inspecting the documents and files used by the business. It is not a complete technique, but rather should be used in conjunction with other techniques, and only with caution. Document archeology entails reverse engineering new requirements from the documents used or produced by the current work. Along the way, you look for requirements that should become part of the new product.

Obviously, not all of the old work will be carried forward; simply because something exists in a document does not mean that it automatically has to be part of a new system. Nevertheless, where a current system exists, it will always provide plenty of material that is grist for your requirements mill (see Figure 5.19).

Inspect the documents you have collected (for simplicity's sake, the term "document" means anything you have collected), looking for nouns, or "things." These can be column headings, named boxes on forms, or simply the name of a piece of data on the document.

For each "thing," ask several of these questions:

- What is the purpose of this thing?
- Who uses it and why?
- What are all the uses the system makes of this thing?
- Which business events use or reference this thing?

Figure 5.19

In document archeology, you start by collecting samples of all documents, reports, forms, files, and so on. Gather anything that is used to record or send information, including regular telephone calls. User manuals are rich sources of material— they describe a way to do work.

- Can this thing have an alphanumeric value? For example, is it a number, a code, or a quantity?
- If so, to which collection of things does it belong? (Data modeling enthusiasts will immediately recognize the need to find the entity or class that owns the attribute.)
- Does the document contain a repeating group of things?
- If so, what is the collection of things called?
- Can you find a link between things?
- Which process makes the connection between them?
- Which rules are attached to each thing? In other words, which piece of business policy covers the thing?
- Which processes ensure that these rules are obeyed?
- Which documents give users the most problems?

These questions will not, in themselves, reveal all the requirements for the product. They will, however, give you plenty of background material and suggest directions for further investigation.

When doing document archeology, you search for capabilities from the current work that are needed for the new product. This does not mean you have carte blanche to replicate the old system—you are, in fact, gathering requirements because you plan to build a new product. Nevertheless, an existing system will usually have some capabilities in common with its replacement.

But be warned: Just because a document is output from a current computer or manual system, it does not mean that it is correct, nor does it mean that it is what is wanted by your client. Perhaps the document serves no useful purpose, or it needs heavy modification before it can be reused successfully.

We suggest that you incorporate document archeology into your data modeling approach, because most of the answers from the questions listed earlier are commonly used in the latter discipline. Of course, some document archeology is used as a foundation for object-oriented development. The current documents, if used cautiously, may reveal the classes of the data. They may also reveal the attributes of data stored by the system, and sometimes suggest operations that should be performed on the data.

As a rule, we always keep artifacts—documents, printouts, lists, manuals, screens, and anything else that is printed or displayed—from our interviews because we often refer back to them (see the earlier section on the murder book). Make a habit of asking for a copy of any document or screen that is mentioned. It is also prudent to log the document with an ID and version number, as it ensures that everyone has the same idea as to the source of their knowledge.

Family Therapy

Family therapists do not set out to make people *agree*. Instead, they aim to make it possible for people to hear and get an understanding of other individuals' positions, even if they do not agree with them. In other words, you should not expect every stakeholder to agree with every other stakeholder, but you should help the stakeholders as a group to accept that other people may disagree without necessarily being wrong, and that the need for choices and compromises will always arise. Early in the project, identify which mechanisms you will use to deal with these situations when they inevitably occur.

The field of family therapy is a rich source of ideas about how to work effectively with a diverse group of people—such as stakeholders in a requirements trawling process. We use ideas from family therapy as a way of helping us to listen to stakeholders and of providing a feedback loop to help avoid misinterpretations.

Family therapists do not set out to make people agree. Instead, they aim to make it possible for people to hear and get an understanding of other individuals' positions.

READING
Goldenberg, Herbert, and Irene Goldenberg. *Family Therapy: An Overview*, eighth edition. Brooks Cole, 2012.

Choosing the Best Trawling Technique

What is the best trawling technique? This is actually a trick question—there is no "best." The technique you should use in any given situation depends on several factors. The first, and most important, is that you feel comfortable with the technique. There is nothing quite as dismaying to a stakeholder audience as to have their business analyst stumbling while trying to learn a technique and at the same time use it. If you are a right-brain person and prefer graphical approaches, then that is what you should do. If you are more of a left-brain thinker—that is, your preference is for serial thinking—then text-based techniques such as scenarios would be more attractive to you.

Similarly, your stakeholders must feel comfortable with whatever technique you have selected. If a stakeholder cannot understand the model you are showing him, then it is simply the wrong model to use.

There are a couple of other considerations:

- Geography: When you are selecting a technique, keep in mind the locations of the stakeholders. Some techniques are more readily adaptable to dispersed teams, or when you have to deal remotely with your stakeholders.

- Legacy: How much of the current implementation has to remain there? How much does this constraint affect possible future implementations? If you have to carry forward a considerable legacy, then some of the more abstract techniques will not be suitable.

- Abstraction: Are you in a situation where you can deal with the business in an abstract or essential way? In some cases your stakeholders are not abstract thinkers, and you have to concentrate more on techniques to deal with physical realities. In contrast, if you are dealing with the desired future state of the business, then techniques involving abstraction are favored.

● Knowledge: What is the domain of your work area? It is worth taking this factor into account when you are selecting a trawling technique. Some domains such as engineering are very physical, while others such as finance are more conceptual and you can use more abstract techniques.

Table 5.1 lists various trawling techniques and summarizes their strengths. Some of these techniques have not yet been discussed; we will encounter them in later chapters. We suggest this table as a useful place for getting started in selecting a technique, or for finding alternative techniques to the ones you are using at the moment.

Table 5.1

Trawling Techniques and Their Strengths

Trawling Technique	Strengths
Business events	Partition the work for external demands
Current situation modeling	Examines the legacy system for reusable requirements
Apprenticing	Spends time working with an expert
Structures and patterns	Identify reusable requirements
Interviewing	Can focus on detailed issues
Essence	Finds the real problem
Business use case workshops	Focus the relevant stakeholders on the best response to the business event
Creativity workshops	Team discovers innovative requirements
Brainstorming	Facilitates creativity and invention
Personas	Use a composite virtual character to represent the user/customer
Mind mapping	An effective planning/note-taking technique
Wikis	Online forums through which stakeholders can contribute
Scenarios	Show the functionality of a use case
Low-fidelity prototypes	Discover undreamed-of requirements
High-fidelity prototypes	Discover usability requirements
Document archeology	Uses evidence from existing documents and files
Family therapy	Uses techniques from psychology to help stakeholders to understand a variety of viewpoints and to make choices clear.

We also refer you to the owls in the margins; they indicate when particular techniques are most effective.

Always use techniques with which you and your stakeholders are comfortable. The best results come when you and the people you are dealing with feel at ease with the way you are working together to discover requirements. If a technique is not working for you, then try a different one.

Finally . . .

Trawling, as we have discussed it here, is concerned with uncovering and understanding the business. At first, the business analyst's study is mainly concerned with the current work. This study should be done as rapidly as possible, and should be no more than is needed to reach a consensus among the stakeholders as to what the work actually is. The techniques presented in this chapter are tools intended to help with this study. Moreover, you have to do this work yourself—no tool has yet been invented that can do it for you.

We have not spent much time with the most critical tools for a business analyst—the ones attached to either side of your head, and the big gray one between those. *Listening* is the most important technique in requirements gathering. If you can listen to what your owner and your other stakeholders are saying, and if you can *think* about what they say and understand what they mean, then the tools described in this chapter will be useful. Conversely, if you don't listen and don't think, then you are highly unlikely to uncover the product that the user really wants.

The trawling techniques are communication tools; they help you open a dialog with your stakeholders and provide the feedback that is so essential to good communication. Use them well and wisely.

You have two ears and one mouth. I suggest that you use them in that proportion.

—G. K. Chesterton

Scenarios

6

*in which we look at scenarios, and how the
business analyst uses them to communicate
with the stakeholders*

At this stage of the requirements process, you have identified the business events, and thereby the business use cases (BUCs) that respond to the events. Here we look at using scenarios to model and record the BUCs. We use scenarios a lot, and find them to be very effective, largely because of their ready acceptance by nontechnical stakeholders.

Formality Guide

Scenarios are useful in most situations—anyone can understand them, and they fit into every development style.

Rabbit projects can use scenarios as a trawling technique. The requirements analysts and the appropriate stakeholders come together to build a scenario for the business use cases. It is usually faster to discover the required functionality by working with scenarios than by coding prototypes. Rabbit scenarios usually overlook non-functional requirements, and capture them later by writing separate non-functional story cards.

Horse projects *might* consider scenarios as an alternative to writing atomic functional requirements. When they have been developed enough, they can serve to inform the developers of the functional needs of the product. However, this approach does not work all the time. If you have complex products, or if you need the functional requirements documented for contractual purposes, for example, you should use scenarios to discover the requirements—but do not use them as your final specification.

Elephant projects make use of scenarios as a discovery tool. The meetings with the stakeholders are occasions for reviewing the desired way of working for each of the business use cases. When the scenario is complete—that is, when the exceptions and alternatives have been discovered and/or decided—it is used as the basis for writing the functional requirements. Elephant projects should keep their scenarios as part of the documentation; usually the developers want to see them when they start programming.

Scenarios

The scenario tells the story of a business use case.

A *scenario,* to give it its proper meaning, is an outline of a plot, or a postulated sequence of steps. In requirements work, we use this term to mean the plot of a section of the work we are studying. The use of "plot" is intended to imply that you break the work into a series of steps or scenes, and by explaining these steps, you explain the work.

In Chapter 4, we discussed how to partition the functionality of the work using business events; each chunk of the work we called a business use case. Now we look at using scenarios as a way of exploring and defining the functionality of the business use case. Consider the following scenario:

> 1. The moviegoer asks for movies based on her previously recorded preferences.
> 2. The moviegoer filters the movies based on the time of screening and the location of the cinema.
> 3. If requested, reviews of the shortlisted movies are provided.
> 4. The moviegoer selects a movie.
> 5. The moviegoer elects to buy the ticket online.
> 6. Ticket details and a quick response code are sent to the moviegoer's mobile phone.
> 7. The moviegoer elects to send e-mails to selected friends with details of the movie and an invitation to join her at the movies.
> 8. The moviegoer checks parking availability, and public transport options, for the cinema.
> 9. The moviegoer sets an alarm to remind her when it is time to leave for the movies.

READING
For information on many other ways to use scenarios, see Alexander, Ian, and Neil Maiden. *Scenarios, Stories, Use Cases Through the Systems Development Life-Cycle.* John Wiley & Sons, 2004.

A business analyst would use a scenario like this to elicit, and then describe, a business use case to its interested stakeholders. The BUC is a discrete amount of functionality; it happens in its own time frame, and can be considered separately from other parts of the work's functionality.

The scenario is a neutral medium, and one that is both simple and understandable to all stakeholders. But you don't have to show it to all the stakeholders. When you are exploring a business use case, we suggest that you identify and invite only the interested stakeholders—those people with knowledge or expertise in the part of the work that you are modeling with your scenario.

You model a scenario and use it to reach agreement on what the work has to do. Once such agreement is achieved, you and the stakeholders decide how much of that work will be done by the product. You then produce one or more scenarios to define the actor's (user's) interaction with the product. This latter scenario is a product use case scenario—but we will put these scenarios aside for the moment and consider them more fully in Chapter 8, Starting the Solution. For the moment, let's concentrate on the work.

We suggest that you write your scenario by breaking the functionality of the business use case down into a series of steps; each step being some meaningful and recognizable activity that forms part of the BUC. Ideally, you should aim for between three and ten steps. There is nothing carved in stone about this range, and nothing untoward will happen to you if you use more steps than ten. However, if you end up with 126 steps, either you have a gigantic business use case (impossible for normal commercial work) or you are writing your scenario with an unnecessarily meticulous level of granularity. The aim is to keep the scenario simple enough to be readily understandable, and three to ten steps usually achieves this goal.

Although a formalized template for a scenario exists (and is provided later in this chapter), your first draft can be simple and informal. As an example, let's leave our IceBreaker case study for the moment and look at something that you are most likely familiar with: the business use case for checking a passenger onto an international flight (see Figure 6.1). Here's Sherri, one of the check-in agents describing the check-in process. Keep in mind that she is describing the current way of working—the How-Now view of the work—which you are using to start your investigation:

> "I call the next customer in line. When he gets to my desk, I ask for a ticket. If the passenger is using an e-ticket, I need the booking record locator. Most of the passengers are not organized enough to have it written down, so I ask them their name and the flight they are on. Most people don't know the flight number, so I usually ask for their destination. They must know that!

> "I make sure I have the right passenger and the right flight. It would be pretty embarrassing to give away someone else's seat or to send a passenger to the wrong destination. Anyway, somehow I locate the passenger's flight record in the computer. If he has not already given it to me, I ask for the passenger's passport. I check that the picture looks like the passenger and that the passport is still valid.

" A formal language for talking about work organizes concepts that help people learn to see work. "

—Beyer and Holtzblatt,
Contextual Design

Write your scenarios using between three and ten steps.

"If there is no frequent-flyer [FF] number showing against the booking, I ask the passenger if he belongs to our mileage scheme. Either he hands me the plastic card with the FF number, or I ask him and if he wishes to join I give him the sign-up form. We can put temporary FF numbers against the flight record so the passenger is credited for that trip.

"If the computer has not already assigned a seat, I find one. This usually means I ask if the passenger prefers a window or an aisle seat, or, if the plane is already almost full, I tell him what I have available. Of course, if the computer has assigned a seat, I always ask if it is okay. One way or another we settle on a seat and I confirm it with the computer system. I can print the boarding pass at this stage, but I usually do the bags first.

"I ask how many bags the passenger is checking and, at the same time, verify that he is not exceeding the carry-on limit. Some people are unbelievable with what they want to carry into a fairly space-restricted aircraft cabin. I ask the security questions about the bags and get the passenger's responses. I print out the bag tags and securely attach them to the bags, and then I send the bags on their way down the conveyor belt.

"Next I print the boarding pass. This means that I have everything done as far as the computer is concerned. But there is one more thing to do: I have to make sure that everything agrees with the passenger's understanding. I read out from the boarding pass where he is going, what time the flight is, and what time it will board, and if a gate has been assigned, I tell him that, too. I also read out how many bags have been checked and confirm that their destination matches the passenger's destination. I hand over the documents, and wish the passenger a good flight."

Now sketch out the scenario. Break the story down to the steps that you consider to be the best ones to capture the normal path through the story.

Figure 6.1

An airline check-in for an international flight. As we go through the scenario for this case, see if it matches your experience of checking in for a flight.

There are no hard-and-fast rules about how you accomplish this—just write whatever seems logical to you. After all, you are the person who is going to use the scenario; it might as well fit with your view of the work. Later you will adjust it with your subsequent activities, but for the moment let us suppose that this is your first draft:

> 1. *Get the passenger's ticket or record locator.*
>
> 2. *Check that this is the right passenger, flight, and destination.*
>
> 3. *Check that the passport is valid and belongs to the passenger.*
>
> 4. *Record the frequent-flyer number.*
>
> 5. *Find a seat.*
>
> 6. *Ask security questions.*
>
> 7. *Check the baggage onto the flight.*
>
> 8. *Print and hand over the boarding pass and bag tags.*
>
> 9. *"Have a nice flight."*

Confirm this scenario with the interested stakeholders. It is in plain English—that is intentional—so all stakeholders can be invited to participate and revise this scenario until it represents a consensus view of what the work should be. Once a consensus is reached on the work, start to formalize the scenario. Along the way, you will learn more about the work.

The first part of the formalized scenario identifies it and gives it a meaningful name.

Stakeholders are invited to participate and revise the scenario until it represents a consensus view of what the work should be.

> *Business Use Case Name: Check passenger onto flight.*

Next, you add the start-up mechanism, or trigger, for the business use case. It usually consists of some data or request (often both) arriving from outside your work area. There are also time-triggered business use cases, in which case you state the time condition (an hour or a date is reached, an amount of time has passed since another business use case, and so on) that initiates the use case.

> *Trigger: Passenger's ticket, record locator, or identity and flight.*

As you model the work with your scenario, you should always be asking whether you can improve on the work. For example, instead of making the passenger wait to get to the desk, could you start before the passenger gets that far? For example, could he check in at home, or on the way to the airport, or while standing in line? All of these options are technologically possible and probably offer a business advantage. For the moment, we leave this question as an open issue.

Now you add any preconditions that must exist when the business use case is triggered. Preconditions indicate the state of the work at initiation. Usually this means certain other business events must have occurred before this business use case makes any sense.

> *Preconditions: The passenger must have a reservation.*

The check-in desk is not the place to be if you do not already have a reservation. While it may seem like good service to allow passengers to make a reservation at the check-in desk, the amount of time needed for this transaction would no doubt annoy the other passengers standing in line.

You might consider adding the interested stakeholders to the scenario. These people have an interest in the outcome of the business use case—they will be affected by the manner in which the work is done and which data is produced by it.

> *Interested Stakeholders: Check-in agent, marketing, baggage handling, reservations, flight manifest system, workflow, security, destination country's immigration.*

There are probably more stakeholders, but this list is adequate to show that you are not only concerned with the immediate problem, but also recognize that whatever you do here has ramifications on a wider scale.

Active stakeholders are the people or systems that do the work of the business use case. Usually, one active stakeholder triggers the business use case, and then one or more others participate in the work.

> *Active Stakeholders: Passenger (trigger), check-in agent.*

The passenger triggers the business use case by arriving at the check-in desk; he is also the recipient of the business use case's output. The passenger interacts with the agent to carry out the work of the business use case. Although the agent manipulates any automated product being used, that action should be thought of as simply the current implementation; it has no binding significance. The essential business is triggered by the passenger, who, in some future incarnation, might be more closely involved. Self-check-in springs to mind here, but we should not leap to the first solution that comes along. The point of the requirements investigation is to fully understand the work before choosing a solution, and there are plenty of other possibilities—checking in by telephone while on the way to the airport, checking in at the club lounge, and using the record locator sent to the passenger's mobile phone by the airline, to name just a few. But let's not get ahead of ourselves.

The Essence of the Business

The scenario, as we now have it, represents the current incarnation of the work. If you think back to the Brown Cow Model from Chapter 5, this scenario belongs to the first quadrant of the model—the How-Now view of the work.

To move above the line and look at the What-Now and Future-What views, you must consider the essence of the problem. To do so, go back over the scenario and eliminate any technological bias, while simultaneously asking the question, "What does the business really need to do?"

The essence is not a better solution to the problem—it is the real problem. You find the real business problem when you eliminate all the technological camouflage that normally makes up a description of some work. There will be more on essence in the next chapter.

> *The essence is not a better solution to the problem—it is the real problem.*

Also, for the moment, consider only the normal case scenario. The normal case (sometimes called the happy case) is when everything works perfectly. Of course, everything does not always work perfectly, so later you go back over the same scenario and explore the exceptions and alternatives.

> *Assume for the normal case that everything works perfectly.*

Let's revisit the check-in scenario, and this time change the language to be technologically neutral.

> 1. *Get the passenger's ticket, record locator, or identity and flight number.*

The ticket and the record locator are both constraints on the work. The ticket comes from outside the work—the passenger has been carrying it up to this point. The record locator is a constraint imposed by the current computer system. In this case it is a real constraint, not because a computer system uses it (the computer system belongs to the airline and, therefore, can be changed), but rather because it is used by travel agents and other bodies outside the scope of the organization. For this reason, we accept that it cannot be changed. However, the ticket and the record locator are merely means to an end—the real work to be done is to find the passenger's reservation. Let's rewrite step 1 to reflect this understanding:

> 1. *Locate the passenger's reservation.*

This is the essence of the first step. Stating it in the essential manner, without the technological artifacts, allows us to think of better ways of implementing it. If you want to rush ahead, you can see that there are several possibilities for the future product. Perhaps passengers could swipe a machine-readable passport, use a credit card, or use any of several other ways to identify themselves.

For now, put those ideas for future technology aside, and consider that the essence of the problem is to connect the passenger with his reservation.

> *2. Check that this is the right passenger, flight, and destination.*

This step focuses on ensuring that the passenger is who he says he is, and that the reservation matches his expectations for the flight. Let's rewrite step 2 accordingly:

> *2. Ensure the passenger is correctly identified and connected to the right reservation.*

Next the scenario checks the passport.

> *3. Check that the passport is valid and belongs to the passenger.*

The passport step is slightly more complex and warrants a few words of explanation. We suggest enhancing this step:

> *3. Check that the passport is valid and belongs to the passenger.*
>
> *3.1 The passport must be current.*
>
> *3.2 The passport must not expire before the end of the complete trip.*
>
> *3.3 The passport must be valid for travel to the destination country.*
>
> *3.4 Visas (where needed) must be current.*
>
> *3.5 There must be no "refused entry" stamps from the destination country.*

Alternatively, you might simply leave this step as it was and refer to notes to complete the business rules for step 3.

> *3. Check that the passport is valid and belongs to the passenger.*
>
> *See procedure guidelines EU-175.*

This is the essence of the problem. There is an unyielding constraint that the passenger has a passport—this is international travel we are dealing with. The airline's management needs to enforce the rules on passports because the airline is responsible for returning the passenger if he is refused entry to the destination country. All in all, this seems like a sensible constraint, so we keep it as part of the essence.

The same technique of scrubbing away the technology and getting to the essence is employed for later steps in the scenario. Keep working through it until you and your interested stakeholders agree that it is an accurate, but not yet detailed, portrayal of the work. When you are finished, it would look something like this:

> *Business Event: Passenger decides to check in.*
>
> *Business Use Case Name: Check passenger onto flight.*
>
> *Trigger: Passenger's ticket, record locator, or identity and flight.*
>
> *Preconditions: The passenger must have a reservation and a passport.*
>
> *Interested Stakeholders: Check-in agent, marketing, baggage handling, reservations, flight manifest system, workflow, security, destination country's immigration.*
>
> *Active Stakeholders: Passenger (trigger), check-in agent.*
>
> *1. Locate the passenger's reservation.*
>
> *2. Ensure the passenger is correctly identified and connected to the right reservation.*
>
> *3. Check that the passport is valid and belongs to the passenger. See procedure guidelines EU-175.*
>
> *4. Attach the passenger's frequent-flyer number to the reservation.*
>
> *5. Allocate a seat.*
>
> *6. Get the correct responses to the security questions.*
>
> *7. Check the baggage onto the flight.*
>
> *8. Print and convey to the passenger the boarding pass and bag tags.*
>
> *9. Wish the passenger a pleasant flight.*
>
> *Outcome: The passenger is recorded as checked onto the flight, the bags are assigned to the flight, a seat is allocated, and the passenger is in possession of a boarding pass and bag claim stubs.*

We add an outcome to the scenario—that is, the desired situation at the successful conclusion of the business use case. Think of it as the stakeholder's objectives at the time he triggered the business use case.

Diagramming the Scenario

Some requirements analysts—and some stakeholders—prefer to use a diagram to explain the functionality of a business use case. This preference is a matter of personal choice, and it depends largely on whether your audience responds more favorably to text or to diagrammatic scenarios. We leave it to you to experiment and decide which form of representation is right for you.

Several diagrams can be used for scenarios. The UML (Unified Modeling Language) activity diagram is a popular choice. BPMN (Business Process Modeling Notation) also has its adherents, as do other styles of diagram. There is no best approach—just pick one that you like, or that your organization already uses. Figure 6.2 shows the airline check-in example as a UML activity diagram.

In Figure 6.2, note the "swim lanes"—that is, the dotted lines that divide the work between the participants. Swim lanes are optional, and they are both good and bad: good because they provide a clear explanation of who is

Figure 6.2

An activity diagram showing the passenger checking in for a flight. This is the equivalent of the scenario shown previously.

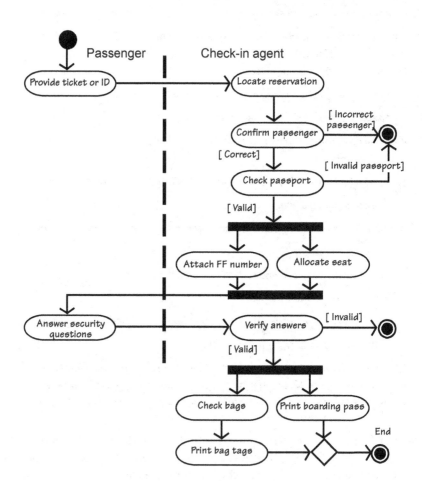

doing what; bad because they tread the dangerous path of inviting readers to believe that they define the way the work must be implemented in the future. Be aware that diagrams like Figure 6.2 are used as explanations. Only after the systems architects and designers have done their work can the swim lanes be taken to mean a specification—more on that in the next chapter.

The activity diagram shows a certain amount of parallel processing. For example, there is no reason why the *Attach frequent-flyer number* and *Allocate seat* activities cannot be performed at the same time. The text scenario does not show this possibility. However, if you want to point out the parallel nature of these two activities, you could amend the scenario as follows:

> *The following two things can be done in any order or in parallel:*
>
> *4. Attach the frequent-flyer number to the reservation.*
>
> *5. Allocate a seat.*

The activity diagram also shows other control aspects. For example, the diamond at the bottom of the model in Figure 6.2 is called a *merge*. This symbol means that all processing must reach this point before proceeding. In the case of the airline check-in, the entire process cannot end until both the bag tags and the boarding pass have been printed. Diamonds are also used to denote decisions, just as they are in traditional flowcharts. We tend to leave them out where the conditions are obvious or can be shown by attaching *guard conditions* (the words in brackets at the exit of an activity). When using activity diagrams during requirements, simplicity is more useful than correct and complete use of the notation.

The book you are reading does not attempt to be a treatise on UML modeling. The reason for including this discussion is so that you can look at the model and the text scenario in a side-by-side fashion, and decide how you can use either models or text to represent scenarios. For more on UML and BPMN, we refer you to the books mentioned in the "Reading" notes and the bibliography.

READING

Allweyer, Thomas. *BPMN 2.0.* Herstellung und Verlag: Books on Demand GmbH, 2010.

Miles, Russ, and Kim Hamilton. *Learning UML 2.0.* O'Reilly Media, 2006.

Alternatives

Alternatives arise when you wish the user to have a choice of possible actions. These choices are intentional, as they are wanted and defined by the business. They usually exist to make the work of the business use case more attractive and convenient to the participants. When you buy books or music online, for example, you can decide whether to place your selected goods in a shopping cart awaiting check-out, or have them sent directly to you when you click "buy." These deliberate choices offered by the vendor are alternatives.

Alternatives arise when you offer an intentional choice of user actions.

The work reacts differently depending on which alternative is selected. Consider step 4 of our example case, to which we have added an alternative:

> **4. Attach the frequent-flyer number to the reservation.**
>
> A4.1 Allow the FF number to be changed to that of a partner airline.

You find alternatives by examining each step of the normal case. Look for instances where the step may be carried out differently, or the active stakeholder (you might call this person an actor) can be given a choice. These choices are sometimes interesting from the point of view of improving the work or providing a better service.

> **4. Attach the frequent-flyer number to the reservation.**
>
> A4.1 Allow the FF number to be changed to that of a partner airline.
>
> A4.2 Allow the FF number to be changed to that of a family member,
>
> A4.3 Allow the mileage of the flight to be donated to a charity of the passenger's choice.

Exceptions

Exceptions are unwanted but inevitable deviations from the normal case.

Exceptions are unwanted but inevitable deviations from the normal case. They are unwanted in the sense that the owner of the work would rather that they did not happen. Nevertheless, we know that they will happen from time to time, so we have to cater for them. For example, a passenger might not know the locator number, an online customer might forget his password, or a passenger could arrive at the airport having forgotten his passport.

We must pause here to urge you to delay looking for exceptions until you are satisfied with the normal case scenario. It is far too easy for stakeholders to get carried away with exceptions, and your review session with them can be quickly derailed by needlessly chasing exceptions that are not guaranteed ever to happen. It is only when you have the normal case that you can methodically work through it by looking for the exceptions and deciding what you will do about them.

The goal of the exception scenario is to show how the work safely handles the exception. In other words, which steps must be taken to rejoin the path of the normal case? You can write a separate scenario to show the exceptions, but in most cases it is more convenient to add the exception steps to your normal scenario.

Consider step 5 as an example:

> **5. Find a seat.**
>
>   **E5.1** *The passenger's choice of seat is not available.*
>
>   **E5.1** *Record a request for a seat change by the gate agent.*

You find the exceptions by examining each step of the normal case and asking questions such as these:

- What happens if this step cannot be completed, or does not go to completion, or comes up with a wrong or unacceptable result?
- What can go wrong at this step?
- What could happen to prevent the work from reaching this step?
- Could any external entity disrupt or prevent this step, or this business use case?
- Could any technology used to implement this step fail or become unavailable?
- Could the end user fail to understand what is required of him, or misunderstand the information presented by the product?
- Could the end user take the wrong action—intentionally or unintentionally—or fail to respond?

There are many questions you can ask, each of which seeks to find a different potential error. We suggest that you make a checklist of the questions pertinent to your particular situation, adding to it each time a new project discovers new questions.

We have also seen some successful attempts to use automation to help with this task. Our colleague Neil Maiden at City University in London is having success using the university's ART-SCENE scenario presenter. This tool works with the normal case scenario to automatically generate a list of potential exceptions. It also uses rich-media scenarios where additional information in the form of photographs, movies, sound, and so on is integrated into the scenario.

We know from experience that the exceptions have the potential to necessitate a great amount of remedial rework if they are not found at requirements time, so look carefully for things that could go wrong. You can ignore the scenario in which the work is struck by a meteor, but almost anything else is possible.

READING
Details of ART-SCENE can be found at http://hcid.soi.city.ac.uk/research/Artsceneindex.html.

What if? Scenarios

What if? scenarios allow you to explore possibilities.

What if? scenarios allow you to explore possibilities and question the business rules. You ask, "What if we did this?" or "What if we didn't do that?" It becomes easier to find the many possibilities if you think about the constraints. Ask what would happen if the constraint did not exist. As an example, suppose that while going over the scenarios for the flight check-in case, you asked, "What if we took away the constraint of the check-in desk?"

This freedom gives rise to all sorts of possibilities. Suppose you wrote your what if? scenario like this:

> 1. The passenger calls the airline while en route to the airport.
>
> 2. Ask the passenger if he wants to check in.
>
> 3. If yes, get the record locator from the passenger's phone (this was sent at the time of the reservation).
>
> 4. Check the passenger onto the flight, and text the seat allocation and passcode (the passenger's phone will be scanned at the gates to allow the passenger to move through the airport).
>
> 5. Text bag checks (these will activate the automated bag tag printers at curbside).
>
> 6. Wish the passenger a pleasant flight.

What if? scenarios are intended to stimulate creativity and guide your stakeholders to come up with more innovative products.

What if? scenarios are intended to stimulate creativity and guide your stakeholders to come up with more innovative products. We shall revisit this topic in Chapter 8, Starting the Solution.

Misuse Cases and Negative Scenarios

Misuse cases (you might like to think of them as "unhappy cases") show negative or harmful possibilities, such as someone abusing the work or attempting to defraud it. Examples include users deliberately entering incorrect data, customers using stolen credit cards, and pranksters making fictitious calls or transactions, planting a virus or other malware, or engaging in any of the myriad other things that can be done to harm the work.

It may be helpful here to think in terms drawn from fiction writing and use the idea of the protagonist and the antagonist. The protagonist is the hero or main character of the story: the good guy, the user, the actor using the product following your normal use case scenario. Winnie the Pooh is the ideal protagonist—he is well intentioned and you want him to win out in the end. But like Pooh, your protagonist might be of very little brain and

> 66 *Maybe 'abuse cases' will always sound jokey, but the idea of the Negative Scenario (e.g., Burglar impersonates householder, Alarm Call Center Operator colludes with Burglar, etc.) is important.* 99
>
> —Ian Alexander

make mistakes: forget his password, choose the wrong option, get honey on the keys, or any of the many unfortunate things a Pooh can do.

Cast your protagonist as someone who is forgetful, slow, distracted, and not paying attention. (You are bound to know someone like that.) Go through the normal case scenario, and for each step, ask what can be done wrongly. It may be simpler to write a new scenario for each misuse, as the ramifications of a misstep may be complex enough to warrant their own separate story.

So much for the protagonist. The antagonist is the person who opposes the work, seeks to harm it, or wants to defraud it. Hackers are the most commonly thought-of example of antagonists. Examine all of the steps for the normal case and ask if there is a possibility of someone opposing or misusing that action. In this case, the ramifications upon discovering an antagonist's misuse may be to simply stop the business use case. For example:

> *Examine all of the steps for the normal case and ask if there is a possibility of someone opposing or misusing that action.*

> 3. Check the passport is valid and belongs to the passenger.
>
> M3.1 The passenger produces a passport that is not his.
>
> M3.2 Call security.
>
> M3.3 Freeze the reservation.

Whether you annotate the normal case with the misuse steps or write a separate misuse scenario depends on the complexity of the situation and the comfort level of the stakeholders.

Some professions have always made use of what if? scenarios. For instance, chess players routinely think, "What would Black do if I moved my knight to e4?", leading to the minimize–maximize algorithms for game-play. Our governments routinely generate what if? scenarios to plan policy: "What if the United States reestablished the gold standard?" "What if Switzerland elects a communist government?" "What if Canada closes the St. Lawrence Seaway?" While these examples are obviously fanciful, most governments generate thousands of likely and unlikely scenarios to explore their reactions to possible future events.

When gathering requirements, try generating several what if? scenarios to experiment with the unforeseen. The intention is to turn the unforeseen into the foreseen: The more you know about eventualities before you build the product, the more robust and long-lasting it will be.

> " *I don't always try to identify the predator flows. I use the same flows as other actors but ask the question, What if a hacker got here? What other precautions need to be implemented? What is the risk to the corporation if they get here? Can the corporation live with the risk of occurrence? How much are you willing to pay to avoid the risk?* "
>
> —Patricia Ferdinandi, *A Requirements Pattern: Succeeding in the Internet Economy*, Addison-Wesley, 200

Scenario Template

You may, of course, write your business use case scenarios in whatever form you and your stakeholders prefer. The template presented in this section is one we have found useful on many assignments. We suggest it as a fairly good compromise between informality and an overly bureaucratic approach.

Business Event Name: The name of the business event to which the business use case responds.

Business Use Case Name and Number: Give each business use case a unique identifier and a name that communicates the functionality—for example, Record Library Loan, Register New Student Enrollment, Make Benefit Payment, Produce Sales Report. Ideally, the name should be an active verb plus a specific direct object.

Trigger: The data or request for a service that arrives from an external source and triggers a response from the work. The trigger may be the arrival of data from one of the adjacent systems—that is, from outside the work area that you are studying. Alternatively, the trigger may be the arrival of the temporal condition that causes the use case to become activated—for example, the end of the month.

Preconditions: Sometimes certain conditions must exist before the use case is valid. For example, a customer has to be registered before he can access his frequent-flyer statement. Note that another business use case usually takes care of the precondition. In the preceding example, the customer would have registered using the Register Passenger business use case.

Interested Stakeholders: The people, organizations, and/or representatives of computer systems that have knowledge necessary to specify this use case or that have an interest in this use case.

Active Stakeholders: The people, organizations, and/or computer systems that are doing the work of this use case. Don't think about users just yet; instead, think of the real people who are involved in the work of the business use case.

Normal Case Steps: The steps that this use case goes through to complete the desired course of its work. Write these steps as clear, natural-language statements that are understandable to business people related to the project. There are usually between three and ten steps.

Step 1 . . .
Step 2 . . .
Step 3 . . .

Note that a business use case can make use of the services or functionality of another business use case as part of its own processing. However, be careful not to start programming at this stage.

Alternatives: Alternatives are acceptable variations on the normal case of processing. For example, gold cardholders may be given an invitation to visit the lounge when they check in. Tell the story in the same way:

Alternative step 1 . . .
Alternative step 2 . . .
Alternative step 3 . . .

If the alternative action is simple, you can make it part of the normal case:

Step 4. Attach the frequent-flyer number to the reservation.
Alternative 4.1 Issue a lounge invitation if the passenger holds a gold card.

Exceptions: These cases are unwanted but inevitable variations. For example, a customer may have insufficient funds for a withdrawal at an ATM. In this case, the procedure has to offer a lower amount, or offer a loan, or do whatever the stakeholders decide is appropriate. Tag each exception to the appropriate step:

Exception 2.1 . . .
Exception 2.2 . . .
Exception 2.3 . . .

Outcome: The desired situation at the end of this use case. You might call this the "post condition." Think of it as the stakeholder's objective at the time when he triggers the use case. For example, the money has been dispensed and taken from the ATM, the customer's account has been debited, and the card has been extracted from the ATM.

Summary

A scenario is a natural language tool for telling a story. We have discussed how to write this story; its intention is to help you and your stakeholders come to a coherent understanding of the functionality of a business use case. Writing the BUC scenario tests whether sufficient study has been done or the business analyst needs to ask more questions and investigate further.

Once the BUC scenario is agreed—that is, you and your stakeholders have come to a consensus that it accurately represents the desired state of the work—it forms the basis for writing the requirements. We shall explore this progression, including the use of scenarios for product use cases, over the next few chapters.

Understanding the Real Problem

7

in which we "think above the line" to
find the true essence of the business,
and so deliver the right product—
one that solves the right problem

I know that's what I asked for, but it's not what I need. You do not have to be part of IT very long to hear that statement and to see the expectant smiles dashed from the developers' faces—it happens all the time. So what is going wrong here? The developers have delivered exactly what the business stakeholders asked for, but it turns out not to solve their business problem. Why not? *Because the real problem was never stated, and so was never correctly understood.*

When stakeholders ask for some feature or capability, they quite often state their request as an implementation. "I want an external disk to back up my laptop's drive." This is a business stakeholder asking for a solution to a problem, but not really saying what that problem is. How can you know if it is the correct solution? You can't; and until you know what the real problem is there is little point in thinking about solutions.

So what is this user's problem? What does he really need?

If our stakeholder is concerned that his laptop's hard drive will crash, then perhaps the correct solution is to replace the hard drive with something more reliable. If the user is concerned that his computer will be stolen from the office, then the thieves will most probably cart away the backup drive as well. And if there is a fire, then the backup drive will melt down at about the same time as this guy's computer.

There's more: The user wants to back up his hard drive, which suggests that at some stage every day or every week he will boot up the backup program and do the backup. But what if he forgets? Is the real business need still being met if the solution relies on fallible human memory?

In this chapter we talk about how to get to the real problem by using *abstraction*—focusing on ideas rather than solutions. To put it another way,

> " *At the end of the day, if the software doesn't meet the user's needs, it is still lousy software regardless of how it was created.* "
>
> —Pete McBreen, *Questioning Extreme Programming*

Figure 7.1

The problem is to back up the hard drive—or is it?

abstraction involves thinking about the *essence* of the subject by discarding the technological and physical components.

Thus, instead of the suggested physical implementation "Back up the hard drive," you look at the essence and say, "Eliminate loss of data" or "Guard the data against theft" or "Guard the data against fire." Once you understand the real problem—the underlying business need—then you are much better placed to find the optimal solution for it. So, dear reader, before you leap to a solution for the backup problem—which can range from frequent, automated uploads to a cloud service, to attaching the laptop to a well-trained attack Rottweiler and giving it an exit from the building in case of fire—we want you to consider the idea of abstraction, and how it can work for you.

The physical reality was that the company rented DVDs. But if you abstract from that, you see that Netflix is in the business of renting out movies.

Let's look at an example of abstraction. Netflix, an American company, had a successful business renting out DVDs though the mail. In return for a monthly fee, customers could have several Netflix DVDs at home, and when they had watched one and returned it, another was sent. At the time when Netflix was founded, this was a new business model for renting movies. But at some point Netflix looked at the abstraction of its business. The physical reality was that the company rented DVDs, but if you abstract from that, you see that Netflix is in the business of *renting out movies*.

Now that we see the real business is about renting movies, we ask if there is a different, more convenient way to do so? Well, yes. Netflix found it and switched its business to providing *downloadable* movies. This model put the customers in direct contact with the Netflix website, and gave the customers even better service by providing a wide choice of instantly available movies, along with the convenience of not having to return their watched DVDs through the mail. By adopting this approach, Netflix changed its operation to be closer to the essence of the problem.

In Chapter 5, Investigating the Work, we considered how you go about studying the current state of the piece of the business you are meant to improve. We said at the time that this initial study is undertaken simply to ensure that you and your stakeholders are talking about the same piece of business, and that you have a reasonable idea of the current state of the work. However, when you looked at the business, you saw the physical artifacts and devices that are used to carry out the work.

In this chapter we intend to eliminate the devices and technology that you encountered, and so uncover the real intent of the work.

Formality Guide

No matter how formal or informal you are, or how agile or how traditional you are, or want to be, you still have to build something that meets the real needs. Otherwise, you are simply wasting your client's money and your own time.

This chapter is of particular importance to rabbits. As a rabbit project, you are likely to be using techniques such as story cards, Post-it notes, or sketches on a whiteboard. These artifacts display, more often than not, proposed solutions to unstated problems. By finding the essence of the problem, your solution will be far more appropriate, and usually more elegant. The essence does not have to be written as the first draft of the story card (it helps if it is) but it must be revealed during the requirements conversation.

Horse projects' aspirations to informality are helped if the business analysts and the stakeholders talk about only the essence of the work. Using this approach, they generate fewer models and possibly cut down on the amount of communication needed.

Elephant projects might involve outsourced development, in which case it is vital that they solve the right problem. If not, the delivered product has to be corrected and the outsourcer charges for the corrections.

Similarly, if the elephant project has more formal internal procedures, and the complete specification is handed to the developers before any construction begins, then a time lag will separate the requirements activity and the software delivery. As repair to the system is now difficult, it becomes vital that the specification is specifying the correct product—one that meets the real needs.

The Brown Cow Model: Thinking Above the Line

The Brown Cow Model, which we introduced earlier in this text, is shown in Figure 7.2. Chapter 5, Investigating the Work, discussed how to study the current business. That investigation is represented by the lower-left quadrant

Figure 7.2

The Brown Cow Model provides four views of the work, each of which provides the business analyst with information that is useful at different stages of the investigation. In this chapter we look above the line.

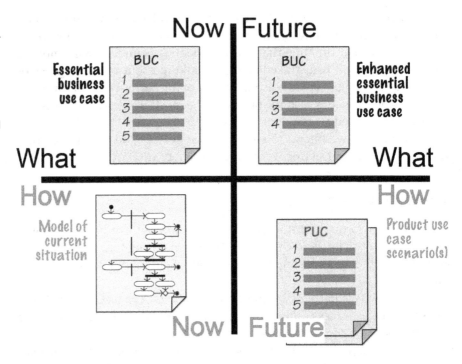

of the model, the How-Now view of the business. In fact, anything below the line—the "how"—shows the physical devices and human organizations used to implement the solution.

The Essence

Now it is time to move above the horizontal line that separates the "how" from the "what." Here's where you see the real business—that which we refer to as the *essence* of the business. Up here the air is rarified and you do not need to deal with the mundane, real-world issues of people and technology; instead, you take an abstract view and discover what the business is really doing. Once you see that, you move to what you would like to be doing in the future. In the Brown Cow Model, these views are shown by the What-Now and the Future-What quadrants.

The reason for spending time above the line is to discover the real problem and avoid what happens in many organizations where people waste their entire 60 minutes building solutions to the wrong problems.

When you are trawling for knowledge, much of what you hear is a stakeholder's idea for a *solution,* not a description of the underlying problem to be solved. This could be a terrific solution, but more likely it is a solution limited by the stakeholder's experience and imagination. Moreover, as yet you (and your stakeholder) have no idea whether it is solving the right problem.

> *If I had an hour to save the world, I would spend 59 minutes defining the problem.*
>
> —Albert Einstein

So your task as the requirements discoverer is to interpret what your stakeholder is saying and uncover its essence.

How the work physically accomplishes its functionality—the technology, the instruments, the computers, the people, and so on—is its implementation. To get to its essence, you must ignore any current or future implementation, and reveal the fundamental reason that the work exists. There are several reasons for doing so: The first, and most important, reason is that you solve the right problem—this is obvious but often overlooked. The second reason is that finding the essence means that you don't inadvertently reimplement outmoded technology. Technology and the organizational structure that were appropriate several years ago when the current system was built will not necessarily be the relevant solution today. And if that is not enough, getting to the essence means that you can avoid the proposed flavor-of-the-month solution that your stakeholder is fixating on.

Separate the essence of the problem from any proposed solution.

The problem, meaning the real business problem you are trying to solve, exists regardless of any technological implementation. This underling business problem—perhaps you prefer to call this the policy—is the essence.

You can reverse engineer the essence from a technological implementation. For example, think of an automated teller machine: What is the essential piece of business that you conduct with an ATM? The actions that you have to take—such as insert a plastic card, enter a PIN, have your retina scanned, and so on—involve interacting with the technology the bank chooses to use. The essence, however, is that you safely access your bank account and withdraw money from it.

The essence exists regardless of any technological implementation.

READING

McMenamin, Steve, and John Palmer. *Essential Systems Analysis.* Yourdon Press, 1984. This was the first book to discuss the essence of the business. Sadly, it is out of print, but you can sometimes find a copy on secondhand book sites.

Note how technology-free that statement is: "You safely access your bank account and withdraw money from it." Consider it, and now consider how many other ways you could "safely access your account and withdraw money from it." Lots of technological possibilities exist. For example, when you use the "cash back" option with your debit card at the supermarket, you are accessing your bank account and withdrawing money from it. That the supermarket forces you to use your debit card and buy something is part of that business's solution; it does not change the essence.

And that is the point: You are looking for the essence of the business. How you implement it—now or in the future—is not part of the essence and so is not important to you at the moment. If you ignore the essence and jump straight to writing a requirement that contains a technological element, then that technology becomes the requirement and as a result will be implemented. For example, suppose that you have a requirement like this:

> *The product shall beep and put a flashing message on the screen if a weather station fails to transmit readings.*

If a requirement contains the means of implementation, then it is a solution, not a requirement.

What's wrong here? Several things. First, the "requirement" contains technology—the screen and flashing message—that might not be the best solution. Additionally, an assumption is made that the operator will see the flashing message, pick up the phone, and call for repairs. The developer is being asked to implement exactly what the requirement says. Even worse, this statement is covering up the real need. If you ask the simple question as to why this requirement exists—in other words, what its essence is—then the answer should be obvious: There is a need to repair a defective weather station.

Now that the essence of the problem is clear, you can think about solutions for it. It is beyond the scope of the IceBreaker work to actually repair the station, but you get a lot closer to the essence if the product sends an alert directly to the repair crew. So you rewrite the requirement as follows:

> The product shall alert the repair crew when a weather station fails to transmit its readings.

Because you have described the real, *essential* requirement, the designer can now cast about and find the most appropriate solution to the correct problem, and the eventual solution will almost certainly be superior.

As another example, consider this requirement for a ticket-selling product for a metro train:

> The traveler shall touch the destination on a route map on a screen.

The stakeholder providing this requirement wanted to employ a touch-sensitive map of the metro network and have the travelers indicate their destination station using their fingers. The product would compute the appropriate fare and, as a bonus, could show an illuminated pathway of the fastest route to the destination. This might be a clever implementation, but the requirement as it now stands does not get to the essence of the problem. The designers could well find better ways to implement a solution if the requirement is expressed in its essential form:

> The product shall determine the traveler's destination.

The designer is now free to find the best way to implement the essence, and can use other technologies to get the traveler's destination into the product. (The touch screen—the stakeholder's first guess at a solution—turned out to be a bad idea: The metro was in a tourist city, and studies showed that many tourists and some regular commuters were not familiar with the rail network and could not locate their destination quickly enough to achieve the target usage speed.)

Simply put, the requirement should not prejudge the implementation, no matter how appealing the technology might be.

Letting go of these preconceptions is not always easy, and over the years we have found the essence to be one of the hardest concepts to convey to our clients and students. It is subtly even more difficult if you are using one of the agile techniques. Agile techniques were developed to produce solutions as efficiently as possible. While these techniques prescribe a conversation between the developers and the business representative, they do not prescribe getting to the essence of the problem and ensuring that your solution is addressing the real problem. You can change this perspective by making the business analyst become part of the conversation, with the responsibility of guiding the participants toward the essence of the problem. An effective way to do so is to have one story card or model containing the suggested solution—there's no reason why you can't start with that—and another story card containing the essence of the problem. Using this quick multiple-viewpoint technique enables you to capture ideas for the solution in parallel with deriving the real essence of the problem. We have found that the more the team members share the understanding of the essence, the more likely they are to change the first idea for solution because they recognize the real problem and almost always find a better solution for it.

When you address the real issues, your solution does not have to be chopped up and changed as successive users tweak it to do the job it should have been doing all along.

If you make the effort to change your process to include discovery of the essence, then you will unearth not only the best solution, but also one that will last even after today's technology falls out of favor. When you address the real issues, your solution does not have to be chopped up and changed as successive users tweak it to do the job it should have been doing all along.

Abstraction

At this stage, it might be helpful to talk a little about *abstraction*. Abstraction and getting to the essence are pretty much the same thing, but possibly abstraction is the more natural way to think about this concept. The word has Latin roots—*abs*, which "means away from," and *trahere*, which means "to draw." Thus abstraction, as we use the term here, is drawing away or removing physical implementation so as to reduce it to its essential characteristics. In other words, an abstraction is the idea, not the implementation.

Perfection is achieved, not when there is nothing more to add, but when there is nothing left to take away.

—Antoine de Saint-Exupery

As an example of abstraction, you probably have several of the following media: CD, vinyl record, cassette tape, iPod, online streaming service, radio, MTV, DVD, and so on. Each of these is an implementation; their abstraction is music. Music is still music no matter how you reproduce it.

Similarly, a business process is a set of activities no matter how you implement it. It does not matter whether the process (now or in the future) is done by a person, computer, robot, mechanical device, or anything else: It is simply a business process. Data is data regardless of whether it is stored in a database, USB flash drive, book, human memory, whiteboard, DVD, the cloud, or any other piece of technology.

Thinking about the abstraction sets you free to find a better implementation. The iPod is a fine MP3 player and for several years has been the preferred player for many people. Even so, if you think of its essence—it plays music—then you are free to find other implementations for that essence, and it is just a small step to find a more convenient implementation. The obvious one is to put this functionality into a telephone, which you are more likely to be carrying about with you. If you think about it, calling it a "telephone" is somewhat of an essential misnomer: A phone today likely plays music, takes photos, organizes your appointments, lets you read books and newspapers, and—inevitably—plays games.

The moral of the story is that for any piece of technology—no matter how beguiling state of the art and attractive it is—you must abstract out the technology and see its underlying essential purpose. Or to paraphrase John F. Kennedy, "Ask not what your technology can do for you, but what the technology is doing."

Swim Lanes Begone

Let's look at a way that business analysts sometimes accidently introduce implementation artifacts into the business problem.

Some business analysts go to a great deal of trouble to add swim lanes to their process models, such as those seen in Figure 7.3. We spoke about modeling the current situation in Chapter 5; while a view of the current implementation is certainly useful, it is also important for the business analyst to ensure that current implementation details are not unnecessarily carried any further. If left there, the swim lanes on the model mislead readers into thinking that the processor boundaries they represent should be preserved for any future implementation. That's probably not what you want. Let's look more closely at the example.

Figure 7.3 shows a model of a business process for a company that processes custom-made furniture. In this model the company's departments show up as swim lanes separating each of the organization's current divisions, and these divisions cover up the essence of the problem.

It works like this: Customers come to the company's website to specify and buy their furniture. From the offered components, customers virtually assemble their desired furniture on-screen, and this mockup acts as the specification for the product they want. Once the customer confirms the order, the Order Control department takes over; it validates the order and processes the customer's payment. The paid-for order is sent to the

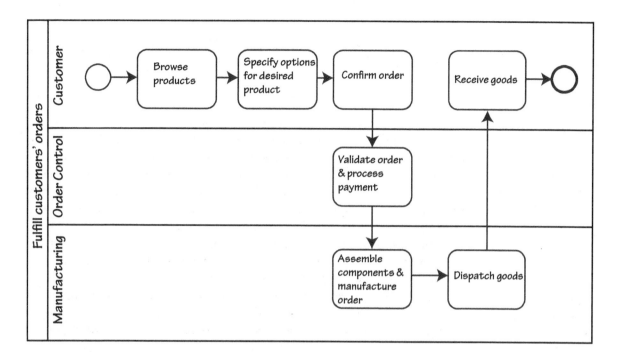

Figure 7.3

A typical process model showing swim lanes; the horizontal lines on the diagram divide the work by current departmental responsibility.

Manufacturing department for construction. At this point the production schedule is updated with the work needed to produce the goods. Herein lies the problem.

Suppose that the Manufacturing department do not have the necessary components and material to complete the order and it will be several weeks or months before the necessary components are available. Or suppose that Manufacturing is so backed up with orders that this new order will not reach the top of the queue for five weeks. Now we have a situation where the customer might want to cancel the order, but, as you can see in the Figure 7.3, the customer has already paid for the goods.

Now delete the swim lanes on this model, and the problem of scheduling becomes quite apparent. At this stage a savvy business analyst would insert a *Prepare Order & Check Inventory* activity *before* the *Confirm Order* activity, as shown in Figure 7.4. By seeing the activities without the swim lanes, the analyst is able to rearrange the process to achieve a better situation, one where the customer knows the delivery time before confirming the order. This could well avert disappointment for customers who are making orders as gifts for birthdays, anniversaries, or Christmas.

When the swim lanes are removed from the model, it is far easier for the business analyst and the stakeholders to see that activities do not have to be carried out in the same place or in the same order in which they have traditionally been done.

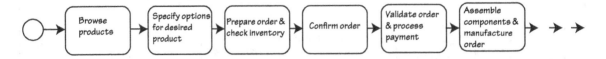

Figure 7.4

The model of the business after removing the swim lanes. Note how the customer can abort the transaction if the inventory is not available. The *Confirm Order* process can now advise the customer of the delivery date.

Remove the swim lanes and see the end-to-end business.

An important step in looking for the essence of the business is to see the end-to-end process and to ignore the current way of dividing the work up among departments. Departments—indeed, any processors (human or automated)—are a result of the way the work was done in the past. Because it arose based on the technology or the business structure available at the time, the current implementation frequently hides the true essence of the business.

Some stakeholders have a problem seeing the work without departmental boundaries, and you may have to convince them that departments are not part of the essence. Step back for a moment and consider why we have departments in our organizations: They exist because we employ humans to do the work. There are very few humans with all the talents needed to do all the tasks in any one organization; as a consequence, we divide the organization up according to the skills of the people we employ. If we did not employ humans, but had a collection of robots that were so multitalented as to be able to carry out all of the tasks needed, then it would be foolish indeed to divide the robots by department (or indeed give them managers). Departments—and please keep in mind that these entities show up as swim lanes in process models—are present merely because of past employment policy.

We urge you to banish your swim lanes and look at the whole of the pool.

Solving the Right Problem

The way of thinking discussed here follows from understanding the abstracted essence. This section is relevant to all requirements analysts, regardless of the size or nature of the project. It is equally applicable to iterative and traditional development methods.

You do not have to be around long before you will observe firsthand the following scenario: The project team builds what they consider to be a really cool product. Yet somehow, despite the project team's enthusiastic cheerleading from the sidelines, not to mention the expense of building the product, the users never seem to put it to use, or use it half-heartedly for a short time and then ask for a truckload of changes. Why, in spite of the project team's best efforts, did this become a pariah product?

Because it solved the wrong problem.

One of our clients, a financial institution, was looking into building a new system that would allow passwords to be reset more efficiently. This task posed a major problem for the organization; the cost of securely establishing its customers' bona fides before resetting their passwords was running at several million dollars per year. The proposed new system would reduce some of the cost of resetting the password.

But what is really happening here? The system producers are looking at a slick new system to establish bona fides more effectively. The real problem—the one they are avoiding or just not seeing—is that *customers forget their passwords*.

The problem the team should be looking at is finding a way for customers to generate secure passwords that they are very unlikely to forget (it can be done). Of course, if you read what we said about essence earlier, you will now be saying, "Hold it! Passwords are a technology for doing something; they are not the essence of the problem." Passwords are not part of the business problem, but rather the bank's chosen technology. Like any other piece of technology, they are less than perfect and appear to be getting in the way of solving the real problem.

Which means that the right problem to solve is this: Allow customers access to their accounts, and do so in a way that is unique for each customer, cannot be guessed or derived by anyone other than the customer, and does not require any special feat of memory on the part of the customer.

The real problem to solve is the real problem; it is not a technological solution. Project teams often set out to solve the wrong problem at the beginning of the project by thinking about the product to be built and the technology they will use, rather than the work to be improved. By looking only at the proposed product, the project team fails to see the larger world—the one that contains the real problem to solve.

READING

Gause, Don, and Jerry Weinberg. *Are Your Lights On? How to Figure Out What the Problem Really Is.* Dorset House, 1990. This book is now quite old and hard to find, but G&W have some delicious things to say about finding the real problem.

READING

Jackson, M. *Problem Frames: Analyzing and Structuring Software Development Problems.* Addison-Wesley, 2001.

Moving into the Future

So far in this book we have been looking at the current implementation of the business, and then deriving the essence of the business and arriving at the correct problem to solve. Of course, all this activity relates to the current business, its current technology, and its current essence. If you refer to the Brown Cow Model, you have achieved respectively the How-Now and the What-Now views of the work.

Once you understand the current essence, it is time to move on to what you want the business to be; this is shown in the Future-What quadrant of the Brown Cow Model. The future business will not be the same as the previous business—your project is meant to improve the work, and here is where you do it. Moving to the Future-What involves questioning and enhancing

Figure 7.5

Having achieved the correct understanding of the work as it is now, we move on to look at what it can be when we finish the project.

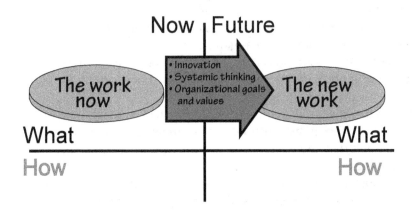

the current business essence to make the business more effective, efficient, and innovative. See Figure 7.5.

Before we get too far into the future, it's worth emphasizing that you must understand the current essence that exists within your work scope—usually defined by a work context diagram, as we discussed in Chapter 3, Scoping the Business Problem. Your thinking about the future might mean that you change this scope because your stakeholders have agreed on some new or changed business policy, and the policy needs a new or different interface with an adjacent system in the outside world.

To start thinking about the Future-What, ask your owner a simple question, "What business do you want to be doing in the future?" While this is a simple question, sometimes it is not so simple to find the answer. At other times, however, it is almost obvious. For example, for many years Amazon was the largest online seller of books printed on paper. Amazon understood that the future of bookselling could be different, so it developed its Kindle reader. This path led Amazon to selling downloadable e-books to be read on the Kindle (or iPad or any of the many other readers that have sprung up), a change that proved to be successful—Amazon now sells more e-books than it does printed books. This change in direction is Amazon's answer to the question, "What business do you want to be doing in the future?"

Moving into the future is not just a matter of wishful thinking; it requires innovative approaches on the part of the business analyst, as well as a willingness to contribute and be open to new ideas on the part of the business stakeholders. What you are doing here is taking the essence of the business as it now stands and changing it to the essence of the business as it will be in the future.

We have to pause here and clarify something. You could say that the essence of Amazon's business did not change—the company is still selling books, just using a different technology to do so. Not quite. What Amazon (or any other bookseller) actually did was to challenge the constraint that a book is always printed on paper. By removing that constraint and saying that the essence of the book is its information content—the words and pictures—then the bookseller can cast about for other, better ways to sell the information content. The ideal bookselling technology would be for the seller to beam the book directly into the brain of the "reader" (no longer the appropriate word). However, until that kind of technology appears, booksellers will have to be content with e-books.

Your innovations for the Future-What state are not necessarily huge changes. When Amazon first started selling (paper) books online, the company quickly gathered information about the book-buying habits of its customers. Amazon also knew the title, genre, author, and other attributes of the books it had for sale. From there, it was not a huge change to develop a new business policy: When a new book arrives from the publisher, compare the attributes of the book with the buying habits of customers and, the next time the customers visit the site, make targeted recommendations.

You can see from this example that sometimes the work possesses some essential knowledge that is not being used to the business's best advantage. Sometimes the business does not recognize its own essential knowledge, or the current implementation makes it difficult to see a new business opportunity.

Similarly, you might be working with stakeholders who are eager and willing to change their business, or you might find that you have to drag them kicking and screaming into the future. Additionally, stakeholders cannot always be relied upon to know exactly what they want. We don't mean that you ignore your customers, but rather be skeptical when they tell you what they want.

Also keep in mind that giving stakeholders exactly what they ask for is often heading down the pathway to oblivion. Customers often ask for incremental improvements to their systems: "I want what I have now, but a few more items of information and a little faster, please." By providing those capabilities and no more, you are turning your back on the innovative leap forward that will result in a superior outcome for the project. Clayton Christensen, in his book *The Innovator's Dilemma*, provides compelling evidence of companies that went out of business by providing exactly what their customers were asking for.

The future work is not just a reimplementation of the current work. You don't find the future work by simply automating all existing manual processes, or by mechanically reimplementing existing computer systems. There is little to be gained by rewriting an old COBOL system in Java.

READING
Christensen, Clayton. *The Innovator's Dilemma: The Revolutionary Book That Will Change the Way You Do Business.* HarperBusiness, 2011.

Nor is the future work the same as the current work with a few extra features tacked on.

To make your project worthwhile, it has to result in some significant step forward for the business. In other words, you and your stakeholders have to innovate and find the significant change, and not just settle for some routine incremental improvement. You are not building just another computer system (the world has plenty of those), but you are improving the work. Granted, that probably means building a computer system, but for maximum value, that system must have its roots in an innovative improvement to the work.

How to Be Innovative

Today's business analyst should always be looking for ways to improve his client's work, and these improvements almost always come about through innovation. Most people do not think of themselves as innovative, but there are some reasonably simple things you can do to encourage yourself to have more and better ideas. Keep in mind that innovation is simply "fresh thinking," and innovation is not the same as invention.

Very few people think of themselves as innovators; but we suggest that almost anybody can be innovative if given the opportunity and some techniques to work with. There are many techniques, and many books discussing these techniques. We will not attempt within the scope of this book to provide a complete treatise on how to be more innovative, but we want to look at a few things you can do that usually result in new ideas to improve the owner's work.

We said a moment ago that your stakeholders might not know what they want; at least they have trouble telling you what they want. But you know that there are three things that people do want and are willing to spend their discretionary[1] money on: *pleasure, prestige,* and *convenience.* Convenience is the most applicable of these for business analysis, but we should quickly look at the other two.

People are willing to pay for pleasure. You simply have to look at the sales of alcohol to see how much people are willing to pay for pleasure (assuming, of course, that people are not merely buying the stuff to drink themselves to oblivion). Going to the movies or watching a movie at home is also an example of people paying for pleasure; as is a woman buying perfume (which is pleasurable to both the woman and other people); as is paying for a properly made cappuccino instead of drinking the brown liquid from the machine in the hall. There are many more examples in our everyday lives. The opportunity for most businesses to provide pleasure is limited, but it should not stop you from asking, "Can we make our customers' interaction with our company more pleasurable?" Most of us would rather part with our money in places where the experience is pleasurable, and we tend to avoid places where doing business is decidedly unpleasant.

People are also willing to pay for prestige. Why do people buy a Mercedes when a Toyota will adequately and comfortably get them to their

FOOTNOTE 1
Discretionary money does not have to be spent—its disposal proceeds at the whim of the spender. It does not include the things that we have to spend money on: food, shelter, transport to work, basic clothing, and so on.

destination? Because a Mercedes makes its owner feel that he has a better car than the other fellow. Apple's iPod captured a huge share of the market because people thought it more prestigious that other, clunky MP3 players. Perhaps iPod owners expressed their feelings for the device as "cool"—but is not being cool a form of prestige, particularly if something makes you cooler than your contemporaries? Leica markets a range of high-quality cameras; Panasonic sells the identical cameras at a significantly lower price. Despite Panasonic's price advantage, the equivalent Leicas continue to sell. Why? Because people want the prestige of owning a Leica: the red spot on the front of the camera that shows that they are using a camera from one of the best optical companies in the world.

Despite their attractiveness, however, such opportunities for providing prestige are generally limited for most companies. That leaves us with convenience as a target for people's discretionary (and nondiscretionary) money.

People are willing to pay—sometimes a considerable amount—for convenience. A ready example is the mobile phone. We put up with some fairly dire quality issues—dropped calls, poor reception, and high prices—just to have the convenience of making and receiving calls wherever we are. As mentioned earlier, Netflix was able to take advantage of people's desire for convenience by providing downloadable movies, and not asking its customers to go to the store to pick up a DVD, and then take it back. Bricks-and-mortar bookshops are (sadly) disappearing with the advent of online shopping for books. The rapid uptake of the Kindle and other e-book readers shows the degree to which we favor convenience.

People are willing to pay for convenience.

Think back over the years of music reproduction. Each new generation of device—the wax cylinder, the shellac disc, the vinyl disc, the cassette, the CD, the MP3 player—was adopted because it provided more convenience. It is debatable whether each of these advances brought better-quality reproduction; many audio enthusiasts still prefer the well-pressed vinyl disc to CD reproduction. MP3s are definitely a retrograde step in the fidelity of a reproduction. Nevertheless, each generation of device provided a step up in the convenience of reproducing and accessing music.

Convenience is something that your business can provide. It is not that difficult a task, but to offer this feature, first you must take a step back from your proposed solution and look at it from the user's point of view. Think of the user's essential objective (use the term "essence" as we earlier discussed) and try to get him to that objective using fewer steps than you have already planned. You can copy ideas if you like: Look at how Amazon does things—it did not become the premier online book retailer by being hard to use. As a small but important piece of convenience, Amazon retains every address in an account to which the user has had purchases shipped: Instead of entering the shipping address, a customer directs the shipment to one of the stored addresses. Convenient? Yes. Easy to do? Yes. Can you do something like that in your business? Yes.

Can you provide an additional service that your user would find convenient? Almost certainly. Take a look at any service that your organization provides. Brainstorm with a few like-minded colleagues, and we guarantee that you will come up with several ideas for adding a service—and thereby convenience—to something that the organization already provides.

There are many things you can do to make your products and solutions more convenient. Such an effort requires not much more than a little time and a little thought. To be successful, however, you have to look at the product through the eyes of the customer, or the person who is to use whatever it is you plan to build. Seeing things through the customer's eyes is not always easy, but the cardinal rule is to disregard what *you* think, and instead come at it from the customer's side. Later in this chapter we discuss personas as a way of understanding things from your customer's way of thinking.

Look at your proposed product through the eyes of the customer—can you make it more convenient?

Systemic Thinking

As well as innovating, moving into the future means *thinking systemically* about the work, the whole problem, the end-to-end system. Sometimes, when you consider the entirety in preference to the parts, you are better able to see how you can rearrange those parts to form a more beneficial system for the future.

It now falls to you in your role as a business analyst to lead the quest for the future work. Often, remarkably often, the future work is apparent as soon as you start applying systemic thinking to the current work. Simply by seeing the bigger picture of the current work, it becomes readily apparent what the future work should be.

Look at the parts, but at the aggregation of the parts.

Systemic thinking, depicted in Figure 7.6 as a series of interlocking cogs, is appropriate at requirements time. The basic idea of systemic thinking is to regard the business as a system—that is, a set of connected parts that produces something none of the parts can do alone. So let's not look at the parts but at the *aggregation* of the parts and the ways in which they interact. This exploration will help us see how they might interact in the future.

" What we have to understand is how the work works. "

—John Seddon

Looking too narrowly, by looking only at the proposed product, inhibits systemic thinking. The product's fundamental functionality and the ways in which it seeks to interact with the user are certainly important, but what the product is doing within the larger scope of the organization is more important. Step back and see how your product affects the rest of the work.

Instead of looking inwardly at the solution, step back and look at the whole of the work that you want to improve.

Suppose you are talking to an engineer as one of the stakeholders in the road de-icing project. The engineer asks for "The product to show a map that marks the roads that need treatment in red, and the roads that are safe in blue." (This was one of the original statements of requirements; we are not making this up.) Note that the engineer is concentrating on the product and his proposed solution for the interface. Now, step back a little and think about the work as a whole—think systemically.

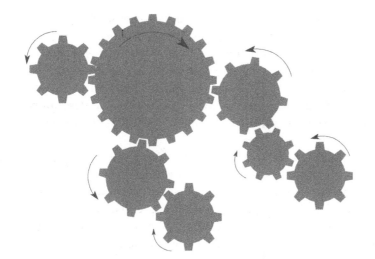

Figure 7.6

Systemic thinking, sometimes called systems thinking, requires that you see the system as a whole. Any system is a set of interconnected functions, and the outcome of one function might have an effect on another. Just as with a set of cogs, when one function does something, it causes others to react.

First consider the request for red roads and blue roads: This engineer has asked for this color scheme because of his personal preferences. But stepping back just a little, you have to ask if everyone will interpret red and blue the same way this fellow does. It is perfectly reasonable to say that blue represents cold and red is the universal color for hot, which means that it is highly likely that another user would make the contrary interpretation, leading to exactly the wrong result.

If you take one more step back and ask why the roads have to be identified on-screen (using *any* color scheme), you get the answer that the engineer has to tell the depot to dispatch a truck to treat the iced-up roads. From a systemic point of view, this answer means that in the wider scope of the whole of the work, there is a need to inform the truck depot of the roads to be treated. Once you see the problem in this way, then you would build a product that informs the depot directly of this need and dispense with color-coded screens and engineers phoning the depot.

Now take one more step back: If a truck has to be dispatched, then there is a need within the work to allocate a truck, and this truck should be the one that makes the most sense when you consider (another step back) that many trucks are attached to the depot. From a systemic point of view, if you are to think about building a product to treat roads, then fleet optimization must be part of the solution.

Let's go even further with our systemic point of view: What if the depot has insufficient resources to treat all of the unsafe roads? Perhaps there is a way of requesting resources from geographically neighboring counties, or asking the police to close the untreated roads and advising the traffic radio service that this has been done? When a road is closed, could the work also recommend an alternative route? We may be getting a little far away from the original screen with its blue and red roads, but along the way systemic thinking has turned up some interesting possibilities.

The idea of systemic thinking is to think about the entirety of the business, how its component parts interact with one another and, most importantly, what *effect* they have on one another. Instead of looking at a neat process flow diagram, or following someone's textual description of a process, think about how the different parts of the system *influence* each other. Figure 7.7 shows this concept.

At this stage you could be thinking, "Wait a minute! My job title is business *analyst*. Analysis involves breaking things up and studying the components." Analytical thinking is, of course, useful and necessary, but we are suggesting—forcefully suggesting—that you enhance your analytical skills with systemic thinking and instead of just analyzing each component, you consider how the components *affect* one another.

John Seddon—an author whose work we recommend—speaks of looking at both *value demand* and *failure demand*. Value demand arises when customers make requests or order whatever your organization sells or provides. Failure demand occurs when those same customers make complaints or ask for repairs to what they have been sold. Obviously, when your product or service fails, it costs you money to put things right or repair the product. Thus finding the points at which the system fails is worthwhile. However, the causes of failure demand are often rooted deeply within the organization, and can be found only by looking at the organization as a whole. This, then, is systemic thinking.

The moral of the story is that instead of concentrating on the first solution that you are given, you step back and look at the problem from a wider scope. By questioning the underlying reason for each of the elements in the solution, and by studying the effect that any one element can have on another, you end up deriving more realistic requirements and, as a result, produce a better end product.

READING

Ackoff, Russell, and Herbert Addison. *Systems Thinking for Curious Managers: With 40 New Management f-Laws.* Triarchy Press, 2010.

Seddon, John. *Systems Thinking in the Public Sector.* Triarchy Press, 2010.

Meadows, Donella. *Thinking in Systems: A Primer.* Earthscan Ltd, 2009.

Senge, Peter. *The Fifth Discipline: The Art and Practice of The Learning Organization,* revised edition. Crown Business, 2006.

Figure 7.7

Some of the activities in this business have an effect on others. This effect, or influence, is shown by the gray arrows. Systemic thinking involves thinking about the outcome of the system as a whole and understanding the consequences of every action.

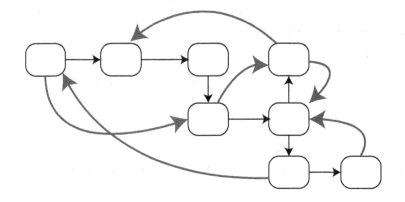

Value

Our premise for doing requirements is that if you build a piece of software, a consumer product, or a service, then it must be valuable to its owner, so let's for a moment consider *value*. We are using the term to mean something that you are prepared to pay for—in other words, you make your decision as to whether to buy something based on its value to you. When you feel that the outlay is worthwhile for whatever it is, then you spend your money on it. If you feel that it is not worth the asking price, then for you it is not good value and you do not buy it.

Sometimes making the value decision is straightforward. For example, your authors travel widely for their work and from time to time we have to get a visa before we can enter a country. We use a visa service that sends a courier to collect the application form and passport from our home, take them to the embassy in question, and return the next day with the visa stamped in the passport. As an alternative, we could choose to stand in line and wait to get the visa application accepted, and then wait again to have it approved, and then come back the next day to pick up the passport. However, we are willing to pay for the visa service because we think that it provides value: We feel that the time it saves us is better spent doing other things—for example, writing this book—and because the visa service achieves faster turnaround than we could do ourselves, we are not stuck without a passport when trips are close together. The point is that we value time enough to warrant paying a moderate fee to someone else to save some of it for us. However, if the cost of the visa service becomes too expensive, or if we are not particularly busy at the time, then it ceases to be valuable to us.

But you, dear reader, do not have to deal with easy stuff like personal preferences and values. Rather, you are focusing on an organization's value—specifically, the organization that is to own the product you are developing. You have to determine what this organization values and what it wants to achieve. If you are dealing with a commercial organization, then the value can usually be expressed in money terms—money saved or money earned. Scientific organizations value the accuracy or the extent of their research. Real-time control organizations value correct and infallible operation. Organizations building products for sale value innovative and useful products that attract their customers' attention.

Perhaps it is easiest to think about value if we look at three factors: *reward, penalty,* and *cost*. There is, of course, an overriding consideration—the *goal* of the project that you established back in the project blastoff. Then, for any unit of work such as a business use case, or for any requirement, you score each of the three value factors based on how much it contributes to the goal.

Value can be thought of as encompassing three factors: reward, penalty, and cost.

For example, suppose you have a requirement that your product must have a secure way of logging on. The reward for this feature is low—perhaps a score of 1 or 2 on a scale of 1 to 5. It doesn't gain you any extra customers or improve the owning organization. Conversely, the penalty for *not* having it is high: Your customers will desert you if they think your product is not secure. Additionally, if sensitive information falls into the wrong hands and it transpires that you did not do enough to protect the information, you could face criminal charges. We would score the penalty for this outcome as 5—very high. The cost of having a secure product is moderate; you can buy off-the-shelf security that will be perfectly adequate for most situations. Let's score cost as a 3. So this requirement is valuable to you: The cost to have it is less than the cost of not having it.

Let's consider a different business use case, one where the customer buys your goods. The reward for having this capability is (obviously) high: You can score that as 5. The penalty for not having it is also high (5 again), and the cost is moderate to high (let's say 4). Collectively, all of this means that this capability is valuable, so you include it in your product.

Alternatively, you might consider the capability of providing free delivery for your product. The reward for this service is high; let's say it scores 4 because customers will appreciate the convenience. The penalty for not doing it is low; nobody really expects free delivery for lower-priced goods. The cost is high—it would eat up a significant portion of the profit from selling the goods, so we score cost as a 5. Is this service valuable? No, the cost exceeds the reward, so you would discard this capability.

For any business use case, you measure value with the objective of including only those facilities that are valuable (taking into account reward, penalty, and cost) to the owner. We suggest that the real problem—the one you are trying to understand—includes only high-value functionality.

Personas

Personas are useful when real users are not available or are too numerous for you to interview all of them. The persona is a virtual character that substitutes for the human users. We strongly sugest using a persona when you do not have access to the real users or customers. Almost always, the persona is a better representation of the user than a human proxy.

A persona is an invented personality; an imaginary but nevertheless archetypical user or customer for whom you are gathering requirements for your product. Why an imaginary character when there are potentially thousands of real users out there? Because, for a mass-market product, or one that is to be used by more than a dozen different people, you don't know, and can't get to know, all of the real users. But you can know one really well, and that imaginary user's attributes guide your requirements: This is your persona.

You don't invent your persona, but rather derive it from market research or other surveys into your likely user population. The degree of precision

needed varies in proportion to both the size of the user base and the critical-
ity of the product to be built. In any event, most teams write a one- or two-
page description that identifies the persona's behavior patterns, goals, skills,
attitudes, and environment. It is also usual, and indeed desirable, to include
enough personal details—including a name—to make the persona seem real
to you and your team. You can, of course, have more than one persona for a
product, but there should be one who is the primary target of the product.
We also find it useful to have a photograph—you can find thousands of
photos in the online stock photo agencies—and you select one that the team
agrees is their image of your persona.

Using a persona makes it easier for business analysts and innovators to
think about their customers' needs. When they can see a photo and speak
about the persona by name as someone real, it puts a human face on what
otherwise would be abstract data about potential customers. The question
to ask is not what a set of data wants, but "What does Emma [or whatever
you have called your persona] want?" or "What would Emma do in this
situation?"

READING
Cooper, Alan, Robert
Reimann, and David Cronin.
*About Face 3: The Essentials
of Interaction Design,* third
edition. Wiley, 2007

Personas avoid what Alan Cooper calls the "elastic user," whereby different stakeholders define the characteristics of the product to be everything
they have in mind, and to accommodate their own assumptions about the
kind of user they are building for. The result is usually too many requirements, many of which conflict with one another, and a product that, by trying to satisfy everyone, satisfies none of its intended audience. Today you can
see some wonderful consumer products that fit exactly our own personal
preferences. This is not because the product's builders know you, but because
they selected a persona whose attributes matched (more or less) yours. In
contrast, if you try to write the requirements for a product to suit everybody
on the planet, the functionality would be so heavy as to make the software
too large to be installed on any known computer—trying to suit everybody
will end up suiting nobody.

Having a persona also prevents stakeholders from defining the user as
themselves. This "self-referential" approach (see Figure 7.8) almost always
yields idiosyncratic results with one stakeholder finding the product easy
and intuitive, but the rest of the audience not responding to the product in
quite the same way.

The realness of the persona gives the business analysts and stakeholders
a target at which to aim their new system. Details such as computer literacy,
attitude toward technology, cultural taboos and viewpoints, gender bias,
and so on act as a guide. This apparent reality also tells the designers what
the normal case is, and what the persona will find to be the exceptions or
edge cases. Such understanding usually prevents the designers from focusing
the product on the abnormal cases or user behavior.

Figure 7.8

The self-referential user considers himself only, and inadvertently disregards the wishes or needs of the wider audience.

READING

Norman, Donald. *The Design of Everyday Things.* Doubleday, 1988. Despite the relative age of this book, Norman's words on clarity of purpose hold true today.

Your authors have a local government client in one of the London boroughs, part of whose responsibilities is to provide meals for aged people and others who are not able to provide for themselves. We worked with the team who manage this service with the aim of finding a new future state of this work. The assignment was to help the team to decide what the borough council could do to improve the service of providing meals for the elderly. The team came up with a persona whom team members considered to be an archetypical recipient of the meals, and then they began asking, "What service does Elsie really want?" The answers were a revelation to many of the team members; until this time they had designed this service to more or less suit their own experience. Elsie—her photo smiled down on the team—gave them answers that made for a far better and well-received service. See Figure 7.9.

When we talk about requirements for software, we often speak of "user requirements." The problem with this term is that requirements are gathered for *anyone* who could be a user. The way to build a successful product is not to gather requirements that mete out something for everyone, but rather to *thrill* the actual users.

Figure 7.9

The team used a persona to represent their customers. By treating the persona as a real person, they were able to devise a far superior Future-What version of their work.

Challenging Constraints

Challenging constraints—seriously questioning constraints and seeking to remove them—is something that every business analyst should be doing. A constraint in this case is an imposed restriction on the problem or solution space—it might be a piece of business policy that says a process must be done in a certain way, a directive about the way in which the solution must be implemented, or about almost anything at all. The problem with constraints is that everyone assumes the constraints are real and immutable.

Let's question that.

Suppose that for any constraint, the business analyst challenges it by asking, "Is this constraint real? What would the result be if I pretended for the moment that this constraint did not exist?" Sometimes the answer is that it is impossible to remove the constraint because lives will be lost (or the corporate equivalent), and sometimes you find that it is entirely possible to remove the constraint, and doing so brings with it an innovation, which is your reason for challenging it in the first place.

Let us suppose that there is a constraint that you have to sell your company's product or service at a profit. Seems reasonable enough. But now let's challenge that truism and see what happens. Better still, let's look at an example where the creator seemed to ignore profit and gave the product away. A little while ago, the rock band Radiohead gave away its recording "In Rainbows." The band posted the song on their website and asked fans to pay whatever they wanted to pay, including nothing at all. The publicity, and the new fans this attracted, meant that when the CD was eventually released, it sold well beyond expectations. Many new musicians mimic this approach by freely giving their music away to generate a fan base, and their return is the money they make from live concerts. Look at your app store—there are lots of free apps available that either offer a taste of the fully featured, payable app or serve as a vehicle for advertising. Either way, these apps are a result of removing the constraint of having to make a profit.

Constraints are often really *assumptions* about the way in which the organization currently does business. For example, it is either an assumption or a constraint that bills are paid by the Accounting department. Analysts at a large American car builder challenged this constraint. Before they did so, the scenario went like this: When parts deliveries were made, the dock foreman would check the delivery, collect and send the paperwork to the accounting people, who, after a certain amount of processing and receipt of an invoice, would pay the supplier. This process is illustrated in Figure 7.10.

When the constraint was challenged and eventually removed, the resultant process was changed to this: The goods would be delivered, the dock foreman would check that the delivery matched the order, and the dock foreman

Figure 7.10

This activity diagram shows the process for receiving goods and eventually paying for them. This is what the process looked like before the constraints were challenged. Note the use of the swim lanes, which made any systemic approach more difficult.

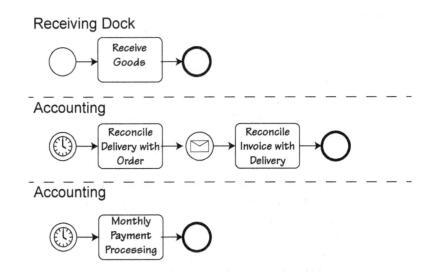

would authorize a check that was immediately printed and handed to the driver. This process is illustrated in Figure 7.11.

The new process has several advantages. It is less expensive because it eliminated the costly processing by the Accounting department. And while traditionally organizations like to pay bills as late as possible, in this case the company saved money by paying the bill immediately. The reason for delaying payment is usually to keep the money in the payer's bank account where it earns interest. However, in these days of low (or zero) interest and poor economy, the discount you get for immediate payment always exceeds any interest that can be earned.

Challenging constraints often results in some surprising (and beneficial) innovations. Consider these constraints: For some countries, you need a visa to visit them; in addition, the visa must be stamped in the passport as proof of having it. The Australian Immigration Department challenged this constraint, and the beneficial result is this: To get a visa, you apply online. If you are the right kind of person, you are granted a visa and informed of that fact while you are online; nothing is stamped in your passport (Figure 7.12). When you arrive at your entry point into Australia, the immigration officer scans the barcode in your passport and his screen tells him that the holder

Figure 7.11

The streamlined process that resulted from challenging the constraints. The check handed to the driver has now been superceded by making an immediate bank transfer.

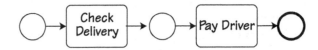

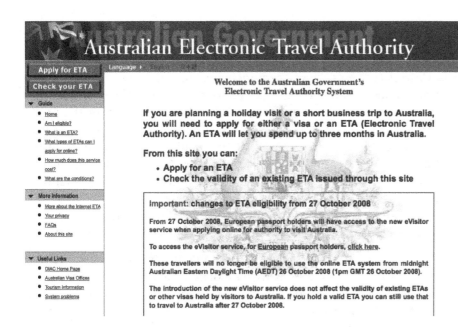

Figure 7.12

The Australian government provides an innovative (and very convenient) facility for online applications for visas. Screenshot used with permission from its source, the Department of Immigration and Citizenship.

has been granted a visa. The net return to the department is that this change cuts down the expense of processing, not to mention the time expended by visa applicants queuing up to get visas stamped in their passport at Australian consulates around the world. Check out the department's website (www .immi.gov.au) to see its innovative approach to immigration and visas.

Innovation Workshops

Innovation workshops are one way of generating ideas. Use them when a large number of stakeholders are involved in the innovation process. These workshops are also appropriate when you want stakeholders to see the advantages of developing a new and better way of working instead of just rebuilding the same old system.

We suggest that as part of moving into the future, you set aside a little time for innovation workshops. These joint sessions are held for the purpose of generating innovations to improve the work. One of the problems we have noticed with innovation is that few people think of themselves as innovative, and fewer people think being innovative is part of their job description. However, we suggest that innovation is part of everyone's job description—it is only through innovation that we progress.

The workshops are a place where you and the stakeholders work together to innovate a better piece of work. You, as the business analyst, have to lead the charge in innovation. We have found that stakeholders are sometimes unwilling to give up time for this activity, but once they experience the improvements generated by the workshop, they become keen participants.

 If there was no innovation, you would be riding a horse to work.

The outcome of the workshops was several hundred innovative requirements.

When Eurocontrol decided to investigate the requirements for the air traffic control systems of the future, the organization found it difficult to think past how things are done now. With our colleague Neil Maiden from City University, we developed requirements creativity workshops as a way of encouraging air traffic controllers, pilots, airline representatives, and systems developers to come up with innovative improvements for the future system. The outcome of the workshops was several hundred innovative requirements. Participants agreed that the requirements coming from the workshops made a significant, almost startling difference to the eventual air traffic product. They also agreed that these requirements would never have seen the light of day but for the creativity workshops.

We suggest something along these lines for planning and running innovation workshops:

1. Set the scope of the innovation. It should not be too narrow, as many innovations are originally thought of as outside the remit of the team. Invite all stakeholders who have an interest in this scope to participate in the workshop.

2. Partition the scope using business events to allow the participants to concentrate on the end-to-end business processes, while keeping in mind that systemic thinking usually involves all of the business events.

3. Plan the workshop. You will probably have to use several innovation techniques. Some of these are discussed in this book, and a number of excellent texts on creativty also available. You will have to facilitate the workshop and lead your stakeholder through the techniques.

4. Record everything that happens in the workshop. *Do not try and assess ideas during the workshop.* Innovating and assessing are two separate activities and should not be tackled at the same time.

5. After the workshop, feed the results back to participants.

6. Incubate. Sometimes the really great idea does not happen for some time. People are quite capable of coming back days later with some profound improvement to one of the workshop innovations.

These workshops are intended to be more structured than regular brainstorming sessions. The intention is to use a mixture of innovation techniques to generate a more interesting outcome.

We cannot recommend one innovation technique over another; people inevitably find that one technique may suit them, yet not others. Innovation is essentially a human activity, so we suggest you use techniques that you are comfortable with and that you like using.

READING
Silverstein, David, Philip Samuel, and Neil DeCarlo. *The Innovator's Toolkit*. John Wiley & Sons, 2009.

Brainstorming

Brainstorming is one way of innovating. It is useful for generating lots of contributions regarding the scope of the problem, or what it could be. This strategy is not intended to promote unconstrained scope creep. Instead, the brainstorming session generates ideas that could lead to a better product without incurring additional expense.

Brainstorming takes advantage of the group effect. That is, you gather a group of bright, willing people, and ask them to generate as many ideas as possible for the new product (Figure 7.13). Tell them that *any* ideas are acceptable, no matter how crazy they may seem, and that they must not slow the process down by criticizing or debating ideas. The aim is to be as imaginative as possible, and to generate as many ideas as possible, often by using the ideas of others to trigger a different idea of their own.

There are some simple rules for brainstorming:

- Participants in the brainstorming session should come from a wide range of disciplines, with as broad a range of experience as possible. This mixture of backgrounds brings many more creative ideas to the fore.

- For the moment, suspend judgment, evaluation, criticism, and, most importantly, debate. Simply record requirements as they are generated. The practice of not stopping the flow is the fastest way to develop a creative and energized atmosphere for the brainstorming group.

- Produce lots of ideas. Come up with as many ideas as possible. Quantity will, in time, produce quality.

- Try to come up with as many ideas as you can that are unconventional, unique, crazy, and wild. The wilder the idea, the more creative it probably is, and often the more likely it is to turn into a really useful requirement.

Figure 7.13

A brainstorming session is a gathering of interested people whose task is to generate new ideas for the product.

- Piggyback a new idea onto an old one. That is, build one idea on top of another.

Ideas disappear faster than water evaporates unless written down.

—Alex Osborne, the founder of brainstorming

- Write every idea down, without censoring.

- If you get stuck, seed the session with a word pulled randomly from a dictionary, and ask participants to make word associations that have some bearing on the product.

- Make the session fun. You cannot mandate creativity; you have to let it come naturally. You won't see many ground-breaking ideas if the boss is present at the session and says something like, "I want to hear only ideas that are marketable."

After the brainstorming session, the lead business analysts and key stakeholders evaluate the list of ideas. Some of them will be worthless, but they will have served their brainstorming purpose—inspiring other, more useful ideas. Some ideas may need to be merged with others—perhaps two half-formed ideas, when put together, will make some useful new idea. Keep the best of the ideas and, providing there is a reasonable chance of implementing them within the project constraints, turn them into requirements.

Back to the Future

Let's return to what we are doing here. Your task is to change the current work into the future work, or as we have described it previously, to transform the How-Now into the Future-What. Looked at it another way, this effort involves changing business policy, and the new policy should be innovative. As we have said several times—and it is worth repeating—there is little value in simply reimplementing some old piece of work. If your project is to provide something valuable to the organization, then it must provide an advance, some fresh thinking, to make the end product as useful as possible.

Our job is to give the client, on time and on cost, not what he wants, but what he never dreamed he wanted; and when he gets it, he recognizes it as something he wanted all the time.

—Denys Lasdon, architect

You must not be afraid to innovate. Customers—both the internal stakeholders and the external business customers—don't always know what they want. Apple, which is by any standard the most innovative company in the world, almost studiously avoids traditional market research. By its own admission, Apple builds not what people say they want, but what Apple thinks its customers are ready for. People usually don't know what they want until they see it, so your task is to give them something to see. Improving the work means delivering a product that when they get it, the users realize it is what they want.

The future work should provide a better response to the business customers, or for products to be used internally, a better way of working for the users. This means giving them something they did not have before, or providing a facility that makes their task easier.

We have suggested using a persona, and looking at the product from the point of view of the persona. This usually results in a change to the work to make it more acceptable—convenient—to the end user or customer. Even eliminating a single step from a buying or ordering process may make a difference. Play through your work from the persona's point of view and see if you can make it more convenient. And remember—you are not trying to please yourself.

The outcome of thinking in the Future-How segment of the Brown Cow Model is a number of models of the future work. These need not be elaborate; we typically use simple scenarios and sketches to elicit the concurrence of the stakeholders. You will, of course, need the full cooperation of the stakeholders, as the Future-What represents a new business policy or the new work to do. Once you have agreed on the extent of the work, define the boundaries of the Future-What view by updating your work context diagram and adding to or changing your event list as needed.

Everybody wants an exciting future—make sure your future work does not disappoint.

Starting the Solution

in which we bring the essence of the business into the technological world of the implementation

We have arrived at the point where we move away from the virtual, abstract, and perfect world that exists above the line, and bring the business requirements into the reality of the technological world that lies below the line. The line we refer to here is the horizontal line of the Brown Cow Model, and we are moving from the third quadrant (Future–What) to the fourth quadrant (Future–How), as illustrated in Figure 8.1. In doing so, we are moving from an abstract world to the physical world; from policy to technology; from

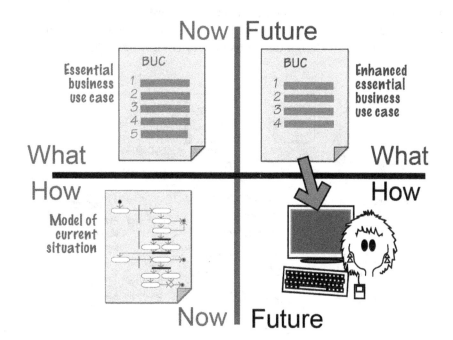

Figure 8.1

You have reached the last quadrant of the Brown Cow Model. Here you decide how you are going to implement the essential business.

problem to solution; from purpose to design. In this fourth quadrant, we begin the design of a solution to the business problem.

Now that you and your stakeholders have a solid understanding of the essence of the business—the real problem to be solved—it is time to determine which parts of that problem would benefit from being automated. To put that another way, how much of the essential business policy can you beneficially carry out with an automated product, be it software, hardware, or otherwise? You can also think of this activity as deciding the automation boundary.

But there is more to it than simply ring-fencing some of the required functionality and declaring that it should be automated. To arrive at an elegant solution, you must consider, and probably design, the experience that results from your choice of automation boundary. In other words, you must deliver the required functionality so that it works in a way that readily fits into the users' work customs, meets the operational needs of the organization, contributes to the organization's goals, and does so at a price that pleases the owner.

Note that we *arrive* at the Future-How view of the product after having first spent some effort discovering what the product is meant to do. Unfortunately, many software projects *begin* with the Future-How; they leap directly to a solution to an as-yet-unstated (and probably not-understood) problem. We sincerely hope that if you are still reading this book, we have been able to show you why it is worth spending the time to understand the real business need before attempting to come up with a solution.

We cannot make this book an exhaustive treatise on the design of software and organizational systems. Each organization has its own unique implementation environment, which means that the designers will come up with a unique design. Nevertheless, we can identify the variables that you need to consider to make the design decisions in your environment. See Figure 8.2.

Figure 8.2

The business analyst juggles many factors to decide the most appropriate product to build.

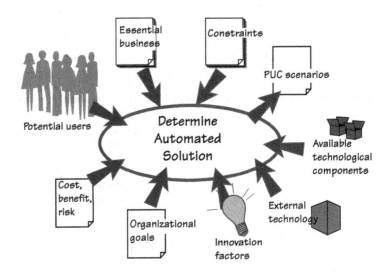

Iterative Development

Iterative development techniques don't always appear to do much in the way of upfront design, relying instead on frequent releases of software to gauge the design's suitability. Although this approach can certainly work, it can be time-consuming if the initial releases are not very close to what is actually needed, or if the problem is so poorly understood or defined by the stakeholders that any solution is bound to be wide of the mark. In any event, it is usually more efficient to begin the discovery of need with abstract models and conversations, instead of concrete implementations.

Unfortunately, many projects begin with a proposed solution—in our terms, this means starting in the fourth quadrant, the Future-How. By starting here, the development team has to hammer and cajole the solution into some semblance of what is needed, and at the same time attempt to discover what is really needed. Many practitioners find that they are forced to start in the Future-How quadrant, move back to the Future-What view to find out what is really needed, and then proceed once more to the Future-How view of the solution.

No matter how you are developing software, the important part of this process is the discovery, by both you and your stakeholders, of the real needs of the solution.

Essential Business

We have discussed the essence of the business in various places throughout this book, most notably in Chapter 7, so there is no need to repeat all of that information here. Suffice it to say that before starting on a solution, you will have collected a good chunk of the functional needs and a significant portion of the non-functional needs for the work that you have been studying. Moreover, you will have collected these as essential, or technology-free, needs.

The functional needs can be presented to you in the form of a business use case (BUC) scenario, a collection of atomic functional requirements, or properly crafted user stories. The level of detail that you address before thinking about the solution will vary depending on your project strategy and the way in which you are working with all the stakeholders. Chapter 9 is devoted to strategies for getting from needs to solutions.

An understanding of the non-functional needs of the essential business is important to crafting a valuable solution. The non-functional requirements—such things as usability, look and feel, operational, environmental, security, and so on—must be taken into account when making choices about the solution. The non-functional needs are largely responsible for specifying the kind of user experience appropriate for the intended audience. We will return to these needs later in the chapter when we look at designing the experience.

As we have said before, it is crucial that the business analyst and the associated stakeholders have a clear understanding of the real needs—that is, the essential requirements—before attempting to find a solution. If the essential requirements are missing, then any solution must be at best a shot in the dark, and at worst a solution for a problem that may not have existed.

Determine the Extent of the Product

It is only by first understanding the work, and then automating part of it, that we achieve a seamless fit between the automated product and the work.

FOOTNOTE 1
Some readers might like to consider using John Hauser and Don Clausing's *House of Quality*. This technique comprises a graphic way of setting out the relationship between the customer's needs/wants and the capabilities of the proposed product. Hauser and Clausing refer to these elements as the "whats" and the "hows," respectively. You can find tutorials and templates on the Web for further reference.

Getting the right product scope is crucial to getting the right requirements.

The task of business analysis is to determine what the work should be in the future and how the product can best contribute to that work. As noted earlier in this text, business use cases are responses to requests from the outside world for the work's service. The optimal response is to provide the most valuable service (from the outsider's point of view) at the lowest cost in terms of time, materials, or effort (from your organization's point of view), and in the most pleasing and encouraging manner (from the end user's point of view). Thus the product you craft should be a contributor to the optimal business use case—one that makes the product cheaper and faster and more convenient and all of the other things your project is to deliver.[1]

Your task in determining the future product is to find the best way to achieve the desired outcome for the business use case—the one closest to the essence of the work. The product is the part of the business use case you choose to automate; so let's look at an example of how we determine what part of the essential work is to become the product.

Consider the situation depicted by a data flow diagram in Figure 8.3. In this typical business use case, we see a customer (an adjacent system) ordering groceries over the telephone. Where is the best place to put the product boundary? Or, thinking of this issue in another and better way, which product boundary would make the best product?

What about the product that would result from boundary number 1? Putting the product boundary here would result in an operator entering the checked order and the product recording the order after the credit card company has authorized it. This choice does not yield a very good product, as it forces the operator to do most of the work and misses several opportunities for automation. It also ignores any potential improvements to the service provided to the customer.

What about boundary number 2? The user—in this case, the telephone representative—takes the order over the telephone and enters it into the product, which then does the credit card check and records the order. Not bad, but perhaps we could do better.

Boundary number 3 automates all of the order-taking work. Customers make a telephone call to a product capable of recognizing voice input or recognizing commands from the telephone keypad. Provided no questions arise and no serious responses are needed, customers get the advantage of calling 24

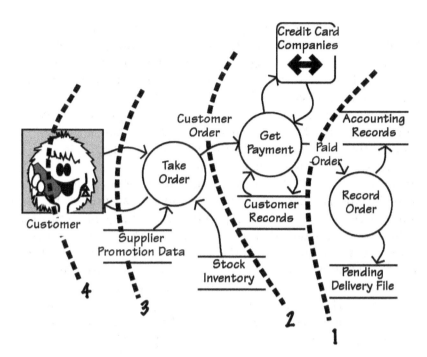

Figure 8.3

Once you understand the complete business use case, you establish how much of it will be done by the product. The dotted lines in the figure represent alternative product boundaries. Each proposed automation is whatever functionality (shown as circles) appears to the right of the dotted line.

hours a day. An alternative solution to boundary number 3 is that customers could log on to the grocery company's website and submit their orders online.

Solution number 3 might be convenient for the grocery company, but what about the customer? Do customers want to talk to machines or click choices on a website? Does this approach depersonalize the shopping experience so much that the customer feels alienated? Alternatively, which type of service should the grocery company provide to keep the customer's loyalty? Also keep in mind that before picking up the phone (or logging on), the customer would have to survey the groceries already in the home to see what is needed.

What about solution number 4? Here we see that the product boundary has been pushed all the way into the customer's home. This solution would take over most of the work previously done by the customer. This solution would count the groceries and trigger the order, perhaps with some collaboration with the customer. This is a higher-risk solution, but it might be attractive enough to the customers to make it a worthwhile approach.

Consider the Users

Whatever it is that you intend to build, someone has to use it. If you alone will use the product, or if you just couldn't give a damn, then feel free to skip ahead and ignore this section. Conversely, if you intend to sell your solution, or if you need people to voluntarily start using it, then it stands to reason that you will want to make the product attractive to its intended audience. With the exception of embedded systems and a few categories of commercial software, everything you design will be used by humans. This simple and unavoidable fact means that it is necessary to consider the human user and what is most appropriate for him.

You know the functionality, but now you have to make it fit seamlessly into the users' expectations, or their perceptions of how it should behave. Of course, you cannot design something that will satisfy people if you don't know those people or understand how they behave.

If you have a substantial budget or if your project has to deliver some absolutely critical product, then it would be appropriate to study the users in significant detail. One way of doing so is to use ethnography—the study of the customs of people and their cultures. The intention of an ethnographical study is to describe the nature of the targeted subjects. Originally ethnography entailed the study of ethnic groups, but for our purposes we are usually not interested in the ethnic background of our users, but rather, as a group, how those users behave and how they think. Ethnographical studies usually involved longish-term close observation, and sometimes interviews and surveys. Ethnographer Bruce Davis describes this type of investigation as "deep hanging out with the subjects."

Unfortunately, most projects do not have the budget to conduct extensive ethnographic studies. Thus you must make do with lesser ways of determining the nature of the users for whom you are constructing a solution.

In Chapter 7, we spoke about personas, and we can make use of them here. Personas are used when you have a large number of in-house users, or a large number of customers who will be using the product. A persona is a virtual person who represents a group of people (see Figure 8.4). Unlike individuals with their idiosyncrasies, personas are constructed from data collected through surveys of your target audience and so represent most of

Figure 8.4

A persona is a virtual character that represents a large number of customers (or users) with similar characteristics or demographics. The business analysts and designers use a persona as their source of user-specific requirements.

your eventual users. It is important that you construct your persona with enough characteristics for you and your team to feel that they understand it well enough to know what it wants.

Naturally if you have only one or two users, then you can interview them directly. However, we urge caution at this stage, as many people cannot be relied upon to say exactly what they do, and observation is the more likely method for you to understand what your users do and how they feel about how they do it. You can also use prototypes and observe the users' reactions to them, thereby discovering how they are most likely to respond to your proposed product.

We urge you to use either observations of real users, or personas. Our experience of customer surrogates or proxies has been less than satisfactory—the representative often states what he imagines is needed, but as he is not a real user, this statement of need is sometimes wide of the mark.

Whatever you do, you must construct a product that is appropriate and well matched to almost all of your users. This might seem obvious, but far too often we have seen project teams constructing the solution that they want or that they feel is appropriate, while forgetting that they will not be the ones using the product. What you or the team want is irrelevant; it is the characteristics of the ultimate end user that determine what the product should be.

At this stage you need to be familiar enough with your target audience to design the appropriate experience for them. We assume that you have studied your potential users, or you have interviewed them in some depth, or you have put together a persona or two; now it is time to design the user experience for them.

Designing the User Experience

Designing the whole of the user experience is the best way to come up with a product that makes people want to buy it and/or use it. Experience design is a significant topic and one that we consider to be beyond the scope of this book. However, we briefly mention it here because this kind of design is beginning to play a larger part in our development activities.

Experience design aims to produce a usage experience that is pleasing and exciting, as well as relevant to the culture and aspirations of the user. Such design focuses much more on how the product makes the user feel than on adding functionality to the product.

Simply put, if you provide a pleasing experience that the users enjoy and wish to repeat, then those users are far more likely to accept your product and—importantly—not ask for changes. At the time of writing, Apple is enjoying remarkable sales figures for its iPad. The iPad is a device that is slightly difficult to justify functionally (other devices can do more or less the same thing, often more cheaply), but it is the experience of using it that makes the iPad the desirable object it is.

Experience design should not be left to amateurs. It comprises a combination of many disciplines and, if it is to be done properly, should be handled by experienced or professional people. Experience design involves ethnography (as noted earlier, the study of how people behave), along with liberal doses of cognitive psychology, user interface design, human–computer interaction, and a liberal amount of prototyping.

The business analyst is not the experience designer, but he has an understanding of the essential business functionality and non-functionality. This knowledge, along with any personas generated or observations of users during the requirements activity, provides the input to experience design. Also, as part of the stakeholder analysis, the business analyst has identified the consultant stakeholders (usability, psychology, graphic design, and cultural experts) who are appropriate for the project in question. The business analyst's task here is to advise and to be an advocate for the business, as opposed to attempting to design the experience himself.

Innovation

This is the time for you to be innovative. If no innovation occurs, then the new product will be much the same as whatever it replaces. It is, of course, important not to disrupt the essential requirements, but there are a number of things that you can do to make a more innovative and acceptable end product.

Innovation, as we use the term here, means thinking differently about the problem to find a new and better way to do the work, or in some cases to find better work to do. Instead of rushing ahead with the first-to-mind solution or the obvious solution, we urge you to spend just a little time with fellow business analysts and other stakeholders to come up with something better, something that will be longer lasting and more appealing, something innovative.

This section introduces some *innovation triggers*. We use these concepts with our project teams to suggest innovations, and to find fresh and better solutions. We suggest using any of these triggers as a way of helping you to think differently and discover an innovative solution.

Convenience

We love convenience; what's more, we are willing to pay for it. We typically pay more for mobile phone calls than we do for landline calls, and we usually pay more for our mobile phones than we do for our landline phones. We are willing to pay more because it is just so wonderfully convenient to carry the phone around with us instead of being limited by a cord connected to the wall.

In several countries, particularly in Australia, Mercedes-Benz dealers are located very close to airports. Why? Convenience. People who buy Mercedes cars are especially likely to be affluent people, and especially likely to be people who fly on business. The near-airport dealer provides a convenience: When the car has to be serviced, the owner takes it to this conveniently located dealer, and the dealer drives the owner to the terminal to catch his flight. When the owner returns, the dealer picks him up at the terminal with the car fully serviced. The car has been washed, and clothing left on the back seat has been dry-cleaned.

These benefits might at first seem trivial, but put yourself in the position of a Mercedes owner: You are most likely affluent and busy. Anything—and that means *anything*—that saves you time and effort is welcome. In other words, you value convenience and are willing to pay for it.

But it is not only the busy Mercedes owner who values convenience; the user of your proposed solution also values his convenience—we all do. Think of the devices and services you own that are there primarily to make your life more convenient. But enough about you: Turn instead to asking what is it that the product you intend to build can do to make life more convenient for its user. Think about your favorite consumer products—they are probably your favorite because they are so downright convenient. Or look at the way that successful software products work, notably those from Apple and Google. But think mostly about what your users want to do, and make it as easy and convenient as you can for them.

The user of your proposed solution values his convenience—we all do.

Connections

We love to be connected. No, let's be honest here: We are *addicted* to being connected. The number of users and the amount of time spent on Facebook, Twitter, and other social networks attest to an almost pathological need to tell our friends and followers about our daily lives. The almost constant attention paid to e-mail speaks of people who don't want to be unconnected. People are busy sending text messages while walking in the street, often while in the midst of crossing the street. As soon as the plane lands, every Blackberry owner turns it on (often before the announcement has been made) and starts checking it to see which messages have come while the devices have been (forcibly) switched off. Surveys in the United Kingdom have found that more than one-third of adults and more than half of teenagers consider themselves to be highly addicted to their smartphones. These people leave their phones on 24/7, and are reluctant to turn them off, even at dinner or in a cinema.

It appears to be so important to remain connected that some people crash their cars while answering their phones, or they risk doing so by texting while driving. Even making the practice illegal—as it is in many countries and states—does not seem to deter addicted phone users.

Given that your customers, if they are like most of the modern world, are people who value connectedness, it seems sensible to give them as much of it as you can. Your next question must be, "What can my product do to build a better connection with my customers or users?"

Keep in mind that your customers measure your organization by the way you respond and connect to them—how you answer their questions, how you support them, how you keep them informed about your products and services. This response is the active part of connecting to the customer. Similarly, remembering the customer's name, preferences, and previous orders is a passive way of remaining connected.

When you are deciding where the product's boundary lies, take a few moments to think of a few ways that your product can more closely connect with its customers or users. Providing more information might be one of them.

Information

Your business customer wants information, wants more of it, and wants it without delay.

Think about your business customer: He wants information, wants more of it, and wants it without delay. If you don't believe that, then look at the astonishing success of Google. What is Google's product? Information. Almost half of the total Internet population uses Google each day to find information. The billions of hits on Google indicate that our thirst for information is relentless and unquenchable.

This dictum also applies to your customers. They know that many organizations are willing to supply as much information as they want, so you must specify your product such that it tells the customer everything he needs or wants to know.

But the product must do more than just pumping information at the customer (or the user); it has to deliver *useful* information. Some of this makes your product more convenient—you provide all the information needed to make it easier for the customer to carry out the transaction.

Moreover, the information must convey only the message intended, and not introduce unwanted side effects from the information. As an example, following are two loudspeaker announcements heard at an airport gate/lounge (these are actual announcements heard by your authors):

"Would all passengers on flight 344 please come to the desk?"

Passengers, being normal airline passengers, predictably responded by assuming the worst, which was that their flight had been cancelled. Anxious passengers stampeded the desk and angry voices were heard in the queue that immediately formed.

Now consider this alternative informative announcement:

"For the attention of passengers on the 3 p.m. flight to Los Angeles. We have had to change the aircraft, which means that your seat assignment *might* have to change. Would all passengers please collect a new boarding pass at the desk before they board the flight? No need to rush—everyone has a comparable seat to the one they had on the previous aircraft."

The second message is much longer, but it provides *all* the information the passengers needed. Note also that it said "3 p.m. flight to Los Angeles" and not just "flight 344." While flight numbers are well known to airline staff, most passengers don't know them; they care only about their destination and departure time. This, then, is the difference between just providing information and providing usable information.

Thus, as you determine your product's boundary, consider which information is available for each of the alternative boundaries you try. A little later we will discuss prototyping, in which you sketch the proposed interfaces and their information content.

Feeling

Systems and products are accepted or rejected based on how the consumer *feels* about them. This might at first seem to be very subjective, but an awful lot of buying decisions and acceptances are subjective. Once again, look at the phenomenal success of Apple's iPad: This product is all about feeling. The shape of it feels right: The screen has a 3:4 ratio that feels right in both portrait (text) and landscape (video) aspects; the touch screen gives a far more pleasing experience than a small and clunky keyboard; its sleekness and simplicity make its users feel good about having one. And note how the curved underside makes it easy to pick up from a table—doesn't that feel good?

There are lots of human feelings, and it is as well to be innovative toward them. This might seem a little idealistic, but do you want your product to be used? Your users or customers are unlikely to use it if they cannot feel good about doing so.

Your users or customers are unlikely to use your product if they cannot feel good about doing so.

Do your users feel they can *trust* your product or service? Does it appear competent enough and secure enough for its purpose? Keep in mind that a secure connection is useful only if your users *feel* that it is secure. It can have "https" in the URL, but if people don't feel safe, then you lose them—no amount of technology can overcome someone's instincts when it comes to security.

Do the users feel that your product has sufficient *speed*? Can you provide some innovation that makes the experience seem fast enough to satisfy your customers' feeling that the product is competent enough to do things quickly?

You can also make your users and customers feel green; they appreciate doing so. That little notice that asks you to consider the environment before printing an e-mail is there to enhance the green credentials of the sender. It does not actually stop you from printing the e-mail, nor does it make it impossible to print on anything except recycled paper, but it does make you *feel* that the sender cares.

Lastly, you have to make your user or customer feel that you are being *responsive* to his needs. That is, your solution must be innovative enough to make your customer feel that you have understood his enquiry and are doing all you can to provide the most appropriate answer. Your response is the strongest message you can send to your customer. Your customers expect marketing messages and are prepared to disregard them, but they measure you by the way you respond to them—how you answer their questions, how you support them, how you keep them informed about your products and services. Responsiveness makes your customer feel better about your product or service.

Sketching the Interface

Earlier in this chapter, we described how you select alternative solutions by drawing the product boundary at various places on a model of the business use case; see Figure 8.3 for an illustration. Each time you draw a different boundary, you create a different interface between the product and what is immediately outside it. In most cases when you select a product boundary, you do so based on the assumption that there will be a human user directly outside the product. Thus it would be useful to be able to show that human your plan for an interface. This is illustrated in Figure 8.5.

There is no need at this time to build elaborate, fully functional proto-types, when sketches on whiteboards and notebooks are almost certain to be sufficient. The intention of the sketch is simply to show the ramifications of putting the product boundary in one place instead of another.

Figure 8.5

Each of the alternative product boundaries is sketched. By doing so, you are able to show potential users what the end result could be.

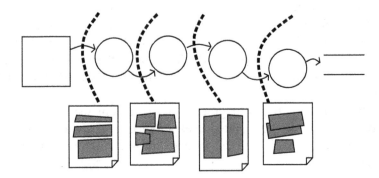

Sketching has certain advantages. It is quick, which is definitely a benefit. Moreover, if the sketch is rudimentary enough, it will dissuade users from trying their hand at screen design. They are not qualified to do so, and it is far too early in the development process to be going into detailed design. There is no point in having a carefully crafted screen layout when you're still unsure of all the functionality (and non-functionality) that could influence the interface. Anything you can do to dissuade business users from designing screens is very much to your advantage.

No one seems to mind if a sketch is changed, but most people mind if their carefully crafted design is changed.

Similarly, when you use rough sketches, no one has too much ego invested. Subsequent tasks in crafting a solution could well mean significant changes to your sketches. No one seems to mind if a sketch is changed, but most people mind if their carefully crafted design is changed.

The Real Origin of the Business Event

In Chapter 4, Business Use Cases, when we discussed business events, we suggested that you look for the real origin of the event. Almost certainly, the origin will not lie within the person normally known as the user; that person is most often part of the work's *response* to the business event, not the origin of it. The business event almost always originates outside the work when the adjacent system does something. Look back at the business event illustrated in Figure 8.3: *The real origin of the business event is when the customer became short of groceries.* When the customer became aware of this fact, he probably went around the kitchen counting groceries and determining what was needed. In short, the origin of the business event occurred quite a while before the customer picked up the phone.

The real origin of the business event often occurs well before our systems think it does.

From the customer's point of view, the most useful product is one that would know when the groceries need to be replenished. In other words, the grocery company is aware (for the moment is does not matter how this is done) of the on-hand levels of groceries and their consumption rates. Now the customer would not need to make the telephone call; instead, the company would call the customer, inform him of what he needs, and arrange a suitable delivery time. This scenario extends the product scope until it is inside the adjacent system, and produces a better—from the service and convenience points of view—product.

Extend the product boundary until it gets into the brain of the adjacent system.

Examine your business events, particularly those that are initiated by humans. By this, we do not mean the human operator or user, but rather the human adjacent system. What is he doing at the time of the event? Can you extend your product scope to include that activity?

As an example of extending the product scope, consider the check-in procedure for passengers flying in Virgin Atlantic's Upper Class. Upper Class (Virgin's first class) passengers are given a limousine ride to the airport (a welcome piece of innovation), but instead of the limo driver dumping the passengers at the terminal and letting them lug their bags to the check-in desk, passengers check in while they are still in the car. The driver phones ahead to the drive-through check-ins that Virgin has installed at some airports and gives the number of bags to be checked. When the car arrives at the drive-through check-in, passengers are handed their boarding passes and baggage-claim checks (the attendant puts the bags into the baggage-handling system), and then driven to a special entrance to the terminal, where they can walk directly to the Upper Class Lounge. From this example, we learn that Virgin Atlantic considers the real origin of the business event to be *when passengers leave their homes*, not when they reach the check-in desk.

Think about your own business use cases. Don't think about the computer, or your user's guess at a solution, but rather think of where the transaction really got started. Often, very often, this point lies outside your organization. By moving your product boundary as close as possible to the real origin, you provide a better solution, one that is more valuable and useful to your customer.

Adjacent Systems and External Technology

In the preceding section, we spoke about extending the product boundary to be as close as possible to the real origin of the business event, which is often inside the adjacent system. Before you extend your products' boundaries to include some (or all) of the adjacent system, it is a good idea to consider the nature and technology of the adjacent system—it may well determine the product you design.

Adjacent systems are just that—systems of some kind (automated or human) that reside adjacent to your work. They are shown as the square symbols on the work context diagram, and looking at the diagram you see that the adjacent systems receive data or services from your piece of work and, in turn, supply data to your work.

The scope of the product you build—that is, the functionality you include in your solution—is partly shaped by the aspirations of the adjacent systems. You need to understand them and their potential role in the work. It helps to think of these systems as belonging to one of three types: active, autonomous, or cooperative.

Active Adjacent Systems

Active adjacent systems are humans.

Active adjacent systems are humans who can interact with, or participate in, the work. When active adjacent systems initiate events, they have some objective in mind, and will collaborate with the work—provide data or biometrics, respond to questions, indicate choices—until their objective is satisfied. Given this fact, you can usually locate your product boundary as close

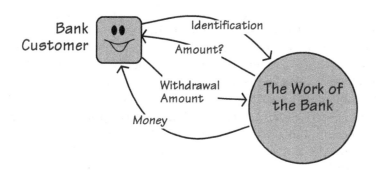

Figure 8.6

An active adjacent system interacting with a bank. In this case the boundary of the product and the boundary of the work are the same. The bank customer initiates a business event, and then supplies information and does whatever is needed until he achieves the desired outcome.

as possible to the adjacent system. Figure 8.6 shows an example of an active adjacent system interacting with the work; in this case a bank customer is using an automated teller machine.

Active adjacent systems are able to interact with the work; this interaction can occur face to face, by telephone, via a mobile device, with an automated machine, or over the Internet. Even though the active adjacent system is technically outside the scope of the work, you should consider whether you might be able to extend the scope of your product to include some of it. Can your product do part of the work that the adjacent system currently does? Or is there an advantage to your work if the adjacent system does some of the functionality that the work currently does?

Back in Chapter 4, we had a list of business events for the IceBreaker system. Business event number 10 on that list is called "Truck Depot reports problem with truck." From time to time, trucks salting the road break down, slide off the road, or somehow get into a situation where they cannot complete the treatment of their allocated roads. In such a case, the driver radios or phones the depot, and the supervisor relays the message to the de-icing work. The work responds by rescheduling trucks so as to disperse the broken truck's allocated tasks among the remainder of the fleet. That seems straightforward enough, as shown in Figure 8.7.

Figure 8.7

Business events are initiated by the supervisors at the truck depots. Because they wish to be more closely involved with the product, we can make the supervisors into active adjacent systems. This choice will probably result in part of the automated product being located in the truck depots so that the supervisors can have direct interaction with it.

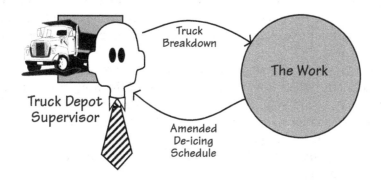

The aim of getting closer to the adjacent system is to provide the opportunity to produce a better end result.

If we inspect this adjacent system a little more closely, we find something is happening that the original systems builders did not take into account. The original designer of the product reasoned that trucks would break down when they were in active duty, but not while they were parked in the garage. It turns out that the supervisor is using business use case 10, "Truck Depot reports problem with truck," not only to handle breakdowns, but also to take trucks out of service for maintenance. This approach causes the supervisor a certain amount of inconvenience. Because it is the only way he is able take his trucks off the active roster so that he can maintain them, however, he puts up with it.

Why did this happen? No one looked closely enough at the work that this adjacent system was doing when the original requirements were gathered. By inspecting this adjacent system more rigorously, you learn more about its needs: You learn that the supervisor needs to schedule truck maintenance. At first glance, this need appears to call for the definition of a new business event, "Supervisor withdraws a truck for maintenance." However, you should consider whether the product itself could do that. Given that the product has data about each truck's activity, it should be straightforward enough for it to schedule the vehicles' maintenance via a time-triggered event, called something like "Time to withdraw trucks for scheduled maintenance."

The result of getting into the brain of the active adjacent system is a product that fulfills more of the requirements that exist in the world surrounding it—in other words, a better, more useful product.

Autonomous Adjacent Systems

An autonomous adjacent system sends and/or receives a one-way data flow to or from the work.

An autonomous adjacent system is some external body, such as another company, a computer system, or a customer, that is not directly interacting with your work. It acts independently of the work being studied, but has connections to it. Autonomous adjacent systems communicate through one-way data flows such as letters or e-mails or online forms where no back-and-forth interaction is possible.

For example, when your credit card company sends you a monthly statement, you (the card holder) are an autonomous adjacent system. You passively receive the statement with no interaction. You are acting independently, or autonomously, as seen from the viewpoint of the work of the credit card company.

Similarly, when you pay your credit card bill, you are again an autonomous adjacent system from the point of view of the work of the credit card company. You send your check by post or make a bank transfer, and you have no expectations about participating in the response the work makes upon the arrival of your payment.

It might at first appear that there are few opportunities to involve the passive autonomous adjacent systems in the work, but you must be certain the adjacent system actually *chooses* to be autonomous, and is not forced to be so by your work's technology. For example, some banks and financial institutions force their customers to fill in forms and mail them whenever they want a new service. That makes the customers autonomous. Most people would much prefer to initiate the appropriate business use case with some direct interaction—telephone, Web, or face-to-face meeting—to give the bank the information it needs and initiate the service. This approach would have the added benefit of using the information the bank already holds about its customers, and not ask them to fill in yet again their name, address, account number, and so on.

There are many opportunities to make better products (from the customer's point of view) by involving the adjacent systems. All it takes is for you to become familiar enough with the autonomous adjacent system to identify an opportunity and a desire to expand the scope of the product to involve the adjacent system more closely in the work.

Cooperative Adjacent Systems

Cooperative adjacent systems are automated systems that collaborate with the work during the course of a business use case, usually by means of a simple request–response dialog. A cooperative adjacent system might be an automated system containing a database that is accessed or written to by the work, an automated system that does some computation for the work, or any other automated system that provides a predictable and immediate service to the work. Because so much of the functionality of our organizations has been automated, several cooperative adjacent systems almost always appear in your context model.

Cooperative adjacent systems are usually computer systems acting as if they are part of the work.

A situation involving a cooperative adjacent system is shown in Figure 8.8. The thermal maps are owned by another organization, which provides the

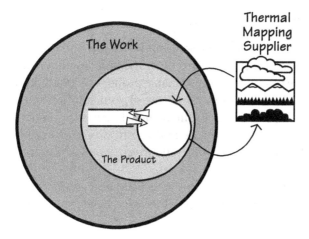

Figure 8.8

An adjacent system maintaining the thermal map database is not owned by the de-icing business, but the de-icing system is allowed access to the data. When it does so, it expects to get data quickly.

Figure 8.9

The processing for a business use case does not stop when it involves a cooperative adjacent system. Even though the adjacent system resides outside the scope of the work, it can be considered part of the work due to its ability to respond immediately. The double arrow indicates a special type of adjacent system, in which the data flow "passes through" the adjacent system. This kind of adjacent system neither initiates events nor acts as an external sink for information flows.

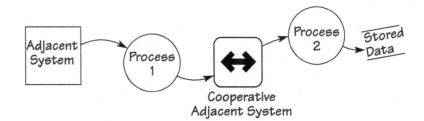

information upon request. When the ice prediction work needs to refer to a thermal map, the adjacent system responds with the requested data in an agreed-upon and timely manner. Thus the cooperative adjacent system receives a single input—the district of the needed thermal conditions—and produces a single output in response. The response is quick enough that the requesting product waits for it.

This immediate and predictable response means that you can think of the cooperative adjacent system as a step or activity in the business use case. In our example, it forms part of the business use case responding to the business event, "Time to predict icy roads." The processing of the business use case does not stop when it reaches the adjacent system—as would normally occur with an autonomous adjacent system—but rather continues until the desired outcome of the business use case has been reached. For the sake of convenience, we generally include it in our models of the business use case, as illustrated in Figure 8.9.

It is unlikely that you will need—or want—to change the interfaces with the cooperative system. Cooperative systems are black boxes, their services are stable, and rarely is there much to be gained from trying to change them. As long as your product can communicate correctly, then the cooperative adjacent system can remain a black box. The only reason for change is if your product needs a different service or different data.

Cost, Benefit, and Risks

Naturally enough, choosing a solution is not just a matter of drawing a few lines on process models and hoping for the best. You have the responsibility to come up with the optimally valuable product—that is, optimally valuable to its owner. This implies that the cost of your solution must be in proportion to the benefit it brings to the owner. There is little point spending $10 to develop the product if the benefit it brings is worth only $1—unless, of course, the $1 saving is part of a repetitive process and is applied thousands of times.

Naturally, you would love to spend $100 and get $1 million in benefits, but that is unlikely to happen. Thus wise heads must prevail, and your assessment of the cost of development and disruption must be reasonable given the benefits that the new product will bring.

Similarly, the risk must be in proportion to the benefit and cost. Risk in this case consists of the likelihood of a potential problem becoming a real problem, together with the downside impact if the problem becomes real.

For example, suppose that your proposed solution includes the use of near-field communication (NFC). You have never used this technology before and have no existing in-house expertise—the risk is that you might not be able to successfully implement NFC. Now add in the risk that even if this technology is successfully implemented, your business customers might refuse to use it, citing a lack of control and lack of privacy. (Never mind whether these are irrational fears; if your business customers feel that way, then listen to them.)

Now look at the downside impact. You face a cost in the form of disruption in getting all your customers switched over to NFC. This process might also involve a cost in the form of a publicity campaign to persuade customers to switch. In addition, the cost of the development of the NFC system could be wasted if your customers do not accept the product.

Now stack that risk up against the benefit. For this level of risk, you would need some substantial benefit to come from the new product. If the benefit is marginal, then you should look at a different solution. Conversely, if the benefit is massive—improved sales, reduced cost of processing, or the opportunity to build on the NFC capability to offer future goods and services to your customers—then the risk is well worth running.

Value is the important thing to remember here—value to the owning organization. Sadly, we don't spend enough time measuring value, because it is too difficult; instead, we measure cost because it is easier to measure. It is safe to say that we measure things only when it is easy to do so: It is easier to measure productivity than it is to measure customer loyalty; it is easier to measure cost than it is to measure effectiveness. As a consequence, we get productivity and ticked-off customers; we get cheap but practically useless systems. Clearly, our projects should decide what it is that provides real value, and build according to that understanding.

When you are considering the automated product to be built, you will likely assess several alternative solutions to see which is the optimal one. We discussed earlier how you evaluate alternative product boundaries—this is where you will spend some time with your stakeholders adjudging which one provides the best mix of cost, benefit, and risk. That option is your optimally valuable product.

Document Your Design Decisions

When you are working on a solution for the business problem, you are designing. As we use the term here, design—and, in fact, any kind of design—means making the optimal product from a set of variables. Technology is not perfect; you have varying capabilities for the different technological devices that are available to you; the cost and skill of labor vary according to the task and rank of the user. These and several other factors mean that design entails juggling a number of factors, none of which can be perfect.

Document the reasons why your product is as it is.

Given these caveats, you must make decisions, and part of your responsibility in providing value to your organization is to document your design decisions—the reasons why the resultant system is as it is. Your responsibility also includes leaving behind documentation for the future generations of people who have to maintain your solution.

Documentation has a bad reputation, and often justifiably so. Usually it is no more than a mirror of the software's functionality, and we see no value in mimicking that when the software itself is the up-to-date documentation of the functionality.

Documentation is not about what the product does, but about *why* the product does what it does and behaves as it does. The documentation, if it is to be useful, records for posterity the rationale for your design decisions. These decisions are often reached at the end of a difficult and sometimes long set of discussions. At such a time the participants are usually too exhausted to set about recording why they have done something. Nevertheless, the small amount of extra time needed to record the rationale for significant design decisions will be paid back many times over the life of the product. Not knowing the reason for features and functionality is the number one complaint we hear from maintenance developers.

As an interesting way of handling this task, Earle Beede told us of a practice at Lucent Technologies: Instead of a written document, one of the designers draws the design and explains its rationale, and this explanation is captured on video. Perhaps future generations of maintainers will be happier with watching this chat on-screen than wading through pages of written explanations.

Product Use Case Scenarios

The product use case sets out the functionality of the product.

The business analyst uses product use case (PUC) scenarios to communicate the intention of the automated product to the stakeholders. Naturally, the PUC scenario is not the only document available to you at this time. Even so, because it shows the functionality of the product, it is an easy document with which to convey your intentions to the stakeholders. We suggest that you *present* the PUC scenario to the stakeholders at some suitable meeting. Do not simply e-mail it to them—you need their feedback.

We suggest this technique as one way of overcoming the problem inherent in many requirements specifications: They are difficult, if not impossible, to read. In many organizations, normal practice is to hand a copy of

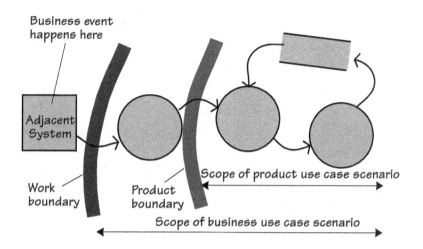

Figure 8.10

This functional model depicts the processes that respond to a business event, as does the business use case scenario; the product use case scenario shows the functionality to be included in the product.

the requirements specification to the stakeholders, and ask them to sign it if they are satisfied that it describes the product they want developed. Unfortunately, this approach ignores the all-too-obvious fact that requirements specifications are rarely read by the business stakeholders.

What does a PUC scenario look like? Not surprisingly, a lot like the BUC scenarios we discussed in Chapter 4. The difference is that the business use case contains all of the functionality that responds to a business event, whereas the corresponding product use case contains only that functionality to be implemented in the product. Figure 8.10 serves as a reminder of the connection between the business use case and the product use case. We will explain how we got to the product use case so that we can point the way from there to the atomic requirements.

To begin, first identify the business events. Pick one of them and trawl to discover the functionality that responds to that event (the business use case). As a way of showing your understanding, write a business use case scenario for this event. When your stakeholders are happy with the scenario, determine how much of that BUC can be implemented as the product. Whatever that turns out to be becomes the product use case. Naturally, we suggest you describe it using a PUC scenario.

Following is an example of this process.

Determine how much of the business use case is to be implemented as the product. The result is the product use case, which you can describe using a product use case scenario.

Business Event Name: *Passenger decides to check in.*

Business Use Case Name: *Check passenger onto flight.*

Trigger: *Passenger's ticket, record locator, or identity and flight.*

Preconditions: *The passenger must have a reservation and a passport.*

Interested Stakeholders: Check-in agent, marketing, baggage handling, reservations, flight manifest system, workflow, security, destination country's immigration.

Active Stakeholders: Passenger (trigger), check-in agent.

1. Locate the passenger's reservation.

2. Ensure the passenger is correctly identified and connected to the right reservation.

3. Check that the passport is valid and belongs to the passenger.

See procedure guidelines EU-175.

4. Attach the passenger's frequent-flyer number to the reservation.

5. Allocate a seat.

6. Get correct responses to security questions.

7. Check the baggage onto the flight.

8. Print and convey to the passenger the boarding pass and bag tags.

9. Wish the passenger a pleasant flight.

Outcome: The passenger is recorded as checked onto the flight, the bags are assigned to the flight, a seat is allocated, and the passenger is in possession of a boarding pass and bag claim stubs.

To make decisions about the product boundary for this BUC, we need to define the constraints. We also need input from the stakeholders who understand the technical and business implications and the possibilities for the product boundary along with the business goals for the project.

Let's suppose that you have that information. That is, you and the stakeholders have decided that the optimal mix of benefit, cost, and risk will be achieved by building a machine that allows passengers to check themselves onto their flights.

The PUC scenario for the machine shows what you intend it to do:

Product Use Case Name: Passenger checks onto flight.

Trigger: Passenger activating the machine.

Preconditions: The passenger must have a reservation.

Interested Stakeholders: Passenger, check-in agent, marketing, baggage handling, reservations, flight manifest system, workflow, security, destination country's immigration.

Actor: *Passenger.*

1. The product asks for the passenger's identity or record locator.

2. The passenger supplies one or the other and the product locates the passenger's reservation.

3. The product asks for a frequent-flyer number if it is not already attached to the reservation.

4. The product asks for and scans the passport if needed.

5. The product shows the allocated seat and accepts the passenger's changes if needed.

6. The product asks for the number of bags and for answers to the security questions.

7. The product checks the baggage onto the flight, and prints the bag tags.

8. The product prints the boarding pass or sends it to the passenger's phone.

9. The product directs the passenger to the bag drop and departure gate.

Outcome: The passenger is recorded as checked onto the flight, the bags are assigned to the flight, a seat is allocated, and the passenger has a boarding pass and bag claim stubs.

Bear in mind that our example PUC scenario reflects a particular set of decisions about the nature and scope of the product. If the stakeholders had made different decisions or different constraints existed, then naturally the PUC scenario would be different.

Now let's consider how you might use this PUC scenario. First, it explains what the intended product does at a level that is suitable for business stakeholders. You might find it necessary to make several revisions of the scenario as you present it, but by the time you and your stakeholders are finished, it should be an accurate portrayal of the product to be built.

The level of detail shown by the scenario is aimed at business stakeholders. If necessary, you can expound on any step and provide the underlying detail. Minor details may remain that need to be worked out, and these can be handled in conversations between the developers, business analysts, and stakeholders.

Putting It All Together

There is no formulaic method for arriving at the optimal solution; you have lots of factors to juggle, and the best design is simply the best compromise among all of them. Figure 8.11 illustrates the idea that these factors are

Figure 8.11

Your solution space
is being stretched
and pulled in many
directions at once. Your
task is to make the best
trade-off between these
sometimes opposing
influences.

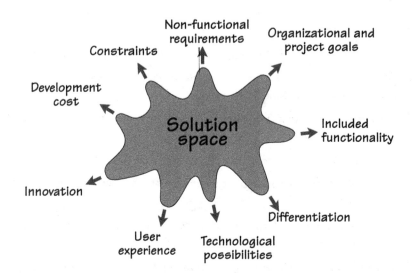

pulling the solution in different directions, and your task is to put together
the best set of compromises to make the optimally valuable product.

You are being pulled in multiple directions. One direction is functionality, and generally speaking, the more functionality you automate, the greater
the benefits. Naturally enough, the cost of development is pulling in exactly
the opposite direction.

Another direction is differentiation. Differentiation does not mean just
being different—you could use a different color and that would be different,
but not particularly beneficial. Instead, differentiation means establishing a
clear separation between your solution and any others, having an end product that represents a distinct leap forward. Generally, the more differentiated
your product is, the higher the benefit it brings.

Your solution should be innovative. If there is no innovation, then your
product will be just more of the same old stuff and will have little benefit
to its owner. Innovation does not mean flashy interface features, but rather
some innovative and beneficial way for the user to work with your solution, or some innovative and beneficial work being done by your solution.
In some cases innovation involves extra cost, but in most cases it brings a
benefit that outweighs any additional implementation cost.

Another factor to be taken into account is the constraints that affect the
design of the product. In some cases these constraints are genuine (always
challenge constraints to ensure they are not just someone's idea of a solution); if so, it means you must develop the solution in the manner prescribed
by the constraint.

The non-functional requirements also influence your solution. These qualitative needs make the difference between a successful and well-accepted product and a product that falls rapidly into disuse.

User experience design also comes into play. Part of the selection of the product boundary consists of ensuring that the intended user of the product has a worthwhile experience while using it.

All of these factors are underpinned by the technological possibilities. New technologies can provide new solutions, and the business analyst should always vigorously investigate the technology available for his solution.

Overriding all of this, and perhaps representing the most important influences of all, are the corporate and project goals. Obviously, you must come up with a solution that contributes to your organizational goals and performs its functions in a way that contributes to the project goals.

We do not pretend that starting the solution is easy, but we do insist that this phase of development is important. A little bit of thought and effort at this stage can mean a longer-lasting and more satisfactory product that over the years requires fewer maintenance changes, provides better customer satisfaction, and delivers greater value to its owner.

Strategies for Today's Business Analyst 9

in which we consider strategies for the
business analyst to guide requirements discovery
in today's changing environments

Things used to be a lot simpler. If you were a business analyst, then the chances were that you worked for a large organization, and large organizations always had their own software development teams. The business analyst who worked in this kind of environment would talk to the users who were part of the same organization, write the requirements, and hand them to the internal software developers. This cozy arrangement meant that the BA and the developers were a lot closer to one another. Because the software was built and used in the same organization, it was simple enough to find a developer to make any necessary or requested changes.

Things have changed. The majority of software used today is not developed by the owning organization, but rather purchased. The development role in large organizations is reserved for specialist tasks.

Today, a huge number of ready-made off-the-shelf (OTS) solutions are available. Enterprise resource management (ERM) software, customer resource management (CRM) software, content management systems (CMS), open-source software, Apple's App Store and similar venues, and a myriad of other applications, components, and solutions are readily available, either freely or for sale.

Given these development and solution options, today's business analyst has the additional task of deciding the best strategy for discovering and communicating the requirements for whatever approach to automation the organization decides to take.

Balancing Knowledge, Activities, and People

A requirements strategy serves as a guide for determining where to start, whether you have sufficient detail, which iterative cycles you need, which form to use when recording your knowledge, when to have reviews, when to involve which stakeholders, when to build prototypes, and when and how to do any of the myriad things that will bring your efforts closer to producing the optimal value for the business. The variations in every project necessitate differences in the order in which you do things, the level of detail to which you do them, and the forms in which you communicate.

Figure 9.1 identifies three variable characteristics that provide useful input for planning your requirements strategy. *Requirements Knowledge* is your understanding of the work, and the product needed to be developed to support that work. It includes the information you obtain from the artifacts you build during the course of your requirements activity and, of course, the requirements you write. *Activities* are the tasks and checkpoints that your project performs to discover and communicate this knowledge. The last characteristic is *People.* Who are the stakeholders—the people whose knowledge you need? What do they know? Where are they? What is their availability?

Common Project Requirements Profiles

Your requirements strategy is a framework for the *Activities* you need to carry out to discover the appropriate level of *Knowledge* and communicate it to the right *People* given the profile of your project. In this chapter, we explore requirements strategies for three project requirements profiles that we commonly encounter in our work: *External, Iterative,* and *Sequential.*

A project with an *External* profile is one where, having discovered the requirements, you send them to an external solution provider. The external profile applies when you are buying a ready-made solution from an external

Figure 9.1

A consistent language for communicating *requirements knowledge,* the *activities* for discovering and disseminating knowledge, and the *people* who are involved are all variables that affect your requirements strategy.

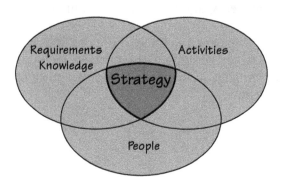

vendor, or you have outsourced the development of the solution, or you are sending a request for proposal to several suppliers. It might involve more than one supplier when you are buying and integrating a number of components.

With a project with an *Iterative* profile, you have the opportunity to iteratively discover the requirements and release partial solutions until the product is complete. The motivation for this profile is wanting to deliver some results to the customer as quickly as possible, and to be responsive to business changes. With this profile you are developing your solution using developers with whom you can work closely; normally (but not always), they are located within your own organization.

Projects fitting the third project profile, known as *Sequential* projects, have more constraints on the specific activities and deliverables; in the most extreme cases, they have rigid phases and documents that must be produced before progressing to the next phase. The requirements must be completely defined before passing them (usually in a prescribed form) to the designers and developers to work on the solution. With this profile, it is difficult to change anything once it has passed through a phase checkpoint.

These descriptions focus on the three profiles in their purest form; your project will most likely be a mixture of the three, or incorporate other activities. It is useful to explore and compare the strategies in their absolute form because it provides the basis for you to combine various aspects of each profile to derive a strategy for your own project.

How Much Knowledge Is Needed Before Each Breakout?

A question that we come across frequently in our consulting work is, "How much detail, or how much information, do I need in my requirements?" The answer is not the same in every case—it depends on your project profile. Even so, you can use this question as the basis for following the requirements strategy most relevant to your project.

All responsible projects have one thing in common—the desire to produce the best result as quickly as possible within the relevant constraints. This means that you don't waste time by following unnecessary procedures, but neither do you take irresponsible shortcuts that cause the project to miss things that bring about inadequate products, or cause extra maintenance and correction work to be done later in the life of the product. To put it another way, the knowledge you have acquired must be sufficient—and no more than is needed—to enable you to break out of your current activity and start the next one.

Each activity in a requirements process builds knowledge; that much is obvious. But how much knowledge is enough? We refer to the accumulation of sufficient knowledge for an activity as meeting its *breakout conditions*. Breakout in this context means that you have reached the point at which the requirements knowledge is sufficient so that moving on to the next activity can be done safely—you have what you need for the next activity to succeed, and as a bonus, you have not wasted time in elaborating requirements that need no more elaboration.

The breakout conditions for an activity vary, naturally enough, according to the strategy you are following. In the rest of this chapter we explore example strategies and define the various breakout conditions for each of the project profiles: External, Iterative, and Sequential.

External Strategy

Figure 9.2

External requirements strategy. This profile applies when the product is to be constructed by an external supplier. The large arrows represent a breakout—a transition from one activity to another. Each arrow is tagged with a key to a breakout condition needed before the transition can be safely made. The smaller dotted arrows represent iteration, both within an activity and within the strategy.

Figure 9.2 summarizes the External project strategy, so named because you are using an external solution provider. In the diagram, note that activities progress from left to right, the arrows show the transitions between activities (which can be jumped over), and are keyed with the breakout condition for the activity.

The first activity is called *Conception*, which happens when someone has an idea for a project. The idea might be that the organization wants to go into a new business area, or to add to or improve its current capabilities, or comply with some legal obligation, or almost anything else. The people involved in the *Conception* discuss the possibilities, make very preliminary estimates of cost and risk, and derive enough requirements knowledge to enable the project to successfully move on to the next activity. But how much is "enough"?

The "enough" is what we call a *breakout condition*. We discussed this before, and the following subsection discusses the breakout conditions for the requirements activities in an External project profile. We suggest that you keep referring to Figure 9.2 as you read the variations within the strategy.

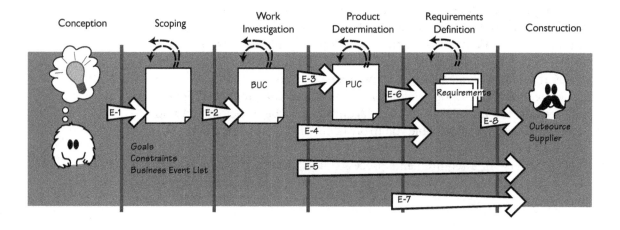

Conception to Scoping

You achieve breakout *E-1* when you understand enough about the purpose of the project to be able to safely and viably move on to subsequent activities. Taking this step means that you have firmly established the strategic goal of the project. Additionally, you have established the project sponsor, who accepts responsibility for the project and will provide the necessary resources. You have also identified the key stakeholders, and they show willingness to participate. You have identified any solution constraints and time and budget constraints. You have probably discussed external suppliers in enough detail to know that at least one is available to build or supply the intended product.

Once this knowledge has been assembled and agreed, then you can break out of the conception activity and proceed to scoping.

Scoping to Work Investigation

Breakout *E-2* conditions for the *Scoping* activity are achieved when you have identified the relevant business area (the work) to be studied. Specifically, you have identified the scope of the work by defining the data interfaces between the work and the rest of the world; that is, you know which data enters the work and which data and services the work produces. We discussed this issue at length in Chapter 3, Scoping the Work. You should know enough about the scope and the work to be able to partition it into stand-alone chunks using business events or features, and these chunks are traceable back to the scope.

You also need to have identified all of the stakeholders (business, users, consultants)—not just the key ones—and have determined what involvement you expect from them. You have also ensured that the project goal is measurable, and that you can use it to help you make decisions about where to focus your efforts as you go into detail.

During the *Conception* activity, you identified the constraints on your project. Now you take them to a more detailed level: Is the constraint justified, and how will you know if it has been satisfied? Understanding the constraints at this stage means that you know what degree of freedom you have in negotiating alternative solutions with your supplier.

You might also have sketched the intended scope of the product that you want your supplier to deliver. This kind of sketch is not obligatory at this stage, as you most likely have not done enough detailed investigation to be able to accurately identify product scope. However, if you have ideas, then it is better to capture them now. It is, of course, important that future requirements investigation is not limited to this sketched idea for the product.

Work Investigation to Product Determination

The transition from the *Work Investigation* activity can occur when you have accumulated sufficient knowledge of the work to begin thinking about the product to be built, and specifically its interfaces. Breakout *E-3* condition happens when you have understood the business carried out by each business use case (BUC) well enough to make choices about what the product should do to enhance each of those BUCs. This probably means that you have recorded the business functionality in a BUC scenario, some kind of process model, or a list of business rules. At this point, it helps to have a dictionary of the business terminology. Once you have stabilized this knowledge, you are in a position to break out of the *Work Investigation* activity and start determining the scope of the product for your supplier to provide.

Work Investigation to Atomic Requirements Definition

In this variation of the External strategy, you have sufficient knowledge of the business and wish to jump directly from work investigation to atomic requirements definition, without doing any product scope determination. Your intention here is to provide your external supplier with the detailed business requirements, with the intention of the supplier (probably multiple suppliers if you are looking for competitive bids) demonstrating to you which of those requirements can be satisfied by its product.

Breakout *E-4* conditions are met when you have defined each business use case to a level of agreement and detail such that it can act as the basis for deriving the atomic requirements. The most common way of achieving this level of detail is to write a business use case scenario for each business event (Chapter 6). Other options are to build some kind of process model; the exact model you select will depend on your own and your supplier's preferences. When writing your business use case scenarios, it is important to use the terms you have defined in your dictionary consistently; after all, the purpose of having such a dictionary is to ensure a consistent and unambiguous interpretation of the requirements.

As mentioned previously, this breakout is commonly used when you want a number of suppliers to bid on your proposal, with the intention of selecting the product that best satisfies your requirements.

Work Investigation to Building

This path is the most radical variation for this strategy: You have accumulated, and documented, sufficient knowledge of the business, and you pass that directly to the supplier with no further elaboration on your part. Your intention is either for the external supplier to design and implement a system to satisfy your business needs, or for the supplier to propose one or more of its products to satisfy as much as possible of your business needs.

Breakout *E-5* conditions are met when you have identified each business event and have reached a consensus on the functionality of each business use case—probably by writing a scenario for each. Your dictionary, which defines your terminology and data, is quite important here, as it will help your supplier to make an unambiguous interpretation of your scenarios.

Product Determination to Atomic Requirements Definition

Breakout *E-6* conditions are met when you have decided on the desired product scope, and you wish to start defining atomic requirements. At this point, you will have some kind of specification for each product use case; we suggest that you use a PUC scenario, but an activity diagram, a collection of user stories, or any other model will also suffice as long as they indicate the scope of the product and its required capabilities. You should also be careful to supply the rationale behind your decisions about this product boundary.

Product Determination to Construction

Breakout *E-7* conditions can be met when you are working closely with your supplier and you both agree that the requirements at PUC level of detail are sufficient for the supplier to develop or supply a satisfactory product. In this variation of the strategy, because you are not writing atomic requirements, you need to have a clear, consistent, and sufficient PUC specification.

You must also supply the non-functional requirements for your product use cases. You might annotate your PUC models with the needed non-functionality, or you might find it necessary to write some or all of the non-functional requirements in the usual form. Don't attempt this breakout unless you have created a dictionary of the terms used in whatever specification you are providing—what you call a "payment" (or anything else) might be very different from what your supplier thinks it is.

Atomic Requirements Definition to Building

Breakout *E-8* conditions occur when you are ready to deliver atomic requirements—functional, non-functional, and constraints—to your supplier. (We describe these requirements in the next few chapters.) Each atomic requirement should have at the very least a description, rationale, and fit criterion (discussed in Chapter 12). It may also have—and should have—other attributes that you are using for your atomic requirements. You need some way of tracing each atomic requirement back to its higher-level chunk (business use case and/or product use case). This kind of traceability is crucial when you reach the stage of acceptance testing of the product your external supplier has delivered.

Iterative Strategy

With an Iterative project profile (Figure 9.3), you are building the product in small increments, and relying to some extent on frequent delivery of these increments, and the feedback they generate, to guide the development of the product. When referring to the diagram in Figure 9.3, note that this is an iterative process—each iteration delivers part of the needed functionality. To put that another way, once you have completed the *Construction* activity for one portion, you cycle back to get the next one, possibly going back as far as *Work Investigation* (the dotted arrows indicate iteration). Please refer to this diagram as you read the variations within the Iterative strategy.

Conception to Scoping

Breakout *I-1* conditions are met when you have sufficient understanding of the purpose of the project and the business value that the project is intended to deliver. In particular, you and your key stakeholders agree on the vision for the project. At this stage you do not need formal models—although they might help—but enough agreement on the problem to be solved to enable you and your team to move on. We suggest that a rich picture—and, of course, a consensus that it is an accurate explanation of the problem—might be sufficient to make this breakout.

Figure 9.3

Iterative requirements strategy. This diagram uses the same activities and conventions as in the previously shown External project strategy (Figure 9.2). In this diagram the breakout condition arrows have the prefix "I"for Iterative. The dotted arrows show iteration, both within and between activities.

Scoping to Work Investigation

Breakout *I-2* conditions occur when you have identified the scope of the work that is appropriate for the business value your project is to deliver. Perhaps when the project begins to iterate in the later activities, this scope may need to be adjusted slightly, but you have to start with something firm and not a vague idea. We strongly suggest that you satisfy the scoping conditions by building a work context diagram. Unless your scope is for a trivial piece of work, you should partition it. We have found that business events (see Chapter 4, Business Use Cases) are the best way of partitioning. The response

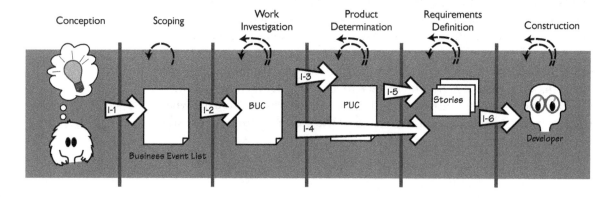

to the business event—a business use case—is the most convenient unit of work to study in the Work Investigation activity.

The business use cases are prioritized based on their value to the business, and naturally enough, you work on the highest-priority business events first. Perhaps it is better to think of breakout condition I-2 as having selected the highest-priority business event from those remaining on the list. This list represents your work backlog.

When you iterate back to this activity, you will probably want to reprioritize the list to reflect changes to business priorities, to include new business events that have been discovered as a result of previous iterations, or because new opportunities have arisen that are best met by adjusting your priorities. At any stage you might need to go back and review your work scope; the changes we are speaking of here can affect it at any time. Keep your knowledge visible and shareable so that people can readily see the impact of any change, and respond to it quickly.

Keep your knowledge visible and shareable so that people can easily see the impact of any change, and respond to it quickly with the minimum amount of administrative overhead.

Work Investigation to Product Determination

Breakout *I-3* conditions are met when you have learned enough about the selected business use case that you are able to decide the optimal product scope. At this point, you know the business rules carried out by the selected BUC, and you have sufficiently investigated how its functionality fits into the overall work.

The knowledge is the important thing here, but it is also necessary to share that knowledge with the rest of the team and the business stakeholders. With an Iterative project profile, you are probably working as a member of a small, co-located team, so we suggest that visible displays are probably the best option for sharing information. You might choose to keep your knowledge on the wall in the form of a mixture of posters, scenarios, business story cards, Post-it notes, or other documents that give visibility to the work knowledge you have accumulated. We find it prudent to regularly photograph the wall.

Of course, this technique won't work for all iterative projects, as organizational constraints sometimes mandate that you translate your knowledge into prescribed documents. The point is to avoid doing any knowledge translation—that is, production of documents—unless it is unavoidable. The important consideration is that you have the necessary knowledge and it is accessible and understandable to the whole team.

Work Investigation to Requirements Definition

Breakout *I-4* happens when you choose to jump from the business use case directly to defining the requirements for that BUC. These requirements will probably take the form of user stories, as stories usually imply the product boundary. The I-4 breakout conditions are similar to those for I-3, with the addition that you need a profile of the users for whom you are building this part of the product. Additionally, you need to understand any constraints that the solution must respect.

Product Determination to Requirements Definition

Breakout *I-5* conditions are met when you have defined the scope of automation for the chosen business use case. Reaching this point implies that you have taken your knowledge of the BUC and, in conjunction with the business stakeholders, decided how much of it can you profitably automate. This decision was discussed in more depth in Chapter 8, Starting the Solution.

You can represent your product scope decision in many ways. We find it effective to draw the product boundary on a graphic model—an activity diagram or whatever you are using—or to sketch the proposed interface (see Chapter 8 for more on this topic).

It is necessary to link your product use case decisions back to your BUCs. This sort of connection enables you to efficiently keep iterating through different ideas and assessing the relative value against the cost for each one.

Requirements Definition to Construction

Breakout *I-6* conditions are satisfied when you have acquired enough knowledge about the part of the work that you are improving to be able to build or assemble the software solution for that piece. Regardless of whether you have chosen to record this knowledge in the form of user stories or atomic requirements (or any other form), you should have captured the functional and non-functional requirements that the product must meet if it is to improve the selected portion of the work.

Important attributes of the atomic requirement or user story are the rationale—the reason for the requirement—and the fit criterion—a measurement that enables the testers to determine that the delivered product meets the requirement (both rationale and fit criteria are discussed in Chapter 12). The reason for including these attributes is to say why the requirement matters, thereby enabling the designers and developers to make the best choices when building the product, and allowing them to decide how much effort to put into testing (requirements with a weak rationale get less attention than showstoppers).

Sequential Strategy

A *Sequential* strategy means that the project has formal project phases, and each phase is expected to be completed before the team can progress to the next one; completion of a phase is usually signaled by the production of a

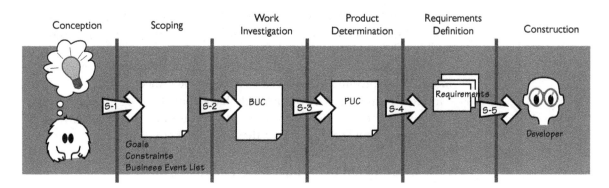

Conception Scoping Work Investigation Product Determination Requirements Definition Construction

Goals
Constraints
Business Event List

Figure 9.4

Sequential requirements strategy. Each of the activities is more or less completed before the next activity begins, making for an orderly progression from beginning to end.

document. This strategy is often used by both large-scale projects and projects characterized by an organizational or statutory need for this kind of formality and documentation. Figure 9.4 illustrates a requirements strategy for sequential projects; this time we have labeled the breakout conditions with an "S" prefix.

Conception to Scoping

Breakout *S-1* conditions are met when you have enough knowledge about the intention of the project and the value that it will deliver to the business so that you are able to identify the work area that is to be affected by the delivery of the product. To do so, you must have determined the strategic goal that drives the project. You also have a sponsor who accepts responsibility for the project, and you must have identified the key stakeholders. Finally, you should have some idea of the design or technical constraints as well as the budget and time constraints.

When these items become known, they are recorded for later guidance of the project. In this type of project, it is likely that you have some kind of specific project strategy document that must be completed before you go to the next phase. When this is done, you are able to break out and move to detailed scoping of the work area.

Scoping to Work Investigation

Breakout *S-2* conditions are met when you have specified the boundaries of the work to be investigated (a task described in Chapter 3). Your product is intended to improve some part of your client's work, so you need to investigate that work to discover the requirements and meet the goal of the project. To correctly scope the work, you specify the interfaces between the work and other parts of the organization, or between the work and relevant external systems or customers. These interfaces also serve as guidelines when you are partitioning this work into cohesive functional chunks that are traceable back to the overall scope of the work—these are the business events.

This scoping knowledge can be represented in any of several ways, but we suggest that a work context diagram and an event list are the quickest and most direct approaches. You also need a stakeholder analysis to define all of your stakeholders (not just the key ones), their responsibilities, and the amount of involvement they need to have in the project.

In sequential projects, you probably have some kind of prescribed high-level business requirements document that you must populate with scope knowledge to show completion of these breakout conditions.

Work Investigation to Product Determination

Breakout *S-3* conditions are achieved when you have completed the analysis of each of the functional chunks of the work, or business use cases as we are calling them. We wrote about this activity in Chapter 5, Investigating the Work. Your accumulated knowledge of the work must be communicated—typically in the form of models and text scenarios, although you should use whatever form is prescribed by standards within your organization.

The breakout conditions are met when you have understood the work well enough to provide satisfactory documentation of it.

Product Determination to Requirements Definition

Breakout *S-4* can happen when you have defined the scope and high-level functionality of the product you intend to build. For each business use case, you have defined which part of that work the product will do; in other words, you have defined the product use cases. This definition can take several forms: swim lane diagrams, use case diagrams, text scenarios, or annotated process models. In addition, you might have added some interface definitions or example interaction diagrams to illustrate the product scope. It is useful—actually, crucial—to record the rationale for each of your decisions on the product scope.

Requirements Definition to Building

Breakout *S-5* conditions are met when you have defined the atomic requirements for the proposed solution. Each of the atomic requirements (functional, non-functional, constraints) must have a description, rationale, and fit criterion to make it unambiguous, measurable, and testable. Each should be traceable back to the relevant product use case and business use case. Each should use terminology that has been defined in your dictionary. The requirements template in Appendix A contains an extensive checklist of the attributes of atomic requirements. We could say that breakout S-5 conditions are met when you have completed the requirements specification according to this template.

Your Own Strategy

It is highly unlikely that your project will exactly match one of the profiles just described; instead, you should think of these profiles as generic. There are many variations on the way that projects are run; we cannot possibly hope to illustrate them all. Some of these variations will fall within the parameters of one of the three profiles, while others will use pieces of different profiles. It is also possible that a project might start out using one strategy and then at some stage determine that it would be beneficial to switch to a different strategy, or that within one project, parts could be run using a different strategy. The possibilities are almost endless.

We have found that the best way to discover the strategy most suitable for your project is to start with the generic profile model that looks most like your current way of working, and then make changes to accomplish the following goals:

- Keep stakeholders involved by having frequent deliveries of artifacts, or working software
- Respond to business changes more quickly
- Make it easier for stakeholders to provide feedback
- Avoid producing deliverables that duplicate existing knowledge, or that provide little or no new knowledge

If there are no obvious changes you want to make, then start using your chosen strategy with a view toward possibly changing it as you achieve a better understanding of the profile of your project. Pointing back to Figure 9.1 at the beginning of this chapter, remember that you are trying to discover and communicate *Requirements Knowledge* in the minimum amount of time, using the level of *Activities* that are most appropriate for the *People* who are involved.

Sharpening Your Requirements Skills

A good business analyst is always looking for ways to be a better business analyst. This section highlights some things that you might consider that would make you a better business analyst.

"Business analyst" is now considered to be a valid job description. And just as other recognized job descriptions—doctor, engineer, project manager, developer, and so on—have their own organizations and qualifications, so do business analysts. A number of organizations contribute to the recognition of business analysis by offering business analysts' paths of study leading to qualifications. The three best known are identified here:

- International Institute of Business Analysts: www.iiba.org
- Information Systems Examination Board of the British Computer Society: certifications.bcs.org
- International Requirements Examination Board: www.certified-re.de (in German)

There are also conferences and Web forums where you can meet other business analysts and exchange experiences and discuss qualifications.

No Longer a Stenographer

Traditionally, the business analyst was seen as someone who wrote requirements. This task was usually described as "Go and interview the users, and write down whatever they say." Thus the business analyst filled a passive role, responding to whatever was asked for.

Today, the business analyst is no longer a stenographer. We can go so far as to say that the today's business analyst is no longer just a requirements writer.

We know from bitter experience that poor requirements contribute to more than half of all project and system failures.

We know from bitter experience that poor requirements contribute to more than half of all project and system failures. This high failure rate suggests very strongly that we must change our approach to discovering requirements. Instead of thinking almost exclusively about a software solution, today's business analyst is much more concerned with the business problem to be solved. As noted earlier (and repeatedly) in this text, it is the failure to identify the *real* problem to be solved that causes projects to deliver up poor results and poor products.

Today, the business analyst must be much more proactive. Doing so means interacting more closely with the business stakeholders, and using a variety of models and techniques to ensure that the business stakeholders give an accurate portrayal of the business they are responsible for.

The question to ask is not "What do you want?" but "What do you do?"

The emphasis is, or should be, on understanding the problem and letting the solution follow along. As part of this approach, the business analyst must prevent his business stakeholders from becoming fixated on a solution. The question to ask is not "What do you want?" but "What do you do?"

The business analyst must now study not just the stakeholders' needs, but also the people who have those needs. The delivered product must match those people, in terms of both the way they work and the skills they have. After all, there is little point delivering a dumbed-down product to a group of scientists, or a standard interface to a group of teenagers who are accustomed to exciting and interesting software products.

Limiting the Number of Requirements That Are Written

A traditional problem with requirements work is the specification. All too often, it is a large, difficult-to-read, and probably ignored document. You know this: When you read a novel, you often skip paragraphs when you think they deal with a topic that has little to do with the development of the story—a lavish description of a room, background information on a protagonist's car, and so on. Knowing that readers tend to skip these pieces, quite a few authors have said that they take care not to write the parts that readers don't read.

We suggest strongly that business analysts emulate these authors and write only requirements that people will read.

Q: How do you write requirements that are certain to be both read and used by all parties?

A: Write fewer requirements.

You can limit the amount of requirements that you have to write by using iteration and prioritization. Let's look at those processes.

When you have identified all of the business events, we suggested that you prioritize them. Prioritization, as we are using the term here, means that you find the business events for which an improved implementation will yield the most value to the owning organization. These would be the business events that, when implemented, will result in the greatest reduction in the cost of a business process, or allow your client to sell more of its goods, or provide a service that will result in a larger, more profitable, customer base.

When you have found these high-value events, implement them using the normal routine of developing the BUC scenario, and from that the requirements. Then go back to the list and do it again. Each time you go back, you are selecting business events that have a lower priority than the last time around.

Continue until you have either exhausted the list of business events, or—and here's where you save time—you find that some business events yield such a low value to the organization that they are not worth developing. Once you encounter these ineffectual events, you stop development.

> *Once you encounter these low-value events, you stop development.*

We are always surprised (and pleased) at how many business events can be discarded this way, and how many unnecessary requirements are avoided.

Reusing Requirements

Within an organization, projects tend to develop the same kind of products. Insurance companies develops insurance applications, a computer-aided design organization develops CAD applications. Indeed, most organizations find themselves building similar products with each new project.

> *Most organizations find themselves building very similar products with each new project.*

In this situation, some overlap between products is likely to occur. Likewise, the business analyst can probably make some use of requirements that have been written for previous projects. To make use of these previously written requirements, you have to create abstractions—look at the requirements and substitute the subject of the current application for the previous one. In other words, instead of a payment for car insurance (the subject of a previous project), the requirement is changed to one that covers paying for house insurance (the subject of the current project). By making these abstractions, the business analyst can often save the effort of rediscovering many of the requirements.

There is considerable potential to save time and effort by reusing requirements. For that reason, we have devoted the entirety of Chapter 15, Reusing Requirements (what else could we call it?), to this very topic.

Innovation and the Business Analyst

Most stakeholders ask for incremental improvements. That is, they want what they have got at the moment, with a few additional changes and features—new buttons on the screen, a little bit more information, the ability to link to one more database, and so on. In other words, people ask for what they've got plus minor, incremental improvements.

Given this fact, it is up to the business analyst to lead the innovation charge. It is not the responsibility of the business analyst to be the only innovator on the project, but he must be the person suggesting innovations and facilitating creativity sessions where the stakeholders are given the opportunity to suggest innovations.

READING
Michalko, Michael.
Thinkertoys: A Handbook of Creative-Thinking Techniques.
Ten Speed Press, 2006.

Having established the need for innovation, the question is obvious: How do you do it? In Chapter 8, we discussed some techniques for innovation, but that coverage was by no means an exhaustive treatment of the subject. Many books on innovation techniques are available, and a good place to start is Michael Michalko's *Thinkertoys*. This author outlines a variety of techniques, several of which you are sure to find suitable for your business analysis work.

Looking for Business Rules

Business rules are directions set down by the organization to direct operations, people, and systems as to what they are to do. Such rules can apply to any aspect of the organization, from top management to the lowest-level process. They can be as all encompassing as "Employees are directed not to commit any crime" or as detailed as "The help desk employees will report to their supervisor any cases that are still unresolved 48 hours after the first contact." Business rules can be written down, or they can be understood by employees and verbally transmitted.

Some organizations have a process to methodically gather and record their rules. Others approach this task less formally, collecting business rules only as they arise during projects. Sometimes, new business rules that are discovered during a project are recorded; at other times, sadly, they are not. In some cases, your work as a business analyst will uncover previously unknown rules, or will lead to the formulation of new rules. If that was not enough, the Business Rules Approach is a development methodology in which the business rules are recorded in natural language and then translated into business processes, and in some cases, into software.

Given this kaleidoscope of business rules, it is little wonder that different business analysts approach them in significantly different ways. But let's consider what we are doing: Business rules are statements of what the business must do. There is no real difference between statements of what the business is to do and the steps in a BUC scenario: The scenario records how the business responds to a business event. That is, it follows the business rules until it has achieved the business objective of the response.

Given the similarity between business rules and BUC scenarios—and, indeed, some of the requirements—our approach to business rules is probably predictable. At the outset of the project, we ask for the business rules. Naturally, these are provided in varying states of completeness and usefulness. As we work through each of the business use cases, we ensure that all appropriate business rules are embedded into the appropriate scenario (or whatever other model we are using). Business process owners are invaluable in helping to find and interpret the applicable rules.

You might consider recording new business rules as a by-product of your business analysis. However, if the organization does not have a formalized way of keeping its business rules, then your BUC scenarios are a sufficient (and probably more useful) repository of the rules.

Your business use case scenarios are a sufficient and useful repository of the business rules.

The Business Analyst as Ideas Broker

We exist in small islands—every organization is made up of them. Most organizations have departments, and the people within one department have limited contact with the people in other departments. This state of affairs leads us to say that a department is an island. Similarly, projects tend to be islands—the people working on one project are usually so busy that they have little time to interact and share ideas with people working on another project. Interaction between different commercial companies is close to nonexistent.

Despite this segregation, some of the best ideas come from outside your own island. Ideas such as new technology, innovative use of existing technologies, new software products, new ways of working, and almost anything else can be thought of as an idea. While ideas exist in abundance, we have limited mechanisms for discovering these external ideas.

Some of the best ideas come from outside your own island.

Most business analysts are already extremely busy, but the role lends itself to external exploration. The role we are suggesting here for the business analysts is that of *broker*. The broker finds ideas, processes, and technology that exist in one island and can be profitably put to use by another island. This type of discovery entails not just an exploration of a problem space, but also a search for useful components and ideas that can be recombined to form new solutions in new problem spaces.

Why a broker? Because sometimes the business analyst is presenting the ideas to others, and not always making use of those ideas himself. Sometimes the idea is one that has to be changed and adapted before it is practical to use on the business analyst's own project. Sometimes the ideas are merely stored for future use.

The business analyst serves as an intermediary, or roving ambassador, between islands. Projects have many stakeholders, who aggregate into islands with their own concerns and interests. Islands—groups of stakeholders—communicate in different ways, and have vastly different levels of skill and knowledge. The accounting people are different from the marketers; the engineers are barely understood by the managers.

The task of the business analyst as broker is to understand the concerns of each island and to interpret and communicate between them. The business analyst also has to ensure that the concerns of each tribe are prioritized and that the genuinely high-priority items become part of the final product.

READING

Hargadon, Andrew. *How Breakthroughs Happen: The Surprising Truth About How Companies Innovate.* Harvard Business School Press, 2003. Hargadon discusses the role of the ideas broker (he calls it "technology broker") and how it works in many different organizations.

Systemic Thinking and the Business Analyst

Systems comprise a set of interconnected components that work together to form a complex whole. Each component (process, machine, person, and so on) plays a part by carrying out some functionality that contributes to the overall goal of the system. Naturally, some of the components will themselves be called a system; looking at these collections from the perspective of the larger context, we can call them a subsystem. Of course, some of these subsystems will contain their own subsystems, and so on.

The point to keep in mind is that modern systems are large and complex. When a business analyst studies a system, he must see not just the components, but also the way in which they work together. Changing one of the components may well have an impact on some relatively distant part of the system. Similarly, malfunctioning of one component could cause another component to fail. In addition, any change to a component might change the overall nature of the larger system.

Systemic (not to be confused with systematic) thinking means looking at how the components play their parts, and considering how one component can disrupt or complement another. Normally the business analyst is concerned with the study of one business area (we refer to this business area

When a business analyst studies a system, he must see not just the components, but also the way in which they work together.

as "the work"). However, taking a systemic view means not only looking at the interconnection of the components of the work, but also seeing how the work fits into the larger system that is the organization itself and, indeed, examining how the organization fits into the wider world.

Systemic thinking is, in one way, the opposite of analysis. Analysis is concerned with partitioning and studying the individual pieces. The word "analysis" comes from the root meaning "to break into constituent parts" or "the process of separating something into its constituent elements." Thus the title business *analyst* is not exactly appropriate for what we are advocating here, but it shall suffice for the person who studies the business.

The task is not just thinking about the interface to some new piece of software or the features that make up that software. Instead, the focus is on exploring how that piece of software will fit into the context of the organization, and whether it has the potential to negatively affect some other part of the organization. Doing so means divorcing yourself from the project for the moment and looking at the project from the organization's viewpoint. Is there anything about this project that could impact—either negatively or beneficially—another part of the organization?

Naturally, you must do the same thing from within the project. That is, you must consider whether all components of the product being built are working harmoniously with one another.

We discussed systemic thinking in Chapter 7, Understanding the Real Problem. A more detailed look at the subject can be found there, and we urge you to consider systemic thinking as part of your business analysis strategy.

> **READING**
> Meadows, Donella. *Thinking in Systems: A Primer.* Chelsea Green Publishing, 2008. See the bibliography for other books on systems thinking.

The Business Analyst as Visualizer

Visualization is a necessary part of any product development activity. As we discussed previously, it is necessary to understand how the various components and processes within your product and your work interact. As the product has not yet been built, this task requires you to visualize these things, and to communicate your visualization to other stakeholders.

Visualization is normally associated with data. By visualizing the data and presenting it in a graphic format, the meaning of the data becomes richer and much more powerful. Edward Tufte has written several wonderful books on the subject. A more immediately resource is the Flowing Data website (flowingdata.com). If you visit this site, you will see how the data is more communicable when it is turned into a visual presentation.

And so it is with systems and products: Words are almost always inadequate to describe them. Your products, systems, and processes are typically multidimensional, and using words alone rarely conveys an accurate picture of their breadth and depth. Yet accuracy is necessary if your stakeholders are to get the right picture of the product you are proposing to build.

> **READING**
> Tufte, Edward. *The Visual Display of Quantitative Information,* second edition. Graphics Press, 2010.

We suggest that to be an effective visualizer, you become a sketcher. Sketching means, naturally enough, drawing pictures, which many of us are reluctant to do. Perhaps this hesitancy arises because people do not feel they are any good at drawing. Of course, if no one is good at drawing, then the fellow looking at your sketches cannot be critical, because his drawings are no better than yours. So lose your inhibition and draw.

Your sketches are intended to convey information about the product you visualize. Part of the business analysis process is to liaise with the stakeholders and ensure that they have the same idea of the product as you do. Without visualizing and sketching, however, it is difficult to convey an accurate notion of what the product is to be.

Visualizing how all the components of the product fit together is not exactly easy; the same is true of visualizing how your product will fit within the larger organization. But it has to be done, and it falls to the business analyst to do it. As we pointed out earlier in this chapter, you are not merely a stenographer who records other people's wishes, but rather an active player who seeks to bring about a product that will improve a piece of work. Without visualizing how the product fits into the piece of work, it is difficult to say whether it will be beneficial.

Summary

This chapter has presented a number of strategies for today's business analyst. Naturally, not all of them will be immediately applicable to you, but we hope that this discussion has provided some guidance on the variables that affect how you carry out your role. Keep in mind that the business analyst is the central player in most projects. True, the business analyst does not have the same amount of control and authority that the project manager does, nor does the business analyst have the detailed technical skills of the developers. Even so, being in the middle of all things makes the job the most interesting one and, in our humble opinions, the most crucial.

Functional Requirements

in which we look at those requirements that
cause the product to do something

Functional requirements specify what the product must do—the actions it must perform to satisfy the fundamental reasons for its existence. For example, this functional requirement describes something the product has to do if it is to complete the work that it is intended to perform:

> The product shall predict which road sections will freeze within the selected time parameters.

The reason for functional requirements is that once the business analyst has understood the necessary functionality of the product, he uses the functional requirements to explain to the developers what has to be built.

In Chapters 5 and 7, we described how to discover the business needs. In Chapter 6, we described how the requirements analyst uses business use case (BUC) scenarios to illustrate the functionality for the interested stakeholders, and product use case (PUC) scenarios to define ideas for the product boundary. Determining the product boundary is discussed in Chapter 8.

Chapters 5 and 7 describe how to discover requirements. Chapter 6 explores how to use scenarios to describe business use cases and product use cases.

We assume that you have read the previously mentioned chapters; the interesting part of them now is the transition from the PUC scenarios to the functional requirements. When the stakeholders reach consensus on the PUC scenarios, the business analyst writes a set of functional requirements to specify the functionality indicated by the scenario. These requirements are then used by the developers to build the product. This process is illustrated in Figure 10.1.

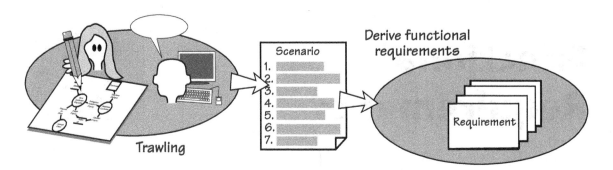

Trawling

Derive functional requirements

Figure 10.1

The functionality of the work is determined during the trawling activity, and you usually communicate this back to the stakeholders by writing a scenario. You then write functional requirements from the scenario. The end result is a set of functional requirements that specify what the product has to do to support the work.

To get the most out of this chapter, it is necessary to understand the difference between a requirement—a need for your product to do something to support the owner's business—and a solution—the technological implementation of that requirement. It is also necessary to understand that while we are describing how to write requirements, the most important thing is to understand what the real business need is, and to communicate it in a way that ensures you get the right product built.

Toward the end of this chapter, we discuss some alternative ways of describing the product's functionality. You may care to jump ahead and preview them, as one (or more) might be suitable for your project.

Formality Guide

Rabbit projects—the small, fast projects—are probably using some form of agile method. These methods emphasize iteration and not producing heavy documentation. We applaud this goal, and suggest that it is not necessary for rabbits to produce the complete requirements specification. Nevertheless, the idea of the description and its rationale contribute greatly to understanding the real requirement and the conversation with the business stakeholders, and should be included in stories. We look at user stories later in the chapter, and discuss alternative ways of specifying the necessary functionality.

Horse projects usually have a need to write their requirements in some communicable form. Compared to rabbits, horses have longer release cycles and geographically scattered stakeholders. This wider distribution of project participants puts greater emphasis on communicating requirements in a more precise and consistent form. It is crucial that team members have a solid understanding of what a functional requirement is, and what the functional requirements mean for the eventual product. That said, horse projects should maximize the potential for communicating the requirements using scenarios and a class model of the work's stored data.

Elephant projects must have a complete and correct requirements specification. All of the information in this chapter is relevant to elephants, and the discussion on level of granularity is particularly pertinent.

Functional Requirements

You have, by this stage, decided how much of your owner's work is to be done by your automated product. Now you have to describe the functionality of that product.

Functional requirements are the things your product does to support the work. They should be, as far as possible, expressed independently from any technology that will be used to implement them. This separation might seem strange, as these requirements apply to an automated product. Keep in mind, however that you, as the business analyst, are not attempting to craft a technological solution, but rather to specify what that technological solution must do. How it achieves that outcome is a matter for the designer.

The functional requirements specify the product to be developed, so they must contain sufficient detail for the developer to build the correct product with only the minimum of clarification and explanation from the requirements analyst and the stakeholders. Note that we do not say *"no* clarification." If the developer has absolutely no questions, then you have done too much work and provided too detailed a requirements specification. We explain this point further as we proceed.

Functional requirements describe what the product has to do to support and enable the owner's work. They should be, as far as possible, independent of the technology used by the eventual product.

Uncovering the Functional Requirements

Several artifacts help to describe the product's functionality. We will look at these items over the course of this chapter, but let's start with the most obvious one—the scenario. You arrive at scenarios by partitioning the work using the business events that affect it. For each business event, there is a business use case that responds to the business event, and a BUC scenario describes this functionality from the business point of view. From this BUC you derive one, and sometimes more than one, product use case.

In Chapter 6, we described writing a scenario that shows the PUC's functionality as a series of steps. The value of the PUC scenario is that it enables you, your business stakeholders, and your developers to have an overview of the functionality for which you are about to write atomic requirements. The steps in the scenario are readily recognizable to the business stakeholders— you write them in the stakeholders' language. Given this fact, the steps are generalized to encapsulate the details of the product's functions. Think of the details contained within each step as its functional requirements; your task now is to expose them by writing them as atomic functional requirements. Figure 10.2 illustrates this progression.

Figure 10.2

The scenario is a convenient way to work with stakeholders to determine the necessary functionality for a product use case. Each of the scenario's steps is decomposed into its functional requirements. The collection of functional requirements reveals what the product has to do to fulfill the product use case.

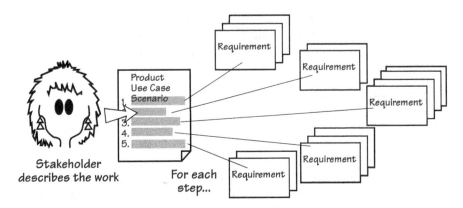

Let's look at how this process works by using an example of a product use case scenario. In the IceBreaker road de-icing system, one of the PUCs is "Produce road de-icing schedule." The actor—the person or thing immediately adjacent to the product (often called a user)—for this use case is the *Truck Depot Supervisor.* He triggers the product to produce the schedule for de-icing the roads in his district. This situation is illustrated in Figure 10.3.

The product must do several things to achieve the outcome needed by the actor. The following scenario describes this product use case:

Product use case: Produce road de-icing schedule

1. Engineer provides a scheduling date and district identifier to the product.

2. Product retrieves the relevant thermal maps.

3. Product uses the thermal maps, district temperature readings, and weather forecasts to predict temperatures for each road section for the district.

4. Product predicts which roads will freeze and when they will freeze.

5. Product schedules available trucks from the relevant depots.

6. Product advises the engineer of the schedule.

Figure 10.3

This use case diagram shows the product generating the road de-icing schedule. This PUC is triggered by the *Truck Depot Supervisor;* the *Thermal Mapping Database* is a cooperative adjacent system providing information to the product use case upon request.

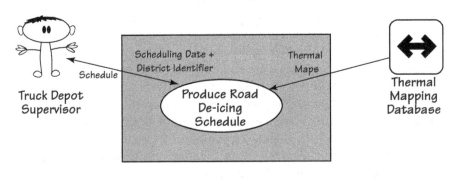

The steps in this product use case are sufficient, in general terms, to describe the work, and, as discussed in Chapter 6, they can be verified with the interested stakeholders. Having a limited number of steps—we suggest between three and ten—in the scenario prevents you from getting enmeshed in details and ensures that the scenario is written in stakeholder-friendly language.

Once you and your stakeholders have agreed on the scenario, for each of the steps ask, "What does the product have to do to complete this step?" For example, the first step in the scenario is

Three to ten steps in the scenario give a reasonable level of detail, without making it too complex for nontechnical stakeholders.

1. Engineer provides a scheduling date and district identifier.

What does the product have to do to complete this step? The first thing is fairly obvious, so this is your first functional requirement:

> *The product shall accept a scheduling date.*

When you ask the stakeholders whether there is anything special about the scheduling date, they tell you that due to imprecise forecasts, scheduling is never done more than two days in advance. This information suggests another functional requirement:

> *The product shall warn if the scheduling date is neither today nor the next day.*

Another requirement from the first step is

> *The product shall accept a valid district identifier.*

You discover another requirement when you inquire what is meant by "valid." The identifier is valid if it identifies one of the districts for which the engineer has responsibility. It would also be valid if it is the identity of a district that is intended by the engineer. This leads us to two more functional requirements:

> *The product shall verify that the district is within the de-icing responsibility of the area covered by this installation.*
>
> *The product shall verify that the district is the one wanted by the engineer.*

The objective is to write enough functional requirements for your developers to build exactly the product your client is expecting and your actor needs to do the work.

The number of requirements you derive from any step is not important, although experience tells us that it is usually fewer than six. If you uncover only one requirement from each step, it suggests either the level of detail in your scenarios is too granular or your functional requirements are too coarse. If you find you are writing more than six requirements per step, either your requirements are too fine-grained or you have a very complex use case. The objective is to write enough functional requirements for your developers to build exactly the product your client is expecting and your actor needs to do the work.

Let's consider another of the use case steps in our example:

4. Product determines which roads will freeze and when they will freeze.

This step in the use case scenario leads us to write three functional requirements:

> The product shall determine which areas in the district are predicted to freeze.
>
> The product shall determine which road sections are in the areas that are predicted to freeze.
>
> The product shall determine when each road section will freeze.

Now continue in the same vein, working through each of the steps from the scenario. When you have exhausted the steps, you should have written the functional requirements for the product use case. You should test whether you have completed the use case by walking through the requirements with a group of colleagues, and demonstrating that the use case provides the correct outcome for the actor.

Level of Detail or Granularity

Requirements are written as a single sentence with a single verb.

Note the level of detail in the preceding examples—the requirements are written as a single sentence with a single verb. When you write this single sentence, you make the requirement much easier to test and far less susceptible to ambiguity. Note also the form "The product shall . . ."; it makes the sentence active and focuses on communicating what the product is intended to do. It also provides a consistent form for the developers and other stakeholders who need to have a clear understanding of what the product is intended to do. You can of course substitute "will" for "shall" (some people claim is it grammatically better), but be consistent with whichever you choose.

Incidentally, the word "shall" does not mean that you will definitely be able to find a solution to satisfy the requirement; it simply means that the requirement is a statement of the business intention. The developers are charged with deriving a technological solution to the requirement, and naturally there will be times when they cannot find a cost-effective solution. In the meantime, the requirement clarifies what the business needs the product to do.

One last word on the form employed to write the requirements description: Sometimes people use a mixture of "shall," "must," "will," "might," "could" and so on, to indicate the priority of a requirement. This practice results in semantic confusion, and we advise against it. Instead, use one consistent form for writing your requirements' descriptions ("The product shall . . ." is the most common) and use a separate attribute of the requirement to identify its priority.

> *Use a separate component of your requirement to indicate the priority of the requirement.*

Description and Rationale

The examples we have given above are what we call the *description* of the requirement. There is more to a requirement than that. We suggest—strongly suggest—that you add a *rationale* to your requirements to show why the requirement exists. In some cases this might be obvious, but in many circumstances it is a crucial component of the requirement.

For example:

> Description: The product shall record roads that have been treated.

This might seem at first glance to be a routine requirement and of no great importance. Now let's add the rationale for this requirement:

> Description: The product shall record roads that have been treated.
>
> Rationale: To be able to schedule untreated roads and highlight potential danger.

Now it looks a little more serious—human lives could possibly be at risk, or at least the owner of this product would not be carrying out his statutory duties. With the inclusion of the rationale, not only have you given the developer the opportunity to build a better solution—one that makes this information readily accessible to the functionality that discovers the untreated roads—but you have also told the tester how much effort to put into testing this requirement. Clearly, the rationale indicates that this requirement is worthy of some attention.

> *The rationale indicates whether the requirement is worthy of some attention.*

Now consider this example:

> Description: The product shall record the start and end time of a truck's scheduled activity.

This is a normal kind of requirement, one that would not cause much comment. But does it contribute any value to the product? Let's look at two possible rationales:

> Rationale: The truck depot foreman wants to know which trucks are being most used.

or:

> Rationale: Trucks are to be scheduled a maximum of 20 out of 24 hours to allow for maintenance and cleaning.

Now we are getting somewhere. The first rationale says that the requirement is very low priority and might not be worthwhile implementing. After all, the depot foreman can discover the trucks' usage simply by reading their tachometers. The second rationale, however, indicates that this is a valuable requirement—if it is not implemented, then the truck fleet will suffer when the trucks are not properly maintained.

By knowing why something is there, the developers and the testers know much more about the effort they should expend on it.

By including a rationale with the description, the requirement itself becomes more useful. By knowing *why* something is there, the developers and the testers know much more about the effort they should expend on it. It also indicates to future maintainers why the requirement exists in the first place.

The rationale also helps to overcome the possibility of inadvertently writing a solution instead of the real need. For example, this requirement description is written for a machine to sell bus tickets for a city bus company:

> Description: The product shall provide the bus network route map on a touch screen.

The description is actually a solution to the problem. When the rationale was added, the real need becomes visible:

> Description: The product shall provide the bus network route map on a touch screen.
>
> Rationale: Passengers have to provide their destination for the fare to be calculated.

The real need—in other words, the real requirement—is for passengers to provide a destination. How they do so is best left to the experience designer and the technology folks. The touch screen might be the best way to accomplish this goal, but then again, it might not. If tourists were prominent users of the buses, then they would not be familiar with the layout of the network, and finding the stop on a map might be a very slow process. This would not please passengers standing behind them in the queue to buy tickets. Also, if the network is divided into zones for charging purposes, then for regular commuters, it might be more efficient to have a way to indicate the number of zones to be covered, and to ignore the actual stops.

Regardless of how the need is finally implemented, it is clear that writing both the description and the rationale leads to discovery of the real requirement.

Why is this aspect of requirements development important? Because it is far too easy to hide important functionality by describing an implementation, and far too easy to select the most obvious implementation when better ones may exist. Regardless of how the need is finally implemented, it is clear that writing both the description and the rationale leads to discovery of the real requirement.

We have not yet talked about how to ensure that each requirement is measurable and hence testable. We do it by adding a *fit criterion*—and this is so crucial that we have devoted Chapter 12 to it. We will also illustrate how the requirement description and rationale both serve as input that help you write the correct fit criterion.

Refer to Chapter 16, Communicating the Requirements, for the other attributes of a requirement; Chapter 12, Fit Criteria and Rationale, for details of how to make the requirements testable; and Chapter 13, The Quality Gateway, for guidelines on testing the requirements.

Data, Your Secret Weapon

As soon as you start to converge on common terminology, you should define what the terms mean in your data dictionary. The first opportunity to do so usually arrives when you have identified the inputs and outputs on the work context diagram. You define these flows by listing their attributes, and these attributes, in turn, enable you to build a business data model. This data model acts as the definition of some of your functional requirements, and provides a common language for your team.

Data Models

Data models—also called class diagrams or entity relationship models— are a rich indicator of the product's functionality. Figure 10.4 shows a data model (using UML class diagram notation) for the IceBreaker product. Take a moment to look at it as we discuss how some of the product's functionality can be derived from this model.

The class model shows the classes (or entities) as rectangles. A class is a logical collection of data attributes that is needed by the product to carry out its functionality. The lines between the classes indicate an association between two classes, and the name on the line indicates the reason for the association. The asterisks and the 1s define the multiplicity of the association. For

Figure 10.4

A class diagram showing the stored data that the business needs to predict the formation of ice on roads. A truck is dispatched to treat a road when the readings from the weather station and the forecast indicate the road section is about to freeze.

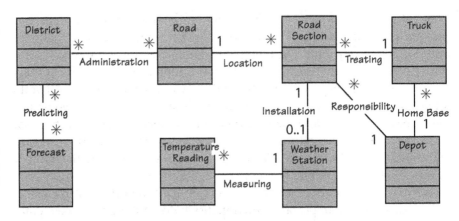

example, a *Road Section* will be recorded as having been treated by one *Truck* (the business policy says that one truck is sufficient to treat a road section, with the sections being about 5 kilometers long), but one *Truck* would be expected to treat many *Road Sections*. The model shows that a *Road Section* has a *Treating* association with one (1) *Truck*, and the *Truck* has the same association with many (*) *Road Sections*.

> *You cannot have stored data unless there is some functionality to store and retrieve it, and functions can only exist if they process data.*

There is a dependency between a product's stored data and its functionality: You cannot have stored data unless there is some functionality to store and retrieve it, and functions can exist only if they process data. Or, as the song goes, "You can't have one without the other."

Note that the class model is a business data model; it represents the data that must be stored so that the business can do its work. It is not a design for a database, so it does not need to show any implementation details—the database designers will add this information later.

Let's examine each of the data classes: *Weather Station* is a data representation of the real-world device installed beside a road. The ice prediction product must have functionality to record the installation of the sensor and its precise location, and to time-stamp and record the *Temperature Readings* as the weather station transmits them. Similarly, there must be functionality to record, change, and delete the *Roads* and their *Road Sections*, and to know which sections are the responsibility of which *Depots*. The product must know which *Trucks* have their home base at a depot, and which are available for scheduling. All of the information we get from the class model indicates the functionality of the product.

Data Dictionary

Your data dictionary defines the meaning of the classes, attributes, and associations on your data model. For example, the data dictionary definition of the class *Road* is

Road = Road Name + Road Number

Thus, whenever you use the term *Road* in this requirements specification, it complies with this definition. To make it clear why we are interested in a road, there should also be a description of each class. For example:

> *A road is stretch of contiguous (but not necessarily linear) highway that can freeze over causing traffic accidents.*

Similarly, your dictionary should also contain a definition of each attribute and association.

The data model is not an indicator of the complete functionality. However, if you routinely build such a model, it will serve as part of the specification of your functional requirements.

The Volere Requirements Specification Template in Appendix A shows an example of the data model and data dictionary for the road de-icing project.

See the section in Chapter 17 on the CRUD check for more about the connection between the data model and the functional requirements.

Exceptions and Alternatives

Exceptions are unwanted but inevitable deviations from the normal case caused by errors of processing and incorrect actions. The exception scenario (which we discussed in Chapter 6) demonstrates how the product recovers from the unwanted happening. The procedure for writing the requirements remains the same: go through each of the exception steps and determine what the product must do to accomplish that step.

For these requirements, you must make it clear that they become reality only if the exception exists. To do so, you might identify a block of requirements as being attached to a particular exception or write each one to include the exception condition:

> *If there are no trucks available, the product shall generate an emergency request to truck depots in adjacent counties.*

Alternatives are allowable variations from the normal case, which are usually provided at the behest of the business stakeholders. A well-known example is Amazon's 1-Click. If you have already saved a credit card with Amazon, you have an alternative path available to you when buying goods: Instead of going through the normal check-out routine, you can have the goods be recorded as sold as soon as you click on them. The normal case would look like this:

> *The product shall add the selected item to the shopping cart.*

Here is the alternative:

> *If 1-Click is used, the product shall record the sale of the selected item.*

Be prepared to create many requirements to handle the exceptions and alternatives for your product; sometimes these nonroutine cases account for the bulk of the requirements. Given that human users of software systems are capable of the most bizarre actions, you will need to specify a great deal of recovery functionality.

Conditional Requirements

Sometimes, you need to add a condition to a requirement. This happens when the requirement comes into play only if certain processing circumstances have occurred. For example:

> If a road scheduled for treatment has not been reported within 30 minutes of its scheduled time, the product shall issue an untreated road alert.

Alternatively, you might find that the requirement reads more easily if you write it with the condition at the end:

> The product shall play the music if requested.

Or even this way:

> The product shall highlight any overdrawn accounts.

This approach works if the conditions rarely appear in your specification—but sometimes that is not true. We discussed alternatives and exceptions earlier, and you will probably find that when these cases arise, many requirements are needed to handle the exception/alternative. Repeatedly writing the condition as an "if" statement is awkward; we suggest that where needed, you tag the requirement with the step of the scenario and write the requirement in the normal imperative way ("The product shall . . ."). You must make your developers aware that the tagged requirements have to be read in conjunction with the scenario to see which are conditional and which are not.

Avoiding Ambiguity

Whether the sources of your requirements consist of written documents or verbal statements from interviews, you should be aware of the enormous potential for ambiguity and the misunderstanding that ambiguity can cause. Ambiguity arises from several sources.

First, the English language is full of homonyms. English contains an estimated 500,000 words in normal usage and about the same number of technical, scientific, and other specialized words. Normal-language words have been almost randomly added by many different people and from many sources over a long period of time. This growth has led to different usages and meanings of the same word.

Consider the word "file," which is used so commonly in information technology. In addition to meaning an automated storage place for information, it means a metal instrument for abrading or smoothing; a collection of documents; a row of people, as in "single file"; a slang term for an artful or shrewd person; a verb meaning to rub away or smooth; and more recently a verb used by lawyers, as when they "file suits." Of course, "suit" itself also means the clothing the lawyer wears in court, as well as a set of playing cards such as hearts, diamonds, spades, and clubs. It is difficult to imagine why, when the language contains a huge number of words, that so many of them have multiple meanings.

It is difficult to imagine why, when the language contains a huge number of words, that so many of them have multiple meanings.

When writing requirements, we have to contend with more challenges than just homonyms. If the context of your product is not clear, then it will also lead to ambiguity. Suppose you have the following requirement:

> The product shall show the weather for the next 24 hours.

The meaning here depends on the type of requirement and what is near it in the specification. Does the requirement mean the product is to communicate the weather that is expected to happen in the forthcoming 24 hours, or must it communicate some weather and continue to do so until one full day has elapsed?

We advise you to group your requirements by product use case, and write your requirements one PUC at a time. This system of organization will, to a large extent, reduce ambiguity. For example, consider this requirement:

> The product shall communicate all roads predicted to freeze.

Does "all" refer to every road known to the product? Or just those roads being examined by the user? The PUC scenario tells us that the actor has previously identified a district or an area within the district. Thus we may safely say that "all" refers to the geographical area selected. In fact, the meaning of almost any requirement depends on its context. This is quite a good thing, because we do not need to waste stakeholders' time by laboriously qualifying every word of every requirement. While anything has the potential to be ambiguous, the PUC scenario, by setting a context for the requirement, minimizes the risk of ambiguity.

We love the example erected by the city traffic authority in New York some years ago when it introduced red zones. Red zones are sections of streets where the authorities are particularly anxious that traffic is not impeded. The zones are designated by red-painted curbs and adorned with signs such as that shown in Figure 10.5.

Although the last directive on the sign is ambiguous, the workers at the traffic authority made a reasonable judgment in taking the ambiguity risk. Taking into account the context, the authority decided that no driver was foolish enough to think the point intended was that drivers should not make jokes in their cars or give birth to baby goats. In other words, the context determines how drivers interpret the sign.

Similarly, when one of the engineers says, "We want to have the trucks treat the roads before they freeze," it is fairly clear that he does not mean that the roads have to be treated before the trucks freeze. At the very least, the context in which it was said should indicate the meaning.

We have already emphasized how progressive definition of terms in your data dictionary (Section 7, The Business Data Model and Data Dictionary, of the Volere Requirements Specification Template) will greatly reduce ambiguity. It's also beneficial to check that the terms defined in the dictionary are being consistently used in the requirements.

Here's another tip: Eliminate all pronouns from your requirements and replace them with the subject or object to which the pronouns refer. (Note the potential ambiguity of the preceding sentence if we had said "they" instead of "the pronouns.")

When you write a requirement, read it aloud. If possible, have a colleague read it aloud. Confirm with your stakeholder that you both reach the same understanding of the requirement. This may seem obvious, but "send the bill to the customer" may mean that the bill goes to the person who actually bought the goods or that the bill is sent to the account holder. It is also

Figure 10.5

A traffic sign in New York. The meaning is very clear. Photo by Kenneth Uzquiano, used with the photographer's permission.

unclear whether the bill is sent immediately after the purchase or at the end of the month. And does "bill" refer to an invoice, a bill of materials, or a bill of lading? A short conversation with the appropriate stakeholders about the definition and consistent use of terminology will clarify the intention.

Keep in mind that you are writing a *description* of the requirement. The real requirement is revealed when you write the fit criterion. Until you add the fit criterion, a good description and its rationale are both worthwhile and sufficient.

Technological Requirements

Technological requirements are functionality that is needed purely because of the chosen technology. In the example of the use case that produces the de-icing schedule, the product interacts with the thermal mapping database. Suppose the designer decides that handling this interaction via an Internet connection is the best option. Because of this technological choice, the product has a need to establish a secure connection. This need is a technological requirement; that is, it arises purely because of the chosen technology. If the designer had selected a different technology to handle this part of the work—say, a direct fiber-optic link—the result would be different technological requirements.

Technological requirements arise purely because of the chosen technology.

The technological requirements are not there for business reasons, but rather to make the chosen implementation work. We suggest that these requirements either be recorded in a separate specification or be identified clearly as technological requirements and recorded along with the business requirements. Stakeholders must understand clearly why a requirement appears in the specification, so it is important that the technological requirements are not introduced before the business requirements are fully understood.

Grouping Requirements

We suggested earlier that you group the functional requirements by use case. The advantage achieved by doing so is that it becomes easy to discover related groups of requirements and to test the completeness of the functionality. Nevertheless, sometimes other groupings may prove more useful.

The word "feature" springs to mind here. The meaning and scope of a feature vary depending on the situation. A feature could be as small as turning on an indicator light or as large as allowing the user to navigate across a continent. Indeed, the feature itself is often important from a marketing point of view. Even so, different features have different degrees of value to the organization. For this reason, you might find it necessary to discard or radically curtail features. Grouping the requirements by feature makes it easier to manipulate them and to adjust your specification when the market

Figure 10.6

A hierarchy of requirements. The work context is the highest-level statement of requirements; it is decomposed into the next level, the business events. The level below the business events comprises the product use cases, each of which is decomposed into a number of product use case steps. The lowest level includes the atomic requirements, each of which can be traced back up the hierarchy. Activity diagrams and user stories are also used to group atomic requirements. Features are a grouping often used by stakeholders from marketing or product version planning.

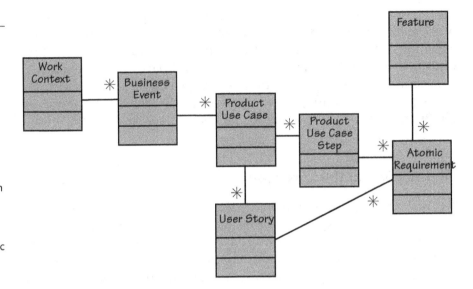

(or the marketing department's request) changes. Bear in mind that a feature will usually contain requirements from a number of different product use cases. Thus, if you are grouping requirements by feature so that you can trace changes from and to the business, it makes sense to be able to group them by product use case as well (as illustrated in Figure 10.6).

It helps to think of the atomic requirements as the lowest level of requirement specification. You group these into a requirements hierarchy for three reasons:

- To be able to involve stakeholders with different depths, breadths, and focuses of interest
- To help you discover the atomic requirements in the first place
- To be able to deal with volume and complexity

Refer to Appendix D for a complete Requirements Knowledge Model that you can use to define your own non-subjective hierarchy.

A leveled requirements specification meets these expectations as long as you have a non-subjective traceable path from one level to another. We have seen people run into trouble when they create "high-level requirements" and "low-level requirements" that do not have a formal, non-subjective link. This practice creates problems and arguments because "high-level" and "low-level" are subjective. To avoid such conflicts, we recommend that you work with a non-subjective hierarchy such as this: work context, business event, product use case, product use case step, and atomic requirement.

Alternatives to Functional Requirements

We have just taken you through most of a chapter that tells you how to write functional requirements, and most of this chapter implies that we think writing functional requirements is a good thing to do. However, just as there is more than one way to skin a cat (we have often wondered why anyone would want to skin a cat, and why they would need several methods for doing it—the cat can participate only once), so there is more than one way to describe the functionality of your product.

Please keep in mind that whatever you do, you must first understand the correct functionality. The alternatives presented here indicate other forms of capturing and communicating that understanding.

Scenarios

In this and a previous chapter, we suggested that you write product use case scenarios. Earlier in this chapter, we described the process of writing the functional requirements using the steps of the BUC scenario. However, if the intended product is routine and the business area well understood, and if your developers are experienced and willing to collaborate, you might consider simply adding implementation details to the scenario, and use that as your specification. With this approach, you might have to revise the scenario a little to make the steps read from the point of view of the product. You and your developers and testers must be confident that they can write and test the product based on this enhanced scenario.

If the scenario becomes too long or too elaborate, then revert to writing the functional requirements in the normal manner.

Do not follow this path if you are outsourcing construction to an external supplier or another department in your organization. For outsourcing, it is better to avoid the increased potential for misinterpretation by writing the atomic functional requirements.

User Stories

User stories are another way to describe the necessary functionality of the product. User stories are used by several agile methods, and you might consider them as an alternative to writing functional requirements.

The user story is written in this form:

> As a [role] I want [functionality] so that [reason for or use of the functionality].

User stories are usually written on story cards by the Product Owner (the representative of the customer), who is part of the agile team and represents the business view. The stories are often about features that the product owner thinks should be part of the product.

> *As a moviegoer I want to have my tickets sent to my mobile phone so that I can avoid the box-office queue at the cinema.*

The intention of the story card is not to specify the requirements, but rather to act as a starting point, or placeholder, for the requirements. These are discovered as development progresses through conversations between the developers and the stakeholders. Stories are usually written on cards, and the developers annotate the cards with their fleshed-out requirements and the necessary test cases.

We have written much more about user stories and their use in Chapter 14, Requirements and Iterative Development. We refer you to that chapter for a full explanation.

Business Process Models

If, as a matter of course, you build activity diagrams (or any other type of process model), then consider whether they, together with their process descriptions, can serve as the functional requirements. Many organizations (perhaps that should be "many business analysts") prefer to use process modeling as a way of arriving at an understanding of the necessary functionality. They find their stakeholders relate more easily to diagrams than to text scenarios.

You can use whatever notation you find most convenient for your process models. There are few bad notations but, unfortunately, many bad ways of using notations. Probably the most popular techniques are the UML activity diagram (Figure 10.7), the BPMN process model (Figure 10.8), and the data

Figure 10.7

An activity diagram showing the product use case "Truck Depot reports problem with truck."

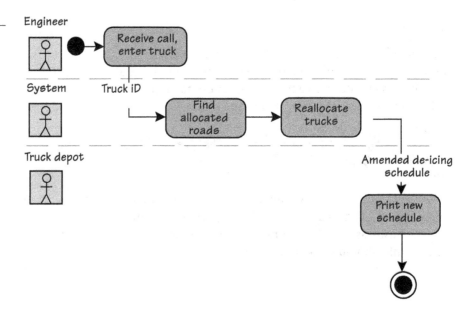

Figure 10.8

A BPMN process model for the BUC that produces the de-icing schedule. Consider how much extra specification your developers need to build the correct product.

flow model of a business use case (Figure 10.9). We have found that analysts have their own preferences when it comes to these diagrams—and these preferences are sometimes expressed with a religious fervor—so we make no attempt to state a preference. Instead, we just ask you to consider them for yourself.

Of course, it is also possible to use the process model as a basis, and then write atomic requirements from each of the activities shown on the diagram.

READING

Robertson, James, and Suzanne Robertson. *Complete Systems Analysis: The Workbook, the Textbook, the Answers.* Dorset House, 1998.

Requirements for COTS

We are using the term COTS (commercial off-the-shelf) product to mean any installable software product. It does not matter whether this item is a commercial off-the-shelf software product, an open-source product, or a product that you found in an abandoned bus shelter; we will refer to it as COTS.

The COTS product is seen as an alternative to building software from scratch. It contains much of the needed functionality, but usually requires a certain amount of post-installation modification. Sometimes this is easily done using parameters; at other times developers have to write additional code to bring the COTS software into line with what is needed.

Figure 10.9

A data flow model of the product use case "Truck Depot reports problem with truck." This diagram is supported by process specifications for each of the processes shown, and a data dictionary to define the data flows and stores.

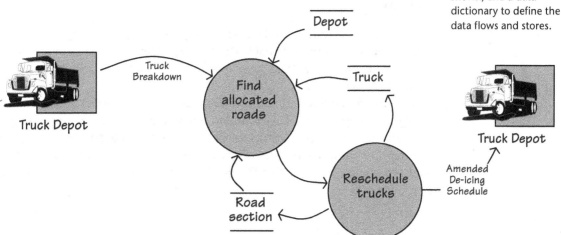

Many organizations buy a COTS product, and then rearrange the organization and their business processes to fit the COTS. Some organizations consider this approach to be the cheapest way of installing software. Sometimes, some of the rearrangement of the organization seeks to change some of the COTS functionality to meet the needed functionality. When this happens, the business analyst must be able to indicate to the organization the areas of deficiency, and the areas where the COTS product is a mismatch with the desired workings of the organization.

There is little point in attempting to document the functionality of the COTS product. However, we recommend that you begin your business analysis by building a context diagram of the work area that will be affected by the COTS product. This activity leads you to the business events of that business area, which you can then compare with the equivalent business event supported by the COTS product. It is not necessary to write a full BUC scenario, as the COTS provider has probably already done so. Nevertheless, you should pay attention to the incoming and outgoing data from each of the business events. Compare this data to the data inputs and outputs of the COTS product, and write requirements for any modifications needed to bring the COTS data in line with the organizational need for data.

We recommend that you begin your business analysis by building a context diagram of the work area that will be affected by the COTS product.

Alternatively, you can choose to change the organization rather than the COTS product. In this case you write a user manual for the people involved in the business area. This document would describe the new work practices necessary to accommodate the COTS product.

Using COTS products does not obviate the need for business analysis. In fact, business analysis is crucial to ensuring that the COTS product functions so that it truly matches the needs of the organization. The task of the business analyst here is to discover and understand the differences between the COTS product and the organization.

Refer to Chapter 9, Strategies for Today's Business Analyst, for more on requirements strategy when you are working with external suppliers.

Summary

The functional requirements describe the product's processing—the things it has to do to support and enable the business. The functional requirements should be a complete and, as far as possible, unambiguous description of the product's functionality.

The functional requirements are derived from the product use cases. The most convenient way we have found to generate the functional requirements is to write a scenario that breaks the product use case into between three and ten steps. Examine each of the steps and ask, "What does the product have to do to accomplish this step?" The things that it does are the functional requirements.

We suggest that you write these requirements (for the moment) using two components: a description and a rationale. The latter is the reason for the former's existence. Elsewhere in this book, we discuss how to formulate the rest of the requirement's attributes.

When you have sufficient functional requirements to achieve the outcome of a product use case, it is time to move on to the next one. As you progress through these PUCs, you may discover that a requirement you defined for one PUC also applies to other PUCs. Reuse the requirement you have already written by cross-referencing it to all relevant product use cases.

When all of the product use cases have been treated this way, you will have defined the requirements that completely and unambiguously specify the functionality of the product.

When all of the product use cases have been treated this way, you will have defined the requirements that completely and unambiguously specify the functionality of the product.

Non-functional Requirements

in which we look at the requirements that specify how well your product does what it does

How can something called "non-functional" be important? Consider this, a story that really happened: The client rejected the delivered help desk software. The functionality was correct—it supported the help desk's activity, and did all that it was supposed to do, but the client didn't want it. Why not? Because the users—the help desk operators—refused to use it, preferring to use the existing manual procedures. Why was the product so bad? Because the requirements team had paid almost no attention to the non-functional requirements.

We should explain that: The help desk staff already had nine other applications running on their desktops. The requirements team did not bother inquiring about the users' look and feel requirements. As a consequence, the new software had a completely different interface style with a different set of icons and screen layouts. The help desk people had to use nine other applications and, quite rightfully, refused to learn a new, non-standard interface. The requirements team also ignored the usability requirements—the new software employed work sequences, metaphors, and terminology unfamiliar to the users.

If that was not bad enough, the requirements team failed to gather the performance requirements, which should have specified the speeds and volumes of data handled. The result? A product with a woefully inadequate database that failed to handle the volume of requests made to the help desk. The operational requirements should have set out the operating environment and collaborating products, but didn't. Security was overlooked, and because cultural requirements were not taken into account, the end product contained several icons considered offensive by some members of the help desk.

Why was the product so bad? Because the requirements team had paid almost no attention to the non-functional requirements.

245

All of these issues were non-functional requirements. In this unfortunate case, their omission meant that the project was a complete failure.

An Introduction to Non-functional Requirements

Projects that pay little or no heed to non-functional requirements often produce a product that we call "Soviet Style." If you recall the heavy-handed, awkward designs of the Soviet era, you get the idea. The Soviet products were almost impossible to use, were inconvenient, and often were downright ugly. The central planners had no time for niceties such as usability—and if the comrades didn't like the look of it, there was always the Gulag.

READING
Soviet Style is one of the patterns of project behavior discussed in our book, *Adrenaline Junkies and Template Zombies: Patterns of Project Behavior.* Dorset House, 2009. Authors: Tom DeMarco, Peter Hruschka, Tim Lister, Steve McMenamin, James Robertson, and Suzanne Robertson.

The non-functional requirements describe the qualities that your product must have or, to put that another way, how well it does the things it does. Such requirements make the product attractive, or usable, or fast, or reliable, or safe. You use non-functional requirements to specify response times, or accuracy limits on calculations. You write non-functional requirements when you need your product to have a particular appearance, or be used by people in particular circumstances, or adhere to laws applicable to your kind of business.

The non-functional requirements describe how well your product does the things it does.

These properties are not required because they are the functional activities of the product—activities such as computations, data manipulations, and so on—but rather are included because the client expects the activities to be performed in a certain manner and to a specific degree of quality.

As an example of non-functional requirements in real life, let's look at Amazon: The Amazon site is easy to navigate, which makes it easier for customers to find things—this, of course, being the purpose of the site. It is also friendly and makes you feel like a valued customer—you can write reviews, get guidance from fellow customers and Amazon's recommendations, check out and arrange delivery easily, and so on. Amazon has made it so incredibly attractive to shop at its site that people do just that; as a result, Amazon has become the world's largest online retailer. Likewise, Apple's iPad is intuitive and a joy to look at; its ease of use is attested to by stories of six-year-old children using iPads without coaching from their parents. As another example, the look and feel of the *New York Times* app boldly says, "This is a newspaper—not a collection of blogs." Everywhere we see successful products, we see clever discovery of their non-functional requirements.

Formality Guide

On some occasions, the non-functional aspects of the product are the prime reason for doing the project. If the users find the existing product difficult to use, slow, or unreliable, then usability, performance, and reliability, respectively, could be considered the most important requirements for the new product. Paradoxically, these non-functional requirements are often overlooked, and sometimes this neglect leads to the downfall of the project.

Some, though not all, of the non-functional requirements should be the earliest to be gathered and understood. They should *never* be assumed, as frequently happens, even when the customers and the developers believe they are obvious.

Rabbit projects should use the requirements specification template (see Appendix A) as a checklist of non-functional requirements types. Go through the list—ensuring that you check the subtypes—with your key stakeholders and determine their priorities regarding non-functional requirements. "All of them" is not an acceptable answer. Keep the project team aware of these high-priority requirements as you work through the user stories. Also keep in mind that you can write non-functional story cards that are a stand-alone requirement, and have no functional component.

Horse projects have multiple stakeholders. The requirements analysts must ensure that they capture everyone's non-functional requirements, as well as identify and deal with the conflicts between non-functional requirements originating from the different and scattered stakeholders.

Elephant projects have a need to capture all of their requirements in written form, including the non-functional ones. We suggest you group the non-functional requirements by type in the specification. Requirements can be grouped by use case, but as there will be overlap between use cases, grouping by type prevents duplication.

Functional Versus Non-functional Requirements

In our ongoing example, we have explored various aspects of the IceBreaker product in earlier chapters. Part of this product's functionality is to record road temperatures and moisture levels each time this data is transmitted by the weather stations. Recording data is a functional requirement—it is part of the fundamental business process. Now suppose that this data has to be recorded within half a second; moreover, once it is recorded, no one except a supervising engineer is allowed to alter the data. These two requirements are non-functional, with the first being a performance requirement and the second a security requirement. Although these requirements are not part of the functional reason for the product's existence, they are needed to make the product perform in the desired manner.

Non-functional requirements do not alter the product's essential functionality. That is, the functional requirements remain the same no matter which properties you attach to them. At the risk of confusing matters, the non-functional requirements might add functionality to the product. In the

Think of the functional requirements as those that cause the product to do the work, and the non-functional requirements as those that give character to the work.

Figure 11.1

Apple's iPad is a runaway success, largely due to its non-functional requirements. The look and feel of the product is simple and elegant, the usability is legendary (very young children use it), and the performance (the capacity of its memory, battery life, and so on) is impressive. Of course, it is also downright cool (another non-functional requirement). While other tablets offer similar functionality, the iPad has won its dominant market share thanks to its superior non-functional qualities. Photo courtesy of Apple.

Non-functional properties may be the difference between an accepted, well-liked product and an unused one.

security example, the product would have to do things to make certain that only supervising engineers alter the data, but that functionality is needed for a non-functional reason—in this case, security. Perhaps it is easier to think of the functional requirements as those that cause the product to do the work and the non-functional requirements as those that give character to the work, and even easier to say that functional requirements are verbs and non-functional requirements are adjectives.

Non-functional requirements make up a significant part of the specification. Provided the product meets the required amount of functionality, the non-functional properties—how usable, convenient, and inviting it is (see, for example, Apple's iPad in Figure 11.1)—may be the difference between an accepted, well-liked product and an unused one. Keep in mind that a large part of what people see or feel with your product is there because of the non-functional requirements.

Use Cases and Non-functional Requirements

A product use case represents a chunk of work the product does when the work is responding to a business event. In earlier chapters, you saw how the scenario breaks the product use case into a number of steps; for each of these steps, you determine the functional requirements.

The non-functional requirements, however, do not fit so neatly into this partitioning theme. Some of them can be linked directly to a functional requirement, some apply to the product use case as a whole, and some apply to the entire product. Figure 11.2 shows the links between the functionality and the associated non-functional requirements.

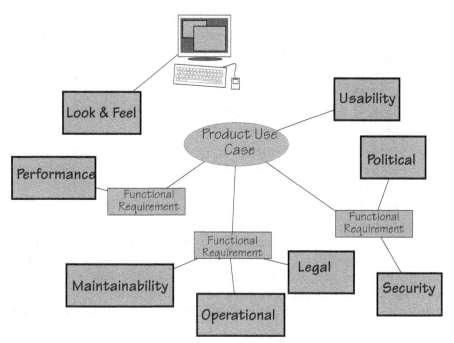

Figure 11.2

Non-functional require-
ments are properties
that the functionality
must have. The function-
ality can be represented
either by a product use
case or by its constitu-
ent functional require-
ments. In this example,
the product use case
has three functional
requirements, each hav-
ing some non-functional
properties. The use case
as a whole must meet
certain usability requirements, whereas the look
and feel requirements
relate to the entire
product.

The Non-functional Requirements Types

We went back over the many requirements specifications we have written
and extracted a list of the most useful properties for products to have. For
the sake of convenience, we grouped them into eight major non-functional
requirement types, and within those, subtypes or variations on the type.
You can see these non-functional types and their identifying numbers in the
Volere Requirements Specification Template.

There is nothing sacred about the categories we have assigned to the non-
functional requirements; feel free to make your own. We assigned categories
because we have found that having a checklist of requirements types makes
it easier to discover all of them—once you are aware of the different types of
requirements, you ask your questions about them.

Following are the non-functional requirement types we use and recommend. Each number is the identifier allocated to that type of requirement in
the requirements specification template.

Appendix A contains
the Volere Requirements
Specification Template.

10 *Look and Feel:* the spirit of the product's appearance

11 *Usability and Humanity:* the product's ease of use, and any special
considerations needed for a better user experience

12 *Performance:* how fast, how safe, how many, how available, and how
accurate the functionality must be

13 *Operational:* the operating environment of the product, and any considerations that must be taken into account for this environment

14 *Maintainability and Support:* expected changes, and the time needed to make them; also specification of the support to be given to the product

15 *Security:* access, confidentiality, recoverability, and auditability of the product

16 *Cultural and Political:* special requirements that come about because of the culture and customs of people who can come in contact with the product

17 *Legal:* the laws and standards that apply to the product

We look at each of these categories in more detail as we go through this chapter. In some cases, the nature of the non-functional requirement suggests how you might go about finding any requirements of the types applicable to your product. If nothing suggests itself, refer to the discussion later in the chapter regarding how to go about eliciting the non-functional requirements.

As you read though these requirement types, keep in mind that sometimes it is difficult to say exactly which type a requirement is. When this sort of uncertainty arises, it could indicate that you have several requirements posturing as one, or that you have one of those not-uncommon requirements that is just too difficult to categorize. If this bothers you, then you can give a requirement multiple types. Don't sweat it—the category is not important; the requirement is.

One other thing to keep in mind as you go through the various non-functional requirements: For the moment, we are dealing only with the description and rationale of the requirement. Some of the examples we give might seem a little vague, ambiguous, or loosely worded. The method of attack is to initially capture the stakeholder's *intention* for the requirement. Later you will add a measurement—we call it a fit criterion—to the requirement to clarify it and make it testable. We discuss fit criteria in Chapter 12, but for the moment we ask you to accept that it is possible to measure such things as "attractive," "exciting," "easy," and other adjectives that appear in the descriptions of non-functional requirements.

The requirement type is a device to help you to find the requirements; think of it as a pointer to questions you have to ask.

Later you will add a fit criterion to the requirement to clarify it and make it testable.

READING

Miller, Roxanne. *The Quest for Software Requirements.* MavenMark Books, 2009. This book contains an extensive list of questions to help you discover the non-functional requirements.

Look and Feel Requirements: Type 10

Look and feel requirements describe the intended spirit, the mood, the style of the product's appearance. These requirements specify the *intention* of the appearance, and are not a detailed design of an interface. For example, suppose you have a look and feel requirement like this:

> Description: The product shall comply with corporate branding standards.

This requirement does not say the company logo must occupy 10 percent of the screen, nor does it talk about the colors or the typefaces to be used. It simply states that the product must comply with the branding standards your organization has established. These standards are published elsewhere—your own organization has a department (usually the communications department) or group responsible for these standards—and the designer has access to them. The fit criterion, when you add it, measures compliance with the standards.

Consider the look and feel requirements that you might build into your next product. Among other appearances appropriate for your product, you might want it to have some of the following characteristics:

- Appears to be simple to use
- Approachable, so that people do not hesitate to use it
- Authoritative, so that users feel they can rely on it and trust it
- Conforming to the client's other products
- Attractive to children or some other specific group
- Unobtrusive, so that people are not aware of it
- Innovative and appearing to be state of the art
- Professional looking
- Exciting
- Cool

In some application areas, software has become a commodity, and the distinction between the functionality of competing products has largely disappeared. In such cases, it falls to the non-functional requirements to differentiate one product from another. Usually, the noticeable and exceptional products have a distinctly superior look and feel.

You should also consider the audience for your product (see Figure 11.3). You are probably not building a product for vampires

Figure 11.3

This is your user—will she be happy with the standard Windows interface? The intended audience for the product largely determines its look and feel requirements. These requirements make it attractive to the audience and sometimes make the difference between a successful product and one that no one wants to use.

and their taste for the dark and the gothic, but even when the product will be used in-house, your users have needs when it comes to the appearance of the software. If your product is for sale, then its appearance makes a major contribution to the customer's buying decision.

Developers of Web products should place a great deal of emphasis on the look and feel requirements.

Developers of products intended for the Web should place a great deal of emphasis on the look and feel requirements. Your client has in mind the kind of experience he wants visitors to the site to have. Your task is to determine these requirements and to specify them with look and feel requirement descriptions such as these:

> *The product shall be conservative.*
>
> *The product shall be intriguing.*
>
> *The product shall appear authoritative.*
>
> *The product shall be attractive to an older audience.*
>
> *The product shall appear simple to use.*
>
> *The product shall appear state of the art.*
>
> *The product shall have an expensive appearance.*

You might be tempted to describe the required look and feel by using a prototype; however, we urge caution because a prototype does not always convey the requirements accurately enough. Prototypes (we usually refer to them as "sketches"), when used to aid requirements discovery, are not intended to be designs for the final product. Instead, they are experiments conducted to find the appropriate functionality, and are usually created before all the requirements are known. Unfortunately, because a prototype is a physical artifact, the developer might assume that the end product is supposed to be an almost exact reproduction of the prototype. He has no way of knowing which of the prototype's features must be implemented exactly as they appear, and which of them are not intended to be definitive. Thus it is important to write the look and feel requirements specifically, and not leave it to someone's interpretation of a prototype.

If you know your product will be implemented using software, then some of your look and feel requirements can be described by citing the appropriate interface standards.

> *The product shall comply with Windows User Experience Interaction Guidelines for Windows 8.*

And here's one other requirement that you should consider:

> *The product shall conform to the established look and feel of the owning organization's products.*

To reiterate the key point, the look and feel requirements describe the intention of the appearance, and are not the design of the interface. To design the product at this stage would be premature—you do not yet know the complete requirements of the product. Designing is the task of the product's designers, once they know the requirements.

Usability and Humanity Requirements: Type 11

These days, usability is crucial. Your users have become accustomed to products for both personal and business use that make for a pleasant, user-oriented experience. To ignore these usability needs is folly—and yet we find that usability requirements are often overlooked owing to the assumption that no sane developer would build a product that is *hard* to use. In the end, the product's usability might be one of the key factors that determine whether the intended users actually use it.

For more on how to define your users, refer to the "Stakeholders" section in Chapter 3, Scoping the Business Problem. Appendix B provides stakeholder templates.

The usability and humanity requirements make the product conform to the users' abilities and expectations. In Section 3 of the requirements specification template, we describe Users of the Product, and explain how to classify their skill levels. What kind of people are they? What kind of product do they need to do their jobs? The usability requirements ensure that you make a successful product for them. (See Figure 11.4.)

The usability of a product affects productivity, efficiency, error rates, and acceptance (i.e., whether people actually use the product). Carefully consider what your client is trying to achieve with the product before writing

Usability requirements make the product conform to the user's abilities and expectations of the usage experience.

Figure 11.4

Consider the capabilities and knowledge of your intended audience when writing the usability requirements.

these requirements. For example, you might write the following usability requirement:

> *The product shall be usable by customers with limited experience of using computers.*

You could also target a different user group:

> *The product shall be easy to use by certified mechanical engineers.*

This requirement captures the intention of your client, and for the moment, it is sufficient; later you will complete it and make it testable. "Easy to use" and "easy to learn" are slightly different characteristics. Easy-to-use products are designed to facilitate an ongoing efficiency, so perhaps some training is necessary before using the product. For example, suppose you were specifying a product to be used for some repetitive task in an office by clerical workers. You would be well advised to make it easy to use, even if the ease of use means training people to use the product, because the ongoing efficiency will pay for this extra effort many times over.

Adobe Photoshop is a case in point. Photoshop is a complex product that offers an amazing wealth of options for the manipulation of digital images to its intended audience of graphic artists and photographers. The Photoshop learning curve is a steep one: There is lot to be learned, and we would venture to say that it is not particularly easy to learn (at least it was not for one of your authors). However, once learned, Photoshop's features make manipulating images a straightforward—even easy—task. Given the depth of functionality needed to do the task and its inherent complexity, Adobe has made its product easy to use once you have learned how to use it.

By contrast, easy-to-learn products are aimed at those tasks that are done infrequently and, therefore, may be forgotten between uses—yearly reports, rarely used features of a software product, and so on. Products that are used by the public—for which no prior training is feasible—must also be easy to learn. For example, telephones, Internet connections in public places, and dispensing machines must be easy to learn.

You might describe your requirement as follows:

> *Description: The product shall be easy to learn.*

Alternatively, you might write this requirement:

> *Description: The product shall be easy to use on the first attempt by a member of the public without training.*
>
> *Rationale: This is a new product and we need our customers to voluntarily switch to using it.*

This description might at first seem blindingly obvious. But it *is* a requirement: Your stakeholder wants the product to be easy to learn, and the rationale gives some insight into why the stakeholder has included the requirement. Later, when you add its fit criterion (which is so important that we have devoted the next chapter to it), you can quantify "easy to use on the first attempt." A suitable fit criterion might be written this way:

> *Fit Criterion: Ninety percent of a panel that is representative of the customer base shall successfully complete [list of tasks] within 90 seconds of their first encounter.*

We once had a client who asked for the product to be "friendly." Because we could not immediately think of a suitable measurement for "friendly," we felt, naturally enough, that we could not write "friendly" as a requirement. Later on, a little questioning revealed that the product the client had in mind would appeal to the personnel consultants who were to use it. He knew that the consultants would be more productive if they switched to the new product, but he also knew that they would not use it, or would use it badly, if they didn't like it.

With that understanding, the requirement began to look like this:

> *The personnel consultants shall like the product.*

We suggested to the client that we could measure the number of consultants who, after an initial training period, preferred to work with the new product rather than their old way. The client agreed with this plan: He said that he would be satisfied if 75 percent of the consultants were using the product after a six-week familiarization period. He decided to use an anonymous survey to poll the consultants.

Thus we had the description and rationale for our usability requirement:

> *Description: The product shall provide the preferred way of working for the personnel consultants.*
>
> *Rationale: To build the consultants' confidence in the product.*

We also had the fit criterion:

> *Fit Criterion: Seventy-five percent of the consultants shall switch to using the product after a six-week familiarization period.*

Usability and humanity requirements can cover areas such as the following:

- Rate of acceptance or adoption by the users
- Productivity gained as a result of the product's introduction
- Error rates (or reduction thereof)
- Use by people who do not speak the language of the country where the product is to be used
- Personalization and internationalization to allow users to change to local spelling, currency, and other preferences
- Accessibility to handicapped people (this is sometimes mandated by law)
- Use by people with no previous experience with computers (an important, albeit often-forgotten consideration)
- Usage during the hours of darkness (this caters to the vampire community)

Politeness is another aspect of usability that is often overlooked. Have you ever used a website that asks you to create an account by filling in all of your personal details and then asks you to enter a password? Once you do so, you get this message: "Your password should be a mixture of 8 alphanumeric characters including one uppercase and one numeric digit; reenter your password." Meanwhile all of the personal details that you entered on your previous attempt to create an account have been obliterated and you are expected to do it all again. We would not tolerate this behavior from another human being, so why should we tolerate it from a piece of software? This sort of behavior toward a user is indicative of a missing politeness requirement:

> *Description: The product shall avoid asking the user to duplicate any entered data.*
>
> *Rationale: To build the user's confidence in the product.*

Usability requirements are derived from what your client is trying to achieve with the operability of the product and from which kind of experience the users expect. Naturally, the users' characteristics make a difference to their expectations. You, as the requirements analyst, have to discover these characteristics and determine which levels of usability will turn the product into a useful and pleasant experience for them.

Before you write your usability requirements, it is helpful to have a very clear picture of who will be using your product. In Chapter 7, we discussed the process of constructing a persona: a virtual person that is a distillation of the majority of your users. You build a persona by surveying your user community, and then derive the archetypical character to represent that community. When the team derives the persona, team members know it so well that they are able to come to a quick consensus of what is appropriate for that persona. As a consequence, you write the usability requirements to suit the persona—the embodiment of almost all of the people who will actually use your product—instead of writing them to suit your own personal preferences, or the preferences of just the one or two loudest users.

Pay attention to usability, as it often leads you to discover the differentiating factor between competing products.

Performance Requirements: Type 12

Performance requirements are written when your product needs to perform some tasks in a given amount of time, some tasks need to be done to a specific level of accuracy, or the product needs to have certain data storage capacity, or it has to achieve a certain volume of throughput.

Consider these requirements carefully. Everyone asks for a product with a quick response time, but the need for speed must be genuine. All too often, we want things to be done quickly when there is no real need to do so. If a task is to produce a monthly summary report, then there is probably no need to complete this job quickly. By contrast, the very success of the product may depend on speed:

> *The product shall identify whether an aircraft is hostile or friendly within 0.25 second.*

Capacity is another performance requirement. This requirement is one of the most critical ones for an ATM network:

> *The product shall support 2,000 concurrent users.*

The client for the IceBreaker product wanted to sell it to road authorities around the world. These authorities are responsible for geographical areas of varying sizes, so the client needed to ensure that the product could handle the largest area covered by any potential client. Initially we would have written the requirement as follows:

> *The product shall accommodate the largest geographical area of any road authority in the world.*

Of course, this is not a practical requirement to hand over to a designer, so eventually we refined it:

> *Description: The product shall have the capacity for 5,000 roads.*
>
> *Rationale: The maximum number of roads in the area of any potential customer for the product.*

When you are thinking about performance requirements, consider such aspects as these:

- Speed to complete a task
- Accuracy of the results
- Safety to the operator
- Volumes of data to be held by the product
- Ranges of allowable values
- Throughput, such as the rate of transactions
- Efficiency of resource usage
- Reliability, often expressed as the mean time between failures
- Availability—the uptime or time periods when users can access the product
- Fault tolerance and robustness
- Scalability of most of the above

Performance requirements include the risk of damage to people or property. If your product is a lawn mower, then there is a genuine need for the product to avoid cutting off the user's toes. Isaac Asimov included this requirement in his laws of robotics:

> *A robot shall not injure a human being.*

Hardware is not the only potential source of damage. You should consider whether your software product could cause damage, either directly or indirectly. The IceBreaker product schedules trucks to spread de-icing materials on roads. Because environmental damage from this material can be serious, the requirement covers this issue:

> *Description: The product shall schedule de-icing activities so that the minimum necessary amounts of de-icing material are spread on roads.*
>
> *Rationale: To minimize environmental damage.*

In some cases, you may want to specify a performance requirement for the outcome of a use case. For example, we found this performance-related requirement:

> *Description: The product shall schedule de-icing activities so that the rescheduled de-icing truck is estimated to arrive at the break-down location within 30 minutes of breakdown notification.*
>
> *Rationale: To resume de-icing as soon as possible.*

The performance requirements come mainly from the operating environment. Each environment has its own set of circumstances and conditions. The people, machines, devices, environmental conditions, and so on all place demands on the product. The way your product responds to these conditions—how fast it has to be, how strong, how big, how often—dictates the appropriate performance requirements.

Operational and Environmental Requirements: Type 13

Operational requirements specify what the product has to do if it is to operate correctly in its environment. In some cases the operating environment creates special circumstances that have an effect on the way the product must be constructed.

> *Description: The product shall be used in and around trucks at night and during rainstorms, snow, and freezing conditions.*
>
> *Rationale: These are the most likely conditions that the truck drivers encounter when de-icing roads.*

Consider the negative impact on the product if this requirement had not been written, particularly if the designer failed to take into account that the truck driver would be wearing gloves.

Not all products must operate in extreme environments—most products are written for personal computers or workstations situated in offices with an uninterruptible power supply. Even the seemingly simple environment may

Figure 11.5

Will the product work in
its intended operating
environment?

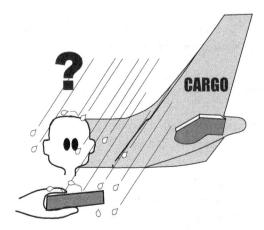

be more demanding than it first appears, however, or it may become more demanding if the operational requirements are not considered carefully.

Figure 11.5 refers to a cargo airline that built its own controller for the high-loader. High-loaders are the machines used to lift the pallets and containers up to the aircraft cargo doors; you have probably watched these devices while staring out the departure gate window waiting for your flight to board. For some reason, the airline's requirements team failed to include the requirement that the product would be used outside for extended periods—the first rainstorm shorted out the electronics of version 1.0 of the controller.

Operational requirements are also written when the product has to collaborate with partner products, access outside databases, or interact with other systems that supply information. These items show up as actors on the product use case diagram, or as adjacent systems on the work context model.

> *The product shall interact in compliance with the Visa International and Regional Operating Regulations issued January 15, 2012.*

To find the operational requirements, look at your product boundary and consider the needs of each of the adjacent systems and/or actors. If necessary, interview each actor or representative of the system to find the requirements resulting from the way that it goes about its product-related work.

You might have to describe the physical environment affecting the users when they use the product. This often means special constraints are placed on the way the product is constructed. For example, if the product will be used by people in wheelchairs or while people are driving their cars, then you must specify that constraint.

Operational requirements can cover these issues:

- The operating environment.
- The condition of the users. Are they in the dark (remember those vampires), in a hurry, and so on?
- Partner or collaborating systems.

Mobile devices have their own special set of requirements:

> *The product shall survive being dropped from shoulder height.*
>
> *The product shall be usable in variable lighting conditions.*
>
> *The product shall conserve battery life.*

If you are building products for sale, you should include any requirements needed to turn the product into a distributable or saleable item. It is also appropriate to describe any requirements that relate to the successful installation of the product.

Maintainability and Support Requirements: Type 14

Usually at requirements time you do not know exactly how much maintenance your product will undergo in its lifetime, nor do you always know which type of maintenance it will need. Nevertheless, maintenance can, to some extent, be foreseen for certain products. Consider whether any expected changes will occur in the following areas:

- Organization
- Environment
- Laws that apply to the product
- Business rules

Might other factors affect your product? If you know or strongly suspect that the product will undergo relatively heavy maintenance due to expected changes, then specify the types of expected changes and the amount of time allowed for those changes.

If you are creating a software product that should be able to run on several different types of operating system, then specify it:

> *Description: The product shall be readily portable to Android and iOS.*
>
> *Rationale: We anticipate moving into the mobile device market.*

Here you are saying to the developer that you want to be able to implement the product on another platform at some point in the future, and that you will hold him accountable for the adaptability of the product to a new device. When you attach the fit criterion to this requirement, you specify the characteristics of the device and the expected time or effort necessary to make the transition.

The IceBreaker product had this requirement:

> *The product shall be translated into various foreign languages. As yet, the languages are unknown.*

This requirement had a major effect on the product's designers. They designed the interface in such a way as to make it easy to add new languages. Also, they took into account the fact that different languages sometimes mean different cultures and different ways of presenting data.

Support requirements are also covered in this section of the requirements specification. In some cases, your client may indicate that the product will be supported by the existing help desk; in other cases, the product must be entirely self-supporting. By making this point clear at requirements time, you ensure that the designer builds in the appropriate mechanisms for contacting the help desk, or providing answers for questions likely to arise with usage.

Security Requirements: Type 15

Security is perhaps the most difficult type of requirement to specify, and potentially the one posing the greatest risk to the owning organization if it is not handled correctly. When you write security requirements, consider the nature of security as it is applied to software and allied products. Shari Lawrence Pfleeger points out that security can be thought of as having three aspects:

- Access: The product's data and functionality are accessible to authorized users and can be produced in a timely manner. Other access requirements focus on denying access to unauthorized people.

- Privacy: Data stored by the product is protected from unauthorized or accidental disclosure.

- Integrity: The product's data is the same as the source, or authority, of the data, and is protected from corruption.

We have added a fourth security aspect:

- Audit: what the product has to do to allow complete verification of its operations and data.

Access

Access also means the data is, well, accessible. In other words, the product stores its data in a way that users can get at it and understand it when they get it.

In a security context, access requirements specify what the product has to do to ensure that the product's data is available *only* to authorized users. We often use software "locks" to prevent anyone except the authorized users from reaching the data. At the same time, any security devices employed must not hinder or delay the authorized users from getting what they want when they want it.

When you write this kind of requirement, you are specifying the allowable access—who is authorized, under which circumstances authorization is valid, and which data and what functions are accessible to each authorized user.

> *The product shall ensure that only authorized users have access to the [name of] data (or function).*

The term "authorized" may also need some further explanation. For example, are all authorized users authorized all the time? Does access depend on the time of day or the location of the user at the time of access? Must a user collaborate with another authorized user to gain access? In other words, is the authorization conditional? If so, write these conditions as a requirement.

Privacy

Privacy is a concern to more and more people, as well as to organizations. We are dealing with privacy under the heading of security, but these requirements could also be envisioned as legal requirements; most Western countries have laws governing privacy of personal information held within computer systems.

Your own concern is most likely writing the requirements for what the product has to do to ensure the privacy of its data. This capability is partly controlled by access, as we discussed earlier, and partly by the product ensuring that its data is not sent or distributed to unauthorized people.

For example, if data held within the product can be printed, the product loses control of that data. Obviously, printed pages can be removed from the organization's office, in which case they are no longer secure and privacy can no longer be guaranteed. In the United Kingdom, there have been several recent cases of sensitive government information being printed and then falling into the wrong hands. In one case—we are not making this up—the documents were left on a commuter train in a folder marked "Top Secret."

You might consider adding this requirement to your specification:

> *The product shall prevent all personal and confidential data from being printed.*

This will prevent any embarrassing (or perhaps illegal) revelations of data. It will also not reveal the existence of any vampires in your records. You might also consider this requirement:

> *The product shall deliver data in a manner that prevents further or second-hand use by unauthorized people.*

If your organization holds personal information about its customers, then a little effort expended at the requirements stage might well prevent significant fines being levied later if that private information is ever released, either accidentally or intentionally, from the organization.

Integrity

Integrity means that the data held by the product corresponds exactly to what was delivered to the product from the adjacent system (the authority for the data). You must consider requirements for preventing the loss or corruption of data and, should the worst happen, recovering lost or corrupted data. Your product, when it goes into production, will hold data that is important to the owning organization—integrity requirements are intended to protect that data.

In our de-icing example, weather stations send data about temperature and precipitation to the IceBreaker product. The weather station originates the data and, therefore, is the authority for it. Any copies of this data, such as those held by IceBreaker, must be faithful to the weather station's version. Here is the integrity requirement for the IceBreaker product:

> *The product shall ensure its road temperature data corresponds to the data transmitted by the weather station.*

You should also consider other integrity requirements, such as those that cause the product to prevent unintentional misuse by authorized users—the most common form of data corruption. Naturally, the product must protect itself against improper usage by outsiders as well.

Integrity also covers those requirements to prove the integrity of the product after some abnormal happening. These events can include such things as a power failure, an exceptional operating condition, or unusual environmental conditions such as fire, flood, or bombing.

Auditing

You should consider normal auditing to be part of the security section of your specification. Most accounting products have a requirement that they be able to be audited, to ensure that no mistakes are made and that the results shown by the product are correct. Audits are also used to detect fraud or misuse, so audit requirements are often written to say that that the product must leave an audit trail. The precise nature of your audit requirements must be negotiated with your own auditors, who, naturally, are stakeholders for your project.

Audit requirements are standard for any product dealing with money or valuables. Their inclusion often results in requirements for the product to retain its records for a given time.

Audit may also mean that the product maintains data on who has accessed which information. The intention of this kind of requirement is to ensure that users cannot later deny they used the product or had access to its information.

> *Description: The product shall retain a journal of all transactions for the statutory period.*
>
> *Rationale: This is required by the auditors and is required by applicable accountancy laws.*

. . . And No More

Consider the effect of adding ". . . and no more" to all of your requirements. This phrase means that the product must do no more than the requirement specifies. For example, if the requirement is to find a name and address from a file, then the product must not delete or change the name and address after finding them.

Consider this access requirement:

> *The product shall allow access to authorized users.*

The ". . . and no more" heuristic yields a complementary requirement:

> *The product shall ensure that only authorized users are able to gain access.*

For security reasons, you might consider adding an overriding requirement to your specification:

> *The product shall not do anything except that which has been speci-*
> *fied as a requirement.*

Sometimes well-meaning product builders make the product perform faster or be bigger than specified, or they add unspecified features. While these properties may be beneficial to one or more parts of the product, they may well have a detrimental effect on the product as a whole or on the security of the product. We know of several cases where unauthorized or unspecified features added to a bank's website opened a serious security loophole. It is necessary to ensure that your development team does not build in extra features or properties without first negotiating their inclusion as requirements.

Immunity is also part of the security requirements. Specify requirements for the product to protect itself against malevolent software such as viruses, worms, Trojan horses, and any of the many other variations on the theme of attacking another computer.

Clearly, security is important, and sometimes essential. It should be assigned a priority that reflects the value of misusing the product. For example, if your product is to be used by a bank, or if it processes credit card or financial trading transactions, then the value of misuse (in financial terms) is high. Similarly, if your product is intended for the military, then misuse may result in loss of life (perhaps even your own) or loss of a military advantage. Thus, for financial, military, or life-support products, security has a higher priority, and consumes more of the budget, than for many commercial systems.

You should consider calling in a security expert as a consultant stakeholder. Software developers are not usually trained in security, and the security of some functionality and data is so important that you need experts to advise you on the security requirements.

READING

Pfleeger, Charles, and Shari Lawrence Pfleeger. *Analyzing Computer Security: A Threat/Vulnerability/ Countermeasure Approach.* Prentice Hall, 2011.

Cultural Requirements: Type 16

Cultural requirements specify special factors that would make the product unacceptable because of customs, religions, languages, taboos, prejudices, or almost any other aspect of human behavior. Cultural requirements are needed when you try and sell a product into a different country, particularly when its culture and language are different from your own.

While "hello" and "stop" are almost universally recognized words and have the same meaning in all cultures, most other words don't. In English we have a single word for "you," whether we are speaking to one or many people (excluding the Southern "y'all"). Many other languages, however, have a different word for the plural and singular "you." Matters become even more complicated in those languages that have a different "you" depending on the familiarity of the contact. In French, you use the formal *vous* to speak with people in a business situation—especially superiors—and *tu* when speaking to family and close friends. To use *tu* too soon in a relationship can be thought of as rude. In Denmark, the familiar *du* is used almost always except when speaking to old people, when you say *de*. To use the formal *de* is considered stiff and unnatural by most people.

The first time your authors went to Italy, looking forward to experiencing the lively Italian atmosphere, we found an elegant, stainless steel coffee bar—the sort of place always full of beautifully dressed people all talking at once. We went to the bar and ordered two *cappuccini* and two pastries. The barman gave us a lengthy explanation in Italian, shook his head and pointed to the cashier. Thus we discovered a cultural requirement: In Italian coffee bars, it is necessary to first go to the cashier and pay, and only then to go to the bar, hand over your receipt, and place your order (Figure 11.6). At the risk of being deprived of our morning coffee, we soon learned to fit into the culture.

We take our own culture for granted, and we don't give a lot of thought to how other people might perceive our products and ourselves. If your product is to be used outside your own country, and in some cases outside your own local region or state, consider whether you should call on the services of a cultural expert. Cultural requirements are often unexpected, and at first glance sometimes appear to be irrational, such as vampires will not enter your house unless you invite them. But you have to keep in mind that the reason behind the requirements lies outside your own culture. If your reaction is "Why on earth do they do it like that?", it is possible that you have discovered a cultural requirement. It is also worth noting that different professions might have cultural differences. The culture of, say, engineering is quite different from that of marketing. Make sure that you do not specify a marketing-type solution for engineers.

READING

Morrison, Terri, and Wayne Conaway. *Kiss, Bow, or Shake Hands: How to Do Business in 60 Countries,* second edition. Adams Media, 2006.

Figure 11.6

Sometimes cultural requirements are not immediately obvious.

Following are some requirements you might consider cultural. Religious observances:

> *The product shall not display religious symbols or words associated with mainstream religions.*

Political correctness:

> *The product shall not use any terms or icons that might possibly offend anyone on the planet.*

Spelling:

> *The product shall use American spelling.*

Forcing political or cultural alignment:

> *The product shall offer the choice of language in the order appropriate for the region of the country.*

This last requirement comes from Belgium, where three or four languages are spoken (depending on whom you are speaking with); each region naturally considers its language to be the most important one. It is considered inappropriate to offer French *before* Flemish if the user is logged in from Flanders.

The more we build products for use in different walks of life, by different professions, and for different socioeconomic groups in different countries, the more we need to consider cultural requirements.

Legal Requirements: Type 17

The cost of litigation is one of the major risks for software-for-sale, and it can be expensive for other kinds of software as well. You must make yourself aware of the laws that apply to your kind of product, and write requirements to ensure that the product complies with these laws. Even if you are building software for use inside your own organization, be aware that laws applying to the workplace might be relevant.

A legal requirement is written like this:

> *The product shall comply with the Americans with Disabilities Act of 1990 as amended.*

You may need to consult with your lawyers to determine which laws are applicable. The law itself may also specify its own requirements. For example, automated products built for drug development use by the pharmaceutical industry must be self-documenting, although the precise nature of this capability varies. Nevertheless, you (or anyone else writing requirements for these applications) have to understand that these legal requirements exist and write them into your specification.

You are required by law to display copyright notices, particularly if you are using other people's products. Products are required by law to display warning messages if there is any danger that some dim-witted user might do the wrong thing with it. For example, a blanket made in a southeast Asian country carries this warning:

> Warning. Do not use blanket as a hurricane shelter.

A label on a child's scooter reads:

> This product moves when used.

Start with your company's lawyers; they have far more experience with the law than you. Here are several things that you can do to facilitate compliance:

- Examine adjacent systems or actors—that is, the entities that have contact with your product. You can use your context diagram to identify them.

- Consider their legal requirements and rights. For example, are any of the disabled-access laws applicable? Does the adjacent system have any rights to privacy for the data that you hold? Do you need proof of transaction? Or nondisclosure of the information your product has about the adjacent system?

- Determine whether any laws are relevant to your product (or to the use case or the requirement). For example, are data protection, privacy laws, guarantees, consumer protection, consumer credit, or right to information laws applicable?

Sarbanes-Oxley Act[1]

The Sarbanes-Oxley Act (SOx), officially titled the Public Company Accounting Reform and Investor Protection Act of 2002, marks a significant change to the U.S. securities laws. This legislation was enacted following a number of large-scale corporate financial scandals involving WorldCom, Enron, Arthur

FOOTNOTE 1
We are grateful for the help provided by Dr. Charles Pfleeger on the subject of U.S. legislation.

Andersen, and Global Crossing. The act requires all publicly traded companies to report on the effectiveness of their internal accounting controls.

SOx has an indirect impact on the requirements activity. That is, it makes it a criminal offense for CEOs and CFOs to neglect the integrity of the internal controls of their companies. As a consequence, traceability between the source of the information and the company's financial reports is now essential. In effect, the executive needs to be able to review your product at some level (presumably not the code) to determine that it presents fair and accurate data about the financial status of the company. To satisfy this need, you may have to present your requirements to the executive. It certainly means that for all internal financial reporting, you must be able to produce the requirements.

The Sarbanes-Oxley Act also includes provisions requiring the organization to have a credible and detailed security policy. (We looked at security previously in this chapter.) Section 404 of SOx is the part most closely tied to IT security.

Even if you are outside the United States, if your product is to be used by an organization that does business with U.S. entities, then there could be SOx implications. Check with your lawyers.

Other Legal Obligations

If you are reading this book in the United States, you should also be aware of the Health Insurance Portability and Accountability Act (HIPAA). This act restricts access and disclosure of personally identifiable medical records: You must not disclose personal medical information to unauthorized parties, and no third party must be able to reengineer statistical data to identify any individual. HIPAA has recently been extended as part of the Affordable Care Act (ACA) of 2010.

The Gramm-Leach-Bliley Act applies to financial institutions and likewise prohibits the unauthorized disclosure of personal information.

If your product is to be used by a unit of the U.S. government, the Federal Information Security Management Act of 2002 (FISMA) probably applies.

If that is not enough to make your head ache, you should also check whether the Dodd-Frank Wall Street Reform and Consumer Protection Act of 2010 applies to your project. This act implements financial regulatory reform, and in some cases is applicable to companies that, while outside the United States themselves, do business with U.S. companies. The act subjects foreign companies to prudential supervision in the United States if the company is adjudged to be carrying on significant financial activity in the United States.

You should also check whether the Privacy and Electronic Communications (EC Directive) Regulations 2003 applies to your product. This directive, which may shortly be updated, applies to non-European Union (EU) countries that are operating within the EU, as it does to EU companies that wish to export data to other countries, particularly the United States.

In the United Kingdom, the Data Protection Act of 1998 prohibits using data—and this includes disclosing it—in any manner that does not comply with your organization's registration under the Data Protection Act. The act prohibits most personal disclosure, but also provides for individuals' access to personal data held about them.

There's more. Lots more. We urge you to consult your organization's lawyers. After all, they are paid to give advice on matters of legal compliance.

Standards

Legal requirements are not limited to the law of the land. Some products must comply with industrial or professional standards. For example:

> *The product shall comply with our ISO 9001 certification.*

Now that we have considered the content of the non-functional requirements, let's look at ideas for finding them.

Finding the Non-functional Requirements

Like all requirements, the non-functional ones can come to light at any time. Nevertheless, there are certain places where we can look that give us better opportunities to discover them.

Blogging the Requirements

When you are trying to elicit non-functional requirements, blogs and wikis can be useful. Start a blog (or any other form of online collaborative thread) using the template's non-functional sections and subsections as headings. That is, instead of limiting your search to "Usability Requirements," instead use the subsections "Ease of Use," "Personalization and Internationalization," "Ease of Learning," "Understandability and Politeness," and "Accessibility." Do not place any limits on what people can contribute, but encourage your team and your stakeholders to contribute what they think are the right properties for the product to have in these categories. You will inevitably receive a number of solutions instead of requirements, and some completely unworkable ideas, but they will provide you with the basis from which to create the abstraction needed to find the underlying requirement.

Use Cases

You can consider each use case from the point of its non-functional needs. For example, the IceBreaker product has a product use case called "Detect icy roads," which produces the road de-icing schedule showing the roads to be treated and the trucks allocated to them. The relevant stakeholders tell you that the schedule will be used by a junior or medium-grade engineer. For each of the non-functional requirements types, interview these stakeholders about the product's needs.

For example—and we list these requirements in the order they appear in the template—the look and feel of the schedule should be such that new engineers (they have a high turnover rate) can immediately feel comfortable with it:

> *Description: The product shall appear familiar to new engineers.*
>
> *Rationale: We frequently have new junior engineers and want the product to have an appearance that is acceptable to them.*

This requirement is slightly more difficult to quantify, but you will be able to write a suitable fit criterion for it after you have read Chapter 12. For the moment, the stakeholders' intention is sufficient.

The usability and humanity requirements for the product use case are next. The stakeholders want the schedule to allow an engineer to easily direct the trucks to the correct roads. The requirement looks like this:

> *Description: The product shall produce a schedule that is easy to read.*
>
> *Rationale: It is important that only the correct roads are treated.*

The rationale shows us that the reason for wanting an easy-to-read schedule relates to accuracy of the road treatment. Thus, when you write the fit criterion for this requirement, you would add a quantification that measures the number of correct roads have been treated, and thereby the success of the product in implementing this requirement.

Performance requirements focus on issues such as how many, how fast, and so on. In this case, the schedule has to be produced within a few seconds of the engineer wanting it:

> *The product shall produce the schedule within 3 seconds of the user's request.*

Here's another performance requirement:

> *The product shall be able to do ice prediction calculations for 5,000 roads.*

Operational and environmental requirements deal with the physical operating environment. In the IceBreaker example, they will be the same for all of the product use cases. Naturally, you need write them only once, as they describe the mandated computers, the database, and so on for the product as a whole.

Maintainability and support requirements specify any special conditions that apply to keeping the product up-to-date or adapting it to another environment. The client for the IceBreaker product intends to monitor roads for different road authorities, so a maintainability requirement is written like this:

> *The product shall enable the addition of new road authority areas within two days.*

Also, given that this product use case is usually activated at night, we have the following requirement:

> *Description: The product shall be self-supporting.*
>
> *Rationale: The help desk will not be manned. There will be no fellow users available to help.*

Security requirements deal with access to the product. For the IceBreaker product, the client does not want unauthorized people running the schedule:

> *The product shall allow access only to junior and higher-grade engineers.*

There is also an audit need here, as road authorities must be able to prove they treated the roads correctly:

> *The product shall retain all ice predictions for all occasions on which the schedule is run.*

Cultural requirements for this product use case are concerned with fitting into the way that the engineers work:

> *The product shall use terminology acceptable to the engineering community.*

Finally, we reach the legal requirements. Many road authorities have a statutory obligation to prove that they have exercised due diligence in monitoring and treating the roads under their control:

> *The product shall produce an audit report of all road schedules and their subsequent treatments. This must comply with ISO 93.080.99.*

The Template

Use the template as a checklist of non-functional requirement types when interviewing your stakeholders. Go through the template looking at each of the subtypes and probe for examples of each. Refer to the template in Appendix A for more explanation and examples of the non-functional requirements.

Prototypes and Non-functional Requirements

You can use prototypes to help drive out non-functional requirements. At requirements time, the prototype usually takes the form of a whiteboard sketch, a paper prototype, or some other quick-and-dirty mockup of what the product *might* be like. The intention here is not to design the product, but rather to ensure you have understood the needs by reverse-engineering the requirements from the prototype. We discussed this process in Chapter 5, Investigating the Work.

In the case of the scheduling product use case, your stakeholders respond favorably to a sketch of a screen showing the roads to be treated in a glowing, cold blue color; the safe roads in green; and the treated roads in yellow. The engineers are delighted that they can see the topography of the district and the roads.

See Chapter 5 for guidance on building requirements prototypes.

> *The product shall distinguish clearly between safe and unsafe roads.*
>
> *The product shall make any unsafe roads obvious.*

You do not yet know that "a glowing, cold blue color" is intuitive—you need some ergonomic input or user surveys for that. Nevertheless, the intention is clear from the prototype.

Go over your own prototypes using the template. For each of the non-functional types, which requirements does the prototype suggest? Go through the prototype carefully, and keep in mind that it is not the requirement, but rather a simulation of the requirement. It is unrealistic to hand over the prototype to the developer and expect the correct product to emerge.

The Client

The client for the product may also have expectations that are relevant here. In many cases, the reason for building a new product is to provide a service to the users or to the customers of the business, and the attractiveness of that service depends on one or more non-functional qualities. For example, providing portable, or highly usable, or secure functionality may be crucial to the development effort. Alternatively, your client may say that if you cannot provide an interactive and graphic display of the current trading position, then he does not want the product. Thus your client becomes the prime source of the critical non-functional requirements.

Once the functional requirements are met, the non-functional qualities may be what persuade a potential customer to actually buy your product. After all, it might well have been its non-functional properties that influenced your own recent buying decisions. Also think about the non-functional requirements of products that you admire.

Table 11.1 summarizes the questions to ask for a use case or a functional requirement. Ask your client to what degree these questions are relevant to the product that you are specifying. Your client, or the marketing department, is the source of information about what will make customers buy the product; make use of them.

Who or What Is (Are) . . .	Do They (Does It) Have These Requirements?	Table 11.1
The users (2)	Look and Feel (10)	Finding Non-functional Requirements
	Usability (11): Are there any special considerations for this kind of user?	
	Security (15): Do you have to protect, or protect against, the users?	
	Cultural (16): Is there a risk of offending, or misleading your users?	
The operating environment (5, 6, 8)	Operational (13): Particularly collaborating products.	
	Performance (12): Demands made by the environment.	
	Maintenance (14): Consider proposed changes to the environment.	
The client, customer, and other stakeholders (2)	Look and Feel (10)	
	Usability (11)	
	Cultural (16)	
The adjacent systems (6, 8)	Legal (17): Include special rights for this kind of adjacent system.	
	Operational (13)	
	Performance (12)	

For each use case or the product as a whole, consider the factor in the first column of Table 11.1. When you have an adequate knowledge of this factor, use it as a trigger to start questioning your stakeholders about the requirement types in the second column. The numbers in parentheses correspond to the sections in the Volere Requirements Specification Template.

We should also mention Roxanne Miller's book, *The Quest for Software Requirements* (cited earlier). It offers an extensive treatment of non-functional requirements; the book can be used as a guide and checklist for the business analyst when uncovering the non-functional needs.

Don't Write a Solution

We have already mentioned the danger of writing a solution instead of a requirement. This problem is so widespread (especially with non-functional requirements) and potentially so serious that you will forgive us if we mention it again.

Don't presuppose a design solution, or enforce a solution, by the way you write your requirement. By the same token, don't adopt a current solution to a problem and write that as the requirement. Suppose, for example, that you write a security requirement like this:

> *The product shall require a password to access account data.*

Now the designer is forced to use a password as the solution. As a result, even if a better security device than passwords is available—and there are many to choose from—the product builder may not use it. In this case, a poorly-written requirement prevents the designer from searching for an alternative, and possibly better, solution.

By writing

> *The product shall ensure account data can be accessed only by authorized users.*

you are asking the product designer or a security consultant—people qualified to do this—to find the most effective security solution.

Apart from potentially solving the wrong problem, one of the main concerns with writing a solution instead of a requirement is that technology is constantly changing. Solutions lock you into one technology or another, and whatever is chosen may be out of date by the time the product is built. By writing a requirement that does not include any technological component, you not only allow the designer to use the most appropriate, up-to-date technology, but also allow the product to change and adapt to new technologies as they emerge.

Consider this usability requirement:

> *The product shall use a mouse.*

We can eliminate the technological component by rewriting the requirement in this way:

> *The product shall use a pointing device.*

Actually, the requirement can be improved even further by writing it as follows:

> *The product shall allow the user to directly manipulate all interface items.*

This non-solution requirement would naturally accommodate touch screen and direct finger manipulation of the content, or even eye-movement detection.

To follow the guideline of not writing solutions, examine your requirement. If it contains any item of technology or any method, rewrite it to avoid mentioning the technology or method. It may be necessary to make several attempts before you reach the desired level of technological independence, but the effect on the design of the end product is worthwhile.

Earl Beede suggests a "three strikes" approach to improving the requirement: List three things wrong with the requirement, and then rewrite the requirement to solve those problems. Do this a total of three times. At that stage the requirement is as good as it is ever likely to be.

Summary

The non-functional requirements describe the qualitative behavior, or the "how well" qualities, of the product—whether it has to be fast, or safe, or attractive, and so on. These qualities come about because of the functions that the product is required to carry out.

Even something as simple as the common bathroom tap shown in Figure 11.7 has non-functional requirements that make the difference between success and failure:

- Look and Feel: The product shall appear to be easy to operate.
- Usability: The product shall be able to be used by someone with wet hands.
- Performance: The full flow of water shall be achievable with fewer than three hand movements.

Figure 11.7

How many non-functional requirements does a common bathroom tap have?

- Operational: The product shall operate correctly with water up to temperatures of 70°C.
- Maintainability: The product shall allow any routine maintenance (such as changing a washer) to be completed in fewer than 4 minutes by a skilled operator.
- Security: The product shall not be able to be operated by a child younger than six years old.
- Cultural: The handle or lever shall turn in the direction dictated by local custom.
- Legal: The product shall conform to the Queensland Plumbers and Drainers Board code of installation.

At this stage you have written a *description* and usually a *rationale* that capture the intention of the non-functional requirements. Some of them may seem a little vague, and some of them may appear to be well intentioned and little more. Please keep in mind that you have not finished with these requirements, because you have yet to write the fit criteria. When you do so, you will write a measurement to quantify the meaning of each requirement. We look at this task in the next chapter.

Fit Criteria and Rationale

12

in which we show how measuring
requirements makes them unambiguous,
understandable, communicable, and testable

Fit, as we use the term here, means a solution completely satisfies or matches the requirement. That is, the solution does exactly what the requirement says it must do or has the property the requirement says it must have—no more and no less. To test whether the solution fits the requirement, however, the requirement itself must be measurable. As a simple example, if the requirement calls for a length of rope "of a suitable size," it is obviously impossible to test any delivered solution. By contrast, if the requirement says the rope shall be "2 centimeters in diameter and 2 meters long," then it becomes a simple matter to test whether the delivered rope fits the requirement.

Of course, attaching a measurement to a length of rope is easy. Attaching a measurement to some requirements is more difficult, but still possible, and absolutely necessary.

The measurement of the requirement is its *fit criterion*. It quantifies the behavior, the performance, or some other quality of the requirement.

So far in this book we have mainly dealt with the *description* of the requirement; the description sets down the stakeholder's intention for the requirement, and is the normal thing that stakeholders say when they are giving you their requirements. But to know precisely what they need, you must quantify the description. Once you measure the requirement—that is, express it using numbers—there is little room for misunderstanding.

> **❝** I often say that when you can measure what you are speaking about, and express it in numbers, you know something about it; but when you cannot measure it, when you cannot express it in numbers, your knowledge is of a meager and unsatisfactory kind. **❞**
>
> —Lord Kelvin

Formality Guide

READING
Beck, Kent, and Cynthia Andres. *eXtreme Programming Explained: Embrace Change,* second edition. Addison-Wesley, 2004.

A pleasing aspect (amongst many) of Kent Beck's eXtreme Programming technique is its insistence on writing test cases before writing the code. The test case defines the yardstick that the implemented code must match. The fit criterion is more or less the same thing: It is a yardstick for the requirement. By adding a fit criterion to the requirement, you are, in essence, writing its test case.

If you are using user stories, then we strongly suggest that you pay particular attention to the reason given for the functionality. This is more or less the same as the rationale, and is an important contributor to ending up with the correct product. Writing test cases on the back of the story card should achieve the same purpose as the fit criterion we speak about here.

We suggested in Chapter 11 that rabbits use a blog or wiki to discover the non-functional requirements. For each of the non-functional requirements yielded by the blog, we now suggest deriving the appropriate fit criterion, confirming it with the stakeholder, and writing the test case using that fit criterion.

Horse projects need to have a precise and easily shareable understanding of the meaning of requirements. It has been our experience that when the project has multiple stakeholders—which is the norm for horse projects— different stakeholders assign different meanings to requirements. Adding a rationale and a fit criterion to each requirement means it is virtually impossible for misunderstandings to occur. We recommend that horse projects include both of these in their requirements.

Elephant projects must use rationales and fit criteria. These projects are forced to produce a written specification to be handed on to some other party, either another part of the organization or an outsourcer. Having a specification containing only unambiguous, testable requirements is crucial to elephant projects if the other party is to understand and then deliver the correct product.

Why Does *Fit* Need a *Criterion*?

When you have a requirement for the product to perform some function or to have some property, the testing activity must demonstrate that the product does, indeed, perform that function or possess the desired property. To carry out such tests, the requirement must have a benchmark such that the testers can compare the delivered product with the original requirement. The benchmark is the fit criterion—a quantification of the requirement that demonstrates the standard the product must reach.

You should also consider the builders of the product. It stands to reason that once they know the criterion for the product's acceptance, they will build to that standard. If they are told their product will be used underwater, and the acceptance criterion is that the product must operate for as long as 24 hours at a depth of 15 meters, then they are unlikely to deliver anything but a waterproof product (see Figure 12.1).

Possibly the most challenging part of testing a requirement against an agreed-upon measurement is defining the appropriate measurement for the requirement. It is tricky, but certainly not impossible.

Let's suppose that your stakeholder is inexperienced and asks for a product that is "user friendly." What that phrase means to you is likely not the same thing as what it means to the stakeholder. However, once you can measure "user friendliness"—that is, put numbers against it—then you and the stakeholder can arrive at the identical understanding.

Additionally, the measurement of friendliness is passed along to the developers, who treat it as a benchmark. They now know how you and your stakeholder are going to test the delivered product: You will measure it against the fit criterion.

So how do you find a measurement for "user friendly"?

First, you need to understand the reason for the requirement. This is where the *rationale* comes into play. You ask the question, "What is the justification for this requirement?", or as that seems a little formal, "Why do you have this requirement?"

Suppose that after some interrogation, your stakeholder reveals that as far as he is concerned, "a user-friendly product will be liked by the customers who are intended to use it." A little more probing reveals that "liked by the customers" means they voluntarily change over to the new product, and don't hesitate before using it.

> " The idea is for each requirement to have a quality measure that makes it possible to divide all solutions to the requirement into two classes: those for which we agree that they fit the requirement and those for which we agree that they do not fit the requirement. "
>
> —Christopher Alexander, *Notes on the Synthesis of Form*

Figure 12.1

If they know the performance criterion that the product must meet before it is accepted, the builders will naturally build a product to meet that criterion.

> *Description: The product shall be user friendly.*
>
> *Rationale: We need customers to voluntarily change to the new product, and not hesitate before using it.*

This explanation gives us something to measure: the duration of hesitation before using the product, the time elapsed before complete adoption of it, or the user satisfaction level after a period of usage.

> *Fit Criterion: Customers, on average, commence using the product within 5 seconds of encountering it for the first time.*

Or:

> *Fit Criterion: Eighty percent of customers are voluntarily using the product within six months of its release.*

Or:

> *Fit Criterion: Customer surveys between six months and a year after launch give a satisfaction rating of greater than 75 percent.*

Some of these criteria might seem a little expensive to test, but this is an important requirement. The rationale tells us that when it says customers should start using the product voluntarily. If customers do not switch over to the new product, then the project will be a failure, so it is worth putting some effort into the development and testing of this requirement.

All of this goes to say that to make it precise, a requirement cannot be just a text description; it needs a rationale and a fit criterion.

The Rationale for the Rationale

Quite often, stakeholders tell you their perceived solution to the problem, rather than their real need.

The rationale is the reason, or justification, for a requirement. We have found that attaching a rationale to the requirement makes it far easier to understand the real need. Quite often, stakeholders may tell you their perceived solution to the problem, rather than their real need. Alternatively, they may state a requirement that is so vague as to be (for the moment) unusable. In the example given previously, the client asked for a "user-friendly" product, but you could make sense of it when you learned that the rationale was that the project needed the users to readily adopt the product.

Suppose the rationale had been different. Say, instead of ready adoption, the client gave you a rationale that indicated a "user-friendly" product is so easy to use that its users make fewer errors than they do with the current product. The corresponding requirement has a different meaning, and the resulting fit criterion is completely different.

> Description: The product shall be user friendly.
>
> Rationale: Users must find the new product easier to use than the current product, so that they make fewer errors.
>
> Fit criterion: The average error rate for all user input shall be less than 1.5 percent.

The rationale is not only a guide to help you find the fit criterion, but also a means to help you know when you have several different requirements masquerading as one. One stakeholder says "user friendly" means the product is pleasant to use, another says "user friendly" means the product is exciting, and yet another says a "user-friendly" product encourages users to make return visits to it. In this case you have three different requirements, each with its own fit criterion that measures the desired property.

Additionally, the rationale provides the basis for making decisions about how to implement the requirement. Put yourself in the developers' shoes: You usually have to choose between several possible solutions, and if you understand the thinking underlying the requirement, you can come up with the most appropriate solution. Also, when you need to make trade-off decisions, it helps if you understand the relative importance of the requirement to the business, and the effect that it will have if the requirement is not correctly implemented.

You have to pass along a way to measure the requirement's real meaning.

> Description: The product shall ensure that the buyer is connecting from an approved country.
>
> Rationale: Some countries do not have copyright laws and our suppliers prohibit us from selling into those countries.

Let's not forget the testers' need for a coherent rationale. There are many ways of designing tests for requirements' fit criteria, some of which involve much more time and expense than others. A tester needs to understand the reason for a requirement if he is to make the best decision about where to spend testing time and money.

Later, when a product is being used and maintained, the rationale still has a vital role. You can work out what a software product is doing by reading the code and observing the people who use it. But suppose you have been asked to make a change to a product: If you do not understand why the product does what it does, it is less likely that you will make the correct change, and more likely that your changes will corrupt some related but distant part of the product—the ripple effect. The problems that arise from a lack of understanding of the rationale partly explain why software maintenance is so expensive.

The rationale is the cognitive thread that connects the business and the delivered product. It is through knowing why something exists that the business analyst is able to discover the correct statement of need, and the developers are able to construct the correct product.

When asking stakeholders for their rationale for a requirement, you might appear to be like the child constantly asking a parent, "Why?" So be it—that is the role of the requirements analyst. You have to ask why, and keep on asking why, until you get to the real reason for the requirement. But you haven't finished yet, because you still have to pass along a way to measure the requirement's real meaning. That is why you derive its fit criterion.

Deriving Fit Criteria

To come up with the appropriate fit criterion, start by analyzing the description and rationale you have established for the requirement.

> *Description: The product shall make it easy for a buyer to find his chosen music.*

This requirement is fairly subjective and slightly ambiguous. The rationale provides more information on what is needed:

> *Rationale: Music buyers are familiar with the Internet and are accustomed to convenience and fast response times. They will not tolerate slow or awkward searches for their chosen tracks.*

Now you know the requirement is about speed—which is fairly easy to quantify—and awkwardness—which is about complexity and perceived ease. For the speed component, imposing a time limit for a search is appropriate. Suppose your market research personnel tell you 10 seconds is the limit of the target audience's tolerance; to be better than the competition, you are shooting for 6 seconds for your own product.

In terms of the awkwardness component of the fit criterion, your ergonomics personnel and market research both say that buyers must be able to find a piece of music in no more than three actions (an action here means a click, a gesture, a menu selection, voice command, or any other conscious action on the user's part).

Your measurement for these things would be this fit criterion:

> Fit Criterion: The average music buyer shall be able to locate any piece of music within 6 seconds, using no more than three actions.

Note that the 6-second time limit also directs the designer to make it obvious to the music buyer what has to be done to buy music—a limit of 6 seconds means that there is very little time for hesitation and figuring out what to do next.

Some fit criteria may, at first, be unattainable because of business or real-life constraints. In other cases, your client may not be willing to spend the amount required for the implementation to meet the criterion. Thus sometimes you might negotiate an adjustment to the fit criterion to allow for the product's operating environment, the intended usage, and the client's budget. Think of these adjustments as *business tolerances*. As we are certain that some of the intended users of the product will be below-average performers, we would adjust the fit criterion to read as follows:

If you can't measure a requirement, it is not really a requirement.

> Fit Criterion: Ninety percent of music buyers shall be able to locate any piece of music within 6 seconds, using no more than three actions.

Scale of Measurement

Any requirement can be measured: All you have to do is find a suitable scale with which to measure it.

The scale of measurement is the unit you use to test the conformance of the product to its requirement. For example, if the requirement is for a certain speed of operation, then obviously the scale is time—microseconds, minutes, months—to complete a given action or set of tasks. For a usability requirement, you can measure the time needed to learn a product, or the time taken before achieving a particular level of competence, or perhaps even the error rate of the work done using the product.

Scales of measurement exist for all sorts of qualities. Color can be measured by specifying its component colors as a percentage of cyan, magenta, yellow, and black. Loudness and softness of sound are measured in terms of decibels. An amount of light is measured in units of lumens. Typefaces can be measured by face names and point sizes. In fact, there is a scale of measurement for almost everything.

You can measure anything.

So far, the only thing that your authors have not been able to find a scale of measurement for is love—we cannot find any way of measuring how much you love someone. Readers are welcome to send suggestions.

Fit Criteria for Non-functional Requirements

A non-functional requirement is a quality that the product must have, such as usability, look and feel, performance, and so on. The fit criterion is, therefore, a measure of that quality. Here we examine fit criteria for all the different types of non-functional requirements.

Let's look at an example. Your authors came across this requirement for a consumer electronics product aimed at a teenage market:

> *Description: The product shall be cool.*

Even vague, ambiguous requirements can be measured.

This requirement at first sight might seem hopeless and unable to be measured—there is no deterministic scale of coolness. If you look little bit more closely, however, you will obviously find that "cool" is a term often used to mean "something that is desirable to have or to be."

When we asked why the product had to be "cool," we were given a rationale that consumers had to be attracted to the product, and to want to own one and be seen to own it. To satisfy this need, we had to first measure the product's attractiveness to its intended audience. The first attempt at a fit criterion was this:

> *Fit Criterion: Forty percent of the people who see the product on display in a store pick it up.*

Naturally you would not go live with the real product and see if it met the test; you would follow the lead of most electronics companies, which test prototypes against representative groups of the target audience.

We improved the fit criterion to this:

> *Fit Criterion: Forty percent of the target audience who see the product on display in the store, pick it up and hold it for at least 5 seconds.*

We also felt that should the picker-upper show the product to somebody else, that action would indicate that he felt that the product was desirable. The "Hey, look at this" gesture indicated the value he put on the product. Thus:

> *Fit Criterion: Forty percent of the target audience who see the product on display in a store, pick it up, hold it for at least 5 seconds, and show it to a companion.*

Of course, an even better fit criterion would have been a measure of whether people actually bought the product, but given the target market we had to take into consideration the fact that not everyone would be able to afford it. Therefore simply picking up, holding, and showing the product was seen as the first test of how desirable it was, or the degree of envy from non-owners it would generate, or as the client called it, its coolness.

Of course, "coolness" must go beyond the store display. We needed to add other requirements that specified how convenient the product was to use. Clearly, a cool product must be very convenient—cool—to use.

Earlier in this chapter, you saw an example of a requirement that specified a "user-friendly" product; the client said that "user friendly" meant the staff liked it. You can measure "like": If the staff likes the product, they will use it. You can measure how quickly they start using it, how much they use it, or how soon word gets around that the product is good and users encourage one another to use it. All of these criteria quantify the client's desire that the staff like the product and use it (see Figure 12.2).

You could write a fit criterion like this:

> *Fit Criterion: Within three months of introducing the product, 60 percent of the users shall be using it to carry out the agreed-upon work. From those users, the product shall receive a 75 percent or more approval rating.*

Figure 12.2

You can measure your users' liking for a product by surveying their work practices before and after the product is introduced, by measuring how long it takes them to start using the product once it is available, or by surveying them after a period of use to ascertain their liking for the product.

Note how you clarify the requirement when you add its fit criterion. By negotiating a measurement, you transform the requirement from a vague and somewhat ambiguous intention into a fully formed, testable requirement.

You will find that it is usually not possible to get the complete, measurable requirement from your first interview. Indeed, it is highly unlikely that your stakeholders will express themselves in such precise terms. We suggest you go with the flow; don't slow down your requirements-discovery processes to make the requirement measurable, but rather get the stakeholders' intention—you write this as the *description*—and the *rationale*. Then analyze your understanding, write your own best interpretation of the fit criterion, and improve it by discussing it with your stakeholder. You both have to agree that your proposed fit criterion is an accurate measurement of the requirement.

Product Failure

The fit criterion might be determined by asking your stakeholder, "What would you consider a failure to meet this requirement?" Suppose you have this requirement:

> *Description: The product must produce the road de-icing schedule within an acceptable time.*

Clearly, the scale of measurement here is time. Your client can tell you how much time he thinks would constitute a failure. For example, the client would consider the product unacceptable if the engineer has to wait for more than 15 seconds for the schedule to become available. This means you have the following fit criterion, with suitable business tolerances applied:

> *Fit Criterion: The road de-icing schedule shall be available to the engineer within 15 seconds from when he makes his request for 90 percent of the times that it is produced. It shall never take longer than 20 seconds.*

Sometimes, however, you may discover there is no agreement on a quality measure, and hence there can be no fit criterion. In these circumstances, it is possible that the original requirement is not really a requirement. Perhaps several requirements have been lumped together in one requirement; in this case, each of the sub-requirements would then have its own measurement. Alternatively, perhaps the requirement is so vague, and its intention so unrealistic, that it is not possible to know whether it has been satisfied. For example, we cannot imagine a fit criterion for this requirement:

> Description: I want a product my grandmother would have liked had she been alive today.

Subjective Tests

Some requirements have to be tested using subjective tests. For example, if a cultural requirement for a product to be used in the public domain is "not offensive to any group," then the fit criterion must be along these lines:

> Fit Criterion: The product shall not be offensive to at least 85 percent of a test panel representing the makeup of the people likely to come in contact with the product. No more than 10 percent of the interest groups represented in the panel shall report that they felt offended.

The business tolerance here allows for the fact that you cannot count on 100 percent of humans passing any test. In this case the business tolerances shield the product from the lunatic-fringe extreme views, while at the same time allowing "offensive" to be measured.

For this kind of testing, it is usually more cost-effective to test prototypes or simulations built specifically for the purpose than to test the delivered product itself. You would hate to put in the effort to build the real thing and then find your audience thought it offensive.

Although fit criteria are measures of the product's performance, it is often more cost-effective to test prototypes built specifically for the purpose.

You can use subjective tests for your fit criteria, but the numbers you use in fit criteria are not subjective. Suppose you have a fit criterion of "reduce the time to perform [some task] by 25 percent of the current time." This means that the current time must be known and documented, not just guessed. The reason for the target of a 25 percent reduction must be well understood and agreed to by the client, and not just your subjective feeling as to what is acceptable. The reasoning behind wanting 25 percent—and not 20 percent or 30 percent—should be backed by empirical data taken from a study of the business.

Standards

Sometimes numbers are not appropriate, or you can create a better fit criterion by citing a standard. For example, the requirement mentioned earlier that the product is "not offensive to any group" could be handled by citing your organization's standards of conduct. Alternatively, your communications department might have standards for what is and what is not allowed to be said or displayed for public consumption. By citing that the product must comply with that standard, you are in effect setting the benchmark for lack of offensiveness.

Sometimes other standards may apply to the kind of products you might be developing. As an example, the ISO 9241 standard covers the ergonomics of human interactions with computer systems. A short glance at the ISO list of standards reveals many others that you might cite in your fit criteria.

Many of the standards you might use are much closer to home. Your organization has branding standards that are usually maintained by the communications department. Many look and feel requirements have their fit criteria written as:

> Fit Criterion: The product shall comply with the branding standard of [name your organization].

You might, as a consideration, add a pointer to where the standard can be found, or the contact in the communications department who looks after the standard.

Legal requirements have a built-in standard—the law. You could cite the appropriate law as your fit criterion, but as it is likely to be unfathomable to you and your development team, the simple approach is to allow your legal department to give their opinion that the solution matches the standard of the law.

Let's look at each type of non-functional requirement and consider how you might write the appropriate fit criterion.

Look and Feel Requirements

Look and feel requirements specify the spirit, mood, or style of the product's appearance and behavior, and the impression the user gets when using the product. Additionally, many companies require their products to be cloaked in company colors. The rationale for this requirement is either adherence to branding standards or a desire to enhance customer recognition. The two points are slightly different, however.

Let's look at branding standards first. Your organization has a communications department, which is responsible for the branding standards. Thus the fit criterion should specify the target standard and state who or what is to certify the product's compliance.

> Fit Criterion: The product shall be certified as complying with this year's corporate branding standards by the head of communications.

Where the rationale is customer recognition, we suggest a fit criterion along these lines:

> *Fit Criterion: Sixty percent of the target audience will recognize the product as belonging to the corporation within 5 seconds of encountering it for the first time.*

Look and feel requirements may start out as "touchy-feely" statements of intent. However, by determining the rationale and looking for its measurable aspects, you will always find a suitable fit criterion.

Usability and Humanity Requirements

Usability and humanity are the requirements for the experience when using the product—in other words, the fitness for use by its intended users. Products are typically required to be easy to use, easy to learn, able to be used by certain types of users, and so on. To write the fit criterion for each of these requirements, you must find a measurement scale that quantifies the objective of the requirement.

Let's look at some examples.

> *Description: The product shall be intuitive.*

To measure "intuitive," you must consider the people to whom the product must be intuitive. In the IceBreaker example, you are told the users/actors are the road engineers; they have engineering degrees and meteorological experience.

> *Rationale: The road engineers must find it easy and intuitive; otherwise, they will not use it.*

Now that you know this rationale, "intuitive" is much better defined.

> *Fit Criterion: A road engineer shall be able to produce a correct de-icing forecast within 10 minutes of encountering the product for the first time without reference to any out-of-product help.*

Sometimes "intuitive" really means "easy to learn." In this case, you ask how much time can be spent in training, and the resulting fit criterion might look like this:

> *Fit Criterion: Nine out of ten road engineers shall be able to successfully complete [list of selected tasks] after one day's training.*

Look and feel requirements may start out as "touchy-feely" statements of intent. However, by determining the rationale and looking for its measurable aspects, you will always find a suitable fit criterion.

Look for the real meaning of the requirement, and confirm it by having your stakeholders agree that your proposed fit criterion is the correct measurement of that meaning.

Fit criteria for usability requirements might also quantify the time allowed for given tasks, the error rates allowed (quantifying ease of use), the satisfaction rating awarded by the users, ratings given by usability laboratories, and so on. Look for the real meaning of the requirement, and confirm it by having your stakeholders agree that your proposed fit criterion is the correct measurement of that meaning.

> *Description: The product should be pleasant to use.*
>
> *Rationale: We want people to enjoy using it so that they continue to visit our site.*
>
> *Fit Criterion: Seventy percent of a representative test panel returns to our site more frequently than they do to the ten other similar sites available to them.*

Accessibility requirements specify how easy it should be for people with common disabilities to access the product. This could result in a fit criterion like this:

> *Fit Criterion: The product shall be certified to be in compliance with the Americans with Disabilities Act of 1990 as amended.*

It may also be necessary to specify the relevant parts of the act and the body responsible for certifying compliance.

Performance Requirements

Most of the time, your performance requirements will be easy to quantify—we tend to use numbers when we describe things such as speed, accuracy, capacity, availability, reliability, scalability, and similar characteristics of the product. Typically, then, the nature of the performance requirements will suggest a measurement scale. Let us look at some examples.

Suppose you have this requirement:

> *Description: The response shall be fast enough to avoid interrupting the user's flow of thought.*

The word "fast" indicates you should measure time. Here is a suggested fit criterion:

> *Fit Criterion: The response time shall be no more than 0.5 second for 95 percent of responses, and no more than 2 seconds for the remainder.*

Similarly, the fit criterion for an availability requirement might be written as follows:

> *Fit Criterion: In the first three months of operation, the product shall be available for 98 percent of the time between 8 A.M. and 8 P.M.*

A fit criterion may be shown as a range. This is particularly appropriate for performance requirements. For example:

> *Fit Criterion: The product shall allow for 3,000 downloads per hour, although 5,000 per hour is preferred.*

The point of using a range is to deter the developers from constructing a product that could be overly expensive, and to make the best design trade-offs to fit the budget and design constraints.

As most performance requirements are themselves quantified, it should be fairly straightforward to write appropriate fit criteria. If the requirement is given to you in correctly quantified terms, then the fit criterion and the requirement are the same. In that case, write one or the other.

If the requirement is given to you in correctly quantified terms, then the fit criterion and the requirement are the same.

Operational Requirements

Operational requirements specify the environment in which the product will operate. In some cases, the product has to be used in adverse or unusual conditions. Recall our example from the IceBreaker product:

> *Description: The product shall be used in and around trucks at night, and during rainstorms, snow, and freezing conditions.*

The fit criterion for an operational requirement is a quantification of the successful usage in the required environment. For the preceding operational requirement, the fit criterion quantifies the ability of the product to withstand the conditions. For example:

> *Fit Criterion: The operator shall successfully complete [list of tasks] within [time allowed] in a simulation of a five-year storm[1] and the product shall function correctly after 24 hours' exposure.*

FOOTNOTE 1
This is an accepted quantification of meteorological conditions. It means that (theoretically) you get this severity of storm only once every five years.

Operational conditions may also specify that the product must coexist with partner, or collaborating, systems. The fit criterion in this case will cite the specification of the partner system or the way to communicate with the partner:

> *Fit Criterion: The interfaces to the Rosa Weather Station shall be certified as complying with the National Transportation Communication ITS Protocol (NTC/IP).*

This criterion is testable—by engineers from NTC—and points the product's builders toward a known and accepted standard.

Additionally, most things in your operating infrastructure have standards:

> *Fit Criterion: The product must comply with HTML5 standard as published April 2011 by W3C.*

Maintainability Requirements

Maintainability requirements specify expectations about the maintenance of the product. Usually the fit criteria for these requirements quantify the amount of time allowed to make certain changes. This is not to say that all maintenance changes can be anticipated, but where changes are expected, then it is possible to quantify the time allowed to adopt those changes.

> *Fit Criterion: All functionality must be migrated to the new website with no more than 10 minutes of unavailability of the site.*

Security Requirements

Security is too important to be left to the whims or the goodwill of the developers. Your organization probably has some security standards in place, either specific to the industry or specific to your type of product. It is important to know which standard applies and to include it in your fit criterion.

Taking this step has an added benefit: CYA. If a breach occurs in the future, at least you can say your product complied with the standard.

Cultural Requirements

Cultural requirements, by their nature, are subjective and slightly more difficult to quantify. The fit criterion is usually based on who will certify the product's acceptability. For example:

FOOTNOTE 2
We are indebted to Ethel Wittenberg for information on the Orthodox Jewish prohibition against wearing a garment made of a mixture of linen and wool.

> *Fit Criterion: The Shatnez Laboratory of Brooklyn shall certify that the product complies with the shatnez rules.[2]*
>
> *Fit Criterion: The communications department shall give the opinion that the product displays no words or symbols that could be construed as religious or political.*

In almost all cases, your communications department can be considered to be the authority when dealing with cultural issues. This fit criterion is a general-purpose one that could be included in most specifications:

> *Fit Criterion: The communications department shall certify that the product is culturally acceptable for the target audience.*

Legal Requirements

Legal requirements specify which laws the product must conform to. As a result, this fit criterion applies to most legal requirements:

> *Fit Criterion: Your client will win a court case brought by someone who uses the product.*

However, fit criteria must be able to be tested in a cost-effective manner, and court cases are too expensive to be indulged in lightly. Thus the majority of fit criteria will be along the following lines:

> *Fit Criterion: The legal department/company lawyers shall certify that the product complies with the [appropriate laws].*

Legal requirements are also written to ensure that the product complies with cited standards. Most standards are written by organizations that either have people who certify compliance—"standards lawyers"—or issue guidelines as to how you can certify compliance for yourself. In either case, fit criteria can be written to specify how compliance with the standard is to be verified.

Fit Criteria for Functional Requirements

A functional requirement is something that the product must do—an action it must take. The fit criterion specifies how you will know that the product has successfully carried out that action. For functional requirements, there are no scales of measurement: The action is either completed or not completed. Completion depends on satisfying an authority that the product has correctly performed the action. The authority in this case is either the source of the data or the adjacent system that initiated the action.

If the action is to record something, then the fit criterion is that the recorded data complies with the data as it is known to the authority. For example:

> Description: The product shall record the weather station readings.
>
> Rationale: The readings are necessary for preparing the de-icing schedule, and must be kept for audit purposes.
>
> Fit Criterion: The recorded weather station readings shall be identical to the readings as recorded by the transmitting weather station.

The authority in this case is the weather station: It initiated the action, and it is the source of the data. You can say the requirement is for the product to faithfully store the data (allow for the product to make necessary manipulations to the data) as sent from the weather station. If this procedure is done correctly, then the product's data conforms to that transmitted by the station.

The fit criterion does not indicate *how* this conformance is to be tested. Instead, it is simply a statement that the tester uses to ensure compliance.

If the functional requirement is to make some calculation, then the fit criterion says the result of the calculation must be consistent with the authority's view of the data. Where the requirement is "the product shall check . . .," the fit criterion is "the checked data conforms with . . ." and again cites the authority for the data. "The product shall calculate . . ." results in a fit criterion of "the result conforms to . . ." and gives the algorithm (or source of the algorithm) for the result.

The general rule for functional requirements is that the fit criterion ensures that the function has been successfully carried out. That brings us to test cases.

Test Cases

You might find it feasible at this stage to think about writing test cases for your functional requirements. This approach is promoted by several agile techniques wherein the tests are written before the code is. The basic idea is to force the programmer to concentrate on learning the fit criterion for any part of the functionality.

Many requirements analysts feel uncomfortable delving into writing test cases. However, the testers for your organization will be—we are sure of this—delighted either to help or to write the test cases for you. Testing is most effective early in the development cycle, and involving the testers in the requirements activity is always beneficial. Testers are the best people to tell you whether your functional requirements are testable.

READING

Beck, Kent. *Test Driven Development: By Example.* Addison-Wesley, 2002.

Merkow, Mark. *Secure and Resilient Software: Requirements, Test Cases, and Testing Methods.* Auerbach Publications, 2011.

Forms of Fit Criteria

The most common way of writing fit criteria is using text and numbers in your natural language. When you follow this route, you need to ensure that all terms that are used in the fit criteria are defined in your specification and consistently used in your requirements. The best way to do so is to create a data dictionary (for examples, see Section 7 of the requirements template in Appendix A) that defines the terms within the scope of your work.

Defining the Data

For example, within the Ice Breaker project requirements often refer to *Road Section*. If you look in the data dictionary, you will find this definition:

Road Section = Road Section Identifier + Road Section Coordinates

You can then expect to find a definition of each of the attributes—for example:

Road Section Identifier = *Unique identifier for 500 meters of road. The maximum number of road sections per road is 10,000.*

Another strategy for defining the data is to define each term as part of the fit criterion of each individual requirement. However, as you will usually reference the same term in more than one requirement, it makes sense to maintain a central dictionary that can act as a cross-reference between requirements. Your growing understanding of the data means that you can progressively build a business data/information model that specifies the essential stored data for the requirements you are specifying.

Graphic Fit Criteria

When writing fit criteria, the aim is to be as implementation neutral as possible, thereby giving the designers and developers the maximum amount of freedom in choosing how to meet each requirement. The problem is that natural language is inherently procedural (you are forced to write words in a serial order) and sometimes that order is interpreted incorrectly as part of the requirement. You might consider the following approaches.

Decision Tables

Suppose that your fit criterion defines the rate of discount that a customer should have depending on how long he has been a customer, what his cumulative spending is, and whether he is a member of the customer loyalty program. Rather than writing all of these rules in text form, it would be clearer to build a decision table, as illustrated in Table 12.1.

In this case, because of the many ways that conditions can be combined, a decision table becomes an effective way of writing the fit criterion. The decision table is less procedural than a text-based fit criterion—you can look at it in whatever order necessary. Also, by identifying all of the possible ways

See Section 7 of the Volere Requirements Specification Template in Appendix A for examples of data dictionary definitions.

For the fit criteria to be complete, the specification must contain definitions of the terms used in the fit criteria.

Table 12.1

Fit Criterion in the Form of a Decision Table

For each combination of conditions, the table identifies which discount rate is applicable and whether to offer a loyalty program membership.

Conditions						
- Customer for more than 12 months	Y	Y	Y	N	N	N
- Cumulative spending greater than n	Y	Y	N	N	N	Y
- Member of loyalty program	Y	N	N	N	Y	Y
Actions						
- 5% discount	X					X
- Offer loyalty program membership		X	X			
- 2% discount		X				
- 0% discount				X	X	X

of combining the conditions, you, together with the business people who are familiar with the discount policy, can see the places where there are missing actions or inconsistent rules.

Graphs

Another pictorial form of fit criterion is to draw a graph. This approach is particularly suitable when you want to express change in values over a period of time, such as for an extensibility requirement. For example, suppose your client wants a product that can cater to a growth in customers from the current 500,000 to 1 million over the next year. Of course, you can write this fit criterion in text form, but drawing it as a graph conveys more information to the developers and testers. In Figure 12.3, you see not just the growth from one number to another but when the peak periods of growth are projected. Just by looking at this picture, the developers and testers get a much better understanding of the business and the nature of the problem that their product has to solve.

Figure 12.3

Projected growth of the business. This graph showing growth over time is the fit criterion for an extensibility requirement.

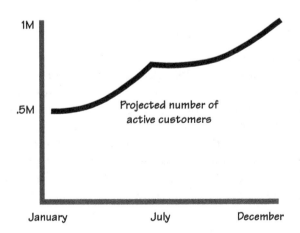

Now that we are in the swing of using a variety of formats for defining fit criteria, we hope that you can see other opportunities for graphical fit criteria. Consider process models, state models, decision trees, dynamics models, or any other technique that best conveys the needed measurement in the least ambiguous way.

Use Cases and Fit Criteria

A use case, whether it is a product use case (PUC) or a business use case (BUC), is a collection of requirements—both functional and non-functional—working toward a desired outcome. While each requirement has its own fit criterion to measure its performance, the fit criterion for the use case as a whole is the benchmark for the collection of requirements when they act together.

You can apply a fit criterion to a use case.

To avoid confusion about this use case criterion, we call it the *outcome*. That is, this criterion is the intended outcome of the (business or product) use case if all works as intended. As we are talking about a collection of requirements, each with a fit criterion, you might prefer to think of the outcome as a summary (or even summation) of all the individual fit criteria. Note that some organizations refer to this as the "end state" or the "post condition" of the PUC.

We suggest that you make use of outcomes very early in your requirements gathering. During the blastoff (or as soon as you identify the business events), try to elicit from your stakeholders the intended outcome for each of their business events. You are asking, "When this business event happens, what does the business need to achieve?" The answer to this question, with a little massaging on your part, can be turned into the outcome or fit criterion for the business use case. As your business use cases evolve into product use cases, the same or very similar criteria can be applied. You will find, as we have, that specifying an outcome criterion early in the development process eliminates a lot of misunderstandings about what each business use case is intended to accomplish.

As you capture individual requirements, and their fit criteria, keep in mind that each of them has to contribute in some way to the purpose of the product. If you have an outcome criterion attached to each use case, it is easier to ensure that all the requirements you are capturing contribute to the use case as a whole.

Fit Criterion for Project Purpose

We have already discussed writing the fit criterion for the project's purpose. Of course, we didn't call it a fit criterion back in Chapter 3 (we called it a measurement), but that is what it is. Let's look quickly at this idea again: The project's purpose is a statement of the reason for making the investment in the project. If you go to the trouble and expense of developing a project to develop a product, then it makes sense to have an objective benchmark to measure the delivered product against.

The measurement of the purpose is exactly the same as a fit criterion for an individual requirement. The only difference is that the fit criterion measures a single requirement, whereas the purpose's measurement is the benchmark for the entire project.

Refer to Chapter 3, Scoping the Business Problem, for information on writing a measurable project purpose.

Fit Criteria for Solution Constraints

Constraints are a special type of requirement—they are global requirements, usually pre-ordained by management—but they still need to be specified correctly just like any other type of requirement. For example, Section 3a of the template includes the solution constraints. These constraints place restrictions on the way that the problem must be solved; you could also say they mandate a solution to the problem. For example:

> *Description: The software part of the product must run on Linux.*

This requirement reflects management's decision to use Linux. It may or may not have a sound technological basis, but that is beside the point for our purposes here. You are being told that any solution you deliver has to comply with this constraint.

We can test compliance—either you comply with the requirement or you don't—as long as whatever it is that you have to comply with is measurable. For example, you can test whether you have complied with a law, but you can't test whether you have complied with a constraint that states, "You shall be happy." In the case of the Linux constraint, you could write the following criterion:

> *Fit Criterion: All functionality of the software shall operate as specified when run using Red Hat Enterprise Linux 5.0.*

Similarly, all other constraint requirements—for example, implementation environment, partner applications, commercial off-the-shelf software, open-source software, workplace environment, time budget, and financial budget—should have fit criteria.

Summary

A fit criterion is neither a test nor the design for a test, but rather a benchmark that the delivered product has to be tested against. It is used as input to building a test case through which the tester ensures that each of the product's requirements complies with its fit criterion.

Quantifying or measuring the requirement gives you a better opportunity to interact with your stakeholders. By agreeing on a measurement, you confirm that you have understood the requirement correctly, and that both you and your stakeholders have an identical understanding of it. As a by-product, you will also find quantifying it ensures that the requirement is both wanted and necessary.

Including a fit criterion in a requirement encourages testers to participate in the requirements process. Testers should be involved early in the development cycle, and they are particularly helpful at requirements time when you are writing your fit criteria. This is not to say that the testers have to write the fit criteria for you, but just that testers are the best source of knowledge about whether something can be tested, and whether the fit criterion contains the appropriate quantification. In other words, the testers are excellent consultants for the fit criteria.

The fit criterion, not the description, is the real requirement. The description you write is the stakeholder's way of stating the intention of the requirement. If your stakeholders are like most of us, they speak using everyday language, which is, unfortunately, often ambiguous and often not precise enough. You need to clarify the requirement with a fit criterion that is stated in unambiguous, precise terms and probably uses numbers or a measurement to convey its meaning.

Fit criteria are also a vehicle for reaching a consensus among multiple stakeholders. Your attempts to clarify and measure will almost always result in hidden meanings becoming visible, hidden requirements bubbling to the surface, and, most importantly, the stakeholders agreeing on what is needed.

Fit criteria are usually derived after the requirement description is written. You derive a fit criterion by examining the requirement's description and rationale, and determining which quantification best expresses the user's intention for the requirement. You may sometimes find that this close examination results in changes to the requirement, but these changes are for the better and should be considered quite normal; their occurrence simply means the requirement was not properly understood in the first instance. With patience and persistence, and with the wise use of measurements, you can ensure that each of your requirements is unambiguous, testable, and real.

The fit criterion is an unambiguous benchmark that the product is compared against.

The fit criterion is the real requirement.

You derive the fit criterion by examining the requirement's description and rationale, and determining which quantification best expresses the user's intention for the requirement.

The Quality Gateway

in which we prevent unsuitable requirements ⇥ ————————
from becoming part of the specification

Consider how requirements come about. It isn't exactly random—we give you trawling techniques to help with your elicitation—and it isn't exactly badly formed—we give you a template and a snow card to help formulate your requirements. But the requirement comes from people who are not always sure of what they need, are not always able to explain what it is that they want, and it cannot always be carefully written so it is unambiguous and complete.

Here is the point of doing requirements: You have to ensure that what is handed to the developers is a precise, complete, and unambiguous statement of the real need. Anything less negates the reason for doing requirements. Your developers can build anything, but first they have to know what it is they have to build.

This, then, is the job of the Quality Gateway—to ensure that from here on, each requirement is as close to perfect as it can be. It achieves this feat by means of the gatekeepers validating each requirement before allowing it to be included in the specification.

Note in Figure 13.1 that the incoming flow to the Quality Gateway process is a *formalized potential requirement,* where "potential" indicates that it is not yet ready to see the light of day. Before it is released into the world, it must be tested (and it must pass the test) by the Quality Gateway. Only then does it become an *accepted requirement.*

When the formalized potential requirement arrives at the Quality Gateway, it should be complete enough that it can undergo tests to determine whether it can be accepted into the specification. Rejected requirements are returned to their originator for clarification, revision, or discarding.

Figure 13.1

(An extract from the Volere requirements process.) The Quality Gateway is the activity where each requirement is tested to ensure its suitability. Suitability in this sense means that the requirement provides downstream activities with a clear, complete, unambiguous description of what to build. To ensure a suitable requirements specification, all requirements must be validated by the Quality Gateway.

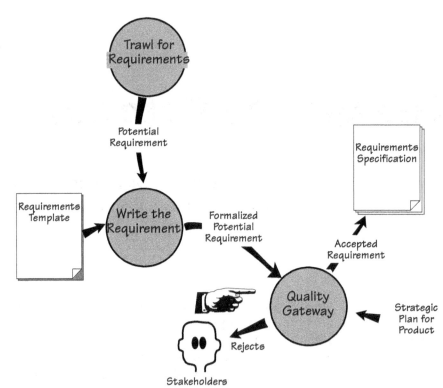

The Quality Gateway tests individual requirements. Later, in Chapter 17, Requirements Completeness, we look at how you can assure yourself that you have a complete set of requirements.

You should also consider the *effect* of the Quality Gateway. When requirements analysts know the standards the gatekeepers use to test the requirements against, they are forced to raise their game and improve the quality of the requirements that arrive at the Quality Gateway.

Formality Guide

This chapter discusses the Quality Gateway in its most formal incarnation. It is worth emphasizing that you can—in fact, you should—apply some or all of the Quality Gateway tests to a requirement at any stage of your requirements gathering. The way that you implement the Quality Gateway depends on the degree of formality needed for your project.

Rabbit projects, because of the proximity and small number of stakeholders, can make good use of verbally communicated requirements. However, the lack of a written requirement makes it slightly more difficult to determine whether the requirement is correct. Before attempting to implement a requirement, the developer must ensure that it is within scope, is testable, is not gold plating, and meets several other criteria that we cover in this chapter. The Quality Gateway is applicable to rabbit projects, but probably not as a formal checkpoint in the sense that we present it here. Rabbit team members should read this chapter and continuously apply its principles when reviewing their user stories.

Horse projects typically use written requirements within an iterative development cycle. This practice results in a short time elapsing between the discovering of requirements and the release of a partial working version of the product. But putting the product in the user's hands quickly should not be viewed as a way of avoiding testing the requirements. Even for the fastest of cycles, it is still far more efficient and effective to test the requirements before attempting any implementation. Horse projects should use a fairly informal Quality Gateway.

Elephant projects produce a written specification, because of either outsourcing, the number of stakeholders, or legal reasons. The sheer size of elephant projects means that even small errors in requirements have the potential to balloon into major problems if not caught early. The size of the final specification precludes effective testing of the entire document—people stop seriously reading at about page 15 and start skimming. The idea of testing individual requirements (or cohesive groups of requirements) as they are generated and before they are allowed into the specification has a much better chance of success.

Requirements Quality

At this stage, let us take a moment to consider the effect of requirements quality and to explain why it matters.

We are about to talk about a specification. Keep in mind that it need not take the traditional form of a written, sometimes long, usually boring document with sign-offs, versions, release dates, and other administrative niceties appended. We recognize the need for this kind of document in some situations, and the lack of a need for it in others. So, for the purposes of this chapter, the word "specification" means the collection of one or more requirements held in whatever manner you choose, including the requirements held inside your head.

The requirements specification is used by several downstream activities and eventually to build your product, whatever it may be. As a result, if the specification is wrong, the product will also be wrong. The Quality Gateway testing is meant to ensure, as far as humanly possible, that the requirements are right.

Approximately 50 to 60 percent of errors in software development originate in the requirements and design activity. Another five percent of software errors originate in the coding part of the development. This distribution

> *For the purposes of this chapter, the word "specification" means the collection of requirements held in whatever manner you use, including the requirements held inside your head.*

implies—strongly implies—that it is beneficial to get the requirements right. Errors in requirements are expensive and, if allowed to continue to the downstream activities beyond the requirements process, become more and more expensive.

The cost of repairing an error increases each time the product reaches a new phase. It is contested as to exactly how much this increase is (some software commentators put it as much as a thousand times if the product reaches the maintenance phase), but whatever the increment is, it is significant. The cost of repairing an error increases regardless of which type of life cycle you use—waterfall, incremental, or any other. All downstream activities have dependencies on the requirements, so an undiscovered error in requirements means a disproportionate effort to correct it later. Capers Jones of Software Productivity Research estimates that the rework needed to remove requirements errors typically accounts for as much as 50 percent of total software development costs.

The earlier an error is discovered, the cheaper it is to correct.

You may dispute some of the research, and you may dispute some of the numbers, but the underlying message remains true: The earlier an error is discovered, the cheaper it is to correct.

The numbers suggest—no, let's be honest here, they scream—that you should spend the time testing and correcting your requirements *during the requirements activity* instead of allowing incorrect requirements to percolate through to a downstream activity. Simply put, testing the requirements is the cheapest and fastest way to develop your product.

Using the Quality Gateway

The Quality Gateway defends the specification against unwelcome, unwanted, and undesirable requirements.

In medieval times, castles and fortified towns had gateways designed to keep invaders and unwanted travelers out. The gateways usually sported a portcullis and were manned by gatekeepers—people charged with the protection of the inner sanctum. The Quality Gateway we describe here has the same role—to defend the specification against unwelcome, unwanted, and undesirable requirements.

To pass through the Quality Gateway and be included in the requirements specification (remember the specification does not have to be a formal, written document), a requirement must pass a number of tests. These tests ensure that the requirements are complete and accurate, and do not cause problems by being unsuitable for the design and implementation stages later in the project. We illustrate this situation in Figure 13.2.

In the next part of this chapter, we discuss the requirements tests. As we do, keep in mind that it takes longer to describe the tests than it does to perform them.

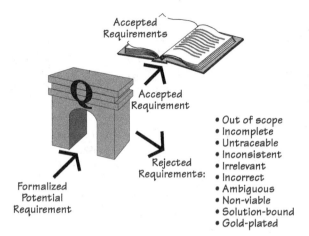

Accepted Requirements

Accepted Requirement

Formalized Potential Requirement

Rejected Requirements:

- Out of scope
- Incomplete
- Untraceable
- Inconsistent
- Irrelevant
- Incorrect
- Ambiguous
- Non-viable
- Solution-bound
- Gold-plated

Figure 13.2

The Quality Gateway tests each requirement for correctness and suitability. Accepted requirements are added to the specification; rejected requirements are returned to their originator.

Within Scope?

A very common problem in projects is out-of-scope requirements. It is all too easy for your stakeholders to become over-enthusiastic and start giving you requirements that are irrelevant to the purpose of your product, or as we talk about it here, out of scope.

This kind of exuberance happens on most projects. Uncontrolled scope creep leads to the project running over time and over budget, and even then it might not deliver the product it set out to build in the first place. We will have more to say about scope creep later in this chapter.

Back in Chapter 3, Scoping the Business Problem, we discussed how to determine the scope of the work by building a context model. Here we present another use for the context model; this time we use it as the arbiter of whether a requirement is in or out of scope.

You have seen how the flows of data in the context model that enter or leave the work area determine its functionality. Naturally enough, if you choose to automate any of this functionality, you must write requirements. Let's see how you can use this link between the flows of data and the requirements.

Suppose you are the gatekeeper, and you have been given this requirement:

> *The product shall pay truck drivers for working overtime.*

Look at the context model in Figure 13.3: There is no data flowing into the work to provide information about drivers. The work knows about trucks, but not who is driving them. The requirement means that a number of flows would be needed—driver information, work hours, rates of pay, deductions,

Chapter 3, Scoping the Business Problem, discusses how to determine the scope of the work, and build a context model to define this scope.

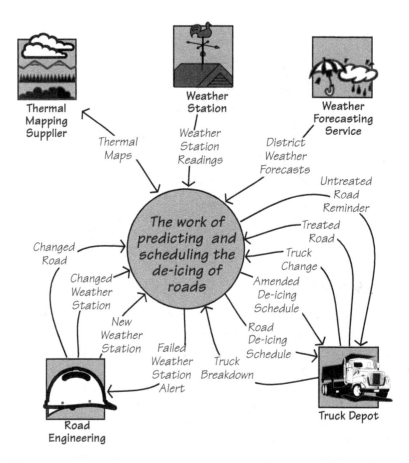

paychecks, and many other things—which would clearly increase the scope
of the work.

You can see that either this requirement is out of scope or the scope of the
work is incorrect. Given the nature of the work being done, you would decide
the requirement is out of scope and reject it.

Now suppose the potential requirement was this:

> *The product shall report on the accuracy of weather forecasts.*

There is no data flow on the context model that has anything to do with
reporting on the weather forecasts. Presumably the report would have to
be sent to some entity outside of the work. By adding a flow to carry that
information, you are increasing the scope of the work. While its subject matter might seem relevant to the work being done, the lack of a data flow says
clearly that it is not part of the work as it stands.

Here is another potential requirement:

> *The product shall record the hours that the trucks are active.*

This requirement could be in or out of scope. To judge it accurately, you need the rationale for the requirement. On the one hand, if the rationale is to provide some kind of report on truck activity, then we can say it is out of scope—there is no flow on the context model that carries such information. On the other hand, suppose we have this situation:

> *Description: The product shall record the hours that the trucks are active.*
>
> *Rationale: Trucks may not be scheduled for more than 22 out of 24 hours to allow for maintenance and cleaning.*

The rationale says that the data is kept and used inside the work, and there is no reason for it to ever leave the work. Given this rationale, you can say that the requirement is within scope.

Relevancy

While the context model is a clear indicator of scope, you also have to consider the relevancy of the requirement.

In Chapter 3, we discussed how to identify the purpose of the project and to record it as quantified project goals. These goals serve as the arbiter of relevancy throughout the project.

Chapter 3, Scoping the Business Problem, discusses how to define the purpose of the product.

To test a requirement for relevancy, compare its intention with the project goals. The test is fairly simple: Does this requirement contribute to the purpose of the project? Does this requirement help make the product, directly or indirectly, meet the project's purpose?

Does this requirement contribute to the purpose of the project?

Let's go back to the IceBreaker project. Suppose you are the gatekeeper and you encounter this requirement:

> *The product shall maintain a lookup table of the times of sunrise and sunset throughout the year.*

At first this requirement appears to be relevant. The product has to predict the formation of ice on roads, and ice usually forms at night. Thus this requirement appears to contribute to the project goal:

> *Project Goal: To accurately predict when ice will form on road surfaces and to efficiently schedule the appropriate de-icing treatment.*

However, if we dig a little deeper, we discover that the temperature of the road surface is the determinant of whether ice will form, and road temperature is monitored and transmitted by weather stations—whether it is night or day does not override the actual temperature. As ice is perfectly capable of forming during the daylight hours, there is no reason for the product to have any knowledge of day or night.

Requirements can contribute indirectly to the product. Sometimes the requirement may call for the product to do something that has no immediate connection to the purpose; however, without this requirement, the product could not achieve its purpose. As an example, consider this requirement:

> *Description: The product shall record the salt capacity of the trucks.*

At first glance, this requirement appears to have nothing to do with the goal of the product, which is to efficiently schedule trucks to treat roads with de-icing material. But look at the rationale for this requirement:

> *Rationale: Different trucks have different capacities. The scheduling of trucks depends on their capacity to treat the number of road sections predicted to have ice formation.*

Now that the reason for the requirement is apparent, the gatekeeper would be correct to allow this requirement to pass: It contributes to the goals of the project.

Many of the non-functional requirements also make an indirect contribution to the project's goals. In contrast, irrelevant requirements indicate a need to talk to the source of the requirement—an "irrelevant" requirement might indicate that a stakeholder has misunderstood the project purpose, or it might signal that a new business area is opening.

When considering relevancy, pay particular attention to the following sections of your requirements specification:

- Users (Section 2): Who are you building the product for, and is it a product suitable for these users?

- Requirements Constraints (Section 3): Is the product relevant within the constraints? Have all the constraints been observed by the requirements?

- Relevant Facts (Section 5): Have the requirements failed to account for any external factors?

- Assumptions (Section 5): Are the requirements consistent with any assumptions you are making about the project?

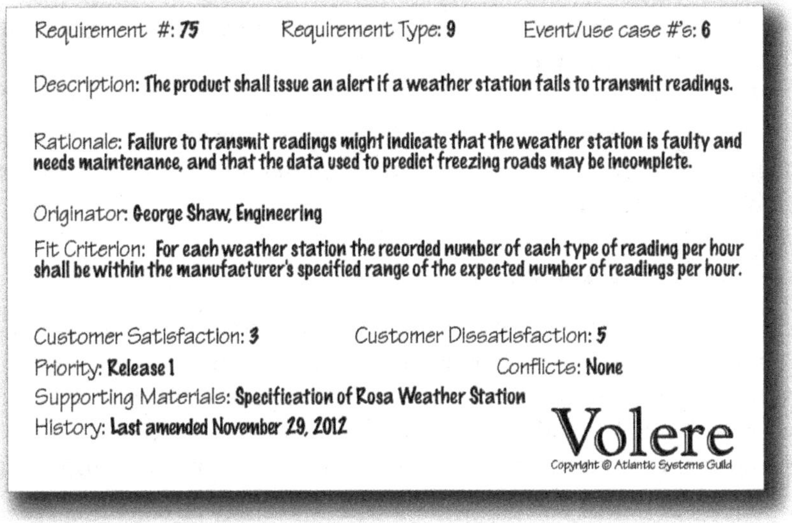
Requirement #: 75 Requirement Type: 9 Event/use case #'s: 6

Description: The product shall issue an alert if a weather station fails to transmit readings.

Rationale: Failure to transmit readings might indicate that the weather station is faulty and needs maintenance, and that the data used to predict freezing roads may be incomplete.

Originator: George Shaw, Engineering

Fit Criterion: For each weather station the recorded number of each type of reading per hour shall be within the manufacturer's specified range of the expected number of readings per hour.

Customer Satisfaction: 3 Customer Dissatisfaction: 5

Priority: Release 1 Conflicts: None

Supporting Materials: Specification of Rosa Weather Station

History: Last amended November 29, 2012

Volere

Copyright © Atlantic Systems Guild

Figure 13.4

An example of a complete atomic requirement using the Volere snow card. All of the attributes are present, and the analyst has marked the requirement as having no known conflicts with other requirements. This requirement passes the completeness tests.

Testing Completeness

In Chapter 16, Communicating the Requirements, we discuss how to use the requirements shell (we also refer to the shell as a "snow card") as an easier way to formulate a complete requirement. We use these cards for training purposes and low-tech requirements gathering. You can see an example in Figure 13.4.

Think of the snow card as a compartmentalized container for an atomic requirement, with each compartment being an attribute of the requirement. Here we use the snow card to test the completeness of a requirement.

Are There Any Missing Attributes?

The first test for completeness is to use the snow card as a checklist to ensure all relevant attributes have been supplied.

Chapter 16 discusses the process of writing the requirements in detail.

Sometimes, not all of the shell attributes are necessary. For example, sometimes the description makes it obvious why the requirement is important, and there is no point writing the rationale. Sometimes the description can be dropped, because a clear and readable fit criterion is provided. Sometimes there are no supporting materials.

The snow card is packaged as part of the Volere Requirements Specification Template in Appendix A.

Naturally, if one of the attributes is missing, then its omission should occur because it is not necessary rather than because it is too difficult or has been overlooked. If the attribute is missing because you are still investigating it (and perhaps waiting for an answer from someone), then include that information in the requirement to keep everyone informed and to forestall unnecessary questions:

> *Supporting Material: Waiting for county engineer to supply details of road treatment volumes.*

The completeness test says that each requirement must have all relevant attributes. If they are not part of the requirement, their absence should be obvious or explained.

Meaningful to Stakeholders?

Once you are satisfied that the requirement has all its needed attributes, you should ensure that the attributes add to the meaning and common understanding of the requirement. To do so, the requirement must be written as clearly as possible. And while we certainly admire conciseness, you must ensure that the requirement is written so that all needed information is included.

Test each attribute of the requirement. Taking the point of view of the appropriate stakeholder, ask, "Is it possible to misunderstand this?" For instance, Figure 13.4 includes the following information:

> *Supporting Material: Specification of Rosa Weather Station*

We ask, "Is it possible to confuse this? Is there more than one specification of the Rosa Weather Station? Is there any doubt about where to find this specification?" The answers to these questions help us to be more precise about exactly what we mean. The resultant entry reads:

> *Supporting Material: Specification of DRS511 Rosa Weather Station, release 1.1, published January 22, 2010.*

Testing the Fit Criterion

Requirements can be ambiguous; in fact, any English-language (or any other language) statement is probably ambiguous in some way, as well as vulnerable to being subjectively understood. This is obviously not the way that we should write requirements. To overcome this ambiguity, we add a fit criterion to measure the requirement and make it accurate and testable.

The task of the gatekeeper is to ensure that the fit criterion is a reasonable measurement of the requirement—one that allows the product to be tested against the requirement.

The first question to ask is, "Does the requirement have a correctly defined fit criterion?" If not, it is probably not well enough understood. The next

> *Everything should be made as simple as possible, but not one bit simpler.*
>
> —Albert Einstein

See Chapter 12 for a full explanation of how to write fit criteria.

question for the fit criterion is, "Can it be used as input when designing acceptance tests?" You should also consider whether a cost-effective (within the project's constraints) way of testing a solution to this requirement exists.

The fit criterion must also meet the purpose of the project. We have discussed how the requirement must conform to the project purpose, so it makes sense that the measurement of the requirement must likewise conform to this purpose.

While the fit criterion uses numbers to express the requirement, the numbers themselves must not be subjective, but rather must be based on evidence. For example:

> *Description: The product shall be easy to learn.*
>
> *Fit Criterion: A user shall be able to learn to process a claim within 30 minutes of starting to use the product for the first time.*

The question to ask about this fit criterion is, "Where did the 30 minutes come from?" Is it simply the whim of a stakeholder or the requirements analyst? Or is it based on evidence that a learning curve longer than 30 minutes means the users will become discouraged and give up? It is, of course, useful if the requirement writer has included a reference to the evidence in the Supporting Materials component of the requirement.

A fit criterion can also be written using a predefined standard. For example, when the requirement specifies that the product is to conform to company branding, the fit criterion should cite the company's branding standards and refer to the communications department for verification.

Security requirements would probably also use a standard as the fit criterion—either an industry-specific security standard or the organization's own internal security standards.

Where a standard is used, the gatekeeper should check that the standard is appropriate for the requirement, and that it is accessible enough for the developers to deliver a product that complies with it.

Whether the criterion uses numbers or cites a standard depends entirely on the type of requirement. Performance and usability requirements normally use numbers, whereas look and feel, security, and cultural requirements mostly use standards.

In any event, the lack of an appropriate fit criterion is sufficient to consign the requirement to the "rejected" bin.

Consistent Terminology

When a poet writes a poem, he intends that it should inspire rich and diverse visions in anyone who reads it. The requirements analyst has the opposite intention: He would like each requirement to be understood in precisely the same way by every person who reads it. Requirements specifications are not poetry—they are not even novels where the reader uses his imagination to see the story being told. Requirements must have only one interpretation; otherwise, there is a high risk of building a product that satisfies the wrong interpretation of the requirement.

To specify a requirement such that it has only one meaning, you need, in addition to a fit criterion, to define the terms, and the meanings of those terms, within the context of the specification. Section 4 of the Volere Requirements Specification Template is called Naming Conventions and Terminology. This section acts as a glossary of the words specific to this project and provides a starting point for understanding the language.

Eventually, each of the terms used in the atomic requirements is formally defined in Section 7, which comprises the data dictionary. The terms are given a non-ambiguous definition that is agreed to by the stakeholders, and these terms are then used to write the requirements.

The next act of consistency is to test that each requirement uses terms in a manner consistent with their defined meanings. As an example of inconsistency, a requirements specification we once audited used the term "viewer" in many parts of the specification. Our audit identified six different meanings for the term, depending on where it was used. Had the requirements using this term been allowed to continue on their ambiguous way, the end product would have included some serious problems.

Without an authority—in this case, a data dictionary—to define the meaning of terms used in requirements, developers and stakeholders will assume different meanings, and different stakeholders will naturally have different meanings, and the project will descend into Babel. [1]

One last word about inconsistency: You should expect it, and you should eliminate it with the Quality Gateway.

Does the specification contain a definition of the meaning of every essential subject-matter term within the specification?

Is every reference to a defined term consistent with its definition?

FOOTNOTE 1
The Tower of Babel is the subject of a biblical story in which construction of a huge tower had to be abandoned because all the builders spoke different languages—something we would like to avoid with software and hardware projects.

Viable within Constraints?

Viable requirements are those for which it is possible to develop and implement a solution in a cost-effective manner, and when implemented, the solution will be operationally successful. In addition, the solution must be able to be implemented within the constraints for both the design of the product and the budget of the project.

Constraints are described in Section 3 of the Volere Requirements Specification Template in Appendix A.

The Quality Gateway rejected the following requirement because it is not viable: It could not be operationally successful.

> *Truck drivers shall receive weather forecasts and schedule their own de-icing.*

Truck drivers do not have the necessary information at hand to predict the time a road will freeze—they do not know which roads have been treated and which are in a dangerous condition. Coordinating a number of trucks treating multiple roads stretching over the whole of a county is a matter for centralized control.

The users for a product might not always be sophisticated computer users. For example, it is probably not viable to pay pensions to the very elderly using cutting-edge, high-tech mechanisms. You would have to wait for today's teenagers to retire before that approach would be viable—and, of course, by that time today's high-tech mechanisms would be replaced by tomorrow's high-tech devices.

You might also consider whether the organization is mature enough to cope with a requirement. There is little point in specifying a product for users who need to have engineering degrees to use it when you are employing minimum-wage manual laborers.

Do you have the technological skills to build the requirement?

Do you have the technological skills to build the requirement? It is an easy matter to write a requirement, but it is sometimes a different, more difficult task to construct a working solution for it. There is little point in specifying a product that is beyond your development capabilities. This test is a matter of assessing—unfortunately, there can be no measurement here—whether the requirement is achievable given the technical capabilities of the development team.

Do you have the time and the money to build the requirement?

Do you have the time and the money to build the requirement? This test asks you to estimate the cost of (or seek advice on) meeting the requirement, and to assess it as a share of the total budget. (The budget should be shown as a constraint in Section 3 of the requirements specification.) If the cost of constructing a requirement exceeds its budget, then the customer value attached to the requirement indicates how you should proceed: High-value requirements are negotiated, while low-value requirements are discarded.

Is the requirement acceptable to all stakeholders?

Is the requirement acceptable to the stakeholders? If a requirement is very unpopular with a large section of the stakeholders, then history tells us that it is futile to include it in the product. Stakeholders have been known to sabotage the development or operation of products because they disagree with part of it. Users have been known to ignore and not use products because not all of the functionality was as they thought it should be.

Do any other constraints make the requirement nonviable? Do any of the partner applications or the expected work environment contradict the requirement? Do any solution constraints—constraints on the way that a solution must be designed—make the requirement difficult or impossible to achieve?

Requirement or Solution?

The more abstract the requirement, the less likely it is to be a solution.

The description of a requirement is unfortunately, often stated in terms of a solution. We all unconsciously talk about requirements in terms of how we think they should be solved, based on our personal experience of the world. The result is a statement that focuses on one possible solution—not necessarily the most appropriate one—and usually hides the real requirement.

Examine the requirement: Does it contain any element of technology? Is it written in a way that describes a type of procedure? Consider this potential solution:

> The product shall use JavaScript for the interface.

You cannot tell if it is the *best* solution. In any event, it is not a real requirement and must be sent back to the originator for clarification.

Sometimes we unconsciously state solutions. For example, this is a solution:

> The product shall have a clock on the menu bar.

Both "clock" and "menu bar" are parts of a solution. We suggest that the real requirement is this:

> The product shall make the user aware of the current time.

This might seem pedantic, but there could well be a better way of implementing the requirement. When you write the requirement in an abstract manner, other solutions become possible. There are ways other than a clock to make people aware of the time—the astrolabe (look it up) is one (albeit not necessarily a better one). Likewise, there are ways other than JavaScript to build usable interfaces.

Examine the requirements for technological content. You must reject any that are a solution and not the requirement, unless that solution is actually a constraint.

Requirement Value

The customer satisfaction/ dissatisfaction ratings indicate the value that the customer places on a requirement.

The customer satisfaction and customer dissatisfaction ratings attached to a requirement indicate the value the customer places on a requirement. The satisfaction rating measures (from 1 to 5) how happy the customer will be if you successfully deliver an implementation of the requirement, and the dissatisfaction rating measures (from 1 to 5) how unhappy the customer will be if you do not successfully deliver this requirement.

The test for the Quality Gateway is whether the requirement carries an appropriate rating of the value that the customer assigns to the requirement.

Gold Plating

The term "gold plating" comes from the domain of bathroom taps—some wealthy people and some rock stars like to have gold-plated taps. The water does not flow out of gold-plated taps any better than it does from chrome-plated ones, and the water is exactly the same water. The difference is that the gold-plated tap costs more and might, to some eyes, look a little better. This term has been taken up by the software industry to mean unnecessary features or requirements that contribute more to the cost of a product than they do to its functionality or usefulness.

Let's look at an example. Suppose a requirement for the IceBreaker product states that it shall play a piece of classical music when an engineer logs on. Our knowledge of the IceBreaker product leads us to suspect that this is a gold-plated requirement. It does not contribute to the goals of the product (to make roads safe from ice).

The gatekeeper must judge this requirement to be gold plating. It is there because it might be "nice to have," but no one would really mind if the requirement were omitted from the product. The first test of gold plating is, "Does it matter if the requirement is not included?" If no one can truly justify its inclusion, then it may be considered gold plating.

The second, and perhaps more reliable, test is to look at the customer satisfaction/dissatisfaction ratings attached to the requirement. A low dissatisfaction rating indicates the requirement is probably gold plating. After all, when the customer says that it does not matter if this requirement is not included, then he is signaling that the requirement does not make a vital contribution to the product.

We hasten to add that there is a difference between unnecessary gold plating and cool features that either sell the product to the consumer or make it far more acceptable to the user. Some of these features could be considered to be gold plating, but before you delete them, ask whether they add to the appeal of the product or merely add to the cost.

The point is that you should know whether a requirement is gold plating. If so, and you decide to include it, then it should be a conscious choice.

See Chapter 16, Communicating the Requirements, for a discussion of customer satisfaction and customer dissatisfaction, and Chapter 17, Requirements Completeness, for a discussion of how to use the customer satisfaction and dissatisfaction ratings to prioritize requirements.

Does it matter if this requirement is not included?

A low dissatisfaction rating indicates a requirement that is probably gold plating.

Requirements Creep

Requirements creep refers to the process in which new requirements enter the specification after the requirements are considered complete. Creep can have a serious impact on the project budget—some commentators put the average creep figure at approximately 30 percent of the total cost of meeting all requirements. This is far too much.

The Quality Gateway has a part to play in controlling creep. We noted earlier that you can use the flows on the context model as a determinant of whether a requirement is in or out of scope. Also, you should ensure that each requirement carries valid customer satisfaction/dissatisfaction ratings. These ratings tell you the value that your customers assign to the requirement. If it is high, then creeping requirements might be tolerated (with a concomitant adjustment to the budget).

The rationale attached to the requirement must also make sense, as often creeping requirements have a rationale that indicates the requirement is out of scope.

A little earlier in this chapter we mentioned the relevancy of requirements, and noted how the requirement must be relevant both to the product purpose and within the scope of the work. If requirements are creeping outside the scope or are not relevant to the product purpose, then we suggest you have serious cause for concern. Is the scope correct? Are the goals for the product correct and realistic? We suggest you look long and hard at the root cause of your requirements creep. Perhaps the scope was set incorrectly in the first place, or perhaps the scope should be changed (in consultation with the business stakeholders and a suitable revision of the budget).

The effect of requirements creep is shown in Figure 13.5, where the graph depicts the cost of delivering functionality. Look at what happens when the size of the product creeps up by 35 percent: The effort needed expands by even more than that percentage—and yet this is the part of the product that somebody expected to get for free. When the requirements grow beyond what was originally anticipated, the budget must grow in tandem. But how often do you hear, "Just one more little thing—it won't affect the budget"?

Requirements creep has a bad reputation, mostly because of the disruption to the schedules and the bloated costs of product delivery associated with this phenomenon. Without wanting to defend requirements creep, we do think it prudent to look at some of the causes of creep and to discuss how we can approach this problem.

Most creep occurs because the requirements were never gathered properly in the first place.

First, most creep occurs because the requirements were never gathered properly in the first place. If the requirements are incomplete, then as the product develops, more and more omissions must of necessity be discovered. The users, aware that product delivery is now imminent, ask for more and more "new" functions. But are they really new? We suggest they are requirements that were really part of the product all along. They were just not, until now, part of the requirements specification.

Similarly, if the users and the clients are not given the opportunity to participate fully in the requirements process, then the specification will

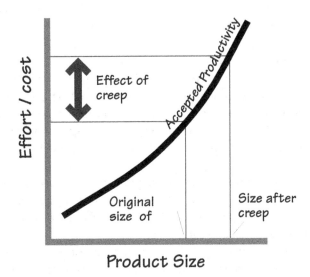

Figure 13.5

When you know the rate of productivity at your organization, it is a fairly simple exercise to convert the size of the product into the amount of effort or cost using a graph such as the one shown here. The ratio of cost to size is not a straight line: Cost increases disproportionally as size increases and more effort is needed in terms of integration work. When the requirements creep occurs, the amount of effort needed also increases, and it is this disproportionate increase that causes many projects to fall behind schedule or fail completely.

undoubtedly be incomplete. Almost certainly the requirements will creep as delivery approaches and the users begin asking for functionality they know they need.

We have also observed creep that arose because the original budget was set unrealistically low (often for political reasons). When the incredibly noticeable creep set in, it was not so much a matter of the requirements creeping, but of the product bringing itself up to its correct functionality.

Requirements also change. Quite often they change for the very good reason that the business has changed, or because new technological advances have made change desirable. These kinds of changes are often seen as requirements creep. In truth, if changes that cause new requirements happen after the official "end" of the requirements process—and they could not have been anticipated—then this type of requirements creep could not have been avoided.

The role of the Quality Gateway in this situation is to make project management aware that requirements creep is happening and, if possible, to help determine the cause of this creep.

Implementing the Quality Gateway

We have described the Quality Gateway as a process for testing requirements. Now you have to decide how you will implement it in your organization.

The first decision focuses on who is involved in the Quality Gateway. Is it one person? If so, who? Should it be a small group? If so, will that group be made up of testers or requirements analysts? Does the group include the project leader? Is the client represented? The answers to these questions are as varied as the organizations that have implemented Quality Gateways.

We suggest you start your Quality Gateway with two people—perhaps the lead requirements analyst and a tester. Keep in mind that this gateway is meant to be a fast, easy test of requirements, not a laborious process involving half of the development team. We have clients who implement their Quality Gateway electronically—the requirements analysts e-mail requirements as they write them to the gatekeepers, who then add the accepted ones to the specification. They report this strategy is both convenient and effective.

We suggest you start your Quality Gateway with two people— perhaps the lead requirements analyst and a tester. This gateway is meant to be a fast, easy test of requirements, not a laborious process involving half of the development team.

Clients who use requirements tools typically assign an attribute to the requirement that indicates whether it has been tested and approved by the gatekeepers. The gatekeepers are, naturally enough, the only people to have write permission for this attribute.

The degree of formality also brings up many questions: How formal does the Quality Gateway need to be? Should you issue inspection reports? Should you hold prearranged Quality Gateway inspection meetings? And so on.

Most of the time we advise clients to keep their Quality Gateway procedures as informal as will allow for the satisfactory checking of their requirements. Some organizations deal with complex, technical subject matter; their Quality Gateways are, of necessity, formal and rigorous. Some clients deal with more accessible subject matter, where all the participants in the requirements-gathering process are well versed in the business; their Quality Gateways are so informal that they happen almost without anybody noticing.

The use of auto- mated tools can help to reduce the amount of human intervention in the Quality Gateway process.

The use of automated tools can help to reduce the amount of human intervention in the Quality Gateway process. Some requirements-gathering tools can do the preliminary mechanical checking ensuring that all the attributes are present, use the correct terminology, are correctly identified, and so on.

Existing procedures may also play a part in your Quality Gateway. If people already have the job of inspecting work, then they are likely to be involved in your Quality Gateway. If inspection procedures exist, then they should be adapted for requirements rather than trying to implement a whole new process.

Alternative Quality Gateways

We have discussed the Quality Gateway as a process whereby appointed gatekeepers test the requirements before they become part of the requirements specification. We have said that this endeavor should be a permanent, but informal process. Of course, there are other ways of testing the quality of your requirements.

Requirements analysts can test each other's requirements, for example. This informal "buddy pairing" approach works well when the analysts are able to approach their work in an ego-free manner. The partners check each other's output and trap errors early in the process. This strategy works best when the "buddies" have learned to be objective about each other's work.

At other times, the process is far more formal and rigorous. One elephant project we worked on implemented the Quality Gateway as a four-stage process. With this approach, in the first stage, each individual developer has a checklist and uses it to informally review and improve requirements throughout the development process.

The second stage is a peer review, in which another member of the team formally reviews each written requirement. We found it very effective for the peer reviewer to be someone from the test team. Rather than examine the entire specification, these reviews concentrate on all the requirements related to a particular use case. The results of the review are recorded for the requirement as part of its history.

The third stage is a team review that includes customers and users. Problem requirements that have not passed the Quality Gateway tests are presented by one person, and are discussed and possibly resolved by the team members.

The fourth, and final, stage is a management review that is mostly concerned with looking at a summary of the Quality Gateway successes and failures. The results of this review are used to manage and fine-tune the requirements project.

Whatever your situation, you should think of the Quality Gateway both as a means of testing the requirements before they become part of the specification, and as a way of improving the quality of your requirements process.

In "buddy pairing," requirements analysts test each other's requirements.

See Chapter 2, The Requirements Process, and Chapter 17, Requirements Correctness and Completeness, for more on tailoring your requirements-development process.

Summary

The Quality Gateway tests the potential requirements, and assesses whether they meet the following criteria:

- Completeness
- Traceability
- Consistency
- Relevancy
- Correctness
- Ambiguity
- Viability
- Being solution-bound

- Gold plating
- Creep

The requirements are tested *during* the requirements activity. By preventing incorrect requirements from slipping into the specification, the Quality Gateway reduces the cost of development—eliminating errors early is the fastest and cheapest way of developing products.

Testing the requirements has a beneficial effect on the writers of those requirements. When an analyst knows his requirements will be subjected to certain tests, then naturally he writes them so they will pass the tests. This greater attention to correctness, in turn, leads to better requirements practices as well as more effective use of analytical time when fewer errors are generated.

The way you implement the Quality Gateway should reflect the particular needs and characteristics of your organization. In any event, be sure to implement your Quality Gateway so that all requirements, with no exceptions, pass through it before they can become part of the specification.

Requirements and Iterative Development

14

in which we look at how to discover and implement requirements in an iterative development environment

The Need for Iterative Development

A significant development in our field is the shared commitment (shared by developers and business people) to doing everything we can to deliver valuable and relevant working product as *quickly* as we can. To be *valuable* and *relevant*, the delivered product must contribute to the business's ability to carry out its work—insurance, retail, communications, medical imaging, banking, government—whatever work is the raison d'être of the organization in question.

Let's look at the "quickly" part of this commitment. The delivery of a working product for a piece of work of any significant size usually involves a wait—sometimes a long wait. Of course, people don't want to wait; if they have a problem, then they want a solution quickly, before the business problem changes once again.

Instead of waiting for every detail of the requirements to be defined, many organizations find it preferable to iterate through the business activities, define some of the requirements, develop part of the solution, define some more requirements, and so incrementally deliver releases until the solution is adjudged complete. This iterative approach means that concerns, ideas, and changes in both the business environment and the development environment are more in synch with each other. The result is that the developers are informed of today's business problem and the working product fits into today's business world.

You have no doubt come across development techniques—usually called "agile"—such as SCRUM, Crystal Clear, eXtreme Programming, Kanban, and others. The common element is that these techniques are designed to deliver a working product iteratively. A core idea is to avoid writing a complete requirements specification upfront (the waterfall process), and instead to build the product iteratively and discover the requirements in parallel with the product's development. The agile techniques advocate using a small, cross-functional team to deliver software frequently in small increments on a regular cycle. They also advocate close cooperation with the customer, including frequent conversations between the customer and the developer to flesh out, clarify, and explore the requirements prior to development. As it is developed, software is delivered incrementally, with each delivery adding some working functionality to the whole product.

We are frequently asked by business analysts how they can make requirements discovery compatible with iterative development:

How can I make my requirements discovery iterative?

- How can I make my requirements discovery iterative?
- How can I communicate the requirements without producing unnecessary documents?
- How can I trace business requirements to iterative development?

An Iterative Requirements Process

Figure 14.1 illustrates an iterative process for integrating the analysis of business needs, discovery of requirements, and development of working product. First let's look at the activities involved in this process; later we will look at variations on who does what and how to manage the iterations.

The Work

The Work, at the top of the diagram, represents the day-to-day operation of an organization. As this operation proceeds, the people involved with it continually discover new business needs and opportunities: "We should make that process faster," "We're going to launch a new service," "Let's update the help desk," "We need to investigate that emerging market," and so on. It is these continuously emerging *Business Needs* that need to be analyzed so that appropriate action can be taken to meet them.

Analyze Business Needs

Analyze Business Needs is a continuous activity that gathers new business needs—these could be in any variety of forms, ranging from a hurried phone call to a detailed business plan—and explores, evaluates, and prioritizes them. The analysis techniques that we have covered previously in this book are the same techniques that are used here to discover the scope, stakeholders, and goals of the problem, and to identify the business events for each new business need. New business events are added to a business event

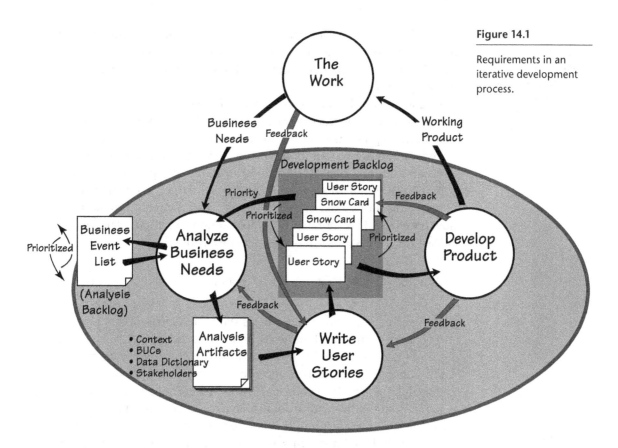

Figure 14.1

Requirements in an iterative development process.

list—the *Analysis Backlog*—that contains all of the identified business events. The analyst prioritizes the events on the list based on the current business situation, demands, and what is considered important at the moment. This analysis of business needs requires the skills of a business analyst along with input from business stakeholders to make the correct choices about the current priorities.

In parallel with helping identify new business needs, the business analyst elaborates the business use cases for the highest-priority business events, producing the *Analysis Artifacts*. These items could be business use case (BUC) scenarios or any other type of model that is acceptable to the stakeholders and the development team.

Write User Stories

The *Analysis Artifacts* provide the foundation for deciding what the product will do to support and improve the work. This determination is made by some combination of the business analyst, the developers, and the business stakeholders.

See Chapter 7, Understanding the Real Problem, and Chapter 8, Starting the Solution, for the core techniques for requirements analysis.

This is the crux of the process. The team members examine the real business, and decide (using the same approach that we described in Chapter 8) what is the most beneficial product to build—the optimally valuable (for the owner) product.

Of course, this decision—this design of the solution—has to be communicated. Most iterative processes use *User Stories* for this purpose. A collection of user stories represents the functionality needed for the next release.

User stories are way of representing a level of requirements that you can envision as being roughly equivalent to a step in a product use case (PUC) scenario, although this can vary and is sometimes equivalent to just the name of the PUC. User stories originate with eXtreme Programming, but now have been incorporated into most iterative methods. The usual form—at least the suggested form—of a user story is this:

As a [role], I want [feature] so that [reason]

For example, the story might be as shown in Figure 14.2.

The story is initially handwritten on an index card, like that shown in Figure 14.2. (Later we will show you how the Volere snow card is used as a slightly more structured container for user stories.) The user story is brief, and at this stage of its evolution, is really a placeholder signaling that there is some functionality whose details have yet to be worked out.

Prioritization is continuous.

As the stories are written, they are added to the *Development Backlog*. Here they are prioritized according to architectural and development demands and, of course, the needs and priorities of the business. This prioritization is continuous, which results in products that are more immediate, and closer to the business's focus of attention.

Develop Product

User stories provide the requirements for developing the next release of the product. If the developers are working closely with the business analysts—and if iterative development is to work well, then these groups will be

Figure 14.2

A user story written on an index card.

"As an insurance adjuster I want a list of outstanding claims so that I can see my workload for the day."

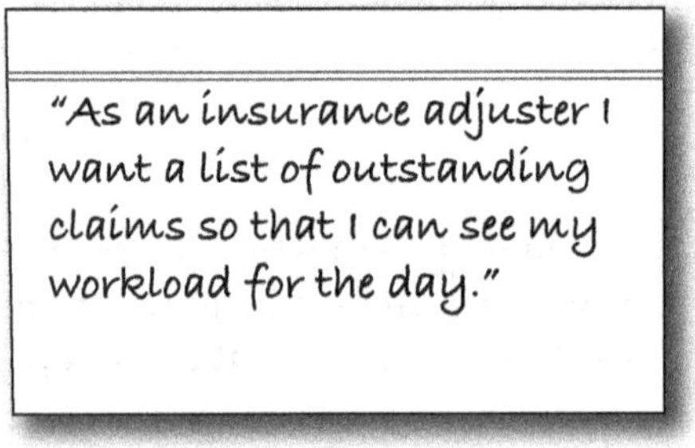

co-located—there is the opportunity for the requirements to be fleshed out of the user stories. Usually test cases are written on the story card, and other development notes added as needed. Naturally, conventional requirements can be written on snow cards, and we suggest doing so for the non-functional requirements. Because there is practically no time delay between the requirements conversation and the development of that part of the product, it is quite feasible for some of the requirements to be communicated verbally and carried in the developer's head.

If the opportunity for interaction is limited by geographical boundaries or divided responsibilities, then it will probably be necessary to derive and write the atomic requirements for each user story. In this case the developers can use the snow card to write the atomic functional and non-functional requirements, and to raise questions for the business.

As you can see in Figure 14.1, discoveries during the development can lead to feedback that might cause changes to the *Development Backlog*. The developers deliver the *Working Product* to *The Work*; it consists of a partial product or, as it is more generally thought of, a release.

Because the product is being developed in piecemeal fashion, the latest-delivered piece of the product might potentially be not quite what the users want; that is, users may provide *Feedback* asking for changes to the *Product*. This flexibility was once trumpeted as the overriding benefit of agile processes—just deliver something and, if the users don't like it, redesign, refactor, and deliver again. This approach approximates the "infinite number of monkeys on word processors eventually producing the entire works of Shakespeare," and has fortunately (and justifiably) fallen out of favor. Nevertheless, there should be some capacity in your process for making minor corrections after delivery.

The point of iterative development is to deal with small pieces—small sets of requirements that can be readily managed, small increments of functionality that can be more easily understood by all concerned, and small pieces of the working product that can be more readily accepted and integrated into the work environment. Moreover, due to the constant rhythm of delivery, the stakeholders become more involved and more interested in the eventual outcome.

READING

Boehm, Barry, and Richard Turner. *Balancing Agility and Discipline: A Guide for the Perplexed*. Addison-Wesley, 2004.

Cockburn, Alastair. *Agile Software Development: The Cooperative Game*. Addison-Wesley, 2006.

Cohn, Mike. *Succeeding with Agile: Software Development Using Scrum*. Addison-Wesley Professional, 2009.

Highsmith, Jim. *Adaptive Software Development: A Collaborative Approach to Managing Complex Systems*. Dorset House, 1999.

Business Value Analysis and Prioritization

The analysis of a new business need might result in the addition of new business events to the analysis backlog, changes to events already on the backlog, or changes in the priority of the analysis backlog.

For each business event and its associated BUC in the analysis backlog, the business analyst, along with the business stakeholders, monitors the relative business value of each—that is, the business value of a BUC relative to

	Business Use Case	Business Value of Investing (1–5)	Damage from Not Investing (1–5)	Current Priority
Table 14.1	BUC 1	3	4	Third
	BUC 2	5	1	
A Business Analysis Backlog	BUC 3	5	5	First
The business analysis backlog shows sample	BUC 4	2	1	
business use cases and the relative business	BUC 5	4	2	
values assigned to them. The purpose of having	BUC 6	5	4	Second
such a list is to prioritize the business events.	BUC 7	5	2	

the others in the backlog (see Table 14.1 for an example). This relative value determines the priority of the BUCs, which dictates the order in which they will be developed.

The following questions are asked about each business use case—and the answers must come from the business:

- Relative to the goal and benefit of this project, how much business value would be provided by investing in a new solution to this BUC? Use a scale from 1 (little or no value) to 5 (highest possible value).

- Relative to the business goal, how much damage would be done or disadvantage would occur if we do *not* provide a new solution to this BUC? Once again, use the scale from 1 (doesn't really matter) to 5 (would seriously damage this part of the business).

This value analysis, at the BUC level, identifies which business functions or processes would benefit most from investing in a new solution.

This value analysis, at the BUC level, identifies which business functions or processes would benefit most from investing in a new solution. The business analyst, as part of his daily work, continues to do value analysis at this level to reflect the current state of the business. The intention is for every new piece of development to truly reflect what is most beneficial to the current state of the business.

It is the business analyst's job to clarify the choices, but making the final choice is the responsibility of the business owner.

It is the business analyst's responsibility to clarify the choices, but making the final choice is the responsibility of the business owner. The business analyst uses the analysis backlog to keep the development teams aware of what is currently most valuable to the business.

An advantage of using BUCs as the source of user stories is that all of the stories are traceable back to a BUC. Whenever the business environment changes, the business analyst can identify which BUCs are affected, and in turn discuss with the developers which user stories might potentially be affected. This connection makes it possible to be aware of and plan for the ripple effect of any changes.

How to Write a Good User Story

The user story identifies the things that the product will do for a user, but it must also address the business problem identified by the business use case. Thus the BUC serves as the starting point for stories, and there are usually one or more stories derived from each BUC.

Questions to Ask

Suppose that your organization is a bank. The first step in a BUC scenario for this bank is summarized here:

> The bank wants to prevent customers from unexpectedly overdrawing their bank accounts. The penalty for non-arranged overdrafts, while profitable, is causing disputes with customers who claim that they need a better way of monitoring their accounts.

To discover the user stories, ask this question: What can the product do for the user (in this case, the bank customer) to satisfy the business intention behind this BUC?

Suppose, as a result of your discussions with the business stakeholders, you decide that bank account holders would be less likely to unexpectedly overdraw their accounts if they could check their account balance. This provides you with a starting point for the story:

> As a bank account holder, I want to check my balance online.

This at first might seem a reasonable and obvious story, but some requirements analysis can make it a lot better. First, there is no "so that" part. Some authors say that this can be omitted, but we suggest very strongly that you *always* include the reason in your stories. When you fail to justify the requirement (that is, when you omit the "so that" part), you reveal only part of the requirement, which puts the developers and testers at a disadvantage. Additionally, without this rationale (it's the same thing as the rationale on the snow card), future maintenance teams are deprived of a valuable clue as to why a particular requirement was included in the software product.

The question is, "Why does the account owner want to check the balance?" Let's revisit the story and this time look at the reason given for the requirement:

> As a bank account holder, I want to check my balance online so that I can access my daily balance 24 hours a day.

This is not exactly a good reason for checking the balance. The "24 hours a day" is slightly more enlightening, but it doesn't really do more than tell us that the account owner may have nocturnal habits. Why does the account owner wish to check the balance? It is not something we do for fun, so there probably is some business reason behind it. We just don't yet know what that is. Let's make some conjectures.

Suppose the reason for the frequent checking is that the account holder is on a tight budget, and is concerned about becoming overdrawn. If so, the owner of the product—that is, the bank—can be more effective and at the same time provide a better service.

Instead of the account owner having to repeatedly check the balance to confirm that it's not going into the red, it would be better to build a capability that notifies the account owner if the normal monthly payments such as rent, electricity, school fees, and so on will reduce the account balance to zero or beyond.

> As a bank account holder I want to be informed if my monthly balance is projected to go to zero or below so that I can arrange for an overdraft.

By arranging for an overdraft, the bank customer avoids the high penalty charges for non-arranged overdrafts, and the bank feels that this is better for customer relations.

Further, we suggest that it is far more useful for the account owner to be periodically informed of the amount of discretionary money in the account.

> As a bank account holder I want to be informed of the discretionary amount after all regular monthly payments have been deducted so that I know how much I can safely spend.

The BUC provides business guidance so that the user stories support the business rather than just identifying user interfaces.

If you try to write the user stories without the BUC for guidance, you could possibly end up with the obvious and simple feature that lets the account owner check the balance online. But, as we have seen, this simplistic approach of writing the first story that comes to mind usually leads to features that do not solve the real business problem. If other banks solve the real problem—that is, if they understand the real needs of their customers—and offer this service to attract more customers, then the original story could hardly be said to providing optimal business value.

There's more. The story is a placeholder and serves as the basis for a conversation that is to follow; if the story starts out poorly, then you can expect that it will be no better than mediocre by the time you have finished with it. In contrast, if you write a good story, then the product that emerges from it will certainly be superior, and provide much better value to the business.

To write a really good story, you must do more than passively listen to the business stakeholders and write down what they think they want. You must apply much of the craft of business analysis that we have been writing about in this book.

- Innovation is important. If your stories are not innovative, then they probably are not providing any advance over what existed previously and, therefore, are probably not providing any real value to the business.

- The innovation triggers should be used as a checklist when writing stories. They are bound to make your story better.

- The real origin of the business event is important. Ask what was happening at the time of the event and try to get your product as close as possible to that point.

- Think of the essence of the problem. By looking at the real underlying need and not the guessed-at solution, you almost always make a better story.

- Think "above the line."

These points were covered previously in Chapters 7 and 8. It is worth looking back at them to explore the advice they offer about writing better stories. The point of good stories is this: The better your story starts out, the better the final product will be. Weak stories lead to weak products—good stories lead to great products.

Good stories lead to great products.

Formalizing Your User Stories

The level of granularity of user stories varies; but it is normally somewhere between, but might be either, a product use case and an atomic requirement. Surprisingly, the precise level of detail in the story is not important, as long as it conveys the intention and can serve as the foundation for prioritization, and for the elaboration conversation that is to follow.

The components of a user story are as follows:

As a [role], I want [feature] so that [reason]

Most iterative development teams write their stories on blank cards, but you can also use the Volere snow card (also used for atomic requirements) for this purpose. Figure 14.3 shows how this works.

The requirement number is substituted with a User Story number—note how User Story number 6.1 traces the story back to BUC 6. The Description contains the "As a [role], I want [feature]," and the Rationale contains the "so that [reason]." Your test conditions are written in the Fit Criterion area of the snow card.

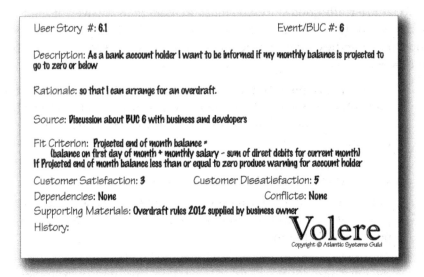

Fleshing out the Story

When stories are selected for development, they are removed from the back-log and augmented. This augmentation usually takes place as the result of conversations between the developers, the business analysts, and various stakeholders. This augmentation is pretty much the same as writing the atomic requirements; the business analyst or the developer adds whatever functional details are needed for correct implementation, and non-functional requirements are attached to the story card or become the subject of a new card. As Figure 14.4 illustrates, augmenting the user story involves input from a number of fields of expertise: the business; non-functional specialties

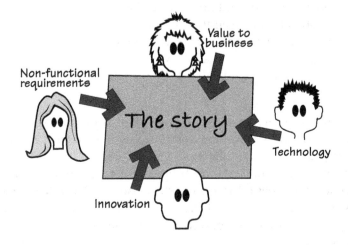

such as usability, security, and look and feel; technology; innovation, and more.

Of course, these specialist areas of knowledge might not be represented by different people; it depends on how, in your organization, expertise is spread between roles. The story card provides a gathering point or a focus for exploring the different types of requirements that the product needs to satisfy the original intention of the story.

The way that you express the requirements details depends on how you are working. In a small co-located team—a rabbit project—you would probably make notes directly on the story card, with those notes then becoming your requirements specification. If you are working on a larger and/or more fragmented project—horses and elephants—you would probably write a snow card for each atomic requirement related to the user story. This latter approach builds a more formal specification, which is particularly critical if you are outsourcing some of the development work.

Iterative Requirements Roles

The iterative requirements and development process shown in Figure 14.1 highlights the need for continuous integration of business and technical knowledge. If only one person had all of this knowledge, then communication would be easy. In the most-likely absence of this superperson, you must find the source of each of the inputs, wherever it lies within your organization. Let's first look at the input that we need and then consider how the appropriate roles can be found.

You need a subject-matter expert who is the source of knowledge about the business or work problem and who is both current on the business/problem and available to answer questions, inform you about changes, and make business-related choices. You also need a source of knowledge about the technical solution space—this source is sometimes called a system architect, and sometimes a developer. This source makes recommendations on the solution and identifies opportunities for how the available technology can be best used to meet the business requirements.

Given the different focuses of the business problem viewpoint and the technical solution viewpoint, it is also necessary to have someone who knows how to connect, analyze, and trace the connections between the business concerns and the technical concerns.

Business Knowledge

A knowledge of the business is important—given that the reason for your project is to improve a part of the owner's business and to provide the optimally valuable product, we can say that business knowledge is the most crucial component of the project. The responsibility for the business knowledge is, reasonably enough, the responsibility of the business. In many cases, however, this knowledge is spread between different stakeholders, each of whom specializes in one or other parts of the business.

On the one hand, it is difficult to perform iterative development if the developers must talk to all these different people. On the other hand, giving responsibility for business knowledge to just one person is problematic, except in very small and simple projects.

One attempt to address this problem is to have a representative of the business who works closely with—in fact, becomes part of—the development team. This person, often called a *product owner*, answers all business-related questions.

The problem is simple: It is rare to find in one person all the skills needed for the role. Consider that the product owner needs to have an in-depth knowledge of the business, be current with technological issues, be innovative and imaginative, be available full-time to the development team, be able to articulate needs, understand the essence of the problem, make the right calls about prioritization, and a lot more. If you have someone in your organization who meets this specification, then you are very lucky indeed. Alas, most teams don't have this luxury.

The product owner role has been abandoned by many iterative development teams—it is just too hard to make it work. Some organizations that develop software for sale have a product manager (sometimes called a program manager) role; as this person is responsible for the financial success of the product, his role comes much closer to that of the ideal product owner. Most teams now use a combination of business analysts and business stakeholders to act as the source of business knowledge.

Analytical and Communication Knowledge

Why is the business analyst a useful source of business knowledge? Because the business analyst is not part of either the business or the development team. The business analyst is a neutral channel who is trained to observe and discover the business needs and to communicate those needs to the developers. The difference between a traditional business analyst's role and that of an iterative business analyst is that the analyst communicates the requirements to the developers in much smaller fragments and the analyst uses techniques to encourage and facilitate feedback.

Technical Knowledge

The technical knowledge is embodied in some combination of the roles of developer, systems architect, tester, and external supplier. It all depends on how you have allocated the responsibilities in your organization. However, there is one big difference here between the business specialists and the technical specialists. The technical specialists are devoted to working on solutions and keeping up-to-date with new technology; their job is to work on projects and solve problems. The business specialists are focused on running the business and doing their day-to-day jobs; they expect the technical specialists to come up with better tools to help them.

Summary

Today's highly dynamic world requires that we iteratively develop and improve solutions to business problems. We need ways to continuously explore the business and its problems, and to communicate those needs to technical specialists, who in turn provide technical solutions for the business.

This ongoing exploration of the work means that the business analyst is continuously analyzing and adding new stories or requirements to the analysis backlog. This backlog, in turn, is continuously analyzed for value, for it is business value that most matters here. The backlog is prioritized according to value and urgencies, with the highest-priority items being handed over to the developers for development.

The developers, with input and explanations from the business analyst and others, write the stories that best meet the business need. The developers prioritize the user stories in their development backlog, and for the selected ones, augment and determine the atomic requirements to be implemented in the next release of working product. Feedback from each release demonstrates to the team if they are, in fact, working toward the optimally beneficial product.

Reusing Requirements

in which we look for requirements that have already been written and explore ways to make use of them

A few days ago, one of your authors needed to know how to do something on his computer—how to type the symbol for degree, as in °C for Celsius temperature. I knew that other people must know this, so I headed to the Mac support forum. I entered my search term and found a thread where some kind soul had previously answered this question. So now I could reuse knowledge that someone else had provided at a previous time.

We all reuse knowledge—the note that you left on the heating system to remind yourself how to restart it; the post that a blogger made about the best way to get a red wine stain out of the carpet; a cooking recipe; the calendar of events on your smartphone. All of these things are knowledge that we put aside for when we need it.

Some of these things were intentionally set down for later reuse, while others were stored without the intention that they be reused (the support thread, for example). Whether it was intended to be reused or not, an amazing amount of knowledge is available to us if only we would make use of it.

A few years ago, it was fashionable to reuse code. A whole movement grew up based on the premise that by reusing code, development time could be considerably reduced. There is no doubt about the veracity of that statement, yet somehow the idea of code reuse never really got off the ground. At least, we see very little of the reuse of in-house code.

One major problem with this approach is illustrated by a conversation overheard at a seminar on code reuse.

Developer: "I get it. From now on I am going to write all my code so that it can be reused."

Developer's manager: "No, you don't get it. From now on you are going to *reuse* code."

Herein lies the problem—everyone wants to build reusable components for others, and no one wants to reuse someone else's components. But this does not have to be a problem.

When you are specifying the requirements for a new product, it is always possible to save effort if you start by asking, "Have these requirements, or similar ones, already been written?"

What Is Reusing Requirements?

Although they might have different names and different features, the products you build are not completely unique. Within an organization, projects tend to build the same or similar products over time—a retail company builds retail software products, a scientific research center builds scientific products. As a consequence, the chances are that someone in your organization has already built a product that contains some—by no means all—of the requirements that are germane to your current project.

By taking advantage of these requirements, your effectiveness as a requirements discoverer increases significantly. Early in your requirements projects, look for requirements that have already been written that, with a little modification or abstraction, can be incorporated into your own project. We illustrate this idea in Figure 15.1.

Figure 15.1

Reusing requirements entails making use of requirements written for other projects. Such requirements can come from a number of sources: a reuse library of specifications, other requirements specifications that are similar or in the same domain, or informally from other people's experience.

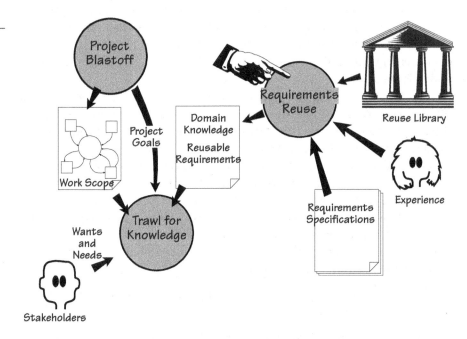

These requirements are not exactly free, however: You have to do something for them. Successful reuse starts with having an organizational culture that consciously encourages reuse rather than reinvention. If you have this attitude—that is, if you are willing to look at existing requirements—then you are in a much better position to include requirements reuse as part of your requirements process.

When you run a project blastoff meeting, use the first seven sections of the requirements template to trigger questions about reuse:

1. The Purpose of the Project: Are there other projects in the organization that are compatible or that cover substantially the same domains or work areas?

2. The Client, the Customer, and Other Stakeholders: Can you reuse an existing list of stakeholders, a stakeholder map, or a stakeholder analysis spreadsheet? Users of the Product: Do other products involve the same users and thus have similar usability requirements?

3. Mandated Constraints: Have your constraints already been specified for another project? Are there any organization-wide constraints that also apply to your project?

4. Naming Conventions and Definitions: You can almost certainly make use of parts of an existing glossary.

5. Relevant Facts and Assumptions: Pay attention to relevant facts from recent projects. Do other projects' assumptions apply to your project?

6. The Scope of the Work: Your project has a very good chance of being an adjacent system to other projects that are underway in your organization. Make use of the interfaces that have been established by other work context models. Consider your work scope and ask whether other projects have already defined similar business events.

7. Business Data Model and Data Dictionary: Are there business data models from overlapping or connected projects that you could use as a starting point?

Don't be too quick to say your project is different from everything that has gone before it. Yes, the subject matter is different, but if you look past the names, how much of the underlying functionality is substantially the same? How many requirements specifications have already been written that contain material that you can use unaltered, or at least adapted, in your own specification? We have found that significant amounts of specifications can be assembled from existing components rather than having to be discovered from scratch. See Figure 15.2.

Successful reuse starts with having an organizational culture that consciously encourages reuse rather than reinvention.

Refer to Chapter 3 for more on how to run a project blastoff meeting.

For more on stakeholder maps and stakeholder analysis, see Appendix B, Stakeholder Management Templates.

Figure 15.2

At project blastoff time, the subject matter of the context, together with its adjacent systems and boundary data flows, should indicate the potential for reusing requirements from previous projects.

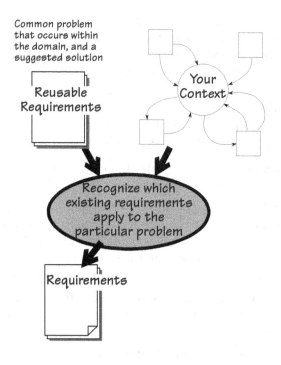

Common problem that occurs within the domain, and a suggested solution

Reusable Requirements

Your Context

Recognize which existing requirements apply to the particular problem

Requirements

The blastoff deliverables provide a focus for identifying reusable knowledge that might not otherwise be found.

The stakeholders who participate in the blastoff meeting are wonderful sources of reusable components. Ask them about other documents that contain knowledge relevant to the work of the project. Ask about related projects that they have participated in. Consider whether someone else might have already investigated subject matter domains that overlap with your project. Closely examine the blastoff deliverables—they provide a focus for identifying reusable knowledge that might not otherwise be found.

When you are trawling for knowledge, continue to look for reusable requirements by asking the people you interview about them: "Have you answered these questions, or questions like them, before? Do you know sources of information that might already contain the answers to these questions?" This fairly informal approach means that you encounter potentially reusable requirements in many different forms. Some are precisely stated and hence directly reusable; others merely provide clues or pointers to sources of knowledge.

The problem with reuse is that unless the knowledge is readily accessible, it lies gathering dust in some database and is not reused. In the past it often took longer to find a reusable component than it did to start from scratch. Today, of course, search technology has greatly accelerated this process. Now everyone, especially in larger companies, has searchable intranets, wikis, SharePoint, requirements tools, and databases that contain a cornucopia of potentially reusable requirements.

We mentioned previously that using the first seven sections of the requirements template to drive your project blastoff provides you with a good starting point for discovering reusable requirements. We recommend that as soon as you have captured your first-cut work context model, you use it as the driver for searching for reusable requirements knowledge within your organization. At the very least, perform a search for each of the interfaces on your model. You will likely discover other places, documents, projects, and people who are connected with each interface and might have already specified requirements that are relevant to your project.

Naturally enough, if everyone structured their requirements and used terminology in a consistent way, such as we are suggesting to you, then all requirements would be more easily reusable by future projects. In this chapter, we explore the thinking behind reuse, development of the ability to spot potential, and the habit of leaving a reusable trail of knowledge.

Sources of Reusable Requirements

When you want to learn to cook the perfect fried egg, one of the best ways to get started is to learn from someone whose fried eggs you admire. They tell you the egg should be less than five days old, and the butter—slightly salted is best—should be heated until it is golden but not brown. You break the egg, gently slide it into the bubbling butter, and then spoon the golden liquid over it until the white turns opaque. You serve the egg with a sprinkling of fresh coriander and, optionally, Tabasco sauce.

Informal experience-related reuse of requirements: We do this when we ask questions of our colleagues. We want to learn from one person's experience so that we do not have to start our own endeavors from scratch.

This example demonstrates informal experience-related reuse of requirements; we do this when we ask questions of our colleagues. We want to learn from one person's experience so that we do not have to start our own endeavors from scratch. We might not always find out everything we want to know, and we might make changes to what we are told, but we use the information discovered to build on other people's knowledge.

More formal reusable requirements for the domain of fried-egg cookery come from cookbooks. For example, Jenny Baker, in her *book Simple French Cuisine,* instructs us to follow these steps:

Once you know the context of your work, you can look for requirements specifications that deal with all or part of that context and use them as the source of potentially reusable requirements.

> "Heat sufficient oil . . . fry the tomatoes with a garlic clove . . . break the eggs on top and cook gently until set."

In *Italian Food,* Elizabeth David advises us to do this:

> "Melt some butter . . . put in a slice of mozzarella . . . break two eggs into each dish . . . cover the pan while the eggs are cooking."

You can think of a cookbook as a requirements specification—it's just written for a different context of study than the one you are currently working on. Even though the preceding examples have some differences, both

READING

Three cookery writers who have made knowledge about cooking accessible and reusable are Jenny Baker, Elizabeth David, and Delia Smith. Any of the books by these writers can help you improve your cooking skills and enjoyment of food.

Baker, Jenny. *Simple French Cuisine.* Faber & Faber, 1992.

David, Elizabeth. *Italian Food.* Penguin Books, 1998.

Smith, Delia. *How to Cook: Book One.* BBC Worldwide, 1998.

have aspects that could be reused as a starting point for generating a new way to fry eggs. Thus, once you know the context of your work, you can look for requirements specifications that deal with all or part of that context and treat them as the source of potentially reusable requirements.

You can reuse requirements or knowledge from any of the sources that we have discussed: colleagues' experiences, existing requirements specifications, domain models, and, of course, books. The only thing necessary is that you can recognize the reusable potential of anything you come across. Recognition itself requires that you perform abstractions, so as to see past the technology and procedures that are part of existing requirements. Abstraction also involves seeing past subject matter to find recyclable components. We will have more to say about abstraction later in this chapter; for now, let's look at making use of the idea of patterns.

Requirements Patterns

A pattern is a guide; it gives you a form to follow when you are trying to replicate, or make a close approximation of, some piece of work. For example, the stonecutters working on classical buildings used wooden patterns to help them to carve the column capitals to a uniform shape. The tailor uses patterns to cut the cloth so that each jacket follows the same basic form, with minor adjustments made to compensate for an individual client's body shape.

But what about patterns in a requirements sense? Patterns imply a collection of requirements that make up some logical grouping of functions. For example, we can think of a requirements pattern for selling a book in a shop: determine the price; compute applicable taxes; collect the money; wrap the book; thank the customer. If this is a successful pattern, then it pays you to use the pattern for any future bookselling activities, rather than reinvent the process of selling a book.

Refer to Chapter 4, Business Use Cases, for more on the connection between business events and use cases.

Typically, we use requirements patterns that capture the processing policy for a business use case (BUC). If we use the BUC as a unit of work, then each pattern is bounded by its own input, output, and stored data. As a consequence, we can treat it as a stand-alone mini-system.

Requirements patterns improve the accuracy and completeness of requirements specifications. You reduce the time needed to produce a specification because you reuse a functional grouping of requirements knowledge that has already been specified by other projects. To do so, look for patterns that may have some application in your project. Keep in mind that a pattern is usually an abstraction and that you may have to do a little work to adapt existing requirements to your own needs. Nevertheless, the time saved in completing your specification and the insights gained by using other people's patterns is significant.

Christopher Alexander's Patterns

The most significant collection of patterns—and one that inspired the pattern movement in software design—was published in *A Pattern Language*, written by a group of architects headed by Christopher Alexander. This book identifies and describes patterns that contribute to functionality and convenience for everyday human life within buildings, living spaces, and communities. The book presents these patterns to architects and builders for use as guides for new building projects. Even if you are neither a builder nor an architect, there is much to learn from this book.

The Waist-High Shelf (illustrated in Figure 15.3) is one of the patterns defined by Alexander and his colleagues. In this case, they looked at many people and observed what happens when we enter and leave our houses. Suppose it is time to leave for work and you are in a hurry. You need your keys, your sunglasses, your building pass, and your phone. If these things are difficult to find, you become irritated, probably forget something, and have a bad start to the day. The Waist-High Shelf pattern is based on the observation that we need somewhere to put our keys and whatever other bits and pieces we are carrying when we arrive, so that we can easily find them again when we leave.

The pattern specifies there should be a horizontal surface at waist height (a convenient height to reach), located just inside the front door (you do not have to carry objects farther than necessary), and big enough for you to deposit items that are commonly transported in and out of the house. In your authors' house, the Waist-High Shelf pattern implemented itself without us realizing it. We noticed that we naturally put our keys and sunglasses on one of the steps of the staircase that is conveniently on your right (we are both right-handed) as you come through our front door. We also noticed that, without being told, our visitors also leave their keys on the "waist-high step."

READING

Alexander, Christopher, et al. *A Pattern Language: Towns, Buildings, Construction.* Oxford University Press, 1977.

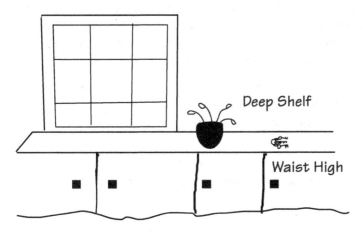

Deep Shelf

Waist High

Figure 15.3

Alexander defined the Waist-High Shelf pattern because, as he observed, "In every house and workplace there is a daily 'traffic' of the objects which are handled most. Unless such things are immediately at hand, the flow of life is awkward, full of mistakes: things are forgotten, misplaced."

Note the role of the pattern: It is a guide, not a rigid set of instructions or an implementation. It can be reused—there is no need to experiment and reinvent the pattern. It is a collection of knowledge or experience that can be adapted or used as is.

Now let us look at patterns as they apply to your requirements.

A Business Event Pattern

Let's start by looking at an example of a requirements pattern. Like most of them, this one is based on the response to a business event:

> *Pattern Name: Customer Wants to Buy Goods*
>
> *Context: A pattern for receiving goods orders from customers, supplying or back-ordering the goods, and invoicing for them.*
>
> *Forces: An organization has demands from its customers to supply goods or services. Failure to meet his demand might result in the customer seeking another supplier. Sometimes the goods or services are unavailable at the time the order is received.*

The following models define this pattern in more detail; we'll start with the context model in Figure 15.4. You would use this diagram to determine whether the details of the pattern might be relevant to the work you are doing. The flows of data (or material) around the boundary of the context indicate the kind of work being done. If the majority of these flows are compatible with the inputs and outputs of your event, then the pattern is potentially reusable within your project.

Context of Event Response

Once you have decided that the pattern is suitable for your use, it's time to move on to the details. These can be expressed in a number of different ways. The technique that you use depends on the volume and depth of your knowledge about the pattern. For example:

- A step-by-step text description or scenario of what happens after a Customer sends an Order for Goods
- A definition of all the individual requirements related to the Fill Order process
- A detailed model that breaks the pattern into subpatterns and their dependencies before specifying the individual requirements

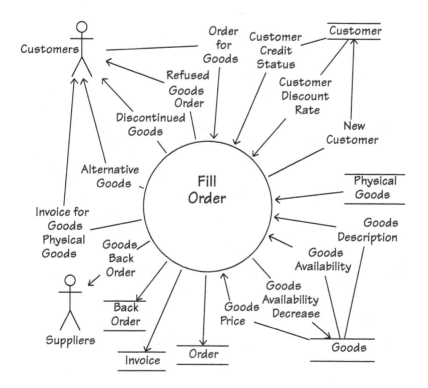

Processing for Event Response

Figure 15.5 illustrates how a large pattern can be partitioned into a number of subpatterns. From this diagram, we can identify other potentially reusable clusters of requirements. For instance, the diagram reveals a subpattern called Calculate Charge along with its interactions with other subpatterns. We can use this subpattern independently whenever we want to specify the requirements for calculating any type of charge. The interactions indicate which other patterns might also be relevant to us when we are interested in the pattern for calculating a charge. Other ways of depicting this pattern are to use a UML activity diagram, a sequence diagram, or a scenario.

Data for Event Response

The class diagram in Figure 15.6 shows the classes that participate in the pattern Customer Wants to Buy Goods, along with the associations between them. We can cluster the attributes and operations unique to each object. For instance, the class Goods has a number of unique attributes, such as its name and price; similarly, it has some unique operations such as calculate discounted price and find stock level. Because we have this cluster of knowledge

Figure 15.5

This diagram breaks the process *Fill Order* (shown in Figure 15.4) into five subprocesses (groups of functionally related requirements) and shows the dependencies between them. Each of the subprocesses (shown with a circle) is connected by named data flows to other subprocesses, data stores, or adjacent systems. Each subprocess also contains a number of requirements. Rather than forcing an arbitrary sequence on the processes, this model focuses on the dependencies between the processes. For example, we can see that the process *Determine Goods Availability* has a dependency on the process *Check Customer Credit*. Why? Because the former needs to know about the *Approved Goods Order* before it can do its work.

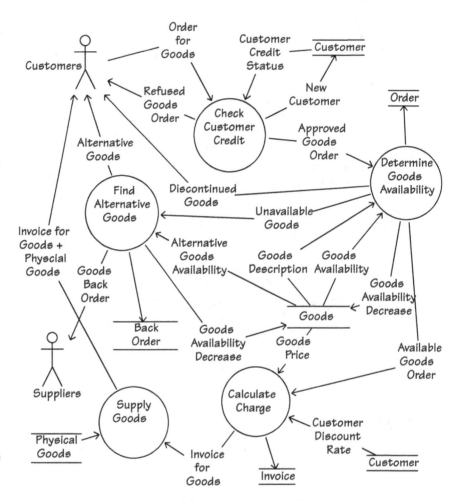

about the class called Goods, whenever we need to specify requirements for goods we can potentially reuse some or all of this knowledge.

Forming Patterns by Abstracting

The requirements pattern we have been discussing is the result of analyzing many business events—quite often from very different organizations—that deal with the subject of a customer wanting to buy something. We derived this pattern by making an abstraction that captures all of the common processing policy, so if your project includes a business event centered on a customer wanting to buy something, then this pattern is a realistic starting point.

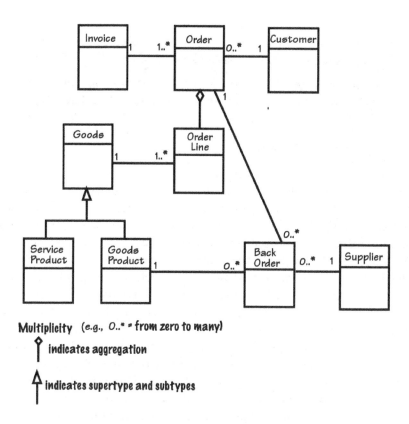

Multiplicity (e.g., 0..* = from zero to many)

⬦ indicates aggregation

△ indicates supertype and subtypes

Figure 15.6

This class diagram shows the classes and associations between them that are part of the pattern Customer Wants to Buy Goods. Consider the business rules communicated by this diagram. A *Customer* may make zero or many *Orders,* each of which is invoiced. The *Order* is for a collection of *Order Lines.* An *Order Line* is for *Goods,* which might be a *Service Product* or a *Goods Product.* Only *Goods Products* can have a *Back Order.* Now consider how many situations in which these business rules, data, and processes might be reused.

The same rubric applies with other events and other domains. Use the idea discussed in Chapter 7, Understanding the Real Problem, and focus on thinking above the line where you find the essence of the problem. Form your patterns by looking past the specific to see the abstract. Look away from the technology that the organization currently uses to see the business policy that is being processed. Think of the work, not in its current incarnation, but rather as a baseline for work that can be done in the future.

Of course, you can have many patterns, covering many business events and domains. To file them so that they are accessible, we organize these patterns in a consistent way according to the following template (which is really a pattern itself):

Use the idea discussed in Chapter 7, Understanding the Real Problem, and focus on thinking above the line.

> Pattern Name: *A descriptive name to make it easy to communicate the pattern to other people.*
>
> Forces: *The reasons for the pattern's existence.*
>
> Context: *The boundaries within which the pattern is relevant.*

> Mechanics: A description of the pattern using a mixture of words, graphics, and references to other documents.
>
> Related Patterns: Other patterns that might apply in conjunction with this one; other patterns that might help to understand this one

Patterns for Specific Domains

Suppose that you are working on a system for a library. One of the business events within your context is almost certain to be Library User Wants to Extend Book Loan. Figure 15.7 shows a model of the system's response to this event. When a *Library User* submits a *Loan Extension Request,* the product responds with either *Refused Loan Extension* or *Loan Extension Approval.*

One of the benefits of using a disciplined process for writing requirements specifications is that you naturally produce requirements that are more easily reusable by future projects.

Your work on the project in the library domain has led to the specification of detailed requirements for a particular product. As a by-product of doing this work, you have identified some useful requirements patterns, clusters of business-event–related requirements that are potentially reusable on other projects in the library domain.

When you specify requirements using a consistent discipline, you make them more accessible to other people and, therefore, reusable. If you or someone else began another project for the library, a good starting point would be the specifications that you have already written. They are usually a prodigious source of recyclable requirements knowledge within this domain.

Now imagine that you are working on a system in a very different domain, that of satellite broadcasting. One business event within this context is Satellite Broadcaster Wants to Renew License. When the satellite broadcaster submits

Figure 15.7

A summary of the library system's response to the event Library User Wants to Extend Book Loan.

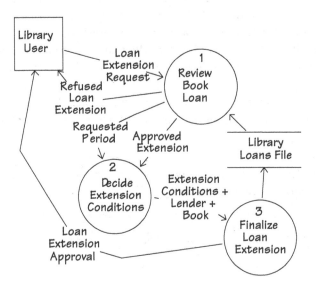

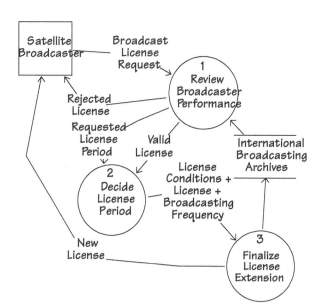

Figure 15.8

A model of the satellite broadcasting product's response to the event Satellite Broadcaster Wants to Renew License.

a *Broadcast License Request,* the product responds with either *Rejected License* or *New License.* Figure 15.8 summarizes the system's response to the event.

When you work on the requirements for the satellite broadcasting project, you also discover requirements patterns that are potentially reusable on products within this domain.

Now let's look a little farther afield. We have talked about the idea of identifying and reusing requirements patterns within a specific subject matter domain. But how can we use patterns outside the originating domain?

Patterns Across Domains

At first glance, the event responses to Library User Wants to Extend Loan and Satellite Broadcaster Wants to Renew License appear to be very different. Indeed, they are different in that they come from very different domains. Nevertheless, let's revisit the two event responses, this time looking for similarities. If we find shared characteristics, then we have a chance of deriving a more abstract pattern that could be applied to many other domains.

Both library books and broadcasting licenses are "things to be renewed." The business decides whether to renew an item in response to requests from a renewer. The business rules for renewing books or licenses share some similarities. For instance, the business checks whether the renewer is eligible to renew the thing; it decides the conditions of renewal; it records the decision and informs the renewer. By looking at several different responses, we can make an abstraction: We have some processing policy that is common to all renewable items. We also discover that some attributes of a "thing to be

Figure 15.9

This business use case
model is the result of
finding the similarities
between a business
use case in the library
domain and a business
use case in the satellite
broadcasting domain.

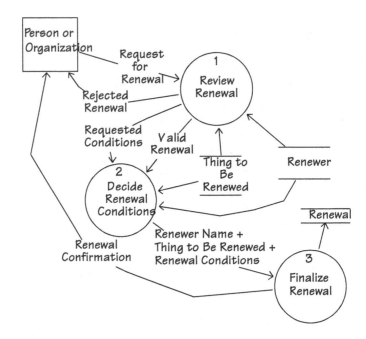

renewed" are the same regardless of whether we are talking about a book or
a broadcasting license. For example, each thing to be renewed has a unique
identifier, a standard renewal period, and a renewal fee.

Figure 15.9 shows the result when we make an abstraction of the processing policy from the two business use cases. Here we are using abstraction to
identify common characteristics. To do so, we look past what we see on the
surface, and find useful similarities or classifications. In addition, we ignore
some characteristics in our quest to find common ones.

When creating an abstract, you ignore the physical artifacts and subject
matters. For example, in Figure 15.9 we have ignored the physical artifacts of
library books and broadcasting licenses. Instead, concentrate on the underlying actions of the two systems, with a view toward finding similarities that
you can use to your advantage. If, for example, a part of a route allocation
system has functional similarities to a container storage system (one of the
authors actually found these similarities), then the work done for one system
can be recycled for the other.

The skill of identifying and using patterns is tied to several other abilities:

- The ability to see work at different levels of abstraction
- The ability to categorize, or classify, in different ways
- The ability to see that lenses and glass spheres filled with water are
  both magnifying devices
- The ability to spot similarities between apparently different things

- The ability to disregard physical artifacts
- The ability to see things in the abstract

Domain Analysis

Domain analysis is the activity of investigating, capturing, and specifying generic knowledge about a subject matter area. You could think of domain analysis as non-project systems analysis: The goal is to learn about the business policy, data, and functionality—not to build something. The knowledge gained about the domain is used, and ideally reused, by any project that builds a product to be used within that domain.

Domain analysis works in the same way that regular systems analysis does. That is, you work with domain experts to extract their hitherto unarticulated knowledge, and you record it in a manner that allows other analysts to reuse the knowledge. This process suggests that regular analysis models—event-response models, activity diagrams, sequence diagrams, class diagrams, state models, data dictionaries, and so on—are the most useful, as these kinds of models have the greatest currency in the analysis world.

Once the domain knowledge has been captured and recorded, it becomes available to anyone who builds a product for that domain. The domain knowledge applies to any product for that domain. The point is not to rediscover knowledge that has always existed, but rather to reuse the models of knowledge.

The point is not to rediscover knowledge, but rather to reuse models of knowledge.

Domain analysis is a long-term project. That is, the knowledge gained is reusable, but this benefit will be realized only if you get the opportunity to reuse that knowledge. An investment in domain analysis is like any other investment: You must have a good idea that the investment will be paid back. In the case of domain analysis, there is no limit to the number of times that domain knowledge can be reused.

Summary

We can informally reuse requirements knowledge by talking to our colleagues and reusing our own experience. Requirements modeling techniques produce deliverables such as work context models, activity diagrams, scenarios, and atomic requirements specifications, among many others; moreover, all of them make requirements visible and, therefore, potentially reusable to a much wider audience.

Requirements specifications that have been written for other projects can also contain material you might find reusable. We have a tendency to disregard anything that comes from another project team, but there is usually something to be gained by looking at the documents of others. Naturally, the clearer and better your requirements documents are, the more likely that someone will find them reusable.

Communicating the Requirements

in which we turn the requirements into
communicable form

At one end of the development universe, you have a business; at the other end, you have developers and technicians who have to build something for that business. The task, which is a lot simpler to say that it is to do, is to communicate the business needs to the development team. Typically, you do this by writing a requirements specification, but there are other ways of getting the needed information, precisely and correctly, to the people who need it. The requirement for the requirements is that they must be conveyed in a style such that the people receiving the information actually read it, understand it, and make use of it.

Writing the requirements is not necessarily a separate activity, but rather something done during the trawling and discovery activities. However, there are some things about writing and packaging your requirements that are significant, and we discuss them in this chapter.

Formality Guide

This chapter is about *communicating* the requirements. You don't always write the requirements in a specification document, but they must be formalized to the point where all concerned stakeholders can see them well enough to agree with your understanding of the requirements.

Rabbit projects usually don't write a formal specification, but you should consider how to communicate some of the attributes of the requirements. In particular, rabbit projects usually write test cases instead of a fit criterion. If you are using story cards, then they *must* contain a rationale, and adding a customer value attribute is useful.

No matter how brilliantly ideas formed in his mind, or crystallized in his clockworks, his verbal descriptions failed to shine with the same light. His [John Harris, who solved the problem of Longitude] last published work, which outlines the whole history of his unsavory dealings with the Board of Longitude, brings his style of endless circumlocution to its peak. The first sentence runs on, virtually unpunctuated for twenty-five pages.

—Dava Sobel, *Longitude*

Keep in mind that getting the requirements right is not making development more bureaucratic, but making it more effective.

Horse projects should start with the requirements knowledge model (shown in Figure 16.2 later in this chapter). Make sure you know where and how these components are recorded. It is not necessary for all of them to reside in one specification, but it is necessary to have them somewhere. Horses should consider the amount of specification they need. We describe here a complete and rigorous specification, but please assess your needs before producing each part of the specification.

Elephant projects build a complete specification and should use some kind of automated tool to contain it. Many such tools are available, and the prime consideration is to allow the team of requirements analysts to access the specification simultaneously. Because of their size, fragmentation, and long lifetime—and, in turn, higher number of rippling changes—elephant projects need to be ultra-concerned with having enough formality (including an agreed-upon requirements knowledge model) to ensure that their requirements are traceable from the product to the work, and from the work to the product.

Turning Potential Requirements into Written Requirements

During the trawling and prototyping activities, the requirements you find are not always precise—they are ideas or intentions for requirements, and are sometimes vague and half-formed. By contrast, the requirements specification you produce is the basis for the contract to build a product. As a consequence, it must contain clear, complete, and testable instructions about what has to be built. The task we tackle in this chapter is turning the half-formed ideas into precise and communicable statements of requirement—a task illustrated in Figure 16.1.

This translation from vagueness to precision is not always straightforward, and we have found it useful to have some help. To do so, we make use of a specification template and a requirements shell. The template is a ready-made guide or checklist for the contents of a specification, and the shell is the container for an individual—we shall call it an "atomic"—requirement. Let's start at the beginning.

Knowledge Versus Specification

Before plunging into a description of how to write requirements and assemble them to make a specification, it is worth spending a few moments to consider the knowledge you accumulate as you progress through the requirements

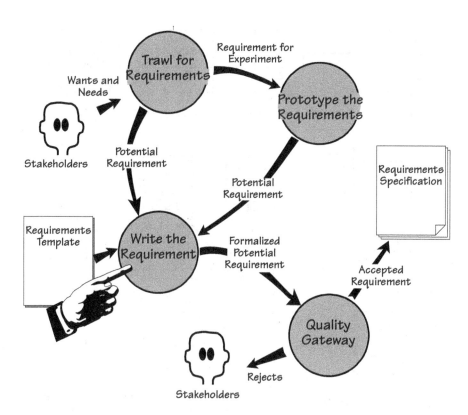

Figure 16.1

You discover the intention of the requirements when you are trawling and prototyping. We refer to these as *potential requirements*. The writing activity transforms the resulting ideas and half-formed thoughts into precise and testable requirements; we call these *formalized potential requirements*. Finally, the Quality Gateway tests the requirements before adding them to the requirements specification.

process. By understanding this knowledge and having a common language for talking about it, you make better decisions on how the requirements specification is written, published, and distributed.

Let's start with the requirements knowledge model shown in Figure 16.2. Think of this model as a conceptual filing system, containing all of the information you have about your requirements. You can also think of it as an abstract way of looking at the contents of the requirements template. Each rectangle in Figure 16.2 represents a class of requirements information. The way in which you store this information is not important, and you should not be overly concerned with its format. Put simply, the *information* is the crucial aspect of this conceptual model. Think facts, not documents or databases.

Think facts, not documents or databases.

The model represents your collected knowledge of the requirements. To make it easier to distribute this information, we suggest that most of it be written as a specification. To that end, the numbers on the classes provide a cross-reference to the specification template.

The classes in the knowledge model (Figure 16.2) are associated with other classes. These associations express the working relationships that give additional meaning to the information held within the class model. For example,

The complete Volere Requirements Knowledge Model is found in Appendix D.

Figure 16.2

The requirements knowledge model represents the information you discover during the requirements process. For convenience, we use a UML class diagram to model this information. Each of the classes (shown as rectangles) is a repository of information about the subject (the name of the class). The associations (lines) between the classes are relationships needed to make use of the information. The numbers attached to the classes correspond to the section numbers in the Volere Requirements Specification Template (see Appendix A).

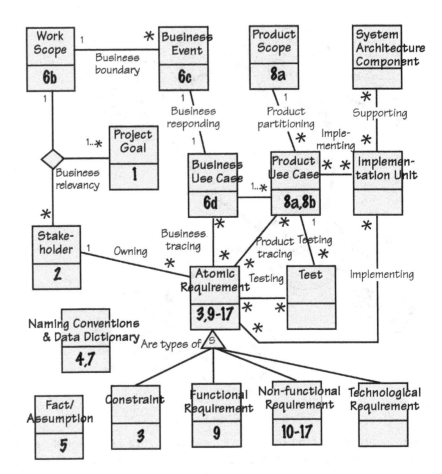

the classes *Work Scope*, *Project Goal*, and *Stakeholder* have three-way association between them. This relationship represents the dependency of one on the others—change the scope and you change the stakeholders; change the goal and you change the scope, and probably the stakeholders. Back in Chapter 3 we discussed the trinity of scope, stakeholders, and goals. Figure 16.2 provides a graphic representation of that trinity; to give it more meaning, we named the association *Business Relevancy* on the model.

Think of the knowledge model as an abstract representation of the requirements information you accumulate, manage, and trace over the course of your development project. Now it falls to you to decide how you will format and store this knowledge. You decide which combination of automated and manual procedures you will use to record and keep track of the content. Typically projects use a combination of spreadsheets, word processors, requirements management tools, modeling tools, and—let us not forget—good, old-fashioned, but still effective cards to manage the information that is represented by the knowledge model.

You should also consider which parts of which classes of knowledge will be published in which of your documents. For example, Figure 16.2 includes an association called *Product Tracing* between the classes called *Product Use Case* and *Atomic Requirement*. An asterisk appears at both ends of the line, indicating that each product use case needs a number of atomic requirements to carry out its functionality and non-functionality, and that each requirement may potentially be used by a number of product use cases.

This association means that when it comes to publishing your documents, you might choose, for example, to publish one or more product use cases and show their details by including all of the associated atomic requirements. The result would be a useful document for implementation purposes. Alternatively, that same association means that you could select a particular requirement and publish a list of all product use cases that contain it. This is useful for determining the impact of changes, and later during system maintenance.

When you have a well-organized knowledge model, you can choose which parts of it should appear in which documents, and provide stakeholders with the information they need.

READING

For more details on building your own tailored requirements knowledge model, see the following source: Robertson, Suzanne, and James Robertson. *Requirements-Led Project Management: Discovering David's Slingshot.* Addison-Wesley, 2005.

The Volere Requirements Specification Template

Thousands of good requirements specifications have already been written. Your task of writing another one becomes easier if you make constructive use of some of the existing good specifications.

We assembled the Volere Requirements Specification Template by "standing on the shoulders of giants." Your authors borrowed useful content and components from specifications of many successfully built products, and packaged the best of them into a reusable template. The intention of the template is that it forms the foundation of *your* requirements specifications. This way, you, too, get to stand on the shoulders of giants.

The Volere template is a compartmentalized container for requirements. We examined requirements documents and categorized their requirements into types that prove useful for the purpose of recognition and elicitation. Each of the types is allocated to a section of the template.

Bernard of Chartres used to say that we are like dwarfs on the shoulders of giants, so that we can see more than they, and things at a greater distance, not by virtue of any sharpness of sight on our part, or any physical distinction, but because we are carried high and raised up by their giant size.

—John of Salisbury

Template Table of Contents

Project Drivers

1. The Purpose of the Project
2. The Stakeholders

The Volere Requirements Specification Template is found in Appendix A. This chapter repeatedly refers to the template.

Project Constraints

   3. Mandated Constraints
   4. Naming Conventions and Terminology
   5. Relevant Facts and Assumptions

Functional Requirements

   6. The Scope of the Work
   7. The Business Data Model and Data Dictionary
   8. The Scope of the Product
   9. Functional Requirements

Non-functional Requirements

   10. Look and Feel Requirements
   11. Usability and Humanity Requirements
   12. Performance Requirements
   13. Operational and Environmental Requirements
   14. Maintainability and Support Requirements
   15. Security Requirements
   16. Cultural Requirements
   17. Legal Requirements

Project Issues

   18. Open Issues
   19. Off-the-Shelf Solutions
   20. New Problems
   21. Tasks
   22. Migration to the New Product
   23. Risks
   24. Costs
   25. User Documentation and Training
   26. Waiting Room
   27. Ideas for Solutions

Template Divisions

The template is set out in five main divisions. First come the *Project Drivers*. These factors cause the project to be undertaken in the first place. Drivers include such things as the purpose of the project—why you are involved in gathering the requirements for a product, and who wants or needs that product.

Next are *Project Constraints*. These are restrictions that limit the requirements and the outcome of the project. The constraints are written into the specification at blastoff time, although you probably have some mechanism in place for determining them earlier.

Think of those first two sections as setting the scene for the requirements that are to follow.

The next two divisions deal with the requirements for the product. Both the *Functional Requirements* and the *Non-functional Requirements* are specified here. Each requirement is described to a level of detail such that the product's constructors know precisely what to build to satisfy the business need, and what to test to ensure the delivered product matches its requirement.

The final division of the template deals with *Project Issues*. These are not requirements for the product, but rather issues that must be faced if the product is to become a reality. This part of the template also contains a "waiting room"— a place to store requirements not intended for the initial release of the product. If you are using an iterative development technique, the waiting room is more or less the same as your backlog.

The complete Volere Requirements Specification Template contains examples and guidance for specifying its content. For each section, the Content, Motivation, Considerations, Examples, and Form provide the template user with guidance for writing the requirements. We recommend that you use the template as a guide to assembling your requirements specification.

Discovering Atomic Requirements

The first eight sections of the requirements specification, which cover the drivers, constraints, and scope of the project, use a mixture of models and free text.

However, the atomic functional and non-functional requirements should be written more formally and with a consistent structure. We call these "atomic" requirements because they do not have to be decomposed. They do contain attributes, just as a real atom is made up of subatomic particles, but are more useful if treated as a single unit. The attributes that make up a complete atomic requirement, are most conveniently thought of as the requirements *shell*.

Snow Cards

Before we discuss the attributes of the shell, we want to introduce the *snow card*. It is simply a card—white, of course—that contains the shell attributes.

We borrowed the idea of using cards from an architect called William Pena. Members of Pena's architectural firm use cards to record requirements and issues relating to buildings they are designing. The team members tape cards containing unresolved issues to the conference room walls, and then use this visual display to get a quick impression of the progress of the building.

We have found a similar use for these cards when gathering requirements. Figure 16.3 shows an example of a snow card. This low-tech approach to requirements gathering is convenient when trawling for requirements, and, of course, the cards can be transferred to an automated tool. Snow cards are also used as story cards—they have attributes in common.

In our requirements seminars, we place small stacks of snow cards on the students' tables, and students use them to record requirements during the workshops. What always surprises us is that, even though the snow card is a low-tech device, the students take away all the unused ones at the end of the seminar. We get e-mails telling us how much they like using snow cards for the early part of the requirements-gathering process.

When working on our own projects, we use cards when we are interviewing stakeholders, and record requirements as we hear them. Initially the requirement is not fully formed, so we might simply capture the description and the originator. As time moves on and we have a better understanding of the requirements, we progressively add more content to the cards.

We were intrigued to receive a snow card with our address and postage stamp on the back.

One advantage of loose cards is that they can be distributed among analysts. We have several clients who make use of cards in the early stages of requirements gathering. They find it convenient to pin them to walls, to hand them to analysts for further clarification, to mail them to users (we were intrigued to receive a snow card with our address and postage stamp on the back), and generally to be able to handle a requirement individually.

Figure 16.3

The Volere shell in its snow card form. Each 8-inch by 5-inch card is used to record an atomic requirement. The requirements analyst completes each of the items as it is discovered, thereby building a complete, rigorous requirement.

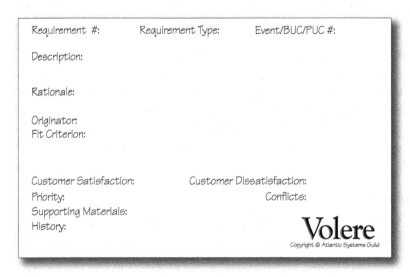

Requirement #:   Requirement Type: Event/BUC/PUC #:

Description:

Rationale:

Originator:
Fit Criterion:

Customer Satisfaction: Customer Dissatisfaction:
Priority: Conflicts:
Supporting Materials:
History:

Volere
Copyright © Atlantic Systems Guild

We also use snow cards for capturing user stories—more on this in Chapter 14, Requirements and Iterative Development.

We also use snow cards for capturing user stories.

Attributes of Atomic Requirements

Now let us look at how a complete, formalized atomic requirement is constructed. As we treat each of the attributes that make up the requirement, consider how you would discover it, and how well it applies to your project. Refer to Figure 16.3 as you go through this list.

Requirement Number

Each requirement must be uniquely identified. The reason for this mandate is straightforward: Requirements must be traceable throughout the development of the product, so it is logical to give each requirement a unique identifier. It is not important *how* you uniquely identify the requirement, just that you do so in some fashion.

Requirement Type

The requirement type comes from the Volere Requirements Specification Template—the template includes 27 sections, each of which contains a different type of requirement. Functional requirements are type 9, look and feel requirements are type 10, usability requirements are type 11, and so on. If you have trouble deciding on one type for an atomic requirement, then it is acceptable to assign multiple types.

Attaching the type to the requirement is useful in several ways:

- You can sort the requirements by type. By comparing all requirements of one type, you can more readily discover requirements that conflict with one another.

- It is easier to write an appropriate fit criterion when the type of requirement is understood.

- When you group all of the known requirements of one type, it becomes readily apparent if some of them are missing or duplicated.

- The ability to group requirements by type helps delineate stakeholder involvement. For example, you can easily identify all of the security requirements and make them available for review by a security expert.

Event/BUC/PUC

The context of the work is broken into partitions using the business events; the response to each business event is a business use case (BUC); and when you decide which part of the business use case is to be handled by the product, then that is your product use case (PUC). All of these items are identified—usually just a number—for convenient referencing.

You can write atomic requirements for any of these elements, but generally business analysts write requirements for the BUC. Whatever level you write the requirement for, you should identify it. The Event/BUC/PUC # allows you—and everybody else—to trace the atomic requirement back to its grouping. Figure 16.4 illustrates how requirements are identified.

Tracing is useful, but being able to assemble the entire set of requirements for a BUC is extremely useful. It allows you to verify that all requirements for the BUC have been written, and, assuming that you are implementing one BUC at a time, allows your developers to see much more clearly the task that lies ahead for them.

Description

The description is the intent of the requirement. It is an English (or whatever natural language you use) statement in the stakeholder's words as to what the stakeholder thinks he needs. Do not be too concerned about whether the description contains ambiguities—but neither should you be sloppy with your language. Your fit criterion will define the precise, testable meaning of this requirement. The objective when you write the description is to capture the stakeholder's wishes. Thus, for the moment, your description should be as clear as you and your stakeholder can make it.

Rationale

The rationale is the reason behind the requirement's existence; it explains why the requirement is important and how it contributes to the product's purpose. Adding a rationale to a requirement helps both you and your stakeholder understand the real need for the requirement. The rationale signals the importance of the requirement, and guides the developers and the testers as to how much effort to put into developing and testing it.

In user stories (story cards), the rationale is the "so that . . ." part of the story. We urge you to *always* include a rationale, omitting it only when the need for the requirement is obvious to even the dullest mind.

Figure 16.4

The requirement number, requirement type, and business event number, business use case number, or product use case number.

| Requirement #: **75** | Requirement Type: **9** | Event/BUC/PUC #: **6** |

Originator

The originator is the person who raised the requirement, or the person who asked for it. You should attach the originator's name or initials to each requirement in case questions arise or clarification is needed, or in case this requirement is found to be in conflict with another. It is also useful if the Quality Gateway rejects the requirement. The originator must have the knowledge and authority appropriate for the type of requirement.

Fit Criterion

A fit criterion is a quantified benchmark that the solution has to meet. Whereas the description and rationale are written in the language of the users, the fit criterion is written in a precise, quantified manner so that the delivered solution can be tested against the requirement.

Fit criteria and rationales are so important that we have devoted an entire chapter to them. If you have not already done so, please visit Chapter 12, Fit Criteria and Rationale, for more on this topic.

Chapter 12 looks in depth at fit criteria.

Customer Satisfaction and Customer Dissatisfaction

Each requirement should carry a customer satisfaction and customer dissatisfaction rating. (See Figure 16.5.) The satisfaction rating measures how happy your client (or panel of stakeholders) will be if you successfully deliver a solution to the requirement; the dissatisfaction rating measures how unhappy the client will be if you fail to deliver a solution for that requirement.

For example, this is a fairly normal and unremarkable requirement:

> *The product shall record changes to the road network.*

Naturally, your client expects the product to be able to record changes to the road network so that it can tell the engineers which roads must be treated. The client is unlikely to get excited over this requirement, so the satisfaction rating may be anything from 3 to 5. However, if the product cannot record changes to roads, you would expect the client to be rather angry, and thus

Figure 16.5

The customer satisfaction and customer dissatisfaction scales measure the client's concern about whether requirements are included in the final product. A high score on the satisfaction scale indicates that the client will be happy if a solution to the requirement is successfully delivered; a high score on the dissatisfaction scales indicates that the client will be very unhappy if a solution to the requirement is *not* included in the product.

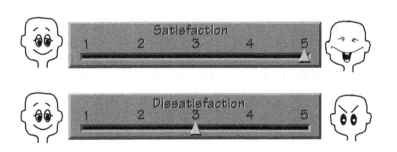

would give a dissatisfaction rating of 5. The high dissatisfaction score gives significance to this requirement.

Now consider this requirement:

> *The product shall issue an alert if a weather station fails to transmit readings.*

This feature of the product would be both useful and nice to have. Your client may give it a satisfaction rating of 5. However, the requirement is not crucial to the correct operation of the product: The engineers would eventually notice if readings failed to turn up from one of the weather stations. In this case the client may well rate the dissatisfaction as 2 or 3. In other words, if the product never performs this task, the engineers will not be too unhappy.

The satisfaction and dissatisfaction ratings indicate the value of the requirement to your client. Although they are typically appended to each atomic requirement, you may elect to attach the ratings to each product use case as a measure of the value that the client assigns to the successful delivery of that part of the work.

The client normally determines the satisfaction and dissatisfaction ratings. As the client is paying for the development of the product, it stands to reason that he should be the one to put a value on the requirements. However, some organizations prefer to have a small group of the principal stakeholders assign the ratings.

Priority

For more on prioritization techniques, refer to Chapter 17, Requirements Completeness.

The priority of a requirement indicates the importance of the requirement's implementation relative to the whole project and governs which requirements will receive priority for development for the next release of the product.

Conflicts

Conflict between requirements means that two (or more) requirements cannot both be implemented; to develop one would prevent the development of the other. For example, a requirement might be to calculate the shortest route to the destination, and another requirement might say the product is to calculate the quickest route to the destination. A conflict arises when you consider that, due to traffic and other conditions, the shortest route is not always the quickest.

Similarly, you may discover a conflict between two or more requirements when you begin to look at solutions—the solution to one requirement might mean the solution to another is impossible, or at least severely restricted.

Conflicts happen. Don't be too concerned if they arise—you can always solve the problem somehow. Chapter 17 has more advice about resolving conflicts.

Supporting Materials

Do not attempt to put everything in the specification. There will always be other material that is important to the requirements, and it can be simply cross-referenced by this item.

> Supporting Materials: Thornes, J. E. Cost-Effective Snow and Ice Control for the Nineties. *Third International Symposium on Snow and Ice Control Technology, Minneapolis, Minnesota, Vol. 1, Paper 24, 1992.*

When you are writing a requirement that would involve many steps to complete—for example, the annual interest calculation for a mortgage—it is almost always easier to not write those steps as requirements, but instead to point to the document that is the authority for calculating interest. Similarly, there are always business rules, standards, laws, regulations, and other situations in which it is more efficient to write the requirement as, for example, "The product shall determine the saline level" and point to the document that tells the developer all he has to do if the product is to successfully find the right salinity.

This is a useful attribute, but don't overdo it. Not all requirements need supporting materials.

History

The History attribute records the date that the requirement was first raised, dates of changes, dates of deletions, date of passing through the Quality Gateway, and so on. Add the names of people responsible for these actions if you think it will help later, but limit the history to only that information necessary and relevant in your environment.

Assembling the Specification

The specification is not so much written, as assembled (see Figure 16.6). The Volere Requirements Specification Template and snow card are convenient guides as to what to assemble to make a complete specification. The template serves as a guide to the topics to be covered by the specification, and the snow card indicates what to write for each atomic requirement.

Keep in mind that it is not always necessary to assemble the entire specification before any other activity can commence. You might decide to publish partial versions, and there are many reasons for doing so.

Figure 16.6

Assembling the specification. The template provides a guide to the types of requirements, and explains how to describe each one. The attributes for each functional requirement and non-functional requirement are compiled using the snow card as a guide. You write the requirements one PUC at a time. You can think of the requirements specification as an assembly of completed snow cards.

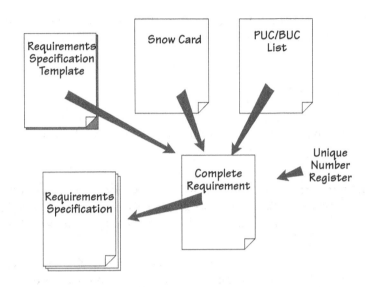

You might also like to think about the way your specification is ordered. The template appears to be saying that requirements are published within a type—all the functional requirements together, all the look and feel requirements together, and so on. In your own work, however, you might find it more useful to publish all the requirements belonging to a product use case together. This has the advantage of making it easier for the developers to do their work, and easier for you to see that you have a complete set of requirements for that PUC.

Naturally, your assembled specification can be published in other ways, and this is where some automation can help.

Automated Requirements Tools

The low-tech approach using cards and pencils is certainly feasible in the early stage of requirements gathering. However, if more than a few analysts are working on your project, you will find that an automated tool pays dividends as the work progresses and the number of requirements grows. Such a tool does not have to be elaborate. In fact, many of our clients find that a word processor or spreadsheet is satisfactory. We do not know this for a fact, but we are strongly of the opinion that the majority of requirements specifications are written using Microsoft Word.

A wide variety of automated requirements tools are available. It would be nice to think that these tools could actually go out and find the requirements for you—but no, you have to discover the requirements; the tool simply records them for you. The features of these tools are quite variable, and we are not about to make any recommendations here. We maintain a list of available requirements tools on our website (www.volere.co.uk/tools.htm). We suggest that it as a starting point for finding which tool or combination of tools is right for you.

Before you commit to any particular tool, try comparing your requirements knowledge model (Figure 16.2) with the tools that are available to you. Which classes of knowledge can the tool help you to record? How about the relationships between the different classes of knowledge—which of these can the tool help you maintain? Bear in mind that you are unlikely to find a single tool that will handle everything on your requirements knowledge model, but you can certainly get as close as possible.

Free tools are also available. Check the open-source sites for the availability of free requirements tools, and also look at the possibility of using Google Docs. The latter is a free word processor (there is also a spreadsheet and a presentation app) that is useful when multiple business analysts and stakeholders need to collaborate on the specification. Microsoft SharePoint is also available as a collaborative way to build requirements specifications.

Look around: You are bound to find something that suits your requirements for recording requirements.

READING
Requirements tools change constantly. We maintain a list of available tools at www.volere.co.uk/tools.htm.

Functional Requirements

Here is an example of a functional requirement for the IceBreaker project:

> The product shall record the new weather stations.

This requirement states an action that, if carried out, contributes to the goal of the product. If the goal is to predict when the roads will freeze, then it is necessary to collect data from weather stations, and thus it is necessary to know the existence and location of the weather stations. When new ones are added to the network, the product must be able to record their details.

Similarly, the following requirement contributes to the product's purpose:

> The product shall issue an alert if a weather station fails to transmit readings.

This requirement is necessary if the product is to know about failures of the stations and the possibility of the product having incomplete data. However, these example functional requirements are not complete. You may also think that they are too casual and possibly ambiguous.

Figure 16.7

A complete functional
requirement written on
a snow card.

> Requirement #: **75**   Requirement Type: **9**   Event/BUC/PUC #: **6**
>
> Description: **The product shall issue an alert if a weather station fails to transmit readings.**
>
> Rationale: **Failure to transmit readings might indicate that the weather station is faulty and needs maintenance, and that the data used to predict freezing roads may be incomplete.**
>
> Source: **V. Appia, Road Engineering**
>
> Fit Criterion: **For each weather station the recorded number of each type of reading per hour shall be within the manufacturer's specified range of the expected number of readings per hour.**
>
> Customer Satisfaction: **3**   Customer Dissatisfaction: **5**
>
> Dependencies: **None**   Conflicts: **None**
>
> Supporting Materials: **Specification of Rosa Weather Station**
>
> History: **Raised by V.A., 28 July 2013**
>
> **Volere**
> Copyright @ Atlantic Systems Guild

To complete each requirement, you use the snow card as a checklist and take the following steps:

- Assign an identification number to the requirement.
- Attach the product use case or business event from which this piece of functionality is derived.
- If the rationale is not self-evident, include it.
- Show the originator.
- Add a fit criterion.
- Describe any conflicts, if they are known.
- Include any supporting materials you consider useful.

Figure 16.7 illustrates a completed functional requirement.

For more on how to derive and write functional requirements, refer to Chapter 10.

Non-functional Requirements

Non-functional requirements are written like other requirements. They have all the usual attributes—they are identified, they have a type, they have a description, they have a fit criterion, and so on. Thus you use the snow card and write them just as you would a functional requirement (see Figure 16.8).

Here you focus on the properties the product must have, such as the spirit of its appearance, how easy it must be to use, how secure it must be, which laws apply to the product, and anything else that must be built into the product, but is not a part of its fundamental functionality.

Chapter 11, Non-functional Requirements, describes these types of requirements and discusses how to write them.

Requirement #: **110**   Requirement Type: **11**   Event/BUC/PUC #: **6,10,13**

Description: **The product shall be easy for the road engineers to use.**

Rationale: **It should not be necessary for the engineers to attend training classes to be able to use the product.**

Source: **Sonia Henning, Road Engineering Supervisor.**

Fit Criterion: **A road engineer shall be able to use the product to successfully carry out the cited use cases within 1 hour of first encountering the product.**

Customer Satisfaction: **3**   Customer Dissatisfaction: **5**

Dependencies: **None**   Conflicts: **None**

Supporting Materials:

History: **Raised by AG, 25 Aug 2013**

Volere
Copyright © Atlantic Systems Guild

Figure 16.8

A non-functional requirement; this one is a usability requirement.

Project Issues

Project issues are concerns that are brought to light by the requirements activity. You can use the Volere Requirements Specification Template Sections 18–27 both as a checklist and as a guide to writing these sections.

We sometimes include project issues in a requirements specification for fear they will become lost if we do not do so. However, if your organization already has procedures in place or suitable documents or files in which to record this information, then please do not add these issues to your requirements specification.

Summary

Writing the requirements specification is not a separate activity, but rather one that is carried out in conjunction with other parts of the requirements process. Requirements analysts write requirements, or parts of requirements, whenever they find them. Not all requirements are completed at the same time.

Even so, writing the specification is not a random activity. Business events, business use cases, product use cases, the template, and the shell enable you to make this an orderly process, and they also measure the degree of completion—and more importantly the areas in need of completion—at any time.

A requirements knowledge model offers an abstract view of your filing system for managing your requirements knowledge. It provides the basis for keeping track of the effect of one piece of knowledge on another. We suggest that you construct your own knowledge model (use ours as a starting point) to guide your requirements discovery activity.

Writing requirements correctly is important. A well-specified set of requirements pays for itself many times over—the construction is more precise, the maintenance costs are lower, and the finished product more accurately reflects what the customer needs and wants.

Requirements Completeness

17

in which we decide whether
our specification is complete,
and set the priorities of the requirements

At some stage during your requirements process, you need to release all or part of your specification—other people, such as developers, testers, marketers, and suppliers, need it. To be released, the specification does not have to contain all the requirements: It could be a partial version with the requirements just for the next iteration, a version of the specification you want to publish for marketing reasons, an extract to use with a request for proposal (RFP), or any portion that you release for any other reason. Nevertheless, before releasing the specification, you need to ensure that it is complete for its intended purpose.

We use the term "specification" here to mean whatever collection of requirements you have. This material does not have to be a formally written specification—it does not even have to be formal. It could be a wiki or a set of story cards; it might hold only the requirements for a partial release of the product. Whatever your intention, this review ensures the specification is sufficient before you hand it over to anyone else.

Figure 17.1 illustrates how the Quality Gateway and the Specification Review work together. The Quality Gateway tests an individual requirement—ensuring that it is correctly stated, unambiguous, within scope, testable, traceable, and not gold plating—thereby confirming that only correct atomic requirements are included in the specification.

Now you have to consider whether the specification is complete, which means reviewing the specification as a whole and ensuring that all the parts that should be there are there. This review makes sense when you consider that it performs these tests:

Chapter 11 discusses the Quality Gateway.

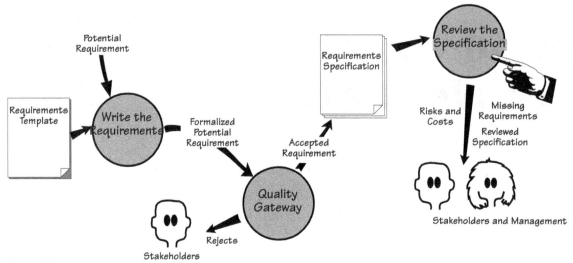

Figure 17.1

You have arrived at the point in the process where you want to consider the specification as a whole. The Quality Gateway has tested and accepted individual requirements, and added them to the specification. Now it is time to assess whether you have a complete specification. This review can be done iteratively—ideally for one product use case worth of requirements at a time.

- Determine whether any requirements are missing.
- Prioritize the requirements so the builders understand their importance and urgency.
- Check for conflicts between requirements that could prevent one or the other from being satisfied.

Additionally, your project management might undertake some other useful tasks at this stage:

- Estimate the cost of construction.
- Evaluate the risks faced by the project.

Reviewing the requirements specification can done at any time, not just before a release—it can be an ongoing activity. You might, for example, review the specification as a check on the progress of the requirements activity. The quality (or lack thereof) of the specification tells you more about progress than the volume of the specification does.

Formality Guide

Rabbit projects rarely package all of their requirements into a complete specification; instead, they act on each tranche of requirements as it comes along. The review process discussed in this chapter is useful for progressively checking completeness in such projects. Rabbits should look at the sections of this chapter covering non-events and the CRUD check. The section on prioritization, while created with written requirements in mind, is also relevant for rabbit projects.

Horse projects almost always have some kind of written specification. It does not have to be as formal as a specification for an elephant project, but knowing it is complete and relevant is desirable. Horses may not build all of the models we describe here, but that's okay: The review process still works without all of them being present. Horse projects should definitely prioritize their requirements.

Elephant projects always need a complete specification. This is either for statutory reasons or because you are outsourcing the development of the product. If there are statutory demands, then it is incumbent upon you to ensure that you have a complete and correct specification, and in some cases to demonstrate how you confirmed its completeness and correctness. If you are outsourcing and you lack an accurate specification, then you will probably be disappointed with the end result—the supplier can do no more than build what you ask for.

In this review process we make use of several models, most notably a model of the stored data (UML class model, entity relationship diagram, or your choice of model). Elephant projects almost always make use of models, so here we present another way that you can reap the benefits from such representations.

Reviewing the Specification

This review process is iterative. Finding errors or omissions, and correcting them, could mean introducing new errors; as a consequence, it might be necessary to iterate through this process once or twice to ensure that the specification is watertight. It is useful to maintain a record of the errors you encounter; the types of errors you discover in this review suggest where you need to improve your requirements process.

This review gives you an ideal opportunity to reassess your earlier decision on whether to go ahead with the project. A seriously flawed or incomplete specification, or measurements that say the costs and the risks outweigh the benefits, are almost always indications that you need to consider project euthanasia.

Inspections

One fairly effective way of reviewing the specification is a formalized process called a *Fagan inspection*. Fagan inspections have been around for quite some time, and much has been written about them, so we do not propose to add much to that body of literature here—a brief outline of the process will be sufficient for our purposes.

The inspection process kicks off with a moderator determining the material to be inspected and the inspectors to inspect it. The inspectors are given an overview of the document under consideration, and they have a day or so to study the material. The inspection meeting proper—limited to two hours—studies the document using checklists of previously found errors. The checklist is applied to the document: "Does this error exist? Does that error exist?" This has proved itself to be a very effective way of trapping errors, yielding a higher detection rate than other review techniques. The checklists are updated when new errors—those not already on the list—are discovered. The author reworks the document, and the moderator ensures all defects have been removed. If necessary, the moderator arranges a follow-up inspection.

You can easily adopt some of the Fagan rules. Try these:

READING

The original paper on Fagan inspection (one of the most cited papers in software history) is this: Fagan, Michael. Design and Code Inspections to Reduce Errors in Program Development. *IBM Systems Journal*, vol. 15, no. 3 (1976): 258–287. (We said this process has been around for a while.)

- Assign a moderator (probably the business analyst) to take responsibility for arranging the inspection and distributing the materials.

- Build a checklist of the most likely errors. You will augment this list with subsequent inspections.

- Give inspectors some time to read the document and prepare for the inspection.

- Limit inspections to two hours and no more than two inspections a day.

- Have between three and eight inspectors.

Fagan inspections can be a very effective weapon to ensure the correctness and completeness of your requirements. Try them.

Find Missing Requirements

The Volere Requirements Specification Template appears in Appendix A.

The review determines whether all of the requirement types appropriate to your product have been discovered. Use the Volere Requirements Specification Template and its requirement types as a guide when determining whether your specification contains the types of requirements called for by the nature of the product. For example, if you are developing a financial product but you have no security requirements, something is definitely missing. Similarly, a Web product that lacks either usability or look and feel requirements is certainly in trouble.

The functional requirements should be sufficient to complete the work of each use case. To check this aspect, play through each of the product use cases as if you were the product. If you do everything the requirements call for, do you arrive at the outcome for the use case? Are your users (you should have them with you when you perform this role-play) satisfied the product will do what they need for their work?

Look for exceptions to the normal things the product must do. Have you generated enough exception and alternative scenarios to cover these eventualities, and do your functional requirements reflect this coverage? Revisit your scenarios and, for each step, determine whether exceptions can occur there or whether an exception might prevent that step from being reached.

Scenarios are discussed in Chapter 6.

Check each product use case against the non-functional requirement types. Does it have the non-functional requirements that it needs and that are appropriate for this kind of use case? Use the requirements template as a checklist. Go through the non-functional requirement types, read their descriptions, and ensure that the correct non-functional requirements have been included.

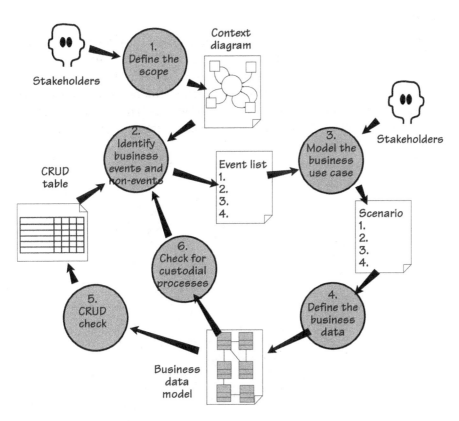

Figure 17.2

The procedure for determining that you have found all of the business events. The process is iterative, going through the activities until the *Identify business events and non-events* activity fails to discover anything new.

Have All Business Use Cases Been Discovered?

For each business event, you determined the business response (the business use case [BUC]) and decided how much of that response will be carried out by the product (the product use case [PUC]). We suggested that you discover the requirements one PUC at a time, and continue until you have covered all of the business events. This approach works well, providing, of course, that you have discovered all of the business events.

So how do you know whether you have discovered all of the business events? There is a short procedure that uses the outputs of your requirements process and system modeling. In other words, you do not have to produce more stuff, but just make more use of what you already have.

You do not have to produce more documents to do the review, but just make more use of what you have.

Figure 17.2 illustrates the procedure for confirming the completeness of your list of business events. Refer to the model of this procedure as we describe its activities.

1. Define the Scope

The scope we are concerned with here is the scope of the work to be studied. In Chapter 3, Scoping the Business Problem, we built a context model to show the scope of the IceBreaker work, and we reproduce it in Figure 17.3. The context model is mainly completed during the blastoff activity, then refined further as requirements discovery progresses. The review process we describe here checks the completeness of your context diagram and, where necessary, updates it.

Figure 17.3

The context diagram of the work shows the data entering and leaving the scope of the work. These data transfers are referred to as boundary data flows. We use these flows to determine the business events.

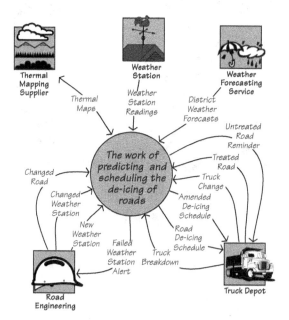

2. Identify Business Events and Non-events

During the blastoff, or at the beginning of trawling, you determined the business events by looking at the boundary data flows on the context diagram. If a business event happens outside the work, the adjacent system sends a data flow (which we are calling a boundary data flow) to the work, and the work responds by processing the data contained in the flow. Thus a business event is associated with each incoming boundary data flow. The outgoing boundary flows are either part of the response to an externally triggered business event (the work responds by processing the incoming flow and produces the outgoing flow) or the result of a time-triggered event (such as reporting and sending out reminders or alerts). In short, each flow on the context model is connected to a business event. When you have found all of the boundary flows from the context model, you have determined all of the possible business events . . . for the moment.

Chapter 4, Business Use Cases, tells you how to determine business events from the context model.

The output of this activity is a list of business events. The list of the Ice-Breaker business events appears in Table 17.1.

Event Name	Input Data Flow	Output Data Flow
1. Weather Station transmits reading	Weather Station Readings	
2. Weather Bureau forecasts weather	District Weather Forecasts	
3. Road Engineering advises changed roads	Changed Road	
4. Road Engineering installs new Weather Station	New Weather Station	
5. Road Engineering changes Weather Station	Changed Weather Station	
6. Time to test Weather Stations		Failed Weather Station Alert
7. Truck Depot changes a truck	Truck Change	
8. Time to detect icy roads		Road De-icing Schedule
9. Truck treats a road	Treated Road	
10. Truck Depot reports problem with truck	Truck Breakdown	Amended De-icing Schedule
11. Time to monitor road de-icing		Untreated Road Reminder

Table 17.1

The Business Event List for the IceBreaker Work

Non-events

Now look for non-events. The term "non-events" is a play on words, and here we use it to mean events that happen if another event does not happen. Table 17.1 lists Event 9, *Truck treats a road*. What happens if the truck does *not* treat the road? The work has to do something, and what it does is a non-event (it happened because another event did not happen), so now we have identified Event 11, *Time to monitor road de-icing*. The work responds to this (non) event by checking whether all roads have been treated as directed and, if they have not, issues an *Untreated Road Reminder*.

A more common example found in many businesses is the business event called "Customer pays invoice." You are no doubt familiar with this event, probably by being the payer rather than the payee. So what happens if the customer does not pay the invoice? There is a corresponding non-event called "Time to send reminder notice to nonpayers."

During your specification review, go through your list of business events and ask, "What happens if this event does not happen?" Not all business events have a non-event—most don't—but checking the list for their existence will reveal missing events.

Add any new business events discovered through this exercise to the list of business events, and update the context model with the appropriate flows. Continue searching the list of existing events for more non-events, but don't be overly concerned if you don't find one for every event. Often when you ask the question, "What happens if this event does not happen?", the answer is "Nothing."

3. Model the Business Use Case

READING
Robertson, James, and Suzanne Robertson. *Complete Systems Analysis: The Workbook, the Textbook, the Answers*. Dorset House, 1998. This book is a thorough treatment of business use case modeling.

Activity 3 (Figure 17.2) is not part of the requirements review, but something you have already done. As part of your requirements investigation, you will have built models or scenarios to help you and your stakeholders understand the desired response to the business event. Given that scenarios are the most commonly used models, we show a scenario in the schematic of the review process. However, many business analysts prefer to use UML activity diagrams or similar forms. The type of model you use is not important. What *is* important is that your model shows the functionality of the business use case; from this information, you can determine the stored data used by that functionality.

4. Define the Business Data

The next part of the review process is a step you might have already performed: building a model of the stored data needed by the work. You can use a class diagram, an entity relationship model, a relational model, or any other data-modeling notation you prefer. As long as it shows classes, entities, or tables, and the associations or relationships between them, it will suffice.

Figure 17.4 shows a sample model of the data used by the IceBreaker work.

If building this kind of model is a task you do not normally tackle, ask one of the database people to do it for you. They have to build such a model at some stage of the development, and they may as well do it now when it can serve more purposes than just aiding the logical database design. However, you must insist that the database person builds a model of the *business data*, and does not start designing a database; these are two different things.

If you don't want to build a model of the stored data, a simple alternative is to make a list of the classes of data used by the business. Data classes (also called "entities") are the subject matter of stored data—they are the things that we store data about. You can think of a class as a collection of elementary data items (their correct name is "attributes") for something that is important to the business. The "something" can be real, such as a customer or goods you sell, or it can be abstract, such as an account, a contract, or an invoice. The important thing to note is that the class does not have an alphanumeric value. For example, an account has no alphanumeric value, but its attributes—the account number, the account balance, and so on—are items that do have alphanumeric values. This is a useful rule for those times when you are wondering whether something is a class or an attribute.

Another, perhaps more useful rule is that classes are uniquely identified. Thus anything to which your organization attaches an identifier is a class— accounts, credit cards, cars, shipments, flights, and so on—and all have unique identifiers.

Classes are uniquely identified.

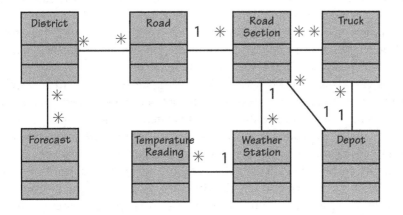

Figure 17.4

This model shows the stored data used to predict and schedule the de-icing of roads. It uses UML class model notation.

Do not agonize too long over identifying the data classes—just do as well as you can without spending the rest of the month on it. Some heuristics are generally helpful in identifying classes by defining their properties:

- Things, concrete or abstract, used by the business
- Things that are identified—accounts, sales opportunities, customers
- Subjects of data, not the data itself
- Nouns with a defined business purpose
- Products or services—mortgages, service agreements
- Branches of organizations, locations, or constructions
- Roles—case officer, employee, manager
- Events that are remembered—agreements, contracts, purchases
- Adjacent systems from the context diagram

You can also find the classes from your context model. The stored data used by the work comes in via data flows and leaves via other data flows. Think about it this way: If data resides inside the work, there must be some flow of data to bring it there. In turn, you can dissect the data flows found on the context model and look at their attributes: "What is this attribute describing?" or "What is the subject of this data?" These subjects are your classes. Analyze all boundary flows, both inward and outward, looking for "things" that conform to the properties of classes listed earlier. When you have analyzed all of the flows, you have most likely identified all of the business data classes.

Now we get to the fun part.

5. CRUD Check

Each class of data must be Created and Referenced. Some are also Updated or Deleted.

Each class of data (check these on your class model) must be Created and Referenced. Some are also Updated or Deleted. Build a CRUD table, such as the one shown in Table 17.2, to show whether every class has all the appropriate actions performed on it. These actions are performed by business use cases, so this step is where you reveal any missing events.

If a class is referenced without first being created, it means the creation event is missing. If a class is created without being referenced, then either an event is missing or some data has been created that does not have to be created. Some classes (but not all) are updated, and some are deleted. Naturally, for either of these last two events to occur, the data must have been created.

Empty cells in the CRUD table reveal missing business events. For example, the classes Depot and District do not have any creating business event, yet they are referenced. Thus the context is incomplete: It does not have the incoming flows needed to create these classes of stored data.

Class	Create	Reference	Update	Delete
Depot		7		
District		2, 8, 10		
Forecast	2	8, 10		
Road	3	4, 8, 9, 10	3	
Road Section	3	4, 8, 10, 11	3, 9	
Temperature Reading	1	6, 8, 10		
Truck	7	8, 9, 11	7, 10	
Weather Station	4	1, 6	5	

Table 17.2

The CRUD Table

Each cell shows the identifier of the business event that creates, references, updates, or deletes the entity. Gaps in the table indicate missing events.

When you find missing business events, you have to revisit your stakeholders to find out more about them. When you determine what the events are, update the context diagram, add them to the event list, update the CRUD table, and continue the process.

The Delete column of the CRUD table shows classes that are deleted for business policy reasons only. This is not the same as archiving or cleaning up the database. For example, if a Depot were to be taken out of service, then it is deleted from a business point of view. However, a Forecast is never deleted—there is no essential business policy reason for doing so.

6. Check for Custodial Processes

The work's processes can be fundamental or custodial. *Fundamental processes* are connected to the reason for the product's existence—for example, analyzing the roads, recording the weather forecasts, and scheduling the trucks to treat the roads. In contrast, *custodial processes* exist to maintain—that is, keep custody of—the stored data. These processes make changes to the data solely to keep it up-to-date and are not part of the fundamental processing.

For example, when you hand over your credit card to make a purchase, the credit card company records the amount and other details of your purchase. That is a fundamental process.

Now imagine that you move to a new home. After doing so, you advise the credit card company of your change of address, and the company updates its records accordingly. This is a custodial process; it exists just to keep the data up-to-date.

To check for custodial processes, go through the class model and the CRUD table, and ensure that you have sufficient business events and their processes to maintain all of the work's stored data. If a class has changeable attributes, then there is probably a custodial business event to change them.

If a class has changeable attributes, there is probably a custodial business event to change them.

Repeat Until Done

Activities 1 through 6 of the business event discovery process are iterative. That is, you continue to go through the process—identifying business events; modeling the business use cases; adding to the class model; checking that the classes are created, referenced, updated, and deleted—until activity 2, *Identify business events and non-events,* fails to reveal any new events. At that point, you can be confident that there are no more business events relevant to your work.

You might also investigate the automated tools at your disposal, as some of this procedure can be automated. It is not that hard to do manually, but if you can get some automated help, why not?

Prioritizing the Requirements

One problem with requirements is that there are always too many of them. Prioritizing gives you a way to choose which ones to implement in which versions of the product. Decisions about prioritization are complex because they involve different factors and these factors are often in conflict with each other. Also, because the various stakeholders probably have different goals, it may prove difficult to reach agreement about priorities.

Despite its difficulty, this task must be done sooner or later, and sooner is best: The earlier you prioritize, the easier it is. But let's go back to being difficult—there are quite a few factors that are considered when prioritizing. We spoke earlier about the customer satisfaction and customer dissatisfaction.

See Chapter 16, Communicating Requirements, for more on customer satisfaction and dissatisfaction.

Each requirement should carry a customer satisfaction and customer dissatisfaction rating. These ratings help the customer to consider the relative value of individual requirements, and to prioritize them.

You can group requirements together and prioritize them as a unit.

To prioritize requirements, you can group them together into logical (to you) groups. These groups are then prioritized as a unit, on the assumption that all of the composing requirements have the same priority as the group as a whole. A group might be a use case, a component, a feature, or any other collection of requirements that it makes sense to prioritize as a unit instead of treating them individually.

To make it easier to read, for the next few pages, we use the term "requirements" to mean "groups of requirements," "features," "product use cases," or any other grouping you care to use.

Prioritization Factors

The following factors commonly affect prioritization decisions:

- The cost of implementation
- Value to the customer or client

- Time needed to implement the product
- Ease of technological implementation
- Ease of business or organization implementation
- Benefit to the business
- Obligation to obey the law

Not all of these factors are relevant to every project, and the relative importance of each factor differs for each project. Within a project, the relative importance of the factors is not the same for all of the stakeholders. Given this combinatorial complexity, you need some kind of agreed-upon prioritization procedure to provide a way of making choices. Part of that procedure is to determine when you will make prioritization decisions.

When to Prioritize

How soon should you make choices? As soon as you have two items to choose between. And keep in mind that the more visible you make your requirements knowledge, the more chances you have to make, and help others make, informed choices.

If your requirements have a well-organized structure, you can prioritize them early in your project. The process described in this book includes a project blastoff (Chapter 3) that advocates building a work context model, and then partitioning it using business events. We strongly suggest that you assign a priority rating to each business use case during the blastoff. You can, if you like, attach customer satisfaction and dissatisfaction ratings to the business events at this time. This early prioritization indicates which parts of the business should be investigated first, and which can be safely ignored until later, or in some cases, abandoned. In addition, you use this first prioritization to guide your iterations and version planning.

As you write atomic requirements, you should progressively consider whether to prioritize them. If any requirements obviously have low value, then tag them as such. Use the customer satisfaction and customer dissatisfaction ratings, discussed in the previous section, to help other people make choices.

Part of the reason for progressive prioritization is to manage expectations. Your stakeholders often assume the term "requirements" means these capabilities will definitely be implemented. "Requirements" are really desires or wishes that we need to understand well enough to decide whether and how to implement them. For example, we might have a requirement that is really high priority but, due to a mixture of constraints, we cannot meet its fit criterion 100 percent. However, we do have a solution that will meet the fit criterion at the 85 percent level.

Your stakeholders often assume the term "requirements" means these capabilities will definitely be implemented. "Requirements" are really desires or wishes that we need to understand well enough to decide whether and how to implement them.

If you have been progressively prioritizing requirements throughout the project, people are able to accept such compromises without feeling cheated. Prioritization prepares stakeholders for the fact you cannot implement all the requirements.

Requirement Priority Grading

You can grade your requirement priority however it suits your way of working. A common way of grading requirements is "high," "medium," and "low," but this approach usually means that all requirements are somehow high priority. There is also the MoSCoW approach, which is popular; this acronym stands for Must have, Should have, Could have, Won't have.

Some organizations assign their requirements to releases: R1, R2, R3, and so on. The idea is that the R1 requirements are the highest priority or have the highest customer appeal, and are intended to appear in the first release. But having assigned your requirements to releases, suppose you discover you have too many requirements in the R1 category. At that point, you need to prioritize further.

The idea of sorting the requirements into prioritization categories is often referred to as *triage*. This term (from the French verb *trier*, meaning "to sort") comes from the field of medicine. It was first adopted during the Napoleonic wars when field hospitals were not capable of treating all soldiers who had been wounded. The doctors used triage to place the patients into one of three categories:

READING
Davis, Al. *Just Enough Requirements*. Dorset House, 2005.

- Those who would live without treatment
- Those who would not survive
- Those who would survive if they were treated

Due to scarce medical resources, the doctors treated the third group only. The idea of triage can be used in project work using the categories:

- Those requirements needed for the next release
- Those requirements definitely not needed or wanted for the next release
- Those requirements you would like if possible

If the first and last categories leave you with more requirements than will fit into your budget, you need to prioritize further.

Prioritization Spreadsheet

A prioritization spreadsheet (Figure 17.5) enables you to prioritize the over-flow requirements. Ideally—and especially if you have done a good job on progressive prioritization—these requirements will fit into the "would like if possible" category.

Earlier in this chapter, we identified seven prioritization factors (or you may use any other prioritization factors relevant to your project). On our spreadsheet (see Figure 17.5), we have limited the number of factors to four, as more than that makes it difficult, if not impossible, to agree on a weighting system.

The *% Weight Applied* column shows the relative importance assigned to each factor. You arrive at this percentage weight by stakeholder discussion and voting.

In column 1, list the requirements you want to prioritize. These might be atomic requirements or recognized groups of requirements. Give each requirement–factor combination a score out of 10. This score reflects the positive contribution to the factor made by this requirement, where 1 means no contribution and 10 means the maximum possible contribution. In the example, for requirement 1, we assigned a score of 2 for the first factor because we believe that it does not make a very positive contribution to *Value to Customer*. The same requirement scores a 7 for *Value to Business,* as it makes a significant contribution to the business. The score for *Minimizing the Cost of Implementation* is 3; we think this requirement is relatively expensive to implement. It scored an 8 in terms of its *Ease of Implementation*, reflecting the relative simplicity of this requirement.

READING

The downloadable Volere Prioritization Spreadsheet (www.volere.co.uk) offers a way to prioritize requirements. This spreadsheet contains some examples that you can replace with your own data.

Figure 17.5

This prioritization spreadsheet can be downloaded from www.volere.co.uk.

Volere Prioritisation Spreadsheet

Copyright © The Atlantic Systems Guild 2006

Requirement/Product Use Case/Feature	Number	Factor - score out of 10 Value to Customer	%Weight applied 40	Factor - score out of 10 Value to Business	%Weight applied 20	Factor - score out of 10 Minimise Implementation Cost	%Weight applied 10	Factor - score out of 10 Ease of Implementation	%Weight applied 30	Priority Rating	Total Weight 100
Requirement 1	1	2	0.8	7	1.4	3	0.3	8	2.4	4.9	
Requirement 2	2	8	3.2	8	1.6	5	0.5	7	2.1	7.4	
Requirement 3	3	7	2.8	3	0.6	7	0.7	4	1.2	5.3	
Requirement 4	4	6	2.4	8	1.6	3	0.3	5	1.5	5.8	
Requirement 5	5	5	2	5	1	1	0.1	3	0.9	4	
Requirement 6	6	9	4	6	1.2	6	0.6	5	1.5	6.9	
Requirement 7	7	4	2	3	0.6	6	0.6	7	2.1	4.9	

For each score, the spreadsheet calculates a weighted score by applying the percent weight for that factor. The priority rating for the requirement is calculated as the total of the weighted scores for the requirement.

You may use a variety of voting systems to arrive at the weights for the factors and the scores for each requirement. To make sure everyone is heard, issue voting tokens (gold stars, Monopoly money, or some such device) and ask each stakeholder to place his voting tokens on his highest-priority requirements. Of course, the spreadsheet is merely a vehicle for enabling a group of stakeholders to arrive at a consensus when prioritizing the requirements. By making complex situations more visible, you make it possible for people to communicate their interests, to appreciate other individuals' opinions, and to negotiate.

Conflicting Requirements

Two requirements are conflicting if you cannot implement them both—the solution to one requirement prohibits implementing the other. For example, if one requirement asks for the product to "be available to all" and another says it shall be "fully secure," then both requirements cannot be implemented as specified.

Prioritization, as we discussed earlier, might prevent some conflicts from happening. However, nothing is perfect, so you might need to take the following steps.

As a first pass at finding conflicting requirements, sort the requirements into their types. Then examine all entries that you have for each type, looking for pairs of requirements whose fit criteria are in conflict with each other. See Figure 17.6.

Of course, a requirement might potentially conflict with any other requirement in the specification. To help you discover these problems, here

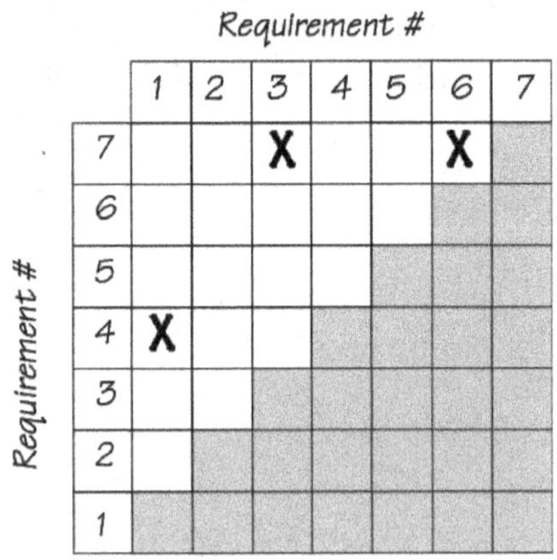

Figure 17.6

This matrix identifies conflicting requirements. For example, requirements 3 and 7 are in conflict with each other. If we implement a solution to requirement 3, it will have a negative effect on our ability to implement a solution to requirement 7, and vice versa.

Requirement #

	1	2	3	4	5	6	7
7			X			X	
6							
5							
4	X						
3							
2							
1							

Requirement #

are some clues to the situations where we most often find requirements in conflict:

- Requirements that use the same data (search by matching terms used)
- Requirements of the same type (search by matching requirement types)
- Requirements that use the same scales of measurement (search by matching requirements whose fit criteria use the same scales of measurement)

For functional requirements, look for conflicts in outcomes. As an example, suppose one requirement for the IceBreaker project calls for a roads section to be treated by the nearest truck, and another specifies that truck scheduling must rotate the trucks to allow for maintenance and driver rest periods. These two requirements would probably result in different outcomes.

Conflicts may arise because different stakeholders have asked for different requirements, or because stakeholders have asked for requirements that are in conflict with the client's idea of the requirements. This type of overlap, which is normal for most requirements-gathering efforts, indicates you need to establish some sort of conflict resolution mechanism.

Conflicts between requirements are normal for most requirements-gathering efforts, and indicate the need for some sort of conflict resolution mechanism.

You, as the requirements analyst, have the most to gain by settling conflicts as rapidly as possible, and as early as possible, so we suggest that you take the lead role in resolving them. When you have isolated the conflicting requirements, approach each of the stakeholders separately (this is one reason why you record the originator of each requirement). Go over the requirement with the user and ensure that both of you have the same understanding of it. Reassess the satisfaction and dissatisfaction ratings: If one stakeholder gives low marks to the requirement, then he may not care if you drop it in favor of the other requirement. Do this with both stakeholders and do not, for the moment, bring them together.

When you talk to each stakeholder, explore his reasoning. What does the stakeholder really want as an outcome, and will it be compromised if the other requirement takes precedence? Also, ensure that the requirement is not a solution, as often stakeholders ask for solutions that are within their own realm of experience, and naturally, experiences differ.

Most of the time we have been able to resolve conflicts by talking to the stakeholders. Note that we use the term "conflict" here, not "dispute." There is no dispute. There are no positions taken, no noses put out of joint by the other guy winning. The stakeholder need not even know who the conflicting party is.

If you, as a mediator, are unable to reach a satisfactory resolution, then we suggest that you determine the cost of implementing the opposing requirements, assess their relative risks, and, armed with numbers, call the participants together and see if you can reach some compromise. Except in cases of extreme office politics, stakeholders are usually willing to compromise if they are in a position to do so gracefully without loss of face.

Ambiguous Specifications

The specification should, as far as is practical, be free of ambiguity. You should not have used any pronouns, and should be wary of unqualified adjectives and adverbs—all of these parts of speech introduce ambiguity. Do not use the word "should" when writing your requirements; it infers that the requirement is optional. Nevertheless, even if you follow these guidelines, some problems may remain.

The fit criterion quantifies a requirement, thereby making it unambiguous. We described fit criteria in Chapter 12, explaining how they make each requirement both measurable and testable. If you have correctly applied fit criteria, then the requirements in your specification will be unambiguous.

This leaves the descriptions of the requirements. Obviously, the less ambiguity they contain, the better, but a poor description cannot do too much damage if you have a properly quantified fit criterion for the requirement. However, if you are concerned about this issue, then we suggest that you select 50 requirements randomly. Take one of them and ask a panel of stakeholders to give their interpretation of the requirement. If everyone agrees on the meaning of the requirement, then set it aside. If the meaning of the requirement is disputed, then select five more requirements. Repeat this review until either it becomes clear that the specification is acceptable or the collection of selected requirements to test has grown so large (each ambiguity brings in five new ones) that the problem is obvious to all.

If the problem is truly bad, then consider rewriting the specification using a better-qualified requirements writer. Or, if it is really, really bad, consider aborting the project. A problem with requirements is the most common problem with crippled projects—there appears no point to proceeding when you know you have poor, ambiguous requirements.

The terms used in the requirements must be those defined in the Data Dictionary section of the specification. If every word has an agreed-upon definition and you have used the terms consistently, then the meanings throughout the specification must be consistent and unambiguous.

Risk Assessment

Risk assessment is not really a requirements problem, but rather a project issue. At this stage of the requirements process, you have a complete specification of a product that you intend to build. You have invested a certain amount of time deriving this specification, and you are about to invest even more time in building the product. Now seems like a good time to pause for a moment and consider the risks involved in proceeding.

As a requirements analyst, you do not have to handle the risk assessment by yourself. This task is more likely to be performed by the project manager, and if your organization is of a reasonable size, there should be someone on staff who is trained in risk assessment.

The role of the business analyst in risk assessment is to consider require-ments from the point of view of whether they contain some risk that could affect the success of the project. Some requirements pose greater risk than others. For example, some requirements might call for a technology or an implementation that the development team has never attempted before. That is not to say that they cannot pull it off, but there is a risk that they can't. Consider the risks that could be present within the following parts of the Volere Requirements Specification Template:

READING

DeMarco, Tom, and Tim Lister. *Waltzing with Bears: Managing Risk on Software Projects.* Dorset House, 2003. This book contains strategies for recognizing and monitoring risks.

Project Drivers

1. The Purpose of the Project

Is the purpose of the product reasonable? Is it something your organization can achieve? Or are you setting out to do something you have never done before, with only hysterical optimism telling you that you can deliver the objective successfully?

2. The Client, the Customer, and Other Stakeholders

Is the client a willing collaborator? Or is he uninterested in the project? Is the customer represented accurately? Are all stakeholders involved and enthusi-astic about the project and the product? Hostile or unidentified stakeholders can have a very negative effect on your project. What are the chances that everyone will make the necessary contributions? Which risks do you run by not gaining the cooperation you need?

2. Users of the Product

Are the users properly represented? While user representative panels are use-ful, experience has shown that they are frequently wrong in their assess-ment of what the real users want and need. Are the users capable of telling you the correct requirements? Many project leaders often cite the quality of user contributions to requirements as their most serious and frequently encountered risk.

Many system development efforts result in substantial changes to the users' work and the way that users work. Have you considered the risk that the users will not be able to adapt to the new arrangements? Remember that humans do not like being changed, and your new product is bringing changes to your users' work. Are the users capable of operating the new product? Consider these risks carefully, as the risk of the users not being prepared to change may turn out to be a substantial obstacle.

Project Constraints

3. Mandated Constraints

Are the constraints reasonable, or do they indicate design solutions with which your organization has no experience? Is the budget reasonable given the effort needed to build the product? Unrealistic schedules and budgets are among the most common risks cited by projects.

5. Relevant Facts and Assumptions

Are the assumptions reasonable? Should you make contingency plans for the eventuality that one or more of the assumptions turns out not to be true? It pays to keep in mind that assumptions are really risks.

Functional Requirements

6. The Scope of the Work

Is the scope of the work correct? Do you run the risk of not including enough work to produce a satisfactory product? If the scope is not large enough, then the resulting product will not do enough for the user to make it truly valuable to him. A failure to define the work scope correctly always results in early requests for modifications and enhancements to the product.

7. Business Data Model and Data Dictionary

Is the terminology defined so that everyone has the same interpretation of the terms contained in the requirements?

8. The Scope of the Product

Does the scope of the product include all of the needed functionality, or just the easy stuff? Is it feasible given the budget and time available? Having the wrong product scope risks having many change requests after delivery.

Other commonly cited risks include creeping user requirements and incomplete requirements specifications. Risk analysis does not make all of these risks disappear, but it does ensure that you and management become aware of problems that might arise and can make appropriate plans for monitoring and addressing them. It is far more preferable to raise the alert early than to watch a disaster unfold while knowing that you might have been able to prevent it.

Measure the Required Cost

Measuring the cost or effort needed is not usually the responsibility of the requirements analyst. We mention this topic here because now that the requirements are known, you have an ideal opportunity to measure the size of the product. Common sense suggests that you do not proceed past this point without knowing its size, and thus the effort needed to build the product.

To this end, we have included a short introduction to function point counting in Appendix C. The appendix shows how this technique works and suggests it as an effective way to estimate size.

Appendix C, Function Point Counting: A Simplified Introduction, gives a brief but sufficient primer on this commonly used technique for measuring the size of your work or your product.

The work you have done in gathering the requirements provides input to the measuring process; your context model is the definitive guide to the size of the work; a data model (if you have one) provides guidance to the effort needed to store the data. You can simply count the number of requirements you have written. All of these are measurements, and any are vastly preferable to guesswork, or blind acceptance of imposed deadlines.

One of the most commonly encountered risks is the risk of poor estimates of time needed to complete the project. This risk almost always manifests itself by turning into a real-world problem—when time starts to run out, the project team usually responds by taking shortcuts, skimping on quality, and ends up delivering a poor product even later than originally planned. It becomes avoidable when you take the short time needed to measure the size of the product, thereby determining—accurately—the required effort to build it.

We suggest that you include some kind of measurement activity in your completeness review.

Summary

The purpose of the review we have been talking about is to assess the correctness, completeness, and quality of the requirements specification. This review also gives you an opportunity to measure the benefit, cost, and risk attached to building the product, and to assess whether it is worthwhile to continue development of the product.

Consider the model shown in Figure 17.7. It provides a composite measure of the overall value of the product by measuring the risk, the cost to build and operate the product, and the benefit it brings along each of the corresponding scales. What does your profile look like? If you have high scores for cost and risk but a low score for benefit, you should consider abandoning the product. Conversely, you would love to have high benefit with low costs and low risks, but you probably won't get it. The point is to map these factors and note whether the overall profile of your product indicates that it is one to build or one to avoid.

Figure 17.7

Each axis represents one of the factors that determines whether the product is worthwhile. The Cost axis, measuring the cost of construction and operation, can be assessed using function points or some other size measurement. The Benefit axis measures the value to the business and reflects the customer ratings placed by the stakeholders on the product. The Risk axis measures the severity of risks determined by the risk analysis activity.

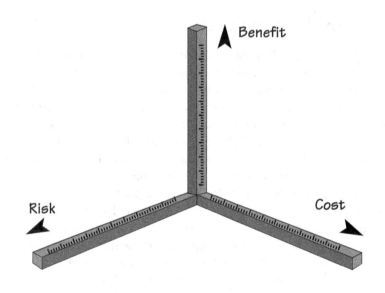

And that brings us to the end of our book. In the course of getting from page one to here, we have tried to inject our experience of requirements projects that spans many years and many continents. If we have been able to pass along some advice, show you a process, give you some tips, suggest a direction, solve a problem, provide a shortcut, and explain the previously unfathomable, then we have succeeded in meeting our goal for this text.

If we have provided you with a reliable companion for your requirements work, then that is what we set out to do. If we have made some noticeable difference to the way that you go about discovering requirements, and if you feel that those requirements are better than they would have been without this book, then the past year will not have been in vain.

Enjoy our book; we hope it makes some difference, and the difference is beneficial to you.

Volere Requirements Specification Template

a guide for writing a rigorous and complete
requirements specification

Contents

14. Maintainability and Support Requirements

15. Security Requirements

16. Cultural Requirements

17. Legal Requirements

Project Issues

18. Open Issues

19. Off-the-Shelf Solutions

20. New Problems

21. Tasks

22. Migration to the New Product

23. Risks

24. Costs

25. User Documentation and Training

26. Waiting Room

27. Ideas for Solutions

Use of This Template

The Volere Requirements Specification Template is intended for use as a basis for your requirements specifications. It provides sections for each of the requirements types appropriate to today's software systems. You may download the template from the Volere site and adapt it to your requirements-gathering process and requirements tool. The template can be used with Yonix, Requisite, DOORS, Caliber RM, IRqA, and other popular tools (see www.volere.co.uk/tools.htm).

The template may not be sold or used for commercial gain or purposes other than as a basis for a requirements specification without prior written permission. It may be modified or copied and used for your requirements work, provided you include the following copyright notice in any document that uses any part of this template:

We acknowledge that this document uses material from the Volere Requirements Specification Template, copyright © 1995–2012 the Atlantic Systems Guild Limited.

Volere

Volere is the result of many years of practice, consulting, and research in requirements engineering and business analysis. We have packaged our experience in the form of a generic requirements process, requirements training, requirements consultancy, requirements audits, a variety of downloadable guides and articles, a requirements knowledge model, and this requirements template. We also provide requirements specification-writing services.

The first edition of the Volere Requirements Specification Template was released in 1995. Since then, thousands of organizations have saved themselves effort by using this template as the basis for discovering, organizing, and communicating their requirements.

The Volere website (www.volere.co.uk) contains articles about the Volere techniques, experiences of Volere users and case studies, requirements tools, and other information useful to requirements practitioners. It also has subsequent updates to this template.

Public seminars on Volere are run on a regular basis in Europe, the United States, Australia, and New Zealand. For a schedule of courses, please refer to www.volere.co.uk.

Requirements Types

For ease of use, we have found it convenient to think of requirements as belonging to a type. This perspective is helpful for two reasons: as an aid to finding the requirements and to be able to group the requirements that are relevant to a specific expert specialty.

Functional requirements are the fundamental or essential subject matter of the product. They describe what the product has to do or which processing actions it must take.

Non-functional requirements are the properties that the functions must have, such as performance and usability. Do not be deterred by the unfortunate name for this kind of requirements—they are as important as the functional requirements for the product's success.

Project constraints are restrictions on the product due to the budget or the time available to build the product.

Design constraints impose restrictions on how the product must be designed. For example, it might have to be implemented in the hand-held device being given to major customers, or it might have to use the existing servers and desktop computers, or any other hardware, software, or business practice.

Project drivers are the business-related forces. For example, the purpose of the project is a project driver, as are all of the stakeholders—each for different reasons.

Project issues define the conditions under which the project will be carried out. Our reason for including them as part of the requirements is to present a coherent picture of all factors that contribute to the success or failure of the project and to illustrate how managers can use requirements as input when managing a project.

Testing Requirements

The Volere philosophy is to start testing requirements as soon as you start writing them. You make a requirement testable by adding its *fit criterion*. This fit criterion measures the requirement, making it possible to determine whether a given solution fits the requirement. If a fit criterion cannot be found for a requirement, then the requirement is either ambiguous or poorly understood. All requirements can be measured, and all should carry a fit criterion.

Atomic Requirements Shell

The requirements shell is a guide to writing each atomic requirement. The components of the shell (also called a "snow card") are identified here. You might decide to add more attributes to provide traceability necessary for your environment—for example, products that implement this requirement, the version of the software that implements this requirement, or departments that are interested in this requirement. Others are possible, though you should be restrained in including them: Do not capriciously add attributes unless they really help you; every attribute you add needs to be maintained.

This requirements shell can, and should, be automated. When you download the template, you will also find an Excel spreadsheet implementation of the snow card.

Here, we discuss and provide examples for each section of the Volere Requirements Specification Template. For each section, the Content, Motivation, Considerations, Examples, and Form provide the template user with some guidance for writing each type of requirement.

The type from
the template

List of events /
use cases that
need this
requirement

Requirement #: **Unique id**   Requirement Type: Event/use case #:

Description: **A one sentence statement of the intention of the requirement**

Rationale: **A justification of the requirement**

Source: **Who raised this requirement?**

Fit Criterion: **A measurement of the requirement such that it is**
possible to test if the solution matches the original
requirement

Customer Satisfaction: Customer Dissatisfaction:

Dependencies: **A list of other requirements that**   Conflicts:
have some dependency on this one

Other requirements
that cannot be
implemented if this
one is

Supporting Materials: —— **Pointer to documents**

History: **Creation, changes,** **that illustrate and**
deletions, etc. **explain this requirement**

Volere
Copyright © Atlantic Systems Guild

Degree of stakeholder happiness if this requirement is
successfully implemented.
Scale from 1 = uninterested to 5 = extremely pleased.

Measure of stakeholder unhappiness if this
requirement is not part of the final product.
Scale from 1 = hardly matters to 5 = extremely
displeased.

1. The Purpose of the Project

The first section of the template deals with the fundamental reason your client asked you to build a new product. That is, it describes the business problem the client faces and explains how the product is intended to solve the problem.

1a. The User Business or Background of the Project Effort

Content

This part of the specification consists of a short description of the business being done, its context, and the situation that triggered the development effort. It should also describe the work that the user intends to do with the delivered product.

Motivation

Without this statement, the project lacks justification and direction.

Considerations

You should consider whether the business problem is serious, and whether and why it needs to be solved.

Perhaps there are no serious problems, just a significant business opportunity your client wishes to exploit. In this case, describe the opportunity.

Alternatively, the project may seek to explore or investigate possibilities. In this case, the project deliverable, instead of a new product, would be a document proving that the requirements for a product can (or cannot) be satisfied.

Form

A short text description is often sufficient to provide an understanding of the project. You can choose to support the description with some combination of a current situation model, business process models, samples of current documents, photographs and videos of the current situation, website addresses, and organization charts.

1b. Goals of the Project

Content

This part of the specification describes what we want the product to do and which advantage it will bring to the overall goals of the work. Do not be too wordy in this section—a brief explanation of the project's goals is usually more valuable than a long, rambling treatise. A short, sharp goal will be clearer to the stakeholders and improve the chances of reaching a consensus for the goal.

Motivation

There is a danger that this purpose may get lost along the way. As the development effort heats up, and as the customer and developers discover more about what is possible, the system could potentially wander away from the original goals as it undergoes construction. This is a bad thing unless there is some deliberate act by the client to change the goals. It may be necessary to appoint a person to act as custodian of the goals, but it is probably sufficient to make the goals public and periodically remind the developers of them. *It should be mandatory to acknowledge the goals at every review session.*

Examples

> We want to give immediate and complete response to customers who order our goods online.
>
> To reduce road accidents by accurately forecasting and scheduling the de-icing of roads.

Measurement

Any reasonable goal must be measurable. This is necessary if you are ever to test whether you have succeeded with the project. The measurement must quantify the *advantage* gained by the business through doing the project. If the project is worthwhile, there must be some solid business reason for doing it. Suppose the goal of the project is this:

> We want to give immediate and complete response to customers who order our goods online.

You must ask which advantage meeting this goal brings to the organization. If an immediate response will result in more satisfied customers, then the measurement must quantify that satisfaction. For example, you could measure the increase in repeat business (on the basis that a happy customer comes back for more), the increase in customer approval ratings from surveys, the increase in revenue from returning customers, and so on.

Ask which type of goal is involved:

- *Service goal:* This is measured by quantifying what it does for the customer.
- *Revenue goal:* Quantify how much revenue or revenue growth occurs over which period of time. Alternatively, a revenue goal could be quantified by market share.
- *Legal goal:* This is not a quantification, but rather a way of knowing that the product conforms to a piece of legislation (this could be the law of the land or it might be a standard of your industry or organization).

It is crucial to the rest of the development effort that the goal is firmly established, is reasonable, and is measured. It is usually the latter that makes the former possible.

Form

You can use the Purpose, Advantage, Measurement (PAM) technique to structure your goal:

- *Purpose:* One sentence that explains the organization's reason for investing in the project
- *Advantage:* One sentence that describes the benefit that the organization will realize if the project is successful
- *Measurement:* One sentence or a graph or diagram that quantifies the benefit the new product is to deliver

Another form for your goals might be to use some kind of goal model. For example, the Extended Enterprise Modeling Language (EEML) includes a goal modeling technique. If your organization is using enterprise modeling then this provides a connection between the enterprise's strategic goals and the goal of an individual project.

2. The Stakeholders

This section describes the stakeholders—the people who have an interest in the product. It is worth your while to spend enough time to accurately determine and describe these people, as the penalty for not knowing who they are can be very high.

2a. The Client

Content

This item gives the name of the client (sometimes referred to as the sponsor). It is permissible to have several names, but having more than three negates the point.

Motivation

The client has the final say on acceptance of the product and, therefore, must be satisfied with the product as delivered. You can think of the client as the person who makes the investment in the product. Where the product is being developed for in-house consumption, the same person often fills the roles of the client and the customer. If you cannot find a name for your client, then perhaps you should not be building the product.

Considerations

Sometimes, when building a package or a product for external users, the client is the marketing department. In this case, a person from the marketing department must be named as the client.

Form

- An annotated organization chart showing where the client fits within the organization
- A list of the decisions for which the client will be responsible

You can also include a chart showing the review checkpoints and itemizing what you will provide for the client as progress indicators for the project.

2b. The Customer

Content

The customer is the person intended to buy the product. In the case of in-house development, the client and the customer are probably the same person. The customer might also be the manager who decides whether the people for whom he is responsible will adopt a new/changed product.

In the case of development of a mass-market product, this section contains a description of the persona developed as the archetypical customer for the product (see Section 2e).

Motivation

The customer is ultimately responsible for deciding whether to buy or recommend the use of the product. The correct requirements can be gathered only if you understand the customer and his aspirations when it comes to using your product.

Form

A list of the decisions for which the customer will be responsible.

You can also include a chart showing the review checkpoints and itemizing what you will provide for the customer as progress indicators for the project. This might include a list of possible prototypes or simulations that you will provide for the customer during the progress of the project.

2c. Other Stakeholders

Content

The roles and (if possible) names of other people and organizations who are affected by the product, or whose input is needed to build the product. These stakeholders might work for your organization but might be external.

Examples of stakeholders:

- Client/sponsor (refer to Section 2a)
- Customer (refer to Section 2b)
- Subject-matter experts
- Members of the public
- Users of the current system
- Marketing experts
- Legal experts
- Domain experts

- Usability experts
- Representatives of external associations
- Business analysts
- Designers and developers
- Testers
- Systems engineers
- Software engineers
- Technology experts
- System designers

For a complete checklist, download the stakeholder analysis template from www.volere.co.uk.

For each type of stakeholder, provide the following information:

- Stakeholder identification (some combination of role/job title, person name, and organization name)
- Knowledge that the project needs from that stakeholder
- The degree of involvement necessary for that stakeholder/knowledge combination
- The degree of influence for that stakeholder/knowledge combination
- Agreement on how to address conflicts between stakeholders who have an interest in the same knowledge

Motivation

Failure to recognize stakeholders results in missing requirements.

Form

A stakeholder map supported by the name of the representative of each role, together with the knowledge to be supplied by that role. The following diagram is a generic stakeholder map that you can use as a checklist and replace the role names with the specific people/roles/organizations for your project.

Another form you can use to identify the stakeholders is a stakeholder analysis spreadsheet. A sample can be downloaded from www.volere.co.uk.

An annotated organization chart is also a useful form for defining stakeholders.

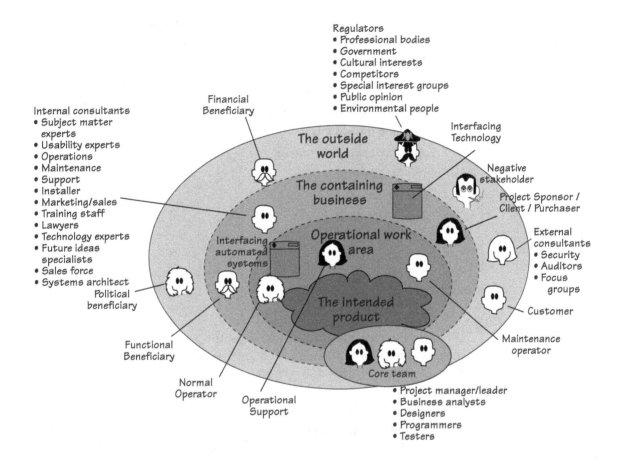

Regulators
- Professional bodies
- Government
- Cultural interests
- Competitors
- Special interest groups
- Public opinion
- Environmental people

Financial
Beneficiary

Interfacing
Technology

Internal consultants
- Subject matter
  experts
- Usability experts
- Operations
- Maintenance
- Support
- Installer
- Marketing/sales
- Training staff
- Lawyers
- Technology experts
- Future ideas
  specialists
- Sales force
- Systems architect

Political
beneficiary

The outside
world

The containing
business

Negative
stakeholder

Project Sponsor /
Client / Purchaser

Interfacing
automated
systems

Operational work
area

External
consultants
- Security
- Auditors
- Focus
  groups

The intended
product

Customer

Functional
Beneficiary

Maintenance
operator

Normal
Operator

Operational
Support

Core team

- Project manager/leader
- Business analysts
- Designers
- Programmers
- Testers

2d. The Hands-on Users of the Product

Content

A list of special types of stakeholders—the potential users of the product. For each category of user, provide the following information:

- User name/category: Most likely the name of a user group, such as clerical users, schoolchildren, road engineers, or project managers.

- User role: Summarizes the users' responsibilities.

- Subject-matter experience: Summarizes the users' knowledge of the subject matter/business. Rate as novice, journeyman, or master.

- Technological experience: Describes the users' experience with relevant technology. Rate as novice, journeyman, or master.

- Other user characteristics: Describe any characteristics of the users that have an effect on the requirements and eventual design of the product. For example:

Physical abilities/disabilities

Intellectual abilities/disabilities

Attitude toward job

Attitude toward technology

Physical location

Education

Linguistic skills

Age group

Gender

Ethnic group(s)

Motivation

Users are human beings who interact with the product in some way. Use the characteristics of the users to define the usability requirements for the product. Users are also known as *actors*.

Examples

Users can come from wide variety of (sometimes unexpected) sources. Consider the possibility of your users being clerical staff, shop workers, managers, highly trained operators, the general public, casual users, passersby, illiterate people, tradesmen, students, test engineers, foreigners, children, lawyers, remote users, people using the system over the telephone or an Internet connection, emergency workers, and so on.

Form

A simple list or a spreadsheet containing the user characteristics for each user role + user name/representative.

2e. Personas

Content

A story about an invented person that includes the persona's name, age, job, family, hobbies, residence, favorite food, favorite music, likes, dislikes, holiday destinations, attitude toward technology, attitude toward money, or any other characteristic that could influence the way that the persona thinks about the product. It helps if you include a photograph (download one from the Internet) to represent the imagined person.

Motivation

By having one or more (limit it to three) personas, you can make the requirements specific to the people whom you are trying to satisfy. This is a particularly effective technique if you are specifying the requirements for a consumer product or a product that will be used by members of the public.

Form

A profile containing the life story of the persona, including a photograph of the person. The profile can take the form of a document that you use to introduce project participants to the persona. You can also put the profile onto a large-format (A3) card that you display at meetings to remind participants about whose requirements you are trying to discover. Another idea is to build a storyboard of the persona's life. In addition, you can make a website for the persona and keep him or her alive by adding more about the persona's everyday life. All of these forms of capturing and communicating the persona are intended to help people think of the persona as a real user with specific—rather than general—real requirements.

2f. Priorities Assigned to Users

Content

Attach a priority to each category of user, which identifies the importance and precedence of the user. Prioritize the users as follows:

- Key users: They are critical to the continued success of the product. Give greater importance to requirements generated by this category of user.

- Secondary users: They will use the product, but their opinion of it has no effect on its long-term success. Where there is a conflict between secondary users' requirements and those of key users, the key users take precedence.

- Unimportant users: This category of user is given the lowest priority. It includes infrequent, unauthorized, and unskilled users, as well as people who misuse the product.

The percentage of the potential customer base represented by each type of user is intended to help you determine the amount of consideration to be given to each category of user.

Motivation

If some users are considered to be more important to the product or to the organization, then this preference should be stated because it should affect the way that you design the product. For instance, you need to know whether a large customer group has specifically asked for the product and that, if they do not get what they want, the results could be a significant loss of business.

Some users may be listed as having no impact on the product. These users will make use of the product, but have no vested interest in it. In other words, these users will neither complain nor contribute. Any special requirements from these users will have a lower design priority.

Form

Include the user importance rating on your user characteristics spreadsheet (see Section 2d) for the information of the core project team. Depending on the culture of your organization, you might need to treat this as sensitive information.

2g. User Participation

Content

Where appropriate, attach to the category of user a statement of the participation that you think will be necessary for those users to provide the requirements. Describe the contribution that you expect these users to provide—for example, business knowledge, interface prototyping, or usability requirements. If possible, assess the minimum amount of time that these users must spend for you to be able to determine the complete requirements.

Motivation

Many projects fail because of lack of user participation, and sometimes because the required degree of participation was not made clear. When people have to make a choice between getting their everyday work done and working on a new project, the everyday work usually takes priority. This requirement makes it clear, from the outset, that specified user resources must be allocated to the project.

Form

Include the estimated user participation time, together with the type of knowledge you expect that user to provide, on your user characteristics spreadsheet (see Section 2d).

2h. Maintenance Users and Service Technicians

Content

Maintenance users are a special type of hands-on users who have requirements that are specific to maintaining and changing the product.

Motivation

Many of these requirements will be discovered by considering the various types of maintenance requirements detailed in Section 14. However, if we define the characteristics of the people who maintain the product, it will help to trigger requirements that might otherwise be missed.

Form

Include the maintenance users on your user characteristics spreadsheet (see Section 2d).

3. Mandated Constraints

This section describes constraints on the eventual design of the product.

Constraints are global—they are factors that apply to the entire product. The product must be built within the stated constraints. Often you know about the constraints, or they are mandated before the project gets underway. They are probably determined by management and are worth considering carefully—they restrict what you can do and, therefore, shape the product. Constraints, like other types of requirements, have a description, rationale, and fit criterion, and generally are written in the same format as functional and non-functional requirements.

3a. Solution Constraints

Content

The content specifies constraints on the way that the problem must be solved. Describe the mandated technology or solution. Include any appropriate version numbers. You should also explain the reason for using the technology.

Motivation

Your goal is to identify constraints that guide the final product. Your client, customer, or user may have design preferences, or perhaps only certain solutions may be acceptable. If these constraints are not met, your solution is not acceptable.

Examples

Constraints are written using the same form as other atomic requirements (refer to the requirements snow card/shell for the attributes). It is important for each constraint to have a rationale and a fit criterion, as these elements help to expose false constraints (i.e., solutions masquerading as constraints). Also, you will usually find that a constraint affects the entire product rather than one or more product use cases.

> *Description: The product shall use the current two-way radio system to communicate with the drivers in their trucks.*
>
> *Rationale: The client will not pay for a new radio system, nor are any other means of communication available to the drivers.*
>
> *Fit Criterion: All signals generated by the product shall be audible and understandable by all drivers via their two-way radio system.*

> *Description: The product shall operate using Windows XP.*
>
> *Rationale: The client uses XP and does not wish to change to a later version.*
>
> *Fit Criterion: The product shall be approved as XP-compliant by the MS testing group.*

> *Description: The product shall be a hand-held device.*
>
> *Rationale: The product is to be marketed to hikers and mountain climbers.*
>
> *Fit Criterion: The product shall weigh no more than 300 grams, it shall be no more than 15 x 10 x 2 centimeters, and there shall be no external power source.*

Considerations

We want to define the boundaries within which we can solve the problem. Be careful when doing so, however, because anyone who has experience with or exposure to a piece of technology tends to see requirements in terms of that technology. This tendency leads people to impose solution constraints for the wrong reason, making it very easy for false constraints to creep into a specification. The solution constraints should be only those limits that are absolutely non-negotiable. In other words, no matter how you solve this problem, you must use this particular technology; any other solution would be unacceptable.

Form

Include the constraint requirements as a specific type of atomic requirement in your requirements spreadsheet or database. For attributes of an atomic requirement, see the atomic requirements shell example at the beginning of this template. Also refer to the article on atomic requirements at www.volere.co.uk.

Another form for constraints can be diagrams of the systems architecture for the new/changed product (see Sections 3b and 3c).

3b. Implementation Environment of the Current System

Content

This section describes the technological and physical environment in which the product is to be installed. It includes automated, mechanical, organizational, and other devices, along with the nonhuman adjacent systems.

Motivation

The goal is to describe the technological environment into which the product must fit. The environment places design constraints on the product. This part of the specification provides enough information about the environment for the designers to make the product successfully interact with its surrounding technology.

The operational requirements are derived from this description.

Examples

Examples can be shown as a diagram, with some kind of icon to represent each separate device or person (processor). Add interfaces between the processors, and annotate them with their form and content.

Considerations

All component parts of the current system, regardless of their type, should be included in the description of the implementation environment.

If the product is to affect, or be important to, the current organization, then include an organization chart.

Form

A diagram that represents each hardware and software component/subcomponent/device/building block that will be used to implement the product. The particular diagrams that you use will depend on your organization and your projects' ways of working. The important issue here is that the implementation environment is unambiguously understandable by the people who must make decisions about how the functional and non-functional requirements will be implemented. Types of UML diagrams commonly used include class, component, component structure, deployment, and package diagrams. Many other home-grown diagrams are possible as well.

3c. Partner or Collaborative Applications

Content

This part of the specification describes applications that are not part of the product but with which the product will collaborate. They can be external applications, commercial packages, or preexisting in-house applications.

Motivation

The goal is to provide information about design constraints caused by using partner applications. By describing or modeling these partner applications, you discover and highlight potential problems of integration.

Examples

This section can be completed by including written descriptions, models, or references to other specifications. The descriptions must include a full specification of all interfaces that have an effect on the product.

Considerations

Examine the work context model to determine whether any of the adjacent systems should be treated as partner applications. It might also be necessary to examine some of the details of the work to discover relevant partner applications.

Form

A diagram or table that identifies all the interfaces between the product to be built and other adjacent systems. Bear in mind that the adjacent systems might be software, human, or hardware. Some adjacent systems are within your organization and hence potentially more easily understood and perhaps influenced. Other adjacent systems may reside outside your organization and might be difficult, if not impossible, to influence. A product scope diagram (see Section 8a for an example) is often used to define interfaces with partner or collaborative applications.

3d. Off-the-Shelf Software

Content

This section describes commercial, open-source, or any other off-the-shelf (OTS) software that must be used to implement some of the requirements for the product. It could also apply to non-software OTS components such as hardware or any other commercial product that is intended to be part of the solution.

Motivation

The goal is to identify and describe existing commercial, free, open-source, or other products to be incorporated into the eventual product. The characteristics, behavior, and interfaces of the package represent design constraints.

Considerations

When gathering requirements, you may discover requirements that conflict with the behavior and characteristics of the OTS software. Keep in mind that the use of OTS software was mandated before the full extent of the requirements became known. In light of your discoveries, you must consider whether the OTS product is a viable choice. If the use of the OTS software is not negotiable, then the conflicting requirements must be discarded.

Note that your strategy for discovering requirements is affected by the decision to use OTS software. In this situation you investigate the work context in parallel with making comparisons with the capabilities of the OTS product. Depending on the comprehensibility of the OTS software, you might be able to discover the matches or mismatches without having to write each of the business requirements in atomic detail. The mismatches are the requirements that you will need to specify so that you can decide whether to satisfy them by either modifying the OTS software, satisfying the requirement in another way, or modifying the business requirements.

Given the spate of lawsuits in the software arena, you should consider whether any legal implications might arise from your use of OTS. You can cover this issue in Section 17, Legal Requirements.

Form

Models or written documentation that specifies the functional and nonfunctional requirements that can be implemented using this OTS software product. If the OTS product has a well-structured requirements specification and systems architecture model, then that model provides you with the basis for identifying which of your requirements can be satisfied by the product. If the product's documentation is not traceable and well organized, then you will need to do more detailed work on your own requirements until you find a level at which you can map your requirements to the OTS product.

Another form is one or more people who are experts in the OTS product and who can answer your questions so that you do not have to puzzle through cryptic or marketing-oriented documents.

3e. Anticipated Workplace Environment

Content

This section describes the workplace in which the users are to work and use the product. It should describe any features of the workplace that could have an effect on the design of the product, and the social and cultural aspects of the workplace.

Motivation

To identify characteristics of the workplace so that the product is designed to compensate for any difficulties.

Examples

> The single office printer is a considerable distance from the user's desk. This constraint suggests that printed output should be deemphasized.
>
> The workplace is noisy, so audible signals might not work.
>
> The workplace is outside, so the product must be weather resistant, have displays that are visible in sunlight, and allow for the effect of wind on any paper output.
>
> The product is to be used in a library; it must be extra-quiet.
>
> The product is a printer to be used by an environmentally conscious organization; it must work with recycled paper.
>
> The user will be standing up and working in positions where he must hold the product. This suggests a hand-held product, but only a careful study of the users' work and workplace will provide the necessary input to identifying the operational requirements.

Considerations

The physical work environment constrains the way that work is done. The product should overcome whatever difficulties exist; however, you might consider a redesign of the workplace as an alternative to having the product compensate for such challenges.

Form

- A written description of the workplace
- Rich pictures showing all the components in the workplace
- Photographs of the workplace
- Videos of the workplace

3f. Schedule Constraints

Content

Any known deadlines, or windows of opportunity, should be stated here.

Motivation

The goal is to identify critical times and dates that have an effect on product requirements. If the deadline is short, then the requirements must be kept to whatever can be built within the time allowed.

Examples

- To meet scheduled software releases.
- Other parts of the business or other software products that are dependent on this product.
- Windows of marketing opportunity.
- Scheduled changes to the business that will use your product. For example, the organization may be starting up a new factory and your product is needed before production can commence.

Considerations

State deadline limitations by giving the date and describing why it is critical. Also, identify prior dates where parts of your product need to be available for testing.

You should also ask questions about the implications of not meeting the deadline:

- What happens if we don't build the product by the end of the calendar year?
- What is the financial impact of not having the product by the beginning of the Christmas buying season?
- Which parts of the product are most critical for the Christmas buying season?

Form

A written statement giving the date of the deadline, the reason for the deadline, and the effect of not meeting the deadline.

3g. Budget Constraints

Content

This section shows the budget for the project, expressed in money or available resources.

Motivation

The requirements must not exceed the budget. This limitation may constrain the number of requirements that can be included in the product.

The intention of this question is to determine whether the product is really wanted.

Considerations

The intention is to restrict the wildest ambitions and to prevent the team from gathering requirements for an Airbus 380 when the budget can buy only a Cessna. Is it realistic to build a product within this budget? If the answer to this question is no, then either the client is not really committed to building the product or the client does not place enough value on the product. In either case, you should consider whether it is worthwhile continuing.

Form

A written statement giving the amount of the budget and the source of the funding.

3h. Enterprise Constraints

Content

This section contains requirements that are specific to the enterprise that is making the investment in your project.

Motivation

The goal is to understand requirements that sometimes appear irrelevant or irrational because they are not obviously relevant to the goals of the project.

Examples

> *The product shall be installed using only American-made components.*
>
> *The product shall make all functionality available to the CEO.*

Considerations

Did you intend to develop the product on a Macintosh, when the office manager has laid down an edict that only Windows-based machines are permitted?

Is a director also on the board of a company that manufactures products similar to the one that you intend to build?

Whether you agree with these enterprise requirements has little bearing on the outcome. The reality is that the system has to comply with enterprise requirements even if you can find a better, more efficient, or more economical solution. A few probing questions here may save some heartache later.

The enterprise requirements might be purely concerned with the politics inside your organization. In other situations, you may need to consider the politics inside your customers' organizations or the national politics of the country. Another way to think about the enterprise requirements is to view them as constraint requirements that have been defined by strategic decisions that are outside the obvious boundary of your project scope.

4. Naming Conventions and Terminology

It has been our experience that all projects have their own unique vocabulary usually containing a variety of acronyms and abbreviations. Failure to understand this project-specific nomenclature correctly inevitably leads to misunderstandings, hours of lost time, miscommunication between team members, and ultimately poor-quality specifications.

4a. Definitions of All Terms, Including Acronyms, Used by Stakeholders Involved in the Project

Content

A glossary containing the meanings of all names, acronyms, and abbreviations used by the stakeholders. Select names carefully to avoid giving a different, unintended meaning.

If the work that you are studying already has a glossary of terms, then use it as your starting point. This glossary should be enlarged and refined as the analysis proceeds, but for the moment, it should introduce the terms that the stakeholders use and the meanings of those terms. This glossary reflects the terminology in current use within the work area. You might also get started by building on the standard names used within your industry.

For each term, write a description. The appropriate stakeholders must agree on this description of the meaning of the term.

We suggest that you add *all* acronyms and abbreviations. We often encounter situations where team members use acronyms, but admit they do not know the meanings of those acronyms. This section gives you a place to register your acronyms.

Motivation

Names are very important. They invoke meanings that, if carefully defined, can save hours of explanations. Giving due attention to names early in the project helps to highlight misunderstandings.

As the detailed work progresses, the glossary provides input to the more precisely specified business/work data model and data dictionary (see Section 7 of the template). As the analysis data dictionary evolves, many of the definitions from the glossary are expanded in the dictionary by adding their data composition.

Examples

> Truck: A vehicle used for spreading de-icing material on roads. "Truck" is not used to refer to goods-carrying vehicles.
>
> BIS: Business Intelligence Service. The department run by Steven Peters to supply business intelligence for the rest of the organization.
>
> Thermal Map: A region or other geographical area is surveyed to determine the temperature differences at various parts of the area. The resulting thermal map means the temperature at any part of the area can be determined by knowing the temperature at a reference point.

Considerations

Make use of existing references and existing data dictionaries. Obviously, it is best to avoid renaming existing items unless they are so ambiguous that they cause confusion.

From the beginning of the project, emphasize the need to avoid homonyms and synonyms. Explain how they increase the cost of the project.

Form

An existing glossary of terms, a pointer to industry dictionaries, or a list of terms commonly used in the problem domain along with a sentence describing the meaning and purpose of each term.

5. Relevant Facts and Assumptions

Relevant facts are external factors that have an effect on the product but are not covered by other sections in the requirements template. They are not necessarily translated into requirements, although they could be. Relevant facts alert the developers to conditions and factors that have a bearing on the requirements.

5a. Relevant Facts

Content

This section identifies factors that have an effect on the product, but are not mandated requirements constraints. Facts provide the reader of the specification with more background for understanding the business problem.

Motivation

Relevant facts provide background information to the specification readers, and might contribute to requirements. They will have an effect on the eventual design of the product.

Examples

> One ton of de-icing material will treat three miles of single-lane roadway.
>
> The existing application is 10,000 lines of C code.

5b. Business Rules

Content

These business rules might have an impact on the work/business/domain that is the source of the requirements. Relevant business rules will be the trigger for requirements.

Motivation

Business rules are mentioned at all stages of the requirements discovery process. It is often difficult to immediately ascertain whether a business rule is or is not relevant to the project that you are doing. This section provides a place to capture the business rules and, as understanding of the work increases, to revisit them and use them as triggers to discover relevant requirements.

Examples

> The maximum length of a truck driver's shift is 8 hours.
>
> The engineers maintain the weather stations once a week.

Form

A written statement describing the business rule, the reason for the rule, the authority for the rule.

At the start of a new project, determine whether at least some relevant business rules have already been defined. If so, their existence sets you on the road to requirements reuse. When your project discovers a new or changed business rule, add it to the *business rule book* for your enterprise. The business rule book then becomes input to, and is updated by, every project.

You might include business process models (many different forms exist) to illustrate how the business rule affects the organization.

5c. Assumptions

Content

This part of the specification lists the assumptions that the developers are making. These assumptions might be about the intended operational environment, but can be about anything that has an effect on the product. As part of managing expectations, assumptions also contain statements about what the product will *not* do.

Motivation

The intention is to make people declare the assumptions that they are making, as well as to make everyone on the project aware of assumptions that have already been made.

Examples

- Assumptions about new laws or political decisions.
- Assumptions about what your developers expect to be ready in time for them to use—for example, other parts of your products, the completion of other projects, software tools, or software components.
- Assumptions about the technological environment in which the product will operate. These assumptions should highlight areas of expected compatibility.
- The software components that will be available to the developers.
- Other products being developed at the same time as this one.
- The availability and capability of bought-in components.
- Dependencies on computer systems or people external to this project
- The requirements that will specifically *not* be carried out by the product.

Some specific examples of assumptions from the IceBreaker project include the following:

> *Roads that have been treated will not need treatment again for at least 2 hours.*
>
> *Road treatment stops at county boundaries.*
>
> *Road Engineering's Apian system will be available for integration testing before November.*
>
> *The treatment trucks being built will be capable of operating at speeds up to 40 mph. They will have a material capacity of two tons.*
>
> *The Bureau's forecasts will be transmitted according to Specification 1003-7 issued by its engineering department.*

Considerations

We often make unconscious assumptions. It is necessary to talk to the members of the project team to discover any unconscious assumptions that they have made. Ask stakeholders (both technical and business related) questions such as these:

- Which software tools are you expecting to be available?
- Will there be any new software products?
- Are you expecting to use a current product in a new way?
- Are there any business changes you are assuming we will be able to deal with?

It is important to state these assumptions upfront. You might also consider the likelihood that the assumption is correct and, where relevant, provide a list of alternatives if something that is assumed does not happen.

The assumptions are intended to be transient. That is, they should all be cleared by the time the specification is released—the assumption should have become either a requirement or a constraint. For example, if the assumption relates to the capability of a product that is intended to be a partner product to yours, then the capability should have been proven satisfactory, and it becomes a constraint to use it. Conversely, if the bought-in product is not suitable, then it becomes a requirement for the project team to construct the needed capability.

Form

A written statement describing the assumption along with the effect on the project if the assumption is false. Depending on the complexity of the assumption, it might be necessary to include references to other documents or people.

Understanding of assumptions can be explored and shared by using cause-and-effect diagrams such as Peter Senge's dynamics models.

6. The Scope of the Work

The scope of the work determines the boundaries of the business area to be studied and outlines how it fits into its environment. Once you understand the work and its constraints, you can establish the scope of the product (see Section 8 of the template).

6a. The Current Situation

Content

This part of the specification is an analysis of the existing business processes, including the manual and automated processes that might be replaced or changed by the new product. In terms of the Volere Brown Cow Model, you refer to this view as the "How-Now" view. Business analysts might already have performed this investigation as part of the business case analysis for the project. This is where it might be appropriate to build some business process models. The models include roles, individuals, departments, technology, and procedures. They illustrate the workflow and the dependencies between the components of the process.

Motivation

If your project intends to make changes to an existing manual or automated system, you need to understand the effect of the proposed changes. The study of the current situation provides the basis for understanding the effects of proposed changes and choosing the best alternatives. Business process modeling does not always lead to building software. Instead, some changes in procedures and the way roles are allocated might be the best way of making a necessary improvement.

Form

Many different notations are suitable for building business process models—for example, activity diagrams, business process diagrams, swim lane diagrams, and data flow diagrams.

6b. The Context of the Work

Content

The work context diagram identifies the boundaries of the work that you need to investigate to be able to build the product. Note that it includes more than the intended product. Unless you understand the work that the product will support, you have little chance of building a product that will fit cleanly into its environment.

The adjacent systems on the example context diagram (e.g., Weather Forecasting Service) indicate other subject-matter domains (i.e., systems, people, and organizations) that need to be understood. The interfaces between the adjacent systems and the work context indicate why we are interested in the adjacent system. In the case of Weather Forecasting Service, we are interested in the details of when, how, where, who, what, and why it produces the District Weather Forecasts information.

Motivation

The goal is to clearly define the boundary for the study of the work and hence the requirements effort. Without this definition, we have little chance of building a product that will fit seamlessly into its environment.

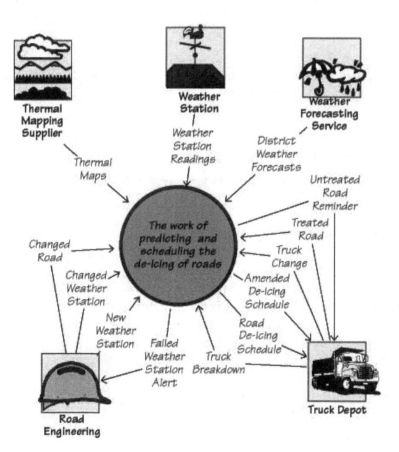

Examples

This work context model defines the connections between the part of the world that is under investigation and other people, organizations, hardware, and software (referred to as adjacent systems). The inputs and outputs represent the data and material that travel between the work and other parts of the world. The work context is the basis for partitioning the investigation and discovering the requirements.

Considerations

The names used on the context diagram should be consistent with the naming conventions (Section 4) and should eventually be defined in the data dictionary (Section 7). Without these definitions, the context model lacks the required rigor, and may be misunderstood. Relevant stakeholders must agree to the definitions of the interfaces shown on the context model.

Form

- A diagram showing the inputs and outputs that flow between the work and the adjacent systems

or

- A table that identifies all the inputs and outputs that flow between the work and the adjacent systems

The names of the inputs and outputs are eventually defined in the data dictionary (see Section 7b).

6c. Work Partitioning

Content

This part of the specification lists all business events to which the work responds. Business events are happenings in the real world that affect the work. They may also occur because it is time for the work to do something—for example, produce weekly reports, remind nonpaying customers, check the status of a device, and so on. The response to each event is called a business use case (BUC); it represents a discrete functional partition of work.

The event list includes the following elements:

- Event name
- Input or triggering data flow from adjacent systems (identical to the name on the context diagram)
- Outputs to adjacent systems (identical to the names on the context diagram)

- Brief summary of the business use case (This is optional, but we have found it to be a very useful first step in defining the requirements for the business use case—you can think of it as a mini-scenario.)

- Classes of business data relevant to this event (You won't know this early in the study of the event; as you go into detail, you will start to understand the essential data and you can add it to the event list.)

Motivation

The goal is to identify logical chunks of the work that can be used as the basis for discovering detailed requirements. These business events also provide the subsystems that can be used as the basis for managing detailed analysis and design. Each business event has a business use case whose details can be studied independently. However, all BUCs connect to each other through the stored business data (see Section 7).

Example

Business Event List

Event Name	Input and Output	Summary of BUC
1. Weather Station transmits reading	Weather Station Readings (in)	Record the readings as belonging to the weather station.
2. Weather Service forecasts weather	District Weather Forecast (in)	Record the forecast.
3. Road engineers advise changed roads	Changed Road (in)	Record the new or changed road. Check that all appropriate weather stations are attached.
4. Road Engineering installs new Weather Station	New Weather Station (in)	Record the weather station and attach it to the appropriate roads.
5. Road Engineering changes Weather Station	Changed Weather Station (in)	Record the changes to the weather station.
6. Time to test Weather Stations	Failed Weather Station Alert (out)	Determine whether any weather stations have not transmitted for two hours, and inform Road Engineering of any failures.
7. Truck Depot changes a truck	Truck Change (in)	Record the changes to the truck.
8. Time to detect icy roads	Road De-icing Schedule (out)	Predict the ice situation for the next two hours. Assign a truck to any roads that will freeze. Issue the schedule.
9. Truck treats a road	Treated Road (in)	Record the road as being in a safe condition for the next three hours.

continues

Event Name	Input and Output	Summary of BUC
10. Truck Depot reports a problem with a truck	Truck Breakdown (in) Amended Gritting Schedule (out)	Reassign available trucks to the previously assigned roads.
11. Time to monitor road treatment	Untreated Road Reminder (out)	Check that all scheduled roads have been treated in the assigned time, and issue reminders for any untreated roads.

Considerations

Attempting to list the business events and create a one-sentence summary of each BUC is a way of testing the work context. This activity uncovers uncertainties and misunderstandings about the project and facilitates precise communications. When you perform an event analysis, it will usually prompt you to make some changes to your work context diagram.

We suggest that you gather requirements for discrete sections of the work. Doing so requires you to partition the work, and we have found business events to be the most convenient, consistent, and natural way to break the work into manageable units and to be able to trace the details back to the scope of the work.

Form

Business event list/table containing the following information for each event: event number, event name, name of input, name of output(s), summary of the business event response. The names on the business event list must match the names on the work context model/table (see Section 6b).

6d. Specifying a Business Use Case

Content

This part comprises a specification of the details of how a business use case (BUC) responds to a business event.

Motivation

The purpose is to understand the detailed business response that must be carried out when a business event takes place and to provide a basis for discovering the detailed requirements. The understanding of the BUC also provides a basis for discussing which parts of the BUC should be carried out by the product that will be built.

Example

In the sample specifications included with the download of this template, you will find examples of BUC scenarios.

Considerations

Whatever approach you use to specify the details of a BUC, you should stay within the boundary of the input and output(s) for that business event. If you discover additional input or output data, then you need to change the input/output data both on the event list and on the work context diagram.

Form

A BUC can be specified using any combination of models that suits the analyst. The most commonly used approaches are activity diagrams, BUC scenarios, process flow diagrams, sequence diagrams, mind maps, and interview notes. The only caveat is that the inputs and outputs on your BUC must be precisely the same and hence traceable to the inputs and outputs on the corresponding business event.

7. Business Data Model and Data Dictionary

7a. Data Model

Content

This part consists of a specification of the essential subject matter, business objects, entities, and classes that are germane to the product. It might take the form of a first-cut class model, an entity relationship model, or any other kind of data model.

Motivation

The goal is to clarify the system's subject matter, thereby triggering recognition of requirements not yet considered. To discover missing requirements, you can cross-check the data model and the events using a Create, Reference, Update, Delete (CRUD) table. The data model is a specification for all business data that is relevant to the scope of the work.

Example

This example is a model of the business system's business subject matter using the Unified Modeling Language (UML) class model notation. It identifies all of the data that is created, referenced, updated, and deleted by processes within the scope of the work being studied. See Section 6 for more on the scope of the work.

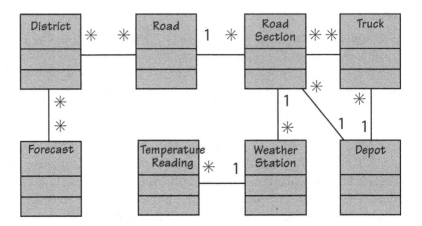

In this model, each of the rectangles represents a class of business data. The attributes of that class are defined in the data dictionary. For example:

District = A geographical area defined by the council

District Name + District Size + District Coordinates

Similarly, each attribute is also defined in the dictionary:

District Name = The unique name used by the engineers to identify a district

You can use any type of data or class model to capture this knowledge. The point is to capture the meaning of the business subject matter and the connections between the individual parts, and to show that you are consistent within your project. If you have an established company standard notation, use that, as it will help you to reuse knowledge between projects.

For more examples of data models, look at the example specifications that are packaged with the download of this requirements template.

Considerations

Are there any data or object models for similar or overlapping systems that might serve as a useful starting point? Is there a domain model for the subject matter dealt with by this system?

Form

You can use many different types of data models to model the business data, although you are most likely to encounter the following models:

- UML class model
- Entity relationship diagrams
- A table showing the class name, associations between classes, and attributes for each class

If your organization prefers a particular model, then you must use that one. Whichever type of model you use, note one important caveat: The data model that you build is a *business data model,* not a design for a database. Your model is concerned with identifying business classes by making a logical partitioning of all data within the work context and the necessary business relationships between those business classes. Your model is used as input to designing how the data will be implemented. The definitions of the attributes in each business class are found in the data dictionary (see Section 7b).

7b. Data Dictionary

The glossary described earlier in Section 4 of the template serves as the starting point for establishing common understanding of terminology. As you begin to define the scope of the investigation, you define the data inputs and outputs in a formal data dictionary. The terms that you define in this dictionary, right down to elemental level, are the same terms that you use when defining detailed atomic requirements.

Content

The data dictionary specifies the content of the following items:

- Classes in the data model
- Attributes of the classes
- Associations between the classes
- Inputs and outputs for all models
- Elements of data within the inputs and outputs

When implementation decisions are made, the technical specifications for the interfaces should be added to the dictionary.

Motivation

The work context diagram provides an accurate definition of the scope of the work being studied, and the product scope diagram (see Sections 8a and 8b) defines the boundary of the product to be built. These definitions can be completely accurate only if the information flows bordering the scope have their attributes defined.

Examples

The following is a partial data dictionary for the road de-icing project we have been using as an example in this template. Note that this version of the dictionary is sorted alphabetically within the type.

Name	Content	Type
Depot	Depot Identifier	Class
District	District Name + District Size	Class
Forecast	Forecast Temperature + Forecast Time	Class
Road	Road Name + Road Number	Class
Road Section	Road Section Identifier + Road Section Coordinates	Class
Temperature Reading	Reading Time + Temperature Measurement	Class
Truck	Truck Identifier	Class
Road De-Icing Schedule	{Road Section Identifier + Treatment Scheduled Date + Treatment Scheduled Start Time + Critical Start Time + Truck Identifier}	Data flow
District Name	Listed in District Catalog	Attribute/element
District Size	Measured in Kilometers	Attribute/element
Forecast Temperature	Measured in Celsius	Attribute/element
Forecast Time	HH/MM/SS 24-hour clock	Attribute/element
Reading Time	HH/MM/SS 24-hour clock	Attribute/element
Road Name	See Road Database	Attribute/element
Road Number	See Road Database	Attribute/element
Road Section Coordinates	See Road Database	Attribute/element
Road Section Identifier	See Road Database	Attribute/element
Temperature Measurement	Measured in Celsius	Attribute/element
Treatment Scheduled Date	YY/MM/DD	Attribute/element
Treatment Scheduled Start Time	HH/MM/SS 24-hour clock	Attribute/element
Truck Identifier	Number between 1 and 1,000; refer to Chief Engineer for list	Attribute/element
Critical Start Time	Treatment started after this time is not guaranteed to be effective	Attribute/element
Treatment Scheduled Date	YY/MM/DD	Attribute/element
Treatment Scheduled Start Time	HH/MM/SS 24-hour clock	Attribute/element

When implementation decisions are eventually made, the format of the data is added to the dictionary by the designers/implementers.

Considerations

The dictionary provides a link between the requirements/business analysts and the designers/developers/implementers. The implementers add implementation details to the terms in the dictionary, defining how the data will be implemented. Moreover, they add terms that are present because of the chosen technology and that are independent of the business requirements.

As you study the work, you will often discover that an entry that you have put in the Naming Conventions and Terminology (Section 4) is actually a specific flow of data or an attribute data. When this happens you should transfer the entry to the data dictionary.

Form

The data dictionary may be maintained in a variety of forms, depending on the tools that you have at your disposal. The important issue is that you make it as easy as possible to cross-reference the use of terms in requirements, documents, and models with their definitions in the dictionary. Forms commonly used for maintaining the data dictionary include spreadsheets, databases, and automated requirements tools.

8. The Scope of the Product

8a. Product Boundary

A use case diagram identifies the boundaries between the users (actors) and the product. You arrive at the product boundary by inspecting each business use case (BUC) and determining, in conjunction with the appropriate stakeholders, which part of the business use case should be automated (or satisfied by some sort of product) and which part should be done by the user or some other product. This task must take into account the abilities of the users/actors (Section 2), the constraints (Section 3), the goals of the project (Section 1), and your knowledge of both the work and the technology that can make the best contribution to the work.

The example use case diagram shows the users/actors outside the product boundary (the rectangle). The product use cases (PUCs) are the ellipses inside the boundary. The numbers link each PUC back to the BUC from which it was derived (see Section 7). The arrows denote usage. In this version of a PUC diagram, we put names on the arrows to make it more precise and traceable. Note that actors can be either automated or human.

You derive the PUCs by deciding where the product boundary should be for each BUC. These decisions are based on your own and appropriate

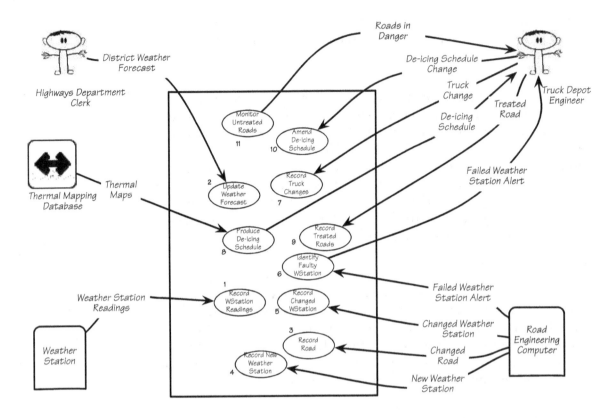

The numbers on this PUC diagram correspond to the BUC numbers on the business event list (see Section 7).

stakeholders' knowledge of the work and the requirements constraints. Your internal design might, and probably will, mean that you will implement a PUC with several system use cases (SUCs).

Example

You can see that the PUC diagram is an effective summary for a small number (fewer than 20 or so) of PUCs. If you have a larger number of PUCs, then a product scope diagram together with a PUC summary table (see Section 8b) is a better approach.

Following is an example of a product scope diagram for the Road De-icing project. The content of each interface on this type of diagram is defined in the data dictionary and can also be supported by a prototype or simulation of some kind. Some projects publish a separate document called the interface specification document. The content of that document would be the definitions of the interfaces on the product scope diagram, often supported by prototypes and models.

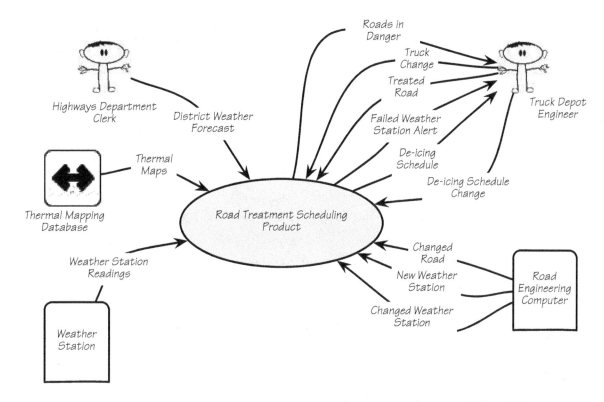

This product scope diagram summarizes the interfaces between the product and the actors/users.

Form

- A product use case diagram
- A product scope diagram supported by individual use case specification
- Specifications and prototypes of the interfaces on the scope diagram

8b. Product Use Case Table

The product scope diagram is a useful summary of all interfaces between the product and other automated systems, organizations, and users. If there are a manageable number of PUCs—say, fewer than 20—then the PUC diagram is useful as a graphical way of summarizing the PUCs relevant to the product. In practice, we have found that a product use case table is more useful because it can handle larger numbers of PUCs and it precisely identifies the input and output data that defines the boundary of each PUC.

PUC Number	PUC Name	Actor(s)	Input and Output
1	Record Weather Station Readings	Weather Station	Weather Station Readings (in)
2	Record Weather Forecast	Highways Department Clerk	District Weather Forecast (in)
3	Record Roads	Road Engineering Computer	Changed Road (in)
4	Record New Weather Station	Road Engineering Computer	New Weather Station (in)
5	Record Changed Weather Station	Road Engineering Computer	Changed Weather Station (in)
6	Identify Faulty Weather Stations	Truck Depot Engineer	Failed Weather Station Alert (out)
7	Record Truck Changes	Truck Depot Engineer	Truck Change (in)
8	Produce De-icing Schedule	Truck Depot Engineer	De-icing Schedule (out)
		Thermal Mapping Database	Thermal Maps (in)
9	Record Treated Roads	Truck Depot Engineer	Treated Road (in)
10	Amend De-icing Schedule	Truck Depot Engineer	De-icing Schedule Change (in)
			Amended De-icing Schedule (out)
11	Monitor Untreated Roads	Truck Depot Engineer	Roads in Danger (out)

Product Use Case
Summary Table

8c. Individual Product Use Cases

This part of the specification is where you define the details about the individual product use cases listed on your PUC table. You can include a scenario or model for each product use case on your list.

Form

- A text scenario
- A storyboard
- A low-fidelity prototype
- A high-fidelity prototype
- A formal use case specification including exceptions and alternatives
- A sequence diagram, activity diagram, data flow diagram, or any other type of model that is familiar to your project group

9. Functional and Data Requirements

9a. Functional Requirements

Content

This section consists of a specification of each atomic functional requirement. As for all types of atomic requirements (functional, non-functional, constraint), you can use the requirements shell as a guide regarding which attributes should be specified. A full explanation of the atomic requirement and its attributes is included in this template's introductory material.

Motivation

The intention is to specify the detailed functional requirements to be carried out by the product.

Examples

Requirement #: **75**   Requirement Type: **9**   Event/BUC/PUC #: **7, 9**

Description: **The product shall record all the roads that have been treated**

Rationale: **To be able to schedule untreated roads and highlight potential**

Originator: **Arnold Snow - Chief Engineer**

Fit Criterion: **The recorded treated roads shall agree with the drivers' road treatment logs and shall be up to date within 30 minutes of the completion of the road's treatment**

Customer Satisfaction: **3**   Customer Dissatisfaction: **5**

Dependencies: **All requirements using road and scheduling data**   Conflicts: **105**

Supporting Materials: **Work context diagram, terms definitions in section 5**   **Volere**

History: **Created February 29, 2010**   Copyright © Atlantic Systems Guild

---

Fit Criterion

Each functional requirement should have a fit criterion or a test case. Whichever is used, it must be a benchmark that the tester uses to objectively determine whether the implemented product has met the requirement.

Considerations

If you have produced an event/use case list (see Sections 6c, 8a, and 8b), then you can use it to help you trigger the functional requirements for each event/use case. If you have not produced such a list, give each functional requirement a unique number and, to help with traceability, partition these requirements into event/use case–related groups later in the development process.

If you have not identified the product boundary and are not in a position to determine the product use cases (PUCs), you should write the functional and non-functional requirements for the business use cases (BUCs). This is an especially good strategy if you are writing business requirements and asking suppliers to tell you which of your business requirements can be satisfied by their product(s).

Form

The form that you use to capture and maintain your atomic requirements (functional, non-functional, and constraint) depends on the tools that you have available. Volere snow cards are often a useful aid to help you in discovering requirements but, due to the volume of requirements and the need to be able to make changes, some kind of automated form is the best way to manage and maintain your atomic requirements. Common forms for atomic requirements include the following:

- A spreadsheet.
- A database provided with whatever requirements tool(s) you have available. A wide variety of tools are available on the market; refer to www.volere.co.uk/tools for a list.
- An intranet set up by you to maintain and make accessible the atomic requirements and their attributes.
- A custom-built database.

Whatever form you use to record and maintain your requirements, it is important to be consistent with your numbering and terminology so that you can check for completeness and respond to change.

Non-functional Requirements

Sections 10–17 describe the non-functional requirements. The form of these requirements is the same as for the functional requirements as described previously.

10. Look and Feel Requirements

10a. Appearance Requirements

Content

The section contains requirements relating to the spirit of the product. Your client may have made particular demands for the product, such as corporate branding, colors to be used, and so on. This section captures the requirements for the appearance. Do not attempt to design it until the appearance requirements are known.

Motivation

The intention is to ensure that the appearance of the product conforms to the organization's expectations.

Examples

> *The product shall be attractive to a teenage audience.*
>
> *The product shall comply with corporate branding standards.*

Fit Criterion

> *A sampling of representative teenagers shall, without prompting or enticement, start using the product within four minutes of their first encounter with it.*
>
> *The office of branding shall certify that the product complies with the current standards.*

Considerations

Even if you are using prototypes, it is important to understand the requirements for the appearance. The prototype is used to help elicit requirements; it should not be envisioned as a substitute for the requirements.

10b. Style Requirements

Content

This part identifies requirements that specify the mood, style, or feeling of the product, which influences the way a potential customer will see the product. Also, it specifies the stakeholders' intentions for the amount of interaction the user is to have with the product.

In this section, you would also describe the appearance of the package, if this is to be a manufactured product. The package may have some requirements as to its size, style, and consistency with other packages put out by your organization. Keep in mind, if applicable, the European laws on packaging, which require that the package not be significantly larger than the product it encloses.

The style requirements that you record here will guide the designers to create a product as envisioned by your client.

Motivation

Given the state of today's market and people's expectations, we cannot afford to build products that have the wrong style. Once the functional requirements are satisfied, it is often the appearance and style of products that determine whether they are successful. Your task in this section is to determine precisely how the product shall appear to its intended consumer.

Example

> The product shall appear authoritative.

Fit Criterion

> After their first encounter with the product, 70 percent of representative potential customers shall agree they feel they can trust the product.

Considerations

The look and feel requirements specify your client's vision of the product's appearance. The requirements may at first seem to be rather vague (e.g., "conservative and professional appearance"), but these will be quantified by their fit criteria. The fit criteria give you the opportunity to extract from your client precisely what is meant, and give the designer precise instructions on what he is to accomplish.

11. Usability and Humanity Requirements

This section is concerned with requirements that make the product usable and ergonomically acceptable to its hands-on users.

11a. Ease of Use Requirements

Content

This section describes your client's aspirations for how easy it is for the intended users of the product to operate it. The product's usability is derived from the abilities of the expected users of the product and the complexity of its functionality.

The usability requirements should cover properties such as these:

- Efficiency of use: How quickly or accurately the user can use the product.
- Ease of remembering: How much the casual user is expected to remember about using the product.
- Error rates: For some products it is crucial that the user commits very few, or no, errors.
- Overall satisfaction in using the product: This is especially important for commercial, interactive products that face a great deal of competition. Websites are a good example.
- Feedback: How much feedback the user needs to feel confident that the product is actually accurately doing what the user expects. The necessary degree of feedback will be higher for some products (e.g., safety-critical products) than for others.

Motivation

The intention is to guide the product's designers toward building a product that meets the expectations of its eventual users.

Examples

> The product shall be easy for 11-year-old children to use.
>
> The product shall help the user to avoid making mistakes.
>
> The product shall make the users want to use it.
>
> The product shall be used by people with no training, and possibly no understanding of English.

Fit Criterion

These examples may seem simplistic, but they do express the intention of the client. To completely specify what is meant by the requirement, you must add a measurement against which it can be tested—that is, a fit criterion. Here are the fit criteria for the preceding examples:

> *Eighty percent of a test panel of 11-year-old children shall be able to successfully complete [list of tasks] within [specified time].*
>
> *One month's use of the product shall result in a total error rate of less than 1 percent.*
>
> *Seventy-five percent of the intended users are regularly using the product after a three-week familiarization period.*

Considerations

Refer to Section 3, Users of the Product, to ensure that you have considered the usability requirements from the perspective of all the different types of users.

It may be necessary to have special consulting sessions with your users and your client to determine whether any special usability considerations must be built into the product.

You could also consider consulting a usability laboratory experienced in testing the usability of products that have a project situation (Sections 1–7 of this template) similar to yours.

11b. Personalization and Internationalization Requirements

Content

This section describes the way in which the product can be altered or configured to take into account the user's personal preferences or choice of language.

The personalization requirements should cover issues such as the following:

- Languages, spelling preferences, and language idioms
- Currencies, including the symbols and decimal conventions
- Personal configuration options

Motivation

The goal is to ensure that the product's users do not have to struggle with, or meekly accept, the builder's cultural conventions.

Examples

> *The product shall retain the buyer's buying preferences.*
>
> *The product shall allow the user to select a chosen language.*

Considerations

Consider the country and culture of the potential customers and users of your product. Any out-of-country users will welcome the opportunity to convert the product's display to their home spelling and expressions.

By allowing users to customize the way in which they use the product, you give them the opportunity to work more closely with your organization as well as enjoy their own personal user experience.

You might also consider the configurability of the product. Configurability allows different users to have different functional variations of the product.

11c. Learning Requirements

Content

These requirements specify how easy it should be to learn to use the product. The learning curve ranges from zero time for products intended for placement in the public domain (e.g., a parking meter or a website) to a considerable amount of time for complex, highly technical products. (We know of one product where it was necessary for graduate engineers to spend 18 months in a training program before being qualified to use the product.)

Motivation

The goal is to quantify the amount of time that your client feels is allowable before a user can successfully use the product. This requirement guides designers to understand how users will learn the product. For example, designers may build elaborate interactive help facilities into the product, or the product may be packaged with a tutorial. Alternatively, the product may have to be constructed so that all of its functionality is apparent upon first encountering it.

Examples

> *The product shall be easy for an engineer to learn.*
>
> *A clerk shall be able to be productive within a short time.*
>
> *The product shall be able to be used by members of the public who will receive no training before using it.*
>
> *The product shall be used by engineers who will attend five weeks of training before using the product.*

Fit Criterion

> *An engineer shall produce a [specified result] within [specified time] of beginning to use the product, without needing to use the manual.*
>
> *After receiving [number of hours] training, a clerk shall be able to produce [quantity of specified outputs] per [unit of time].*
>
> *[Agreed percentage] of a test panel shall successfully complete [specified task] within [specified time limit].*
>
> *The engineers shall achieve [agreed percentage] pass rate from the final examination of the training.*

Considerations

Refer to Section 2d, Hands-on Users of the Product, to ensure that you have considered the ease of learning requirements from the perspective of all the different types of users.

11d. Understandability and Politeness Requirements

This section is concerned with discovering requirements related to concepts and metaphors that are familiar to the intended end users.

Content

This section specifies the requirement for the product to be understood by its users. While "usability" refers to ease of use, efficiency, and similar characteristics, "understandability" determines whether the users instinctively know what the product will do for them and how it fits into their view of the world. You can think of understandability as the product being polite to its users and not expecting them to know or learn things that have nothing to do with their business problem. Another aspect of politeness is that the product should not expect the user to input any information to which the product already has access.

Motivation

The intention is to avoid forcing users to learn terms and concepts that are part of the product's internal construction and are not relevant to the users' world. Another goal is to make the product more comprehensible and, therefore, more likely to be adopted by its intended users.

Examples

> *The product shall use symbols and words that are naturally understandable by the user community.*
>
> *The product shall hide the details of its construction from the user.*

Considerations

Refer to Section 2d, Hands-on Users of the Product, and consider the world from the point of view of each of the different types of users.

11e. Accessibility Requirements

Content

These requirements specify how easy it should be for people with common disabilities to access the product. These disabilities might be related to physical disability or visual, hearing, cognitive, or other abilities.

Motivation

In many countries it is required that some products be made available to the disabled. In any event, it is self-defeating to exclude this sizable community of potential customers.

Examples

> *The product shall be usable by partially sighted users.*
>
> *The product shall conform to the Americans with Disabilities Act.*

Considerations

Some users have disabilities other than the commonly described ones. In addition, some partial disabilities are fairly common. A simple, and not very consequential, example is that approximately 20 percent of males are red-green color-blind.

12. Performance Requirements

12a. Speed and Latency Requirements

Content

This section specifies the amount of time available for the product to complete specified tasks. Such requirements often refer to response times, but they can also refer to the product's ability to operate at a speed suitable for the intended environment.

Motivation

Some products—usually real-time products—must be able to perform some of their functionality within a given time slot. Failure to do so may mean catastrophic failure (e.g., a ground-sensing radar in an airplane fails to detect an upcoming mountain) or the product will not cope with the required volume of use (e.g., an automated ticket-selling machine).

Examples

> *Any interface between a user and the automated system shall have a maximum response time of 2 seconds.*
>
> *The response shall be fast enough to avoid interrupting the user's flow of thought.*
>
> *The product shall poll the sensor every 10 seconds.*
>
> *The product shall download the new status parameters within 5 minutes of a change.*

Fit Criterion

Fit criteria are needed when the description of the requirement is not quantified. However, we find that most performance requirements are stated in quantified terms. The exception is the second requirement shown above, for which the suggested fit criterion is this:

> *The product shall respond in less than 1 second for 90 percent of the interrogations. No response shall take longer than 2.5 seconds.*

Considerations

The importance of different types of speed requirements varies widely. If you are working on a missile guidance system, then speed is extremely important. By contrast, an inventory control report that is run once every six months has no need for a lightning-fast response time.

Customize this section of the template to give examples of the speed requirements that are important within your environment.

12b. Safety-Critical Requirements

Content

This part of the specification quantifies the perceived risk of damage to people, property, and environment. Different countries have different standards, so the fit criteria must specify precisely which standards the product must meet.

Motivation

The intention is to understand and highlight the damage that could potentially occur when using the product within the expected operational environment.

Examples

> The product shall not emit noxious gases that damage people's health.
>
> The heat exchanger shall be shielded from human contact.

Fit Criterion

> The product shall be certified to comply with the Health Department's standard E110-98. It is to be certified by qualified testing engineers.
>
> No member of a test panel of [specified size] shall be able to touch the heat exchanger. The heat exchanger must also comply with safety standard [specify which one].

Considerations

The example requirements given here apply to some, but not all, products. It is not possible to give examples of every variation of safety-critical requirements. To make the template work in your environment, you should customize it by adding examples that are specific to your industry and type of product.

Also, be aware that different countries have different safety standards and laws relating to safety. If you plan to sell your product internationally, you must be aware of these laws. A colleague has suggested that for electrical products, if you follow the German standards, the largest number of countries will be supported.

If you are building safety-critical systems, then the relevant safety-critical standards are already well specified. You will likely have safety experts on your staff; they are the best source of the relevant safety-critical requirements for your type of product. They will almost certainly have copious information that you can use in this part of the template.

Consult your legal department. Members of this department will be aware of the kinds of lawsuits that have resulted from product safety failure. This is probably the best starting place for generating relevant safety requirements.

12c. Precision or Accuracy Requirements

Content

This section of the specification quantifies the desired accuracy of the results produced by the product.

Motivation

The goal is to set the client's and users' expectations for the precision of the product.

Examples

> All monetary amounts shall be accurate to two decimal places.
>
> Accuracy of road temperature readings shall be within ±2°C.

Considerations

If you have done any detailed work on definitions, then some precision requirements might be adequately defined by definitions in the dictionary in Section 7.

You might consider which units the product is intended to use. Readers will recall the spacecraft that crashed on Mars when coordinates were sent as metric data rather than as imperial data.

The product might also need to keep accurate time, be synchronized with a time server, or work in UTC.

Also, be aware that some currencies have no decimal places, such as the Japanese yen.

12d. Reliability and Availability Requirements

Content

This section quantifies the necessary reliability of the product. The reliability is usually expressed as the allowable time between failures, or the total allowable failure rate.

This section also quantifies the expected availability of the product.

Motivation

It is critical for some products not to fail too often. This section allows you to explore the possibility of failure and to specify realistic levels of service. It also gives you the opportunity to set the client's and users' expectations about the amount of time that the product will be available for use.

Examples

> The product shall be available for use 24 hours per day, 365 days per year.
>
> The product shall be available for use between the hours of 8:00 a.m. and 5:30 p.m.
>
> The escalator shall run from 6 a.m. until 10 p.m. or until the last flight arrives.
>
> The product shall achieve 99 percent uptime.

Considerations

Consider carefully whether the real requirement for your product is that it is available for use or that it does not fail at any time.

Consider also the cost of reliability and availability, and determine whether the requirement is justified for your product on those bases.

12e. Robustness or Fault-Tolerance Requirements

Content

Robustness specifies the ability of the product to continue to function under abnormal circumstances.

Motivation

The goal is to ensure that the product is able to provide some or all of its services after or during some abnormal happening in its environment.

Examples

> The product shall continue to operate in local mode whenever it loses its link to the central server.
>
> The product shall provide 10 minutes of emergency operation should it become disconnected from the electricity source.

Considerations

Abnormal happenings can almost be considered normal. Today's products are so large and complex that there is a good chance that at any given time, one component will not be functioning correctly. Robustness requirements are intended to prevent total failure of the product.

You could also consider disaster recovery in this section. Such a plan describes the ability of the product to reestablish acceptable performance after faults or abnormal happenings.

12f. Capacity Requirements

Content

This section specifies the volumes of data that the product must be able to deal with and the amount of data stored by the product.

Motivation

The intention is to ensure that the product is capable of processing the expected volumes.

Examples

> The product shall cater to 300 simultaneous users within the period from 9:00 a.m. to 11:00 a.m. Maximum loading at other periods will be 150 simultaneous users.
>
> During a launch period, the product shall cater to a maximum of 20 people who are in the inner chamber.

Fit Criterion

In this case, the requirement description is quantified and, therefore, can be tested.

12g. Scalability or Extensibility Requirements

Content

This part specifies the expected increases in size that the product must be able to handle. As a business grows (or is expected to grow), software products must increase their capacities to cope with the new volumes.

Motivation

The intention is to ensure that the designers allow capacity for future growth.

Examples

> The product shall be capable of processing the existing 100,000 customers. This number is expected to grow to 500,000 customers within three years.
>
> The product shall be able to process 50,000 transactions per hour within two years of its launch.

12h. Longevity Requirements

Content

This section specifies the expected lifetime of the product.

Motivation

The intention is to ensure that the product is built based on an understanding of the expected return on investment.

Examples

> The product shall be expected to operate within the defined maximum maintenance budget for a minimum of five years.

13. Operational and Environmental Requirements

13a. Expected Physical Environment

Content

This section specifies the physical environment in which the product will operate.

Motivation

The intention is to highlight conditions that might need special requirements, preparations, or training. These requirements ensure that the product is fit to be used in its intended environment.

Examples

> The product shall be used by a worker, standing up, outside in cold, rainy conditions.
>
> The product shall be used in noisy conditions with a lot of dust.
>
> The product shall be able to fit in a pocket or purse.
>
> The product shall be usable in dim light.
>
> The product shall not be louder than the existing noise level in the environment.

Considerations

Consider the work environment: Will the product operate in some unusual environment? Does this lead to special requirements? Also see Section 11, Usability and Humanity Requirements.

13b. Requirements for Interfacing with Adjacent Systems

Content

This section describes the requirements to interface with partner applications and/or devices that the product needs to operate successfully.

Motivation

Requirements for the interfaces to other applications often remain undiscovered until implementation time. You can avoid a high degree of rework by discovering these requirements early.

Examples

> *The products shall work on the last four releases of the five most popular browsers.*
>
> *The new version of the spreadsheet must be able to access data from the previous two versions.*
>
> *The product must interface with the applications that run on the remote weather stations.*

Fit Criterion

For each inter-application interface, specify the following elements:

- The data content
- The physical material content
- The medium that carries the interface
- The frequency
- The volume
- The trigger
- The standards/protocols that apply to the interface

13c. Productization Requirements

Content

This section specifies any requirements that are necessary to make the product into a distributable or saleable item. It is also appropriate to describe here the operations needed to install a software product successfully.

Motivation

The goal is to ensure that if work must be done to get the product out the door, then that work becomes part of the requirements. Also, this section is intended to quantify the client's and users' expectations about the amount of time, money, and resources they will need to allocate to install the product.

Examples

> *The product shall be downloadable.*
>
> *The product shall be able to be installed by an untrained user without recourse to separately printed instructions.*
>
> *The product shall be of a size such that it can fit on one DVD.*

Considerations

Some products have special needs to turn them into a saleable or usable product. You might consider that the product has to be protected such that only paid-up customers can access it.

Ask questions of your marketing department to discover unstated assumptions that have been made about the specified environment and the customers' expectations of how long installation will take and how much it will cost.

Most commercial products have needs in this area.

13d. Release Requirements

Content

This section specifies the intended release cycle for the product and the form that the release shall take.

Motivation

The goal is to make everyone aware of how often you intend to produce new releases of the product.

Examples

> The maintenance releases will be offered to end users once a year.
>
> Each release shall not cause previous features to fail.

Fit Criterion

The fit criterion describes the type of maintenance as well as the amount of effort budgeted for it.

Considerations

Do you have any existing contractual commitments or maintenance agreements that might be affected by the new product?

14. Maintainability and Support Requirements

14a. Maintenance Requirements

Content

This section quantifies the time necessary to make specified changes to the product.

Motivation

The intention is to make everyone aware of the maintenance needs of the product.

Examples

> *New BI reports must be available within one working week of the date when the requirements are agreed upon.*
>
> *A new weather station must be able to be added to the system overnight.*

Considerations

Sometimes there may be special requirements for maintainability, such as that the product must be able to be maintained by its end users or by developers who are not the original developers. These requirements have an effect on the way that the product is developed. In addition, there may be requirements for documentation or training.

You might also consider writing testability requirements in this section.

14b. Supportability Requirements

Content

This section specifies the level of support that the product requires. Support is often provided via a help desk. If people will provide support for the product, that service is considered part of the product: Are there any requirements for that support? You might also build support into the product itself, in which case this section is the place to write those requirements.

Motivation

The goal is to ensure that the support aspect of the product is adequately specified.

Considerations

Consider the anticipated level of support, and which forms it might take. For example, a constraint might state that there is to be no printed manual. Alternatively, the product might need to be entirely self-supporting.

14c. Adaptability Requirements

Content

Describe other platforms or environments to which the product must be ported.

Motivation

The goal is to publicize the client's and users' expectations about the platforms on which the product will be able to run.

Examples

> *The product is expected to run on iOS and Android.*
>
> *The product might eventually be sold in the Japanese market.*
>
> *The product is designed to run in offices, but we intend to have a version running in restaurant kitchens.*

Fit Criterion

- Specification of system software on which the product must operate
- Specification of future environments in which the product is expected to operate
- Time allowed to make the transition

Considerations

Question your marketing department to discover unstated assumptions that have been made about the portability of the product.

15. Security Requirements

15a. Access Requirements

Content

This part of the specification indicates who is authorized to access the product (both functionality and data), under which circumstances that access is granted, and to which parts of the product access is allowed.

Motivation

The goal is to understand the expectations for confidentiality aspects of the system.

Examples

> *Only direct managers can see the personnel records of their staff.*
>
> *Only holders of a current security clearance can enter the building.*

Fit Criterion

- Security standards to be complied with
- User roles and/or names of people who have clearance to access specified data
- User roles and/or names of people who have clearance to add, change, delete specified data

Considerations

Is there any data that management considers to be sensitive? Is there any data that low-level users do not want management to have access to? Are there any processes that might cause damage or might be used for personal gain? Are there any people who should not have access to the system?

Avoid stating how you would design a solution to the security requirements—for instance, don't specify a password system. Your aim here is to identify the security requirement; the design will flow from this requirement.

Consider asking for help. Computer security is a highly specialized field, and one in which improperly qualified people have no business meddling. If your product has need of more than average security, we advise you to make use of a security consultant. Such consultants are not cheap, but the unhappy results of inadequate security can be even more expensive.

15b. Integrity Requirements

Content

This part specifies the required integrity of databases and other files, and of the product itself.

Motivation

The goals are twofold: (1) to understand the expectations for the integrity of the product's data and (2) to specify what the product will do to ensure its integrity in the case of an unwanted happening such as attack from the outside or unintentional misuse by an authorized user.

Examples

> *The product shall prevent incorrect data from being introduced.*
>
> *The product shall protect itself from intentional abuse.*

Considerations

Organizations are relying more and more on their stored data. If this data should become corrupt or incorrect—or disappear—then it could be a fatal blow to the organization. For example, almost half of small businesses go bankrupt after a fire destroys their computer systems. Integrity requirements are aimed at preventing complete loss, as well as corruption, of data and processes.

15c. Privacy Requirements

Content

This section specifies what the product has to do to ensure the privacy of individuals about whom it stores information. The product must also ensure that all laws related to privacy of an individual's data are observed.

Motivation

The intention is to ensure that the product complies with the law, and to protect the individual privacy of your customers. Few people today look kindly on organizations that do not respect and protect their privacy.

Examples

> The product shall make its users aware of its information practices before collecting data from them.
>
> The product shall notify customers of changes to its information policy.
>
> The product shall reveal private information only in compliance with the organization's information policy.
>
> The product shall protect private information in accordance with the relevant privacy laws and the organization's information policy.

Considerations

Privacy issues may well have legal implications, and you are advised to consult with your organization's legal department about the requirements to be written in this section.

Consider which notices you must issue to your customers before collecting their personal information. Also, do you have to do anything to keep customers aware that you hold their personal information?

Customers must always be in a position to give or withhold consent when their private data is collected or stored. Similarly, customers should be able to view any private data and, where appropriate, correct or ask for correction of the data.

Also consider the integrity and security of private data—for example, when you are storing credit card information.

15d. Audit Requirements

Content

This content specifies what the product has to do (usually retain records) to permit the required audit checks.

Motivation

The goal is to build a system that complies with the appropriate audit rules.

Considerations

This section may have legal implications. You are advised to seek the approval of your organization's auditors regarding what you write here.

You should also consider whether the product should retain information on who has used it. The intention is to provide security such that a user may not later deny having used the product or participated in some form of transaction using the product.

15e. Immunity Requirements

Content

These requirements indicate what the product has to do to protect itself from infection by unauthorized or undesirable software programs, such as viruses, worms, malware, spyware, and any other undesirable interference.

Motivation

The intention is to build a product that is as secure as possible from malicious interference.

Considerations

Each day brings more malevolence from the unknown, outside world. People buying software, or any other kind of product, expect that it can protect itself from outside interference.

16. Cultural Requirements

16a. Cultural Requirements

Content

This section contains requirements that are specific to the sociological factors that affect the acceptability of the product. If you are developing a product for foreign markets, then these requirements are particularly relevant.

Motivation

The goal is to bring out in the open requirements that are difficult to discover because they are outside the cultural experience of the developers.

Examples

> The product shall not be offensive to religious or ethnic groups.
>
> The product shall be able to distinguish between French, Italian, and British road-numbering systems.
>
> The product shall keep a record of public holidays for all countries in the European Union and for all states in the United States.

Considerations

Question whether the product is intended for a culture other than the one with which you are familiar. Ask whether people in other countries or in other types of organizations will use the product. Do these people have different habits, holidays, superstitions, or cultural norms that do not apply to your own culture? Are there colors, icons, measurement units, or words that have different meanings in another cultural environment? If your reaction to a requirement is "That's rather odd/unusual/weird," then likely you have a cultural requirement.

17. Legal Requirements

17a. Compliance Requirements

Content

This section consists of a statement specifying the legal requirements for this system.

Motivation

The intention is to comply with the law so as to avoid later delays, lawsuits, and legal fees.

Example

> Personal information shall be implemented so as to comply with the Data Protection Act.

Fit Criterion

Obtain a lawyer's opinion that the product does not break any laws.

Considerations

Consider consulting lawyers to help identify the legal requirements.

Are there any copyrights or other intellectual property that must be protected? Conversely, do any competitors have copyrights on which you might be in danger of infringing?

Is it a requirement that developers have not seen competitors' code or even have worked for competitors?

The Sarbanes-Oxley (SOX) Act, the Health Insurance Portability and Accountability Act (HIPAA), and the Gramm-Leach-Bliley Act may have implications for you. Check with your company lawyer.

Might any pending legislation affect the development of this system?

Are there any aspects of criminal law you should consider?

Have you considered the tax laws that affect your product?

Are there any labor laws (e.g., working hours) relevant to your product?

17b. Standards Requirements

Content

This statement specifies applicable standards and references detailed standards descriptions. A standard does not refer to the law of the land—instead, think of it as an internal law imposed by your company or by your industry.

Motivation

The intention is to comply with standards so as to avoid later delays.

Examples

> *The product shall comply with MilSpec standards.*
>
> *The product shall comply with insurance industry standards.*
>
> *The product shall be developed according to SSADM standard development steps.*

Fit Criterion

Have the appropriate standard-keeper certify that the standard has been adhered to.

Considerations

It is not always apparent that there are applicable standards because their existence is often taken for granted. Consider the following:

● Do any industry bodies have applicable standards?

- Does the industry have a code of practice, watchdog, or ombudsman?
- Are there any special development steps for this type of product?

Project Issues

Sections 18–27 deal with issues that must be faced if the requirements are to be met and the product is to become a reality. These sections also connect the requirements with the project activities that discover and progress the requirements. If you are using a consistent language for communicating requirements, then project managers can use the requirements as input to steering the project. The Volere requirements knowledge model (included with the download of version 16 of the template) provides the basis for a requirements common language by identifying classes of requirements knowledge and the associations between them. Each of the classes of knowledge is cross-referenced to sections in this template.

18. Open Issues

Open issues have been raised but do not yet have a conclusion.

Content

Provide a statement of factors that are uncertain and might make significant difference to the product.

Motivation

The goal is to bring uncertainty out in the open and provide objective input to risk analysis.

Examples

> Our investigation into whether the new version of the processor will be suitable for our application is not yet complete.
>
> The government is planning to change the rules about who is responsible for ice treatment on the motorways, but we do not know what those changes might be.
>
> The feasibility study to determine whether to use the Regional Weather Center's online database is not yet complete. This issue affects how we should handle the weather data.
>
> Planned changes to working hours for drivers may affect the way that trucks are scheduled and the length of the routes that drivers are permitted to travel. The changes are still in the proposal stage; details will be available by the end of the year.

Considerations

When you are probing around the user's business, questions often come to the surface that cannot for the moment be answered. Similarly, as you are gathering the requirements for a future product, it may well be that your stakeholders are unsure of how the work should be done in the future. Have any issues bubbled up from the requirements-gathering process that have not yet been resolved? Have you heard of any changes that might occur in the other organizations or systems on your context diagram? Are there any legislative changes that might affect your system? Are there any rumors about your hardware or software suppliers that might have an impact?

Form

Provide a list of open issues containing the following data:

- Cross-reference to affected requirements (business events, BUCs, PUCs, atomic requirements, dictionary definitions)
- Summary of the issue
- Stakeholders involved
- Action
- Resolution

19. Off-the-Shelf Solutions

This section looks at available solutions and summarizes their applicability to the requirements. This discussion is not intended to be a full feasibility study of the alternatives, but it should tell your client that you have considered some alternatives and determined how closely they match the requirements for the product.

19a. Ready-Made Products

Content

List the existing products that should be investigated as potential solutions. Reference any surveys that have been done on these products.

Motivation

The intention is to give consideration to whether a solution can be bought.

Considerations

Could you buy something that already exists or is about to become available? It may not be possible at this stage to make this determination with a great deal of confidence, but any likely products should be listed here.

Also consider whether some products must *not* be used.

19b. Reusable Components

Content

This section includes a description of the candidate components, either bought from outside or built by your company, that could be used by this project. List libraries that could be a source of components.

Motivation

Reuse, rather than reinvention, is the goal.

19c. Products That Can Be Copied

Content

List other similar products or parts of products that you can legally copy or easily modify.

Motivation

Reuse, rather than reinvention, is the goal.

Example

> Another electricity company has built a customer service system. Its hardware is different from ours, but we could buy its specification and cut our analysis effort by approximately 60 percent.

Considerations

While a ready-made solution may not exist, perhaps something, in its essence, is similar enough that you could copy, and possibly modify, it to better effect than starting from scratch. Note that this approach is potentially dangerous because it relies on the base system being of good quality.

This question should always be answered. The act of answering it will force you to look at other existing solutions to similar problems.

Form

For each of Sections 19a, 19b, and 19c, identify the alternatives that you think are suitable. If your findings are preliminary, then say so. It is useful to add approximate costs, availability, time to implement, and other factors that may have a bearing on the decision.

20. New Problems

20a. Effects on the Current Environment

Content

This section describes how the new product will affect the current implementation environment. It should also cover things that the new product should *not* do.

Motivation

The intention is to discover early any potential conflicts that might otherwise not be realized until implementation time.

Example

> Any change to the scheduling system will affect the work of the engineers in the divisions and the work of the truck drivers.

Considerations

Is it possible that the new system might damage some existing system? Could people be displaced or otherwise affected by the new system?

Form

These issues require a study of the current environment. A model highlighting the effects of the change is a good way to make this information widely understandable.

20b. Effects on the Installed Systems

Content

This part includes a specification of the interfaces between new and existing systems.

Motivation

Very rarely is a new development intended to stand completely alone. Usually the new system must coexist with some older system. This question forces you to look carefully at the existing system, examining it for potential conflicts with the new development.

Form

Provide a model identifying the interfaces between the new and existing systems supported by data dictionary definitions of the interfaces. The interfaces might also be supported by prototypes or sketches of format.

20c. Potential User Problems

Content

This section provides details of any adverse reaction that might be suffered by existing users.

Motivation

Sometimes existing users are using a product in such a way that they will suffer ill effects from the new system or feature. Identify any likely adverse user reactions, and determine whether we care about those reactions and what precautions we will take.

20d. Limitations in the Anticipated Implementation Environment That May Inhibit the New Product

Content

This section states any potential problems with the new automated technology or new ways of structuring the organization.

Motivation

The intention is to make early discovery of any potential conflicts that might otherwise not be realized until implementation time.

Examples

> The planned new server is not powerful enough to cope with our projected growth pattern.
>
> The size and weight of the new product do not fit into the physical environment.
>
> The power capabilities will not satisfy the new product's projected consumption.

Considerations

This requires a study of the intended implementation environment.

20e. Follow-Up Problems

Content

This part identifies situations that we might not be able to cope with.

Motivation

The goal is to guard against situations where the product might fail.

Considerations

Will we create a demand for our product that we are not able to service? Will the new system cause us to run afoul of laws that do not currently apply? Will the existing hardware cope with the anticipated demand?

There are potentially hundreds of unwanted effects. It pays to answer this question very carefully.

21. Tasks

Which steps have to be taken to deliver the product? This section highlights the effort required to build the product, the steps needed to buy a solution, the amount of effort to modify and install a ready-made solution, and so on.

21a. Project Planning

Content

This section provides details of the life cycle and approach that will be used to deliver the product.

Motivation

The intention is to specify the approach that will be taken to deliver the product so that everyone has the same expectations.

Considerations

Depending on the maturity level of your process, the new product will be developed using your standard approach. However, some circumstances are unique to a particular product and will necessitate changes to your life cycle. While these considerations are not product requirements, they are needed if the product is to be successfully developed.

If possible, attach an estimate of the time and resources needed for each task based on the requirements that you have specified. Attach your estimates to the events, use cases, and/or functional requirements that you specified in Sections 6, 8, and 9.

Do not forget issues related to data conversion, user training, and cutover. These needs are usually ignored when projects set implementation dates.

Form

A high-level process diagram or a task list showing the tasks and the interfaces between them is a good way to communicate this information. Here you can also identify the strategy that you intend to use to maximize your potential for agility.

21b. Planning of the Development Phases

Content

This section specifies each phase of development and the components in the operating environment.

Motivation

The goal is to identify the phases necessary to implement the operating environment for the new system so that the implementation can be managed.

Considerations

Identify which hardware and other devices are necessary for each phase of the new system. This list may not be known at the time of the requirements process, as these devices may be decided at design time.

Form

This section usually consists of a mixture of diagrams and text. For each phase of the project, provide the following information:

- Name of the phase
- Value/benefit of delivery to the user
- Required operational date
- Operating environment components included
- Functional requirements included
- Non-functional requirements included

22. Migration to the New Product

When you install a new product, some things always have to be done before it can work successfully. For example, databases often have to be converted to a different format. There are usually new data to be collected, procedures to be completed, and many other steps to be taken to ensure the successful transition to the new product.

In many situations, the organization will run both the old product and the new product in parallel for some period of time until the new one has proved that it is functioning correctly.

This section of the specification is where you identify the tasks necessary for the period of transition to the new product. It serves as input to the project planning process.

22a. Requirements for Migration to the New Product

Content

This section lists the conversion activities and provides a timetable for project implementation.

Motivation

The goal is to identify conversion tasks as input to the project planning process.

Considerations

Will you use a phased implementation to install the new system? If so, describe which requirements will be implemented by each of the major phases.

Which kind of data conversion is necessary? Must special programs be written to transport data from an existing system to the new one? If so, describe the requirements for these programs here.

Which kind of manual backup is needed while the new system is installed?

When are each of the major components to be put in place? When are the phases of the implementation to be released?

Is there a need to run the new product in parallel with the existing product?

Will we need additional or different staff?

Is any special effort needed to decommission the old product?

This section is the timetable for implementation of the new system.

Form

A cross-reference between the development tasks, your project phases, and the product use cases and atomic requirements.

22b. Data That Must Be Modified or Translated for the New System

Content

This section lists data translation tasks.

Motivation

The intention is to discover missing tasks that will affect the size and boundaries of the project.

Considerations

Every time you make an addition to your dictionary (see Section 7), ask this question: Where is this data currently held, and will the new system affect that implementation?

Form

- Description of the current technology that holds the data
- Description of the new technology that will hold the data
- Description of the data translation tasks
- Foreseeable problems

23. Risks

All projects involve risk—namely, the risk that something will go wrong. Risk is not necessarily a bad thing, as no progress is ever made without taking some risk. Risk becomes a bad thing when the risks are ignored and they evolve into problems. Risk management entails assessing which risks are most likely to apply to the project, deciding a course of action if they become problems, and monitoring projects to give early warnings of risks becoming problems.

Content

This section of the specification contains a list of the most likely and the most serious risks for your project. For each risk, include the probability of it becoming a problem and any contingency plans.

Motivation

The intention is to discover and manage the risks.

Considerations

Risks will undoubtedly change during the lifetime of a project. The better you understand the requirements, the better you can identify which risks are most serious for your project. Although the project manager determines how to manage the risks, the requirements specialists and developers provide input on new risks and help identify which risks are turning into problems.

Use your knowledge of the requirements as input to discover which risks are most relevant to your project. Use the Volere requirements knowledge model (included with the download of version 16 of the template) as a trigger for identifying relevant risks.

Another useful input for project management is the impact on the schedule, and/or the cost, if the risk does become a problem.

As an alternative, you may prefer to identify the single largest risk—the showstopper. If this risk becomes a problem, then the project will definitely fail. Identifying a single risk in this way focuses attention on the single most critical area. Project efforts are then concentrated on not letting this risk become a problem.

This book is not intended to be a thorough treatise on risk management, nor is this section of the requirements specification meant to be a substitute for proper risk management. The intention here is to assign risks to requirements and show clearly that requirements are not free—they carry a cost that can be expressed as an amount of money or time, and as a risk. Later, you can use this information if you need to make choices about which requirements should be given a higher priority.

Form

Use a risk list or log. Risk models as defined in the following source: DeMarco, Tom, and Timothy Lister. *Waltzing with Bears: Managing Risk on Software Projects.* Dorset House, 2003.

For each risk, include the probability of that risk becoming a problem. Capers Jones's *Assessment and Control of Software Risks* (Prentice-Hall, Englewood Cliffs, NJ, 1994) gives comprehensive lists of risks and their probabilities; you can use these lists as a starting point. For example, Jones cites the following risks as being the most serious:

- Inaccurate metrics
- Inadequate measurement
- Excessive schedule pressure
- Management malpractice
- Inaccurate cost estimating
- Silver bullet syndrome

- Creeping user requirements
- Low quality
- Low productivity
- Cancelled projects

24. Costs

The other cost of requirements is the amount of money or effort that you have to spend building them into a product. Once the requirements specification is complete, you can use one of the estimating methods to assess the cost, expressing the result as a monetary amount or time to build.

There is no best method to use when estimating costs. The important point is to create your estimates using metrics directly related to the requirements. If you have specified the requirements in the way we have described, you will have the following metrics:

- Number of input and output flows on the work context
- Number of business events
- Number of product use cases
- Number of functional requirements
- Number of non-functional requirements
- Number of requirements constraints
- Number of function points

The more detailed the work you do on your requirements, the more accurate your estimates will be. Your cost estimate comprises the amount of resources you estimate each type of deliverable will take to produce within your environment. You can create some very early cost estimates based on the work context. At that stage, your knowledge of the work will be general, and you should reflect this vagueness by making the cost estimate a range rather than a single figure. You can use these metrics as the basis for estimating the time, effort, and cost of building the product. First you need to determine what each of these metrics means within the environment in which you are building the product. For example, do you know how long it will take you to do all the work necessary to implement a product use case? If you do not, then you can take one of the use cases and benchmark it.

As you increase your knowledge of the requirements, we suggest you try using function point counting—not because it is an inherently superior method, but because it is so widely accepted. So much is known about function point counting that it is possible to make easy comparisons with other products and other installations' productivity. For details on how to estimate requirements effort and costs, refer to Appendix C, Function Point Counting: A Simplified Introduction.

At this stage, your client should be told what the product is likely to cost. You usually express this amount as the total cost to complete the product, but you may also find it advantageous to point out the cost of the requirements effort, or the costs of individual requirements.

Whatever you do, do not leave the costs in the lap of hysterical optimism. Make sure that this section includes meaningful numbers based on tangible deliverables.

25. User Documentation and Training

This section specifies the user documentation that will be produced as part of the product-building effort. It is not the documentation itself, but rather a description of what must be produced. The reason for including this description is to establish your client's expectations, and to give your usability people and your users the chance to assess whether the proposed documentation will be sufficient.

25a. User Documentation Requirements

Content

This section lists the user documentation to be supplied as part of the product. Be careful not to waste time defining anything that has already been defined. Bear in mind that the requirements—especially the product use cases, atomic requirements, and definitions of data—provide the input for the user documentation.

Motivation

The intention is to set expectations for the user manuals and to identify who will be responsible for creating them.

Examples

- Technical specifications to accompany the product
- User manuals
- Service manuals (if not covered by the technical specification)
- Emergency procedure manuals (e.g., the card found in airplanes)
- Installation manuals

Considerations

Which documents do you need to deliver, and to whom? Bear in mind that the answer to this question depends on your organizational procedures and roles.

For each document, consider these issues:

- The purpose of the document
- The people who will use the document
- Maintenance of the document

Which level of documentation is expected? Will the users be involved in the production of the documentation? Who will be responsible for keeping the documentation up-to-date? Which form will the documentation take?

Use the requirements that you have already specified as input to writing the user documentation. For example, you have defined all the terms used in the requirements, so then take advantage of this information and use the same definitions and dictionary in the user documentation. Use the product use case (PUC) scenarios as the core of describing how a user can do a particular task. If other people are writing the user documentation, then show them how they can use a lot of the work that has already been done as the basis for user manuals.

25b. Training Requirements

Content

This section describes the training needed by users of the product. Be careful not to waste time defining anything that has already been defined. Bear in mind that the requirements—especially the product use cases, atomic requirements, and definitions of data—provide the input for the user training.

Motivation

The goals are twofold: (1) to set expectations for the training and (2) to identify who is responsible for creating and providing that training.

Considerations

Which training will be necessary? Who will design the training? Who will provide the training? What are the plans for holding the training sessions?

Use the requirements that you have already specified as input to designing the training. For example, you have specified what a PUC must do; use that PUC scenario or model as the basis for building training for the users who will be carrying out that task. Likewise, you have defined all the terms used in the requirements, so take advantage of this information and use the same definitions and dictionary in the user training.

26. Waiting Room

The waiting room holds requirements that will not, for one reason or another, be part of the initial release of the product. If you are competent at gathering requirements, your users may often be inspired to think of more requirements than you can fit within the constraints of the project. While you may not want to include all of these requirements in the initial version of the product, neither do you want to lose them.

If you are doing iterative development, then the waiting room serves as your backlog.

Content

This section may include any type of requirement at any level of detail.

Motivation

The goal is to capture all requirements, even though some will not be part of the current development. The waiting room ensures that good ideas are not lost and provides a way to manage a backlog.

Considerations

The requirements-discovery process often throws up requirements that are beyond the sophistication of, or time allowed for, the current release of the product. This section holds these requirements in waiting. The intention is to avoid stifling the creativity of your users and clients, by using a repository to retain future requirements. You are also managing expectations by making it clear that you take these requirements seriously, although they will not be part of the agreed-upon product.

Many people use the waiting room as a way of planning future versions of the product. Each requirement in the waiting room is tagged with its intended version number. As a requirement progresses closer to implementation, then you can spend more time on it and add details such as the cost and benefit attached to that requirement.

You might also prioritize the contents of your waiting room. "Low-hanging fruit"—requirements that provide a high benefit at a low cost of implementation—are the highest-ranking candidates for the next release. You would also give a high waiting room rank to requirements for which there is a pent-up demand. You can think of the waiting room as a way of managing your backlog.

The waiting room has a calming effect on everyone because it shows their ideas are being taken seriously. Your users and client know the requirements are not forgotten, but merely parked until it is time to review them and make decisions about whether they will be incorporated in the product.

27. Ideas for Solutions

Ideas for solutions are obviously not requirements, but it is impossible when gathering requirements not to get ideas for how they might be implemented. Rather than discarding the ideas or—even worse—writing them as if they are requirements, a practical idea is to simply set aside a section of your specification to hold these ideas. Record each one faithfully in this area, and then hand them over, along with the requirements, to your designer.

Content

This section includes any idea for a solution that you think is worth keeping for future consideration. It can take the form of rough notes, sketches, pointers to other documents, pointers to people, pointers to existing products, prototypes, and so on. The aim is to capture, with the least amount of effort, an idea to which you can return later.

Motivation

The intention is to make sure that good ideas are not lost, while keeping requirements separate from solutions.

Considerations

While you are gathering requirements, you will inevitably have solution ideas; this section offers a way to capture them. Bear in mind that this section will not necessarily be included in every document that you publish.

Form

The ideas for solutions are an ideal subject for a blog. This is, after all, the place for ideas, and blogs are a great place for creativity and building on one another's ideas.

Stakeholder Management Templates

This appendix contains templates that are designed to help you to manage your stakeholders. Its aim is threefold:

- To help you discover the relevant stakeholders for your project
- To help you identify gaps without stakeholder representation
- To help you agree on your decision-making structure

Stakeholder Map

Figure B.1 is a generic stakeholder map showing the potential classes of stakeholders. Use it as an aid for discovering your stakeholders. Refer to Chapter 3, Project Blastoff, for a discussion of each of the stakeholder classes.

Figure B.1

This generic stakeholder map shows the various classes of stakeholders. Use it as an aid in identifying your stakeholders.

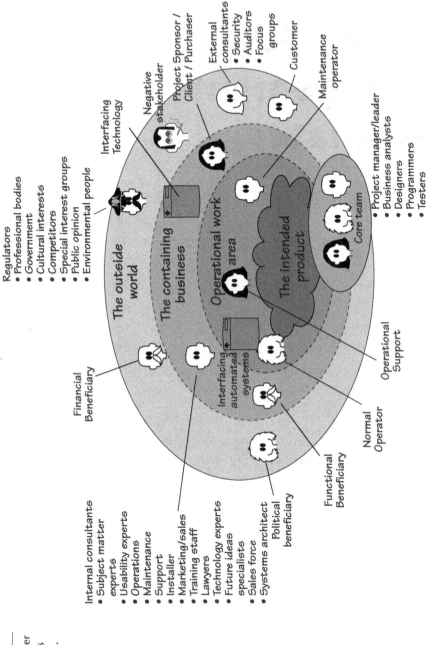

Regulators
- Professional bodies
- Government
- Cultural interests
- Competitors
- Special interest groups
- Public opinion
- Environmental people

Internal consultants
- Subject matter experts
- Usability experts
- Operations
- Maintenance
- Support
- Installer
- Marketing/sales
- Training staff
- Lawyers
- Technology experts
- Future ideas specialists
- Sales force
- Systems architect

- Project manager/leader
- Business analysts
- Designers
- Programmers
- Testers

Stakeholder Template

The following template is a sample checklist you can use to identify and analyze your stakeholders. Note that the template's stakeholder classes correspond to those on the stakeholder map shown in Figure B.1. For each stakeholder class, we have suggested common roles that represent the class. Of course, you will want to modify this list to include role names that are appropriate for your organization. It will probably be more convenient for you to do so using a spreadsheet. A complete version of the template in the form of an Excel spreadsheet can be found at www.volere.co.uk.

Volere Stakeholder Analysis Template

Identify your stakeholder roles, the representative(s) of each role and the type(s) of knowledge that you need from them

Bear in mind that you might choose to add additional roles and classes of knowledge. You might also have several Stakeholder Names for the same role.

For each stakeholder role, identify the relevant classes of knowledge. The classes of knowledge are suggestions, you will need to replace the suggestions with classes of knowledge for your particular project.

Classes of Knowledge

Stakeholder Class (Class of education stakeholder sharing a particular stakeholding in the project)	Stakeholder Role (The job title, department or organisation that might indicate a role for this class of stakeholder)	Stakeholder Name (The name(s) of the responsible stakeholder(s) or their representatives)	Stakeholder Rationale (Why does this stakeholder need to be involved? Consider benefits and impacts)	Necessary Involvement (Estimate of when and how much time)	Goals	Business Constraints	Technical Constraints	Functionality	Look and Feel	Usability	Performance	Safety	Operational Environment	Portability	Security	Cultural Acceptance	Legal	Maintenance	Estimates	Risk	Design Ideas

Operational Work Area, Stakeholder Classes

Interfacing Technology (Any system within the operational area, software, hardware or mechanical - that must have a defined interface with the eventual solution)

Interfacing Technology - Existing Software Systems
Interfacing Technology - Existing Hardware
Interfacing Technology - Existing Machines

Maintenance Operator (Keeps the product operational according to agreed requirements)

Maintenance Operator - Hardware maintainer
Maintenance Operator - Software maintainer
Maintenance Operator - Mechanical part maintainer

Normal Operator (Directly uses the product to do work or to accomplish some purpose)

Normal Operator - Operational Technical Users
Normal Operator - Operational Business Users
Normal Operator - Members of the Public

Operational Support (Helps the normal operators to make effective use of the product)

Operational Support - Help Desk
Operational Support - Coach/Mentor
Operational Support - Trainer
Operational Support - Installer

Containing Business, Stakeholder Classes

Client (Responsible for making the investment to do the project)

Client - Investment Manager
Client - Product Manager
Client - Strategic Programme Mgr.
Client - Chief Executive

Functional Beneficiary (Does not have direct, hands-on contact with the product but benefits from the fact that it exists)

Functional Beneficiary - Manager of Operators
Functional Beneficiary - Business Decision Maker
Functional Beneficiary - Relative of Operator
Functional Beneficiary - Product Manager
Functional Beneficiary - Programme Manager
Functional Beneficiary - Another Department
Functional Beneficiary - User of Reports

Interfacing Technology (Any system in the containing business environment - software, hardware or mechanical - that must have a defined interface with the eventual solution)

Interfacing Technology - Meta manager

Internal Consultant (People inside your organisation who provide knowledge and expertise necessary to necessary to quantify technical and business constraints)

Internal Consultant - Business/Subject Expert
Internal Consultant - Business Data Modeller
Internal Consultant - Future Ideas Specialist
Internal Consultant - Current Automation Specialist
Internal Consultant - Usability Expert
Internal Consultant - System Architect
Internal Consultant - Marketing Specialist
Internal Consultant - Sales Specialist
Internal Consultant - Technology Expert
Internal Consultant - Standards Specialist
Internal Consultant - Testing Specialist
Internal Consultant - Organisational Architect
Internal Consultant - Aesthetics Specialist
Internal Consultant - Graphics Specialist

Sponsor (The link between the project and the rest of the organisation. Helps to resolve problems and make decisions)

Sponsor • Sponsor
Sponsor • Project Champion

Wider Environment, Stakeholder Classes
Customer (Purchasers your product or influences other people to purchase or use your product)

Customer • Department Manager
Customer • Another Organisation
Customer • Member of the Public

Interfacing Technology (Any system in the wider environment – software, hardware or mechanical – that must have a defined interface with the eventual solution)

Interfacing Technology • External Meta Manager

External Consultants (People outside your organisation who provide knowledge and expertise necessary to quantify technical and business constraints)

External Consultant • Auditors
External Consultant • Focus Group
External Consultant • Security Specialist
External Consultant • Environmental Specialist
External Consultant • Safety Specialist
External Consultant • Outsources
External Consultant • Cultural Specialist
External Consultant • Legal Specialist
External Consultant • Packaging Designer
External Consultant • Manufacturer
External Consultant • Negotiator
External Consultant • Public Opinion
External Consultant • COTS Supplier
External Consultant • Inspector

Negative Stakeholders (People or organisations who do not want your project to succeed)

Negative Stakeholder • Competitor
Negative Stakeholder • Hacker
Negative Stakeholder • Political Party
Negative Stakeholder • Pressure Group
Negative Stakeholder • Public Opinion

Core Project Team, Stakeholder Classes
Core Team Members (People who are dedicated to working on the project. These people are concerned with all the rings on the stakeholder map)

Core Team Member • Project Manager
Core Team Member • Business Analyst
Core Team Member • Requirements Analyst
Core Team Member • Systems Analyst
Core Team Member • Tester
Core Team Member • Technical Writer
Core Team Member • Systems Architect
Core Team Member • Systems Designer

Function Point Counting: A Simplified Introduction

 in which we look at a way to accurately measure the size or functionality of the work area, with a view toward using the measurement to estimate the requirements effort

Measuring the Work

This primer on function points is an appendix because it is, strictly speaking, outside the scope of the business analyst's normal responsibilities. That said, being able to measure the work area so as to estimate the effort needed for business analysis is definitely a benefit to any business analyst. Thus, with the idea of making you interested in measuring, or making you interested in making your organization interested in measuring, here is a simplified (but not simplistic) introduction to counting function points.

The requirements activity is an investigation of a piece of work, with the potential to cause a change to that work, probably by automating some of it. The work to be investigated can be automated, manual, scientific, commercial, embedded, a combination of these, or anything else. The reason for measuring that work is to learn how "large" it is. The bigger the work—that is, the more functionality and data it contains—the longer it takes to study it. You would expect to spend more time studying an airline reservation system than you would studying a system for taking bar orders. Why? The airline reservation system contains more functionality, and it takes longer to discover and record it.

Function points are a measure of the size or the amount of functionality contained within a work area. If you have drawn a context diagram, function points measure the functionality inside the central bubble.

Think of function points like this: Imagine that the work is being done by Lilliputians, the small people whom Gulliver visited on his travels. The Lilliputians work hard, very hard, so the volume of work is not important. However, they have one shortcoming—they can do only one task and are

 *To measure is to know.*
—Lord Kelvin

 *You cannot control what you cannot measure.*
—Tom DeMarco

single-minded to the point that whenever you have a new task to do, you have to hire a new Lilliputian. Of course, some tasks are more complex and require more work to be done, so you hire several Lilliputians for these tasks. Sometimes the task is simple and one or two Lilliputians can handle it. By now you are imagining the workplace peopled by these tiny, hard-working people, each one doing part of a task. How many Lilliputians are there in the workplace? Well, it depends on the amount and complexity of the work being done. So that brings us to counting function points, which is just the same as counting the number of Lilliputians you need to do the work.

Function points are a neutral measure of functionality. That is, the type of work being done does not influence them. You can count the function points for air traffic control, car traffic control, or car cruise control; in so doing, you count in exactly the same way.

Once you know the function point count of a work area, you apply your metric to determine how long it takes to study that size of work area.

Over the years our industry has established that for most sizing metrics, there is a standard amount of work to be done to implement one unit of the metric. For example, if you use function points as your sizing metric, then there are industry-standard figures of the number of hours, or the number of dollars, it takes to implement one function point. Thus, if you know the size of the work area in function points, then it is a relatively straightforward matter to translate size into effort required to build the product.

For example, Capers Jones of Software Productivity Research gives us this rule of thumb:

Effort in staff months = (function points / 150) * function points$^{0.4}$

So for a 1,000-function-point work area (this is a substantial, but not overly large area) the effort in person-hours is (1,000 / 150) * 1,0000.4, which is 105.66 staff-months.

Jones's rule of thumb applies to the complete development effort, and includes the effort expended by everybody on the development side of the project. He is talking about typical software projects where roughly half the effort is spent debugging (most of which entails correcting ill-gathered requirements), so it is safe to say that if you take about one-third of Jones's number that would cover a thorough requirements effort.

Besides, we do not advocate attempting to measure the complete implementation—there are too many variables in implementation and development environments to make that kind of count reliable. Instead, we suggest that you limit yourself to estimating the effort needed for requirements analysis.

Please take a moment to consider whether your current estimation process is accurate enough to persist with, or whether you should start to count function points.

You can, of course, measure the size of your work area any way you and your organization think is appropriate. The key word here is "measure." If you are not already using a measuring method, then we suggest you start with function point counting. While it is by no means the ultimate measuring method, it is widely used, so a lot is known about it, and a lot of information and statistics on function points are available.

The key word here is "measure."

READING
Jones, Capers. *Applied Software Measurement: Global Analysis of Productivity and Quality,* third edition. McGraw-Hill Osborne Media, 2008.

Function points are not the only way to measure the size of a work area. You can use Mark II Function points (these are a variation of standard function points), Capers Jones's Feature Points (also a variation), Tom DeMarco's Bang, or any of dozens of measuring methods. However, at the requirements stage of development, function points are convenient, and given what you know of the product at this stage, probably the most appropriate.

So if you do not already use another method, and would like to get started with function points, then please join us for this . . .

READING
Pfleeger, Shari Lawrence. *Software Cost Estimation and Sizing Methods, Issues, and Guidelines.* Rand Publishing, 2005.

A Quick Primer on Counting Function Points

This is definitely not all there is to know about counting the size of a piece of work using function points. However, it is sufficient to get started, and could possibly make you better at estimating than many organizations are at the moment.

Function points are a measure of functionality, which is useful on the simple premise that the more functionality contained within the work, the more effort is needed to study it and gather its requirements. This functionality within the work is a direct result of the data it processes. The more data there is, and the more complex it is, the more functionality is needed to process it. Because data is more visible and more readily measurable, it makes sense to measure the data and extrapolate the functionality from it.

READING
Garmus, David, and David Herron. *Function Point Analysis: Measurement Practices for Successful Software Projects.* Addison-Wesley, 2001.

As the development proceeds, your models will become more accurate, and thus your measuring can become more accurate along with them. But we are still at the requirements stage, so it is appropriate to follow these guidelines:

- Count function points quickly. As you are at an early stage of the project, acceptable measurements at this stage are more useful than perfect measurements later.
- Count the function points for the work in its entirety, or for each of the business use cases.

Scope of the Work

Let's start counting function points by using what you already have. During the blastoff you built a context model of the work area. We discussed this model in Chapter 3, so to save you flipping back many pages, we reproduce it in Figure C.1.

Figure C.1

The context model is one of the inputs to function point counting. The context model shows the flows of data entering and leaving the work area. Each of these flows triggers some functionality, or is the product of some functionality. The amount of functionality is in proportion to the amount of data carried by the flow.

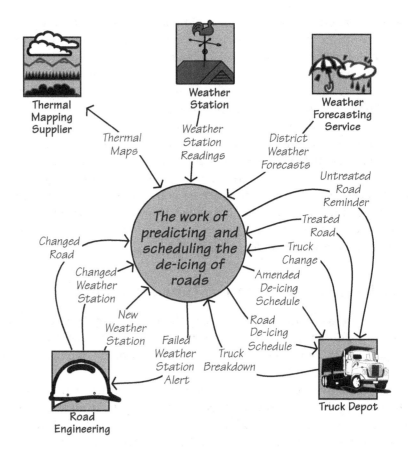

The context diagram shows the flows of data entering and leaving the work; each flow that enters the work has to be processed. The amount of functionality needed to process it depends on the amount of data—the number of data elements—carried by the flow. Thus one of the measurements used by function point counting is the number of data elements in the flow. Determining this number is easier if you have already written a data dictionary entry for each flow. If not, it is simple enough to do without.

Data Stored by the Work

Another determinant of the needed functionality is the data to be stored by the work. Each database, file, or any other storage medium for data requires some functionality to maintain it. Again, the amount of functionality depends on the amount of data (expressed as the number of data elements) and the complexity of the data (in other words, the number of records or tables the data is organized into). This is easy enough to discover if you have a class model of the data, such as that shown in Figure C.2.

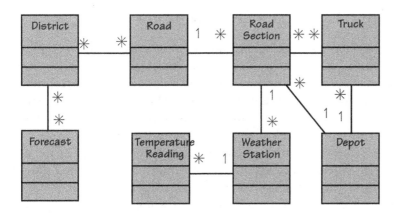

Figure C.2

The stored data model for the work area. There are a number of classes in the model; each one represents something about which the work stores data. Each class has a number of attributes. The function point counting procedure uses both of these numbers.

Each of the classes shown in the data model contains attributes—that is, the elementary items of data that together describe the class. The simple way to think of elements is that they have alphanumeric values, and classes are the subjects of the data.

If you look at both the context model in Figure C.1 and the class model in Figure C.2, you can imagine how the work uses the incoming data to process and maintain the stored data. The two models should be seen as two views of the same piece of work.

If you do not have a data model, then it sufficient for our purposes here to simply list the classes—these are anything that is uniquely identified by the work. If it carries an identifier (such as a credit card, a telephone, an account, an employee, a bank transfer, or a motor car), then consider it to be a class. Considering that speed is more important than hyper-accuracy at this stage, a simple list of classes will suffice.

Classes are anything that is uniquely identified by the work.

Business Use Cases

Again, we can make use of what you already have to count the function points. In Chapter 4, we examined the idea of partitioning the work using business events. A business event is either some happening outside the work or some happening caused by the passage of time that triggers a response (we call it a business use case) from the work. Business use cases are not only a convenient way to gather requirements, but also a convenient way to count function points. Let's assume you have partitioned the work into business use cases, and show how they are measured.

Unfortunately, the UML use case diagram is of no help to us here, as it does not contain any information about the inputs, outputs, or stored data. Instead, we will use a data flow model of a business use case to illustrate how function points are counted. We hasten to add there is no need for you to draw these diagrams to count function points; we are using them purely for illustrative purposes.

Counting Function Points for Business Use Cases

We said earlier that you could count function points either for the work as a whole or for each business use case at a time. It is usually more convenient to count for each business use case, so we will illustrate that technique here.

The counting procedure varies slightly depending on the primary intention of the business use case. Think of this as what the adjacent system wants or needs when it triggers the business event. If it simply intends to supply data to be stored within the work—an example of this is when you pay your utility bill—then it is called an *input* business use case. When the primary intention of the adjacent system when it triggers the business use case is to receive some output, then we call it an *output* business use case. Time-triggered business use cases are referred to as *inquiries*; the data stored by the work is being inquired upon, so this name makes sense.

To measure the amount of functionality of a business use case—recall that you are trying to figure out how long it will take to analyze it—you count the data elements of the incoming and/or outgoing data flows, and the number of classes referenced by the business use case. We will show how this is done for each type of business use case.

Counting Input Business Use Cases

One of the business events we mentioned in Chapter 4 is called *Weather station transmits reading*. This is a simple enough event—we show it in Figure C.3—and its primary intention is to update some internally stored data. Outputs from this kind of business use case, if any, are trivial and can safely be ignored. In the model of the business use case, you see the incoming flow of data *Weather Station Reading* and the functionality it triggers inside the work. The result of the functionality is two classes of data are referenced. "Referenced" in this context can mean either the class is written to or read; it does not matter which one.

The model of the business use case shown in Figure C.3 provides all that is needed to count the function points.

First, count the data elements or attributes that make up *Weather Station Reading*. This is easier if you have a data dictionary entry for it, but failing that, estimate the number. We could say it is likely to have an identifier for the weather station, the temperature, the moisture content of the road surface, the data, the time, and possibly one or two others. That makes seven attributes. Hold on to that number.

The business use case references two classes of data. Even without any detailed study of the work, it is easy enough to see that there is no need for more stored data to be involved.

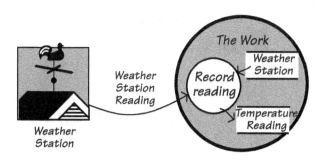

Figure C.3

The primary intention of this input business use case is to alter internally stored data. It references two classes. It does not matter whether they are written to or read.

Next, you convert those two numbers to function points. To do so, we use the matrix shown in Figure C.4. The example business use case has 7 data attributes in the input flow, and references 2 classes. The cell at the intersection of these counts gives a result of 4 function points.

That's it for this business use case. The official function point counting practices have an additional step of assigning a complexity measure and using it to adjust the function point count. However, as few people bother with it and the increment in accuracy is marginal, we shall not bother with it here.

The process outlined previously is repeated for each of the input business use cases. The function point count can be aggregated to give you the count for the whole of the work, or you can use the counts to compare the relative expense for analyzing each of the business use cases.

Of course, not all the business use cases are inputs.

Counting Output Business Use Cases

An *output* business use case is one where the primary intention of the business use case is to achieve the output flow. That is, when the adjacent system triggers the business event, it wants the work to produce something. The oncoming data flow is a request for the output, and it contains whatever information is needed for the work to determine what is wanted. The work

Data attributes of input flow

		1-4	5-15	16+
Classes referenced	<2	3	3	4
	2	3	4	6
	>2	4	6	6

Figure C.4

The function point counts for an *input* business use case. The correct function point counting terminology for these is *external inputs*.

Figure C.5

This is an *output* business use case. The primary goal of the adjacent system when triggering this business use case is to obtain the output information.

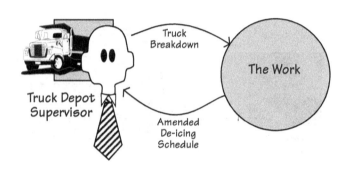

produces the significant output flow, and in so doing, makes some calculations, or it updates stored data, or both.

When measuring an output business use case, you count the *data elements* in the output flow: These are the individual data items. You can also call them "attributes" of the flow. It would be helpful to have a data dictionary at this stage, but simply looking at the flow leads you to take an educated guess at what it contains. For example, the *Amended De-icing Schedule* in Figure C.5 would be expected to contain data elements such as the following:

Road

Road section

Truck identifier

Starting time

Latest possible time

Distance to treat

And maybe one or two others. Let's say eight. It might seem a little cavalier to be taking guesses like this, but when you look at the matrix in Figure C.6, you see the data elements arranged in ranges of 1 to 5, 6 to 19, and 20 and

Figure C.6

The function points for *output* business use cases.

Data Elements

		1-5	6-19	20+
Classes Referenced	<2	4	4	5
	2-3	4	5	7
	>3	5	7	7

greater. Your real need here is to determine, as best you can, which range the data element count for the output flow falls into.

The next step in the count is to look at the data referenced by the business use case. In Figure C.3, we were kind enough to show the classes referenced by the business use case; we won't be so kind this time. Go back to the class model in Figure C.2, and imagine the processing for this business use case. You are rescheduling a truck to cover for a broken-down truck, so all that is needed is to find the roads and road sections allocated to the broken truck, find another truck attached to the same depot, and reallocate the roads and sections.

That's four classes: *Road*, *Road Section*, *Truck*, and *Depot*. Now refer to the matrix in Figure C.6. The number of elements in the output flow is 8, and the number of classes referenced is 4. The matrix shows 7 function points. These function points are added to your accumulated total, and you continue with the rest of the business use cases.

Counting Time-Triggered Business Use Cases

Time-triggered business use cases are almost always reports. They are produced when a predetermined time is reached—we report sales on the last day of the month; we send out invoices five days after the purchase—or because someone wants to see a report or get some information from the work. The function point counting people know this kind of business use case as an *inquiry*. This is not a bad name, as such use cases start by inquiring on the stored data.

The underlying assumption with this kind of business use case is that there are no significant calculations. If the processing is more than just the simple retrieval of stored data, then it must be classified as an *output* business use case. That is, the stored data is updated and/or nontrivial calculations are involved. Your count must reflect this action by allowing for its greater complexity.

The example shown in Figure C.7 is triggered by time. That is, every two hours it is time for the work to generate a schedule of the roads to be treated, and send it to the Depot.

If the business use case shown in Figure C.7 were to be an on-demand report, then it would be possible for someone at the *Truck Depot* to enter parameters to get the schedule he wanted. Unless nontrivial processing goes on as a result or data stores are modified, this is still considered a time-triggered, inquiry type of business use case. For on-demand reports, count the data elements in both the input parameter flow and the resultant output flow. However, if a data element appears in both the input and output flows, count it only once.

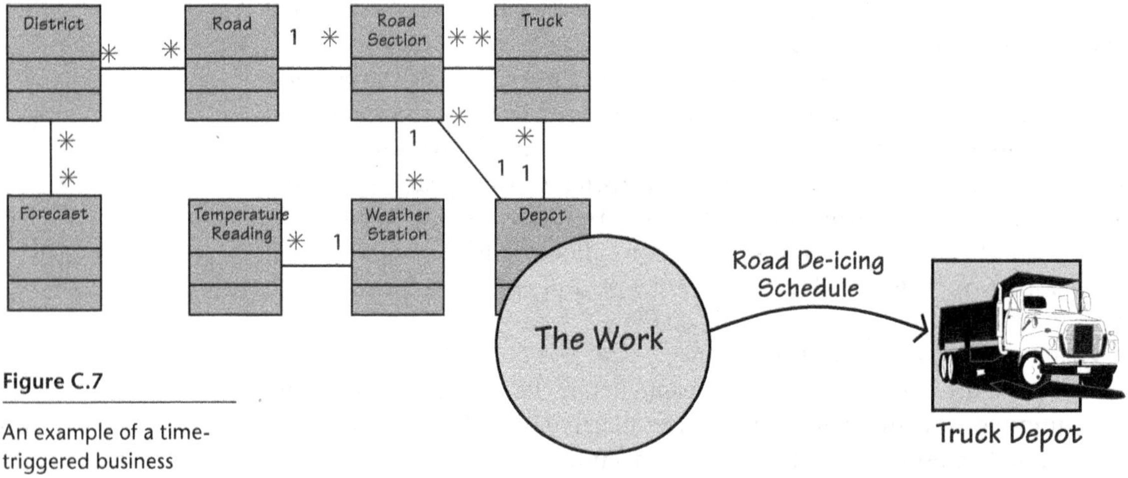

Figure C.7

An example of a time-triggered business use case. This kind of business use case, in which there is no input from an adjacent system, is also called an *inquiry*. It gets this name because the stored data is simply retrieved and not modified, and there are no calculations. This business use case references all the stored data classes.

To count the function points for the time-triggered business use case shown in Figure C.7, use the inquiry matrix shown in Figure C.8. This business use case has to reference all eight of the classes to make its predictions about ice formation. The amended schedule we saw a little while back had eight data elements; this output would have the same number.

Note that these are *unduplicated* elements. You are counting unique data elements, which you might also call *data element types*.

Turning to the matrix shown in Figure C.8, the combination of 8 data elements and more than 3 classes referenced yields 6 function points. Add the 6 function points to your total and continue counting the other business use cases.

Figure C.8

The function points for *inquiries* or time-triggered business use cases.

Classes Referenced	Data Elements 1-5	6-19	20+
1	3	3	4
2-3	3	4	6
>3	4	6	6

Counting the Stored Data

The data stored within the work area has to be maintained. This task naturally requires an amount of functionality, which can also be counted by measuring the amount and complexity of the data. For this part of the count, you take pretty much the same steps as before, except that now you count only the stored data—business use cases do not figure in this count at all.

Internal Stored Data

The first of the stored data to be counted is the data held inside the work area. Function point counting manuals refer to such data as *internal logical files*. These items include the databases, flat files, paper files, or whatever else is part of your work area. Keep in mind that any files that are there for implementation reasons are not counted—for example, backups and manual files that are identical (or close) to automated files.

You count from the class model of the data. This time, for each entity, count its *attributes*. Skip any attributes that are there for purely technological reasons, but count foreign keys (pointers from one class to another). The count should be accurate enough to assign the class to one of the three columns shown in Figure C.10.

The next count is *record elements*. These are either the class itself or subtypes of classes. That is, if the class has no subtypes, it is one unit of data and counts as one record element. If there are subtypes, then you must count those as record elements. We do not have any subtypes in the IceBreaker class model, so let us invent some. Suppose that weather stations come in various types. One special type does not have a surface moisture sensor, so predictions made with the data from this kind of weather station are done differently. Moreover, the work needs to keep special data relating to this kind of weather station. The stations also fail from time to time. When they do, the work needs to store special data relating to past predictions from this station.

The result of these changes is that we have created two subtypes of the weather station class (you can also call these subclasses). The resulting model is shown in Figure C.9.

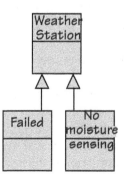

Figure C.9

The *Weather Station* entity has two subtypes. The *Failed* subtype contains attributes about past predictions that are used in lieu of current readings. The *No moisture sensing* subtype has attributes describing adjustments to be made to compensate for the weather station not being equipped with a moisture sensor. These subtypes are necessary, as their attributes do not apply to all stations.

Figure C.10

The function point counts for *internally stored data*, or *internal logical files* as they are known in function point terminology.

Attributes

		1-19	20-50	51+
Record Elements	<2	7	7	10
	2-5	7	10	15
	>5	10	15	15

In function point terms, the *Weather Station* entity counts for 2 record elements. You count only the subtypes, not the parent entity. For the other entities in the class model, count them as having 1 record element.

The next step is to count the number of attributes in each class. This task is not as arduous as it might at first seem. According to the matrix shown in Figure C.10, you need to know only if there are between 1 and 19 attributes to the class, or between 20 and 50, or more than 51. Given the range of these numbers, and given the desire to do this step quickly, it is permissible to make some inspired guesses about the number of attributes for the entity.

Pick a class—say, *Truck*. How many attributes does the *Truck* class have? Or, as you could say here, does it have more than 19? Unlikely. So let us say that the *Truck* class has 19 or fewer attributes, and no subclasses so it counts as 1 record element. That means it needs 7 function points worth of functionality to support it.

Do the same thing for the remainder of the stored data. Most items will also have a count of 7, as none of them should have more than 19 attributes, and only *Weather Station* has two subtypes, and even has few enough attributes to count for 7 function points. There are 8 entities in the stored data model, so the *internal* stored data attracts 56 function points.

Externally Stored Data

Most pieces of work you study make use of data stored and maintained outside of the work. For example, almost every project has to reference stored data that is owned by some other part of the organization or, in some cases, by another organization.

References to external stored data show up on the context diagram as interactions with *cooperative adjacent systems*—that is, adjacent systems that receive requests for data and immediately send back a response. The IceBreaker work makes use of thermal maps that are maintained by an outside body. When the scheduling business use case needs this data, it makes a request for the map of the appropriate district, and the thermal map supplier responds with the requested information. This situation is illustrated in Figure C.11.

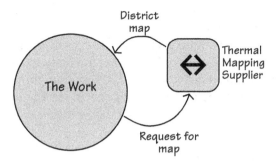

Figure C.11

The *Thermal Mapping Supplier* is an external system that maintains a database of the temperature differentials within areas. This data is too volatile for the IceBreaker work to maintain, so it elects to query this cooperative adjacent system whenever it needs the data.

Although external data does not have to be maintained by the work, the need for the data adds functionality to the work; as a consequence, external data is also counted. You can make such a count in the same way as you did for the internal data; however, instead of building a data model, let's use educated guesses to size the data.

The external stored data deals with the temperatures of roads. Specifically, it consists of the road surface temperature for every meter of every road. However, even though the data is repetitive, you count a just single iteration.

No, don't even count. Look at the matrix in Figure C.12 and note that once again you just need to guess whether the number of attributes is 19 or fewer, 20 to 50, or more than 50. The thermal mapping database would fall into the first column. Further educated guesswork would suggest there are fewer than 2 record elements—the number could have been as large as 5, as it would make no difference to the count—so this external data adds 5 function points to the functionality of the work.

Repeat this process for each of the classes in the externally stored data. In the case of IceBreaker, it appears there is only one class in the database. This situation is a little unusual, as you will normally find more than that in your databases.

A small aside: Figure C.11 shows the use of externally stored data. The flows to and from the adjacent system are *not* counted for function point

Attributes

Record Elements		1-19	20-50	51+
	<2	5	5	7
	2-5	5	7	10
	>5	7	10	10

Figure C.12

The function point counts for *external interface files*, or data stored held by a cooperative adjacent system.

purposes. They are omitted because the adjacent system is a cooperative system; that is, it provides some service in collaboration with the work area. Thus the flows would be parameters to query the database, and the resultant data comes from that database. For both flows, their attributes would be the same as the attributes of the stored data. For function point counting purposes, think only about the use of the adjacent system's database—in this case, it is providing data as if it were inside the work area.

Adjust for What You Don't Know

You are counting function points during the requirements activity. You may not have all the data you need to create a completely accurate function point count. Earlier, we explained how you count the function points using the inputs, outputs, inquiries, internal files, and external files. Even if you do not have all five of these parameters, you can still count function points. The count is simply adjusted according to how many of these parameters you have available to count.

Figure C.13 provides the *range of uncertainty* depending on the number of parameters used in your count. For example, if you used only 3 parameters— say, the inputs, outputs, and inquiries (the easiest options to find, as they are the data flows that show up on the context model)—then your function point count is accurate within a range of ±15 percent.

Now That I Have Counted Function Points, What's Next?

The function point count for the requirements activity for the project is simply the aggregation of the counts for all the business use cases and the stored data. Now you must convert that count into some indication of effort needed for the requirements activity. In the early part of this appendix, we showed a rule of thumb used by Capers Jones. So many people use this rule

Figure C.13

This table, courtesy of Capers Jones, shows the uncertainty ranges based on the number of parameters you use in your function point counting. This information comes from the study of many software projects.

Number of parameters used	Range of uncertainty
1	+ or - 40%
2	+ or - 20%
3	+ or - 15%
4	+ or - 10%
5	+ or - 5%

that we believe it is worth trying on your project. Of course, data that comes from your own organization is preferable, but obtaining it requires you to count the function points for previous projects to come up with your own metric of hours (or money) needed per function point.

You can also get help. Following are some resources that have useful information. As we said at the beginning of this appendix, our aim is to give you a gentle introduction to counting function points, and to make you interested enough to want to carry the subject further.

A lot of material is available on the Web, much of it free. These organizations are good places to start for more information on function points, as well as productivity metrics:

- International Software Benchmarking Group: www.isbsg.org
- International Function Point Users Group: www.ifpug.org
- Quality Plus Technologies: www.qualityplustech.com
- Software Productivity Research: www.spr.com
- United Kingdom Software Metrics Association: www.uksma.co.uk/

Additionally, we recommend the following resources:

Bundschuh, Manfred, and Carol Dekkers. *The IT Measurement Compendium: Estimating and Benchmarking Success with Functional Size Measurement.* Springer, 2010.

Dekkers, Carol. *Demystifying Function Points: Clarifying Common Terminology.* http://www.qualityplustech.com. This source is used internally at IBM as one of its definition standards.

Dekkers, Carol. *Function Point Counting and CFPS Study Guides Volumes 1, 2, and 3.* Quality Plus, 2002. http://www.qualityplustech.com. In addition to case studies, all of these study guides provide logistics/hints for the IFPUG Certified Function Point Specialist (CFPS) Exam.

Fenton, Norman, and Shari Lawrence Pfleeger. *Software Metrics: A Rigorous and Practical Approach,* second edition. Thomson Computer Press, 1996. This book looks at several ways of measuring the software development process. The case studies alone—on Hewlett-Packard, IBM, and the U.S. Department of Defense—are worth the price of the book.

Garmus, David, and David Herron. *Function Point Analysis: Measurement Practices for Successful Software Projects.* Addison-Wesley, 2001. This book provides a thorough treatment of function point counting using the IFPUG rules.

Pfleeger, Shari Lawrence. *Software Cost Estimation and Sizing Methods, Issues, and Guidelines.* Rand Publishing, 2005. This book covers function points and several other measuring methods. Recommended for its breadth of coverage.

Putman, Lawrence, and Ware Myers. *Five Core Metrics: The Intelligence Behind Successful Software Management.* Dorset House, 2003. Not function points but some other and very good ways and things to measure. The authors demonstrate how the five core metrics—time, effort, size, reliability, and process productivity—are used to control and adjust projects.

That's not really all there is to function point counting, but it is enough for the quick counts needed at requirements time.

Volere Requirements Knowledge Model

The Volere Requirements Knowledge Model (Figure D.1) provides a language for the knowledge that you discover and accumulate during your requirements activities. We present it as a guide to the information you need to discover, and as a tool for communication between the various stakeholders on your project. The model can also serve as your specification for which requirements knowledge you plan to discover and trace. Your own process must define who gathers which information, to what degree of detail, and how it will be packaged and reviewed.

If you are not familiar with this notation:

- A rectangle represents a *class* of knowledge. The name of the class is written in the rectangle.
- A line represents an *association* between two or more classes.
- *Multiplicity* is shown by 1 and *. This means if you have only one of a class, there are * (many) of the class at the other end of the association.

Definitions of Requirements Knowledge Classes and Associations

The purpose of the knowledge model is to provide you with a common of language for communicating and managing requirements. Use the model as a starting point and then, if you need to, add other classes and associations to reflect the way that you need to manage your requirements knowledge.

It is, of course, necessary for everyone using the knowledge model to have the same understanding of what the names of the classes mean. This means

Figure D.1

The knowledge model identifies the classes of knowledge concerned with requirements and the associations between them.

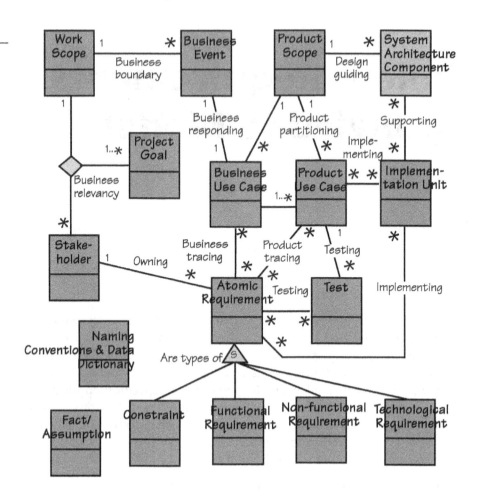

you need a dictionary to support the model. The following is a definition of the classes of knowledge and their associations; the classes are listed before the associations.

Knowledge Classes

Knowledge class: Atomic Requirement

Purpose:

A Requirement specifies a business need; it has a number of attributes.

Attributes:

Requirement Number
Requirement Description

Requirement Rationale

Requirement Type

Requirement Fit Criterion

Requirement Source

Customer Satisfaction

Customer Dissatisfaction

Conflicting Requirements

Dependent Requirements

Supporting Material

Version Number

Considerations:

Also see the subtypes of requirements—namely, Constraint, Functional Requirement, Non-functional Requirement, Technological Requirement.

Suggested Implementation:

Sections 9 though 17 of the Volere Requirements Specification Template. There are various automated tools available; these allow team access to the requirements.

Knowledge class: Business Event

Purpose:

A Business Event is some happening outside the work scope that is, in effect, a demand for some service provided by the work. Examples: a motorist passes an electronic tollbooth, a customer orders a book, a doctor asks for the scan of a patient, a pilot lowers the landing gear.

Business events can also happen because of the passage of time. Examples: if a customer's bill is not paid in 30 days, then it is time for the work to send a reminder; it is two months before an insurance policy is due to expire.

Attributes:

Business Event Name

Business Event Adjacent Systems/Actors

Business Event Summary

Considerations:

It is important to recognize the business event. Its nature, the circumstances that exist at the time the event happens, and the activity of the adjacent system at the time of the business event are all important indicators of the appropriate response.

Suggested Implementation:

Section 6 of the Volere Requirements Specification Template. A list of the business events and their associated input and output flows will suffice. It is practical to give each business event a unique identifier.

Knowledge class: Business Use Case

Purpose:

A Business Use Case (BUC) is the processing done in response to a business event. Example: a policyholder decides to make a claim is a business event. The business use case is all the processing done by the work to approve or deny the claim. Also see Product Use Case.

Attributes:

Business Use Case Name

Business Use Case Description

Business Use Case Input

Business Use Case Outputs

Business Use Case Rationale

Business Use Case Priority

Normal Case Scenario

Exception Case Scenarios

Preconditions

Post or exit conditions

Considerations:

Business use cases are self-contained portions of the work, and can be studied independently. For this reason they are an important unit that project leaders can use to structure the analytical work.

Suggested Implementation:

Section 6 of the Volere Requirements Specification Template. BUCs can be represented using any combination of business process models, sequence diagrams, activity diagrams, scenarios, or any other representation that is acceptable to the people involved—providing the BUC is within the boundaries declared for the Business Event.

Knowledge class: Constraint

Purpose:

A Constraint is a type of requirement. It is a limit placed on the design of the product, or on the project itself, such as budget or time restrictions.

Considerations:

We treat constraints as a type of requirement that must be met. However, we highlight them, as it is important that you and your management are aware of them.

Suggested Implementation:

Section 3 of the Volere Requirements Specification Template. Design constraints should be recorded in the same way as the other requirements. See the Knowledge class **Requirement** for the attributes.

Knowledge class: Fact/Assumption

Purpose:

An Assumption states an expectation on which decisions about the project are based. For example, it might be an assumption that another project will be finished first, or that a particular law will not be changed, or that a particular supplier will reach a specified level of performance. If an assumption turns out not to be true, there might be far-reaching and unknown effects on the project.

A Fact is some knowledge that is relevant to the project and affects its requirements and design. A Fact can also state some specific exclusion from the product and the reason for that exclusion.

Fact/Assumption is a global class and could have an Association with any of the other classes in your knowledge model.

Attributes:

Description of the Assumption/Fact

Reference to people and documents for more details

Considerations:

Assumptions indicate a risk. For this reason they should be highlighted and all affected parties made aware of the assumption. You could consider installing a mechanism to resolve all assumptions before implementation starts.

Suggested Implementation:

Section 5 of the Volere Requirements Specification Template; these can be written in free text. They should be regularly circulated to management and the project team.

Knowledge class: Functional Requirement

Purpose:

A Functional Requirement is something that the product must do. Examples: calculate the fare, analyze the chemical composition, record the change of name, find the new route. Functional requirements are concerned with creating, updating, referencing, and deleting the essential subject matter within the context of the study.

Attributes:

This is a subtype of **Atomic Requirement** and inherits its attributes.

Suggested Implementation:

Section 9 of the Volere Requirements Specification Template. See the Knowledge class **Atomic Requirement** for the attributes.

Knowledge class: Implementation Unit

Purpose:

The unit for packaging your implementation.

Attributes:

Implementation Unit Name

Considerations:

This could be what your customers refer to as a "feature"; if your product is a consumer item, then it might be called a "function." The choice of implementation unit is driven by a combination of your implementation technology and your implementation process. When you tailor this part of the knowledge model, you might find that you replace your implementation unit with several classes. The important issue is that you can unambiguously trace your implementation unit back to the relevant requirements.

Knowledge class: Naming Conventions & Data Dictionary

Purpose:

A dictionary that defines the meaning of terms used within the requirements. This dictionary will be expanded throughout the project to include terms that are related to the implementation. This global class could have an association with any of the other classes in your knowledge model. Consistent use of the same terminology—as defined in the dictionary—helps to minimize misunderstandings.

Attributes:

Name of the Term

Definition of the Term

Suggested Implementation:

Section 4 of the Volere Requirements Specification Template; this should be in the form of a **glossary**. Along with the work context and the product context, it provides a good introduction for new team members.

Section 7 of the Volere Requirements Specification Template; there is a formal **dictionary** that defines all of the data in the inputs, outputs, and attributes within the scope of the work and the scope of the product. The dictionary provides a mechanism for connecting business terminology and implementation terminology.

Knowledge class: Non-functional Requirement

Purpose:

A Non-functional Requirement is a quality that the product must have. Examples: fast, attractive, secure, customizable, maintainable, portable. Non-functional requirements types are Look and Feel, Usability, Performance and Safety, Operational Environment, Maintainability and Portability, Security, Cultural and Political, and Legal.

Attributes:

This is a subtype of **Atomic Requirement** and inherits its attributes.

Considerations:

The non-functional properties are important if the user or buyer is to accept the product.

Suggested Implementation:

Sections 10 though 17 of the Volere Requirements Specification Template. It is vital that you give all non-functional requirements the correct fit criteria.

Knowledge class: Product Scope

Purpose:

The product scope identifies the boundaries of the product that will be built. The scope is a summary of the boundaries of all the product use cases.

Attributes:

> User Names
> User Roles
> Other Adjacent Systems
> Interface descriptions

Suggested Implementation:

Section 8 of the Volere Requirements Specification Template. This should preferably be a diagram, either a use case diagram or a product scope model supported by a product use case summary table. Some interface descriptions might be supported by prototypes or simulations.

Knowledge class: Product Use Case

Purpose:

A Product Use Case (PUC) is a functional grouping of requirements that will be implemented by the product. It is that part of the business use case that you decide to build as a product.

Attributes:

> Product Use Case Name
> Product Use Case Identifier
> Product Use Case Description
> Product Use Case Users
> Product Use Case Inputs
> Product Use Case Outputs
> Product Use Case Stories
> Product Use Case Scenarios
> Product Use Case Fit Criterion

Product Use Case Owner

Product Use Case Benefit

Product Use Case Priority

Suggested Implementation:

Section 8 of the Volere Requirements Specification Template. The product use cases are a good mechanism for communication within the extended project team. They might take the form of models, user stories, scenarios, or anything else that suits the people involved. Whatever the type of representation, the details of the PUC should be within the boundaries declared by the PUC inputs and outputs.

Knowledge class: Project Goal

Purpose:

To understand why the company is making an investment in doing this project. There might be several project goals.

Attributes:

Project Goal Description

Business Advantage

Measure of Success

Suggested Implementation:

Section 1 of the Volere Requirements Specification Template. This is the basis for making decisions about scope, relevance, and priority; it is the guiding light for the project. Ideally, this goal should be defined as part of the project initiation. All project goals should be unambiguously defined and agreed to by stakeholders before putting effort into discovering detailed requirements.

Knowledge class: Stakeholder

Purpose:

Identifies all the people, roles, and organizations that have an interest in the project. This population includes the project team, direct users of the product, other indirect beneficiaries of the product, specialists with technical skills needed to build the product, external organizations with rules or laws pertaining to the product, external organizations with specialist knowledge about the product's domain, opponents of the product, and producers of competitive products.

Attributes:

> Stakeholder Role
>
> Stakeholder Name
>
> Types of Knowledge
>
> Necessary Participation
>
> Appropriate Trawling Techniques
>
> Contact information (e.g., e-mail address)

Suggested Implementation:

Section 2 of the Volere Requirements Specification Template. Use the stakeholder map and stakeholder analysis template to define the attributes for each stakeholder.

Knowledge class: System Architecture Component

Purpose:

A piece of technology, software, hardware, or abstract container that influences, facilitates, or places constraints on the design.

Knowledge class: Technological Requirement

Purpose:

A Technological Requirement exists because of the technology chosen for the implementation. These requirements are there to serve the purposes of the technology, and are not originated by the business.

Attributes:

This is a subtype of **Atomic Requirement** and inherits its attributes.

Considerations:

The technological requirements should be considered only when you know the technological environment. They can be recorded alongside the business requirements, but it must be clear which is which.

Knowledge class: Test

Purpose:

The design for Test is the result of a tester reviewing a requirement's fit criterion (precise measure) and designing a cost-effective test to prove whether a solution meets the fit criterion.

Considerations:

You might consider having your testing people write the test cases as the requirements are being written. Also consider that the requirement's fit criterion is the basis of the test case.

Knowledge class: Work Scope

Purpose:

Defines the boundary of the investigation necessary to discover, invent, understand, and identify the requirements for the product.

Attributes:

    Adjacent Systems

    Input Data Flows

    Output Data Flows

    Work Context Description

Considerations:

The work scope should be recorded publicly, as our experience indicates that it is the most widely referenced document. A context model is an effective communication tool for defining the work context.

Suggested Implementation:

Section 7 of the Volere Requirements Specification Template. This is best illustrated with a context model.

Associations

Association: Business boundary

Purpose:

    To partition the work context according to the functional reality of the business.

Multiplicity:

    For each Business Event, there is one Work Context.

    For each Work Context, there are potentially many Business Events.

Association: Business relevancy

Purpose:

To ensure that there are relevant business connections between the scope of the investigation, the project purpose, and the stakeholders.

Multiplicity:

The trinary Association is as follows:

> For each instance of one Work Context and one Stakeholder, there are one or more Project Purposes.
>
> For each instance of one Project Purpose and one Stakeholder, there is one Work Context.
>
> For each instance of one Project Purpose and one Work Context, there are potentially many Stakeholders.

Association: Business responding

Purpose:

To reveal which business use cases are used to respond to the business event.

Multiplicity:

> For each Business Event, there is usually one, but could be more than one, Business Use Case.
>
> For each Business Use Case, there can be only one triggering Business Event.

Association: Business tracing

Purpose:

To keep track of which requirements are generated by which business use cases. Note that this is a many-to-many association because a given requirement might exist in more than one business use case.

Multiplicity:

> For each Business Use Case, there are potentially many Atomic Requirements.
>
> For each Atomic Requirement, there are potentially many Business Use Cases.

Association: Implementing

Purpose:

To keep track of which product use cases are implemented in which implementation units.

Multiplicity:

For each Product Use Case, there are potentially many Implementation Units.

For each Implementation Unit, there are potentially many Product Use Cases.

Association: Owning

Purpose:

To keep track of which stakeholders are the originators of which requirements. The idea of "ownership" is to identify a person who takes the responsibility for helping to get answers to questions about the requirement.

Multiplicity:

For each Requirement, there is one Stakeholder.

For each Stakeholder, there are potentially many Requirements.

Association: Product partitioning

Purpose:

All the product use cases together form the complete scope of the product. The product scope is partitioned into a number of product use cases.

Multiplicity:

For each Product Use Case, there is one Product Scope.

For each Product Scope, there are potentially many Product Use Cases.

Association: Product tracing

Purpose:

To keep track of which requirements are contained in which product use cases for the purpose of traceability and dealing with change.

Multiplicity:

> For each Requirement, there are potentially many Product Use Cases.
>
> For each Product Use Case, there are potentially many Atomic Requirements.

Association: Supporting

Purpose:

To keep track of which systems architecture components support which implementation units for the purpose of tracking tests and assessing impact of change.

Multiplicity:

> For each System Architecture Component, there are potentially many Implementation Units.
>
> For each Implementation Unit, there are potentially many System Architecture Components.

Association: Testing

Purpose:

To keep track of which atomic requirements or PUC-related groups of atomic requirements are covered by which tests.

Multiplicity:

> For each Test, there are potentially many Atomic Requirements.

Knowledge Model Annotated with Template Section Numbers

The Volere Requirements Knowledge Model is a formal structure for identifying and relating classes of requirements knowledge. In the view of it presented in Figure D.2, the numbers on the classes provide cross-references to the relevant sections of the Volere Requirements Specification Template.

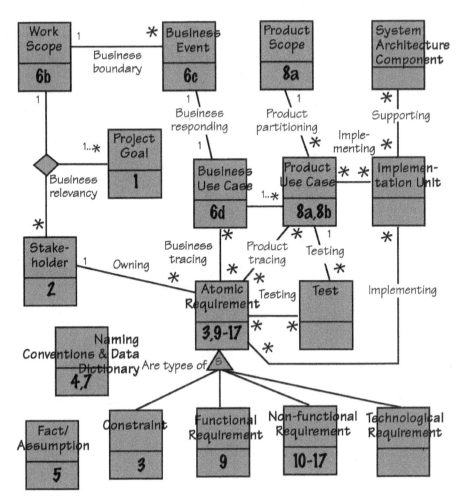

Figure D.2

The Volere Requirements Knowledge Model with cross-references to the relevant sections of the Volere Requirements Specification Template

Glossary

Actor The person or automated system that interacts with a product use case. Actors are also known as *users* and end users.

Adjacent system A system (person, organization, computer system) that provides information to, or receives information from, the work that you are studying.

Agile development A way of developing software using *iterative development*. A variety of agile techniques exist, including Scrum, eXtreme Programming, and Crystal. We use the term *iterative* to mean any agile or iterative technique.

Agile Manifesto A set of principles that focuses on the delivery of working software to the customer, collaborative working practices, and the ability to respond rapidly to change.

Atomic requirement A requirement that is testable and does not need further decomposition. See also *Functional requirement, Non-functional requirement, Constraint, Snow card.*

Attribute A data element that describes (and has been attributed) to a class. Also used to mean the components of an *atomic requirement.*

Blastoff A technique for building the foundation for the requirements activity by establishing the scope–stakeholders–goals trinity, and verifying the viability of the project.

Brown Cow Model A technique for discussing and modeling the work by using different system viewpoints. The viewpoints are permutations of now, future, how, and what.

Business analyst The role responsible for discovering and communicating requirements among the project's stakeholders. Also referred to as requirements analyst, requirements engineer, and systems analyst.

Business data model   A model of the essential classes of business data and associations between them necessary to support the functional requirements within the scope of the work.

Business event   Something that happens to the business (usually called "the work"), that makes it respond. Examples: "Customer pays an invoice," "Truck reports all roads have been treated," "Time to read electricity meters," "Surfer wants to search website."

Business process model   A model of the processes within a business; often used to understand the current processes so that they can be improved. A variety of notations can be used for such models.

Business use case (BUC)   The work's response to a business event. It includes the processes and the stored data needed to satisfy the request implicit in the business event. See also *Product use case*.

Class   A physical or abstract entity within a context of study that has one or more attributes of stored data.

Client   The person who pays for the development of the product, or who has organizational responsibility for the project. Also known as the *sponsor*.

Constraint   A requirement, either organizational or technological, that restricts the way you produce the product. It may be a management edict on the way the product must be designed—"It must work on a 4G mobile phone"—or a budget that limits the extent of the product or a characteristic of the current technology that constrains the possible solutions.

Context   The subject matter, people, and organizations that affect the requirements for the product. The context of study, or the work context, identifies the business being studied and the adjacent systems that interact with this work. The product context identifies the scope of the product and its interactions with users and other actors.

Context diagram   A graphic model of the *work scope* showing how the work to be investigated connects to the outside world.

Commercial off-the-shelf (COTS) products   Products (usually software) developed by external organizations to carry out a specified range of functionality.

Customer   A person who buys the product.

Data dictionary   Specification (to the elemental level) of the terms used in the requirements specification.

Data element   A piece of data that has a defined range or set of values within a context of study. Also called an *attribute*.

Data flow   Data that moves from one process to another; usually represented by a named arrow.

Data model   A model showing *classes* of data and the associations between them. This is also known as a class model. See also *Business data model*.

Design   The act of crafting a technological solution to fit the requirements, within the constraints.

Developer   Someone who is part of the technological development or building of the product. Examples: programmer (often called a developer) designer, architect.

Domain analysis   The activity of investigating, capturing, and specifying generic knowledge about a subject-matter area.

Essential viewpoint   A viewpoint that focuses on the rules, policy, and data independent from any implementation of those rules, policy, and data. Also referred to as *thinking above the line*.

External event   An event triggered by a happening in an adjacent system outside the work context. Example: "Customer wants to open an account." See also *Time-triggered event*.

Fit criterion   A quantification or measurement of the requirement such that you are able to determine whether the delivered product satisfies (fits) the requirement.

Function point   A measure of the functionality of the work or a piece of software. Function points were first proposed by Allan Albrecht; today the method for counting function points is specified by the International Function Point User Group.

Functional requirement   Something that the product must do. Functional requirements are part of the fundamental processes of the product.

Innovation   Fresh thinking, or thinking differently, about the problem to find a new and better way to do the work.

Iterative development   Strategies that facilitate repetitive and continuous delivery of software solutions.

Naming conventions   The terminology (including abbreviations and acronyms) that the stakeholders use when talking about the work. This terminology is usually captured in a glossary such as the one you are reading.

Non-functional requirement   A property or quality that the product must have, such as an appearance, speed, security, or accuracy property.

Persona   A virtual person, archetypical of your users, invented to help you to discover the requirements.

Product   The thing you are writing your requirements for. In this book, "product" usually means a software product, but the requirements can be for hardware, consumer goods, a service, or any other thing you need to specify.

Product use case (PUC)   The part of the business use case you decide to automate. You write the requirements for the product use case. See also *Business use case*.

Project blastoff   See *Blastoff*.

Project goal   The reasons for doing the project. The goal must include a quantification of the expected benefit.

Prototype   A simulation of the product using software prototyping tools, low-fidelity whiteboards, or paper mockups. Also referred to as a *sketch*.

Quality Gateway   Application of a set of tests (relevance, ambiguity, viability, fit, and so on) to assure the quality of individual requirements before the requirements become part of the requirements specification.

Rationale   The justification for a requirement. It is used to help understand a requirement, and usually reveals the underlying reason for the requirement.

Requirement   Something that the product must do, or a property that the product must have, that is needed or wanted by the stakeholders.

Requirements analyst   The person who has responsibility for producing the requirements specification. The analyst does not necessarily do all of the requirements elicitation, but is responsible for coordinating the requirements effort. Depending on how roles are defined in an organization, this individual might be referred to as a *business analyst*, systems analyst, or requirements engineer.

Requirements creep   The uncontrolled addition of new requirements to the product after the requirements are considered complete.

Requirements knowledge model   A conceptual filing system—usually implemented as a data model—that establishes a common language for communicating requirements. (An example appears in Appendix D.)

Requirements pattern   A cohesive collection of requirements that carry out some recognizable and potentially recurring functionality.

Requirements specification   A complete collection of requirements knowledge for a specific project. The specification defines the product and may be used as a contract to build the product.

Requirements specification document   A document that contains all or part of the requirements specification knowledge, depending on who and why the knowledge is being communicated.

Requirements specification template   A guide for gathering and organizing requirements knowledge. (An example appears in Appendix A.)

Requirements tool   A software tool capable of maintaining all or part of the requirements specification.

Retrospective   A review designed to gather experience and provide input into improving the requirements process. Also known as "lessons learned."

Scenario   A breakdown of a business use case, or a product use case, into a series of stakeholder-recognizable steps. Scenarios are used for discovering and communicating work knowledge.

Sketch   A quick and dirty model or *prototype* of a piece of work or a proposed product. Sketches can be created on any medium—paper, electronic, whiteboard—and are intended to make it easier for stakeholders to understand and discuss their requirements.

Snow card   A paper card showing the attributes of an atomic requirement. Most requirements teams use an electronic version of the snow card.

Solution   A way of implementing the requirements. Also called the *product*.

Sponsor   See *Client*.

Stakeholder   Any person who has an interest in the product and who therefore has requirements for it, such as the client, a user, and someone who builds the product. Some stakeholders are remote, such as an auditor, a safety inspector, and the company lawyer.

System   In the context of this book, a business or work system, and not just a computer or software system.

Systemic thinking   The technique of understanding how things affect one another within a whole.

Systems analysis   The craft of modeling the system's functions and data. Systems analysis can be done in several ways: data flow modeling, as defined by DeMarco; event response modeling, as per McMenamin and Palmer; use cases, as per Jacobson; or any of the many object-oriented methods, most of which use the Unified Modeling Language notation.

Technological requirement   A requirement that is necessary only because of the chosen technology; it is not there to satisfy a business need.

Thinking above the line   Deriving and discussing the essence of the work. The "thinking" refers to an exploration of the possibilities without being constrained (for the moment) by technological realities. The "line" is the horizontal line on the *Brown Cow Model* that separates the physical reality (how) from the essential policy (what).

Time-triggered event   An event triggered by some time-related policy. Examples: "Time to produce sales report," "Time to remind driver to renew license." See also *External event*.

Trawling techniques   Techniques for discovering, eliciting, determining, and innovating requirements.

Use case   A chunk of functionality describing the interaction between a *user/actor* and an automated system. See also *Business use case* and *Product use case*.

User   The person or system that uses the product to do work. Also known as an *actor* or end user.

User story   A technique for discovering requirements by using the guide: "As a [. . .] I want [. . .] so that [. . .]." Sometimes called a story card.

Volere   A set of principles, processes, templates, tools, and techniques developed to improve the discovery, communication, and management of requirements. (*Volere* is the Italian verb for "to wish" or "to want.")

Work   A business area of the organization that your product is meant to improve. The business analyst studies the work before making decisions on the optimal product to do some or all of the work.

Work scope   The extent of the business area under investigation, and the real world that surrounds it. It is usually shown using a *context diagram*.

Bibliography

Ackoff, Russell, and Herbert Addison. *Systems Thinking for Curious Managers: With 40 New Management f-Laws.* Triarchy Press, 2010.

Alexander, Christopher. *Notes on the Synthesis of Form.* Harvard University Press, 1964.

Alexander, Christopher, et al. *A Pattern Language.* Oxford University Press, 1977.

Alexander, Ian, and Ljerka Beus-Dukic. *Discovering Requirements: How to Specify Products and Services.* Wiley, 2009.

Alexander, Ian, Neil Maiden, et al. *Scenarios, Stories, Use Cases Through the Systems Development Life-Cycle.* John Wiley, 2004.

Alexander, Ian, and Richard Stevens. *Writing Better Requirements.* Addison-Wesley, 2002.

Allweyer, Thomas. *BPMN 2.0.* Herstellung und Verlag: Books on Demand, 2010.

Beck, Kent, with Cynthia Andres. *Extreme Programming Explained: Embrace Change,* second edition. Addison-Wesley, 2004.

Beyer, Hugh, and Karen Holtzblatt. *Contextual Design: Defining Customer-Centered Systems.* Morgan Kauffmann, 1998.

Boehm, Barry. *Software Risk Management.* IEEE Computer Society Press, 1989.

Boehm, Barry, and Richard Turner. *Balancing Agility and Discipline: A Guide for the Perplexed.* Addison-Wesley, 2004.

Booch, Grady, James Rumbaugh, and Ivar Jacobson. *Unified Modeling Language User Guide,* second edition. Addison-Wesley, 2005.

Brooks, Fred. *The Mythical Man-Month: Essays on Software Engineering.* Addison-Wesley, 1979.

Brooks, Fred. *No Silver Bullet Refired. The Mythical Man-Month: Essays on Software Engineering,* 20th anniversary edition. Addison-Wesley, 1995.

Buzan, Tony, and Chris Griffiths. *Mind Maps for Business: Revolutionise Your Business Thinking and Practise.* BBC Active, 2009.

Carroll, John. *Scenario-Based Design.* John Wiley & Sons, 1995.

Checkland, Peter. *Systems Thinking, Systems Practice.* John Wiley & Sons, 1981.

Checkland, Peter, and J. Scholes. *Soft Systems Methodology in Action.* John Wiley & Sons, 1991.

Christensen, Clayton. *The Innovator's Dilemma: The Revolutionary Book That Will Change the Way You Do Business.* HarperBusiness, 2011.

Cockburn, Alastair. *Agile Software Development: The Cooperative Game.* Addison-Wesley, 2006.

Cohn, Mike. *User Stories Applied: For Agile Software Development.* Addison-Wesley, 2004.

Cooper, Alan. *The Inmates Are Running the Asylum: Why High Tech Products Drive Us Crazy and How to Restore the Sanity.* Sams Publishing, 2004.

Cooper, Alan, Robert Reimann, and David Cronin. *About Face 3: The Essentials of Interaction Design,* third edition. Wiley, 2007.

Davis, Alan. *Just Enough Requirements Management.* Dorset House, 2005.

DeGrace, Peter, and Leslie Hulet Stahl. *Wicked Problems, Righteous Solutions: A Catalogue of Modern Software Engineering Paradigms.* Yourdon Press, 1990.

DeMarco, Tom, Peter Hruschka, Tim Lister, Steve McMenamin, James Robertson, and Suzanne Robertson. *Adrenaline Junkies and Template Zombies: Patterns of Project Behaviour.* Dorset House, 2009.

DeMarco, Tom, and Tim Lister. *Waltzing with Bears: Managing Risk on Software Projects.* Dorset House, 2003.

DeMarco, Tom, and Tim Lister. *Peopleware. Productive Projects and Teams,* second edition. Dorset House, 1999.

Fagan, Michael. Design and Code Inspections to Reduce Errors in Program Development. *IBM Systems Journal* 15, no. 3 (1976): 258–287.

Fenton, Norman, and Shari Lawrence Pfleeger. *Software Metrics: A Rigorous and Practical Approach.* International Thomson Computer Press, 1997.

Ferdinandi, Patricia. *A Requirements Pattern: Succeeding in the Internet Economy.* Addison-Wesley, 2001.

Fowler, Martin. *UML Distilled: A Brief Guide to the Standard Object Modeling Language,* third edition. Addison-Wesley, 2003.

Function Point Counting Practices Manual. International Function Point Users Group, Westerville, OH.

Garmus, David, and David Herron. *Function Point Analysis: Measurement Practices for Successful Software Projects.* Addison-Wesley, 2000.

Gause, Donald, and Gerald Weinberg. *Are Your Lights On? How to Figure Out What the Problem Really Is.* Dorset House, 1990.

Gause, Donald, and Gerald Weinberg. *Exploring Requirements: Quality Before Design.* Dorset House, 1989.

Gilb, Tom. *Competitive Engineering: A Handbook for Systems Engineering, Requirements Engineering, and Software Engineering Using Planguage.* Butterworth-Heinemann, 2005.

Goldenberg, Herbert, and Irene Goldenberg. *Family Therapy: An Overview,* eighth edition. Brooks Cole, 2012.

Gottesdiener, Ellen. *Requirements by Collaboration: Workshops for Defining Needs.* Addison-Wesley, 2002.

Gottesdiener, Ellen. *Software Requirements Memory Jogger.* Goal/QPC, 2005.

Hass, Kathleen, and Alice Zavala. *The Art and Power of Facilitation: Running Powerful Meetings (Business Analysis Essential Library).* Management Concepts, 2007.

Hauser, John R., and Don Clausing. The House of Quality. *Harvard Business Review,* May–June 1988, 63–73.

Hay, David. *Data Model Patterns: Conventions of Thought.* Dorset House, 1995.

Highsmith, James. *Adaptive Software Development: A Collaborative Approach to Managing Complex Systems.* Dorset House, 2000.

Holtzblatt, Karen, Jessamyn Burns Wendell, and Shelley Wood. *Rapid Contextual Design: A How-to Guide to Key Techniques for User-Centered Design.* Morgan Kaufmann, 2004.

Hull, Elizabeth, Ken Jackson, and Jeremy Dick. *Requirements Engineering,* second edition. Springer, 2005.

International Institute of Business Analysts. *The Agile Extension to the BABOK Guide.* IIBA, Canada, 2012.

International Institute of Business Analysts. *The Business Analysis Body of Knowledge BABOK Version 2.* IIBA, Canada, 2009.

Jackson, Michael. *Problem Frames: Analyzing and Structuring Software Development Problems*. Addison-Wesley, 2001.

Jackson, Michael. *Software Requirements and Specifications: A Lexicon of Practice, Principles, and Prejudices*. Addison-Wesley, 1995.

Jacobson, Ivar, Magnus Christerson, Patrik Jonsson, and Gunnar Övergaard. *Object Oriented Software Engineering: A Use Case Driven Approach.* Addison-Wesley, 1992.

Jones, Capers. *Applied Software Measurement*. McGraw-Hill, 1991.

Jones, Capers. *Assessment and Control of Software Risks*. Prentice Hall, 1993.

Kerth, Norman. *Project Retrospectives*. Dorset House, 2001.

Kovitz, Benjamin. *Practical Software Requirements: A Manual of Content and Style*. Manning, 1999.

Kruchten, Philippe. *The Rational Unified Process: An Introduction,* third edition. Addison-Wesley, 2003.

Laplante, Phillip. *Requirements Engineering for Software and Systems*. Auerbach Publications, 2009.

Lauesen, Soren. *Software Requirements: Styles & Techniques*. Addison-Wesley, 2002.

Lawrence-Pfleeger, Shari. *Software Engineering: Theory and Practice,* fourth edition. Prentice Hall, 2009.

Leffingwell, Dean. *Agile Software Requirements: Lean Requirements Practices for Teams, Programs, and the Enterprise*. Addison-Wesley, 2011.

Leffingwell, Dean, and Don Widrig. *Managing Software Requirements: A Use Case Approach,* second edition. Addison-Wesley, 2003.

Maiden, Neil, and Suzanne Robertson. *Integrating Creativity into Requirements Processes: Experiences with an Air Traffic Management System*. International Conference on Software Engineering, May 2005.

McConnell, Steve. *Software Estimation: Demystifying the Black*. Microsoft Press, 2006.

McMenamin, Steve, and John Palmer. *Essential Systems Analysis*. Yourdon Press, 1984.

Meadows, Donella. *Thinking in Systems: A Primer*. Chelsea Green Publishing, 2008.

Merkow, Mark. *Secure and Resilient Software: Requirements, Test Cases, and Testing Methods*. Auerbach Publications, 2011.

Michalko, Michael. *Thinkertoys: A Handbook of Creative-Thinking Techniques.* Ten Speed Press, 2006.

Miller, Roxanne. *The Quest for Software Requirements.* MavenMark Books, 2009.

Norman, Donald. *The Design of Everyday Things.* Basic Books, 2002.

Pardee, William J. *To Satisfy and Delight Your Customer.* Dorset House, 1996.

Pfleeger, Charles, and Shari Lawrence Pfleeger. *Security in Computing,* fourth edition. Prentice Hall, 2006.

Pilone, Dan, and Neil Pitman. *UML 2.0 in a Nutshell.* O'Reilly, 2005.

Podeswa, Howard. *The Business Analyst's Handbook.* Course Technology, 2008.

Pohl, Klaus. *Requirements Engineering: Fundamentals, Principles, and Techniques.* Springer, 2010.

Prieto-Diaz, Rubén, and Guillermo Arango. *Domain Analysis and Software Systems Modeling.* IEEE Computer Society Press, 1991.

Robertson, James, and Suzanne Robertson. *Complete Systems Analysis: The Workbook, the Textbook, the Answers.* Dorset House, 1994.

Robertson, Suzanne, and James Robertson. *Mastering the Requirements Process,* second edition. Addison-Wesley, 2006.

Robertson, Suzanne, and James Robertson. *Requirements-Led Project Management: Discovering David's Slingshot.* Addison-Wesley, 2005.

Rumbaugh, James, Ivar Jacobson, and Grady Booch. *Unified Modeling Language Reference Manual,* second edition. Addison-Wesley, 2004.

Seddon, John, *Systems Thinking in the Public Sector.* Triarchy Press, 2010.

Senge, Peter. *The Fifth Discipline: The Art and Practice of the Learning Organization,* revised edition. Crown Business, 2006.

Sommerville, Ian, and Pete Sawyer. *Requirements Engineering: A Good Practice Guide.* John Wiley & Sons, 1998.

Spolsky, Joel. *Joel on Software: And on Diverse and Occasionally Related Matters That Will Prove of Interest to Software Developers, Designers, and Managers, and to Those Who, Whether by Good Fortune or Ill Luck, Work with Them in Some Capacity.* Apress, 2004.

Sullivan, Wendy, and Judy Rees. *Clean Language: Revealing Metaphors and Opening Minds.* Crown House Publishing, 2008.

Tockey, Steve. *Return on Software: Maximizing the Return on Your Software Investment.* Addison-Wesley, 2004.

Tufte, Edward. *The Visual Display of Quantitative Information,* second edition. Graphics Press, 2010.

Weinberg, Jerry. *Quality Software Management. Volume 1: Systems Thinking. Volume 2: First-Order Measurement. Volume 3: Congruent Action. Volume 4: Anticipating Change.* Dorset House, 1992–1997.

Wiegers, Karl. *More About Software Requirements: Thorny Issues and Practical Advice.* Microsoft Press, 2006.

Wiegers, Karl. *Software Requirements,* second edition. Microsoft Press, 2003.

Wiley, Bill. *Essential System Requirements: A Practical Guide to Event-Driven Methods.* Addison-Wesley, 1999.

Yourdon, Ed. *Death March,* second edition. Prentice Hall, 2003.

Index

Volere

Requirements Resources

The authors and creators of the Volere techniques, Suzanne and James Robertson, conduct training courses and work with organizations to improve their requirements effectiveness. Please see their web site **www.volere.co.uk** for course outlines, consulting arrangements, and the current schedule of public seminars.

The authors also host a LinkedIn discussion forum for both the techniques discussed in this book, and the wider world of requirements in general. Visit **http://www.linkedin.com/groups/Volere-Requirements-2491512**.

For college instructors who adopt this book for their courses, some of the graphics used herein are available in the **Pearson Instructor Resource Center (www.pearsonhighered.com)** for your use in preparing course materials.

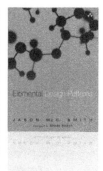

The type from the template

List of events / use cases that need this requirement

Requirement #: **Unique id**   Requirement Type: Event/use case #'s:

Description: **A one sentence statement of the intention of the requirement**

Rationale: **A justification of the requirement**

Originator: **The person who raised this requirement**

Fit Criterion: **A measurement of the requirement such that it is possible to test if the solution matches the original requirement**

Customer Satisfaction: Customer Dissatisfaction:

Priority: **A rating of the customer value**   Conflicts:

Other requirements that cannot be implemented if this one is

Supporting Materials: — **Pointer to documents that illustrate and explain this requirement**

History: **Creation, changes, deletions, etc.**

Volere
Copyright @ Atlantic Systems Guild

Degree of stakeholder happiness if this requirement is successfully implemented.
Scale from 1 = uninterested to 5 = extremely pleased.

Measure of stakeholder unhappiness if this requirement is not part of the final product.
Scale from 1 = hardly matters to 5 = extremely displeased.

PROJECT DRIVERS

1 The Purpose of the Project

1a The user business or background of the project effort

1b Goals of the project

2 Client, Customer and other Stakeholders

2a The client

2b The customer

2c Other stakeholders

2d Hands-on users of the product

2e Personas

2f Priorities assigned to users

2g User participation

2h Maintenance users and service technicians

3 Mandated Constraints

3a Solution constraints

3b Implementation environment of the current system

3c Partner or collaborative applications

3d Off-the-shelf software

3e Anticipated workplace environment

3f Schedule constraints

3g Budget constraints

3h Enterprise constraints

4 Naming Conventions and Terminology

4a Definitions of all terms, including acronyms, used by stakeholders involved in the project

5 Relevant Facts and Assumptions

5a Relevant Facts

5b Business Rules

5c Assumptions

6 The Scope of the Work

6a The current situation

6b The context of the work

6c Work partitioning

6d Specifying a business use case (BUC)

7 Business Data Model and Data Dictionary

7a Business data model

7b Data dictionary

8 The Scope of the Product

8a Product boundary

8b Product use case table

8c Individual product use cases